Every Day in the Kitchen

ESSENTIAL RECIPES FOR THE MODERN HOME

Allan Campion and Michele Curtis

Hardie Grant Books

Our thanks to:

Tracey Campion for babysitting duties above and beyond the call of duty

The Chadwicks for being the best neighbours, and always hungry

Henry the fat dog for eating the leftovers

Ruth Wirtz for her recipes and keen interest

Our foodie friends for technical advice and information

And everyone who has ever eaten at our house, particularly if they brought a bottle of wine with them.

Published in 2003 by
by Hardie Grant Books
12 Claremont Street
South Yarra, Victoria
3141, Australia
www.hardiegrant.com.au
Reprinted in 2003

All rights reserved. No part of this publication may be reproduced, stored in a retrieval system or transmitted in any form by any means, electronic, mechanical, photocopying, recording or otherwise, without the prior written permission of the publishers and copyright holders.
The moral right of the authors has been asserted.

Copyright text © Michele Curtis and Allan Campion 2001
Copyright photographs © Matt Harvey 2001

Every Day in the Kitchen was previously published in 2001 as Campion & Curtis in the Kitchen.

National Library of Australia Cataloguing-in-Publication Data:
Campion, Allan.
  Every day in the kitchen.
    ISBN 1 74066 097 8.
    1. Cookery. I. Curtis, Michele. II. Title. III. Title :
    Every day in the kitchen.
641.5

Edited by White Kite Productions
Photography by Matt Harvey
Cover design by Klarissa Pfisterer Design
Text design by Danie Pout Design
Typeset by J & M Typesetting
Printed and bound in Australia by Australian Book Connection

Preheat oven to 180°C (350°F).

Heat a heavy-based frying pan over medium heat, add a generous splash of olive oil and cook onion and garlic with red capsicum until softened. Add potatoes and cook until these just begin to colour.

Place into a 28 cm (11 in) cake tin and cook in preheated oven for 20–30 minutes, until potatoes are soft and slightly brown, stirring often.

Beat together eggs, salt, pepper and chopped parsley. Pour egg mixture over potatoes, stir gently and bake for 20 minutes, or until risen and golden brown. Test as you do a cake: insert a skewer or cake tester into the centre of the potato omelette. The skewer should come out free of raw egg mix. If it doesn't, cook for a further 5 minutes, then try again.

Best served warm. Serves 8–10.

Smoked salmon and prawn kedgeree

Traditionally a kedgeree is made with smoked haddock, but this can be hard to find, so we tend to make it with salmon and prawns. It's a great rice dish that's good for brunch or even supper.

1 tbsp olive oil
2 onions, diced
2 tsp mild curry paste
400 g (14 oz) long grain rice
750 ml (1¼ pt) water
200 g (7 oz) green (raw) prawns, shells removed

2 medium eggs, hard boiled, peeled and cut into wedges
60 g (2 oz) butter, diced
150 g (5 oz) smoked salmon, cut into wide strips
2 tbsp chopped parsley

Preheat oven to 180°C (350°F).

Heat a medium-sized saucepan over a medium–high heat. Add oil and onion and cook until tender. Add curry paste and stir together for 1 minute. Add rice and water and bring to the boil. Reduce heat to low, cover and cook until all water is absorbed. Place rice in a buttered casserole dish and add the prawns and egg wedges on top. Dot rice with butter and cover casserole with foil. Place in the preheated oven and cook for 15 minutes. Remove foil and gently stir in the smoked salmon. Scatter parsley on top. Serves 4.

Blueberry pikelets

Pikelets are one of our son Luke's favourite breaky foods. We vary the fruit according to the season. In winter we cook the pikelets with no fruit and serve them with poached quinces or rhubarb and with yoghurt on top.

250 ml (8 fl oz) milk
1 medium egg
150 g (5 oz) self-raising flour

Olive oil for cooking
150 g (5 oz) blueberries
Maple syrup and natural yoghurt to serve

Beat milk, egg and flour together until smooth. Heat a heavy-based pan over medium–low heat. Add a splash of oil and wipe it with kitchen paper so it is a thin coating. Add 3–4 spoonfuls of batter to the hot pan. Add 4 or 5 blueberries to each pikelet and cook until bubbles start to form on the surface. Turn pancakes over and continue to cook for 2–3 minutes.

Repeat with remaining batter.

Serve with maple syrup and natural yoghurt. Makes 12–15 pikelets.

Banana pikelets
Replace blueberries with banana slices.

Summer berry pancakes pikelets
Omit adding blueberries from the mix, instead serve pikelets with 250g (8 oz) mixed berries and a generous spoonful of mascarpone.

Ricotta hotcakes with banana and maple syrup

These are a bit trickier to cook than pikelets. As hotcakes are thicker, you may want to cook them in the pan, then pop them in a warm oven for 5 minutes to ensure they're cooked through.

2 medium eggs
250 g (8 oz) ricotta
60 ml (2 fl oz) milk
125 g (4 oz) natural yoghurt
2 tbsp caster sugar
150 g (5 oz) self-raising flour

½ tsp baking powder
½ tsp salt
Olive oil for cooking
4 bananas, sliced
Maple syrup

Beat eggs and ricotta. Add milk, yoghurt and sugar and beat until smooth. Sift flour with baking powder and salt and add to ricotta base, stir until combined.

Heat a heavy-based pan over a low heat. Add a splash of oil and wipe it with kitchen paper so it has a thin coating, then 6 ladlefuls of ricotta mix. Mixture should spread to about 6 cm (2 in) wide. Cook until base is golden brown. Turn over and cook for a further 2–3 minutes. Keep warm until all hotcakes are cooked.

Turn heat up slightly, add a splash more oil and add bananas, cook for 1–2 minutes on each side. Serve hotcakes with bananas on top and drizzle with maple syrup. Serves 4–6.

Corn fritters v

Corn fritters are marvellous for breakfast with grilled bacon and tomatoes. Or smaller fritters can be served as an entrée or pre-dinner nibble with smoked salmon and horseradish cream on top.

75 g (2⅔ oz) self-raising flour
150 g (5 oz) polenta
½ tsp salt
½ tsp baking powder

1 medium egg
250 ml (8 fl oz) milk
2 corn cobs
Olive oil for cooking

Combine flour, polenta, salt and baking powder. Add egg and milk and mix until batter is smooth. Remove kernels from corn with a sharp knife and add to mixture.

Heat a heavy-based frying over medium heat. Add 1–2 tbsp olive oil and spoonfuls of batter and cook on one side until golden brown. Turn fritters over and cook until golden brown on other side.

Repeat until mixture is used up, keeping cooked fritters warm in the oven. Serves 4.

Smoked salmon with polenta pancakes

The Rolls Royce of pancakes is now on the menu for breakfast.

110 g (3½ oz) self-raising flour
165 g (5½ oz) polenta
½ tsp salt
½ tsp baking powder
1 medium egg
250 ml (8 fl oz) buttermilk, or milk soured with lemon juice

Olive oil for cooking
200 g (7 oz) snow pea shoots
100 g (3½ oz) rocket
8 slices smoked salmon, cut in half
Crème fraîche or sour cream to serve
Chopped chives to garnish

Combine flour, polenta, salt and baking powder. Whisk egg and buttermilk together lightly, then stir dry mixture through. Allow to stand for 30 minutes before cooking.

Heat a heavy-based pan over medium heat. Add olive oil, then ¼ of the polenta mixture – enough to make a 15 cm (6 in) pancake. Cook until golden, about 2 minutes, turn and cook on the other side. Keep each pancake warm while you prepare the others.

Place warm pancakes on individual plates. Mix together snow pea shoots (trimmed of long stems) and rocket, and divide evenly between pancakes. Top with four half-slices of smoked salmon each. Add a spoonful of crème fraîche, top with chives and serve. Serves 4.

French toast

Another firm favourite in our house as it's very quick to make and sets the children up for the day – perfect! Luke, master of the breakfast table, calls this eggy bread.

4 medium eggs
90 ml (3 fl oz) milk
Salt and freshly ground black pepper

4 pieces day-old bread
Olive oil for cooking
Maple syrup and yoghurt to serve

Whisk eggs, milk, salt and pepper together until combined. Take each piece of bread and soak first one side, then the other (turned over), in egg mixture until all of it is absorbed.

Heat a large heavy-based pan over a medium–high heat. Add a generous splash of oil and add bread (you may need to cook in two batches, depending on size of bread). Cook for 3–4 minutes on each side until well browned. Serve immediately with maple syrup (or honey) and yoghurt. Serves 4.

Croque monsieur

Croque monsieur is an up-market toasted sandwich dish with a rich filling of cheese, mustard and smoked ham. It'll help bring a taste of Paris to your breakfast table.

90 g (3 oz) mix of grated cheese, such as gruyère, cheddar and parmigiano
2 tbsp sour cream
Freshly ground black pepper
Pinch of grated nutmeg

1 tsp Worcestershire sauce, optional
½ tsp Dijon mustard
4 slices smoked ham
8 slices white bread
Soft butter

Mix cheese with sour cream, pepper, nutmeg, Worcestershire sauce and mustard to form a smooth paste. Spread the cheese mixture on four slices of bread, top each with a ham slice and another slice of bread to form sandwiches. Butter the outside of both slices of bread.

Heat a heavy-based pan over a medium–high heat. Add sandwiches and cook for 3–4 minutes on each side until golden brown and crisp. Serves 4.

Grilled tomatoes with basil butter and bacon

Most people love the flavours of tomatoes, bacon and basil together. In summer we cook the tomatoes and bacon on the barbecue and enjoy breakfast outside. It's called driving the neighbours wild.

60 g (2 oz) soft butter
2 tbsp chopped basil leaves
Freshly ground black pepper
2–4 ripe tomatoes, stalks removed, and cut in half

8 thin slices bacon
Olive oil for cooking
4 slices sourdough bread

Mix butter, basil and a little pepper until well combined. Turn basil butter onto a square of greaseproof paper and roll paper around butter to form a sausage shape. Refrigerate until firm.

Place tomatoes and bacon on grill tray and drizzle tomatoes with olive oil. Place under a medium–heat grill and cook for 6–7 minutes, or until tomatoes soften and bacon is crisp. Turn regularly to ensure even cooking.

Toast sourdough until golden. Serve toast topped with grilled bacon and tomatoes and sliced rounds of basil butter. Serves 4.

Mushrooms on toast ⓥ

Mushrooms are one of the simplest things to pan-fry. In autumn wild mushrooms such as pines and slippery jacks are excellent. Try mixing wild mushrooms with button mushrooms, or use your favourite mix of exotics such as oyster or shiitake.

500 g (1 lb) mushrooms of your choice
2 tbsp olive oil
Salt and freshly ground black pepper
Fresh chopped herbs
Toast for serving

Cut mushrooms to a similar size if necessary, to allow even cooking. Heat a heavy-based frying pan over medium–high heat, then add oil. Add mushrooms and toss to coat. Continue cooking, moving mushrooms so that they cook evenly, until they start to soften. Add salt, pepper and fresh chopped herbs to taste. Serve straight away on toast. Serves 4.

Apricot and almond muesli

Easy to make and much more delicious than brought pre-mixes. We vary the flavours every time we make it, often adding additional ingredients such as desiccated coconut, wheat germ and sunflower seeds. Make a huge batch, divide into smaller bags and give these to your friends as Christmas presents.

1 kg (2 lb) rolled oats
90 g (3 oz) toasted almonds, chopped
200 g (7 oz) sultanas
125 g (4 oz) dried apricots, chopped
150 g (5 oz) bran

Combine all ingredients. Divide into plastic containers with tight-fitting lids and store in a cool dark place. Will keep for 2–3 months. Makes just over 1.5 kg 3lb.

Apple and hazelnut muesli
Substitute hazelnuts for almonds and dried apple rings for apricots.

Date and walnut muesli
Substitute walnuts (or pecans) for almonds and dried dates for apricots.

Bircher muesli

This is a decadent muesli that you soak overnight and serve chilled with fresh fruit the next morning. It makes you feel healthy, but you're not kidding anyone.

150 g (5 oz) rolled oats
60 g (2 oz) sultanas
30 g (1 oz) flaked almonds
250 ml (8 fl oz) milk
250 ml (8 fl oz) natural yoghurt

1 apple, grated
150 g (5 oz) berries, cut if necessary
1 banana, sliced
90 ml (3 fl oz) cream
Honey, optional

Mix oats with sultanas, almonds, milk and yoghurt. Refrigerate overnight.
    In the morning add apple, berries, banana and cream. Add honey to taste and if needed more milk or yoghurt to adjust consistency; it should be moist, but not runny. Serves 6–8.

Moroccan spiced breakfast couscous

A very sophisticated and exotic way to start the day. It is also delicious served with poached or stewed fruit (see page 258) on top.

250 ml (8 fl oz) orange juice
½ tsp ground cinnamon
¼ tsp ground nutmeg
2 tsp caster sugar

250 g (8 oz) instant couscous
100 g (3½ oz) natural yoghurt
2 tbsp honey
60 g (2 oz) flaked almonds

Place orange juice, cinnamon, nutmeg and sugar in a small saucepan. Heat to almost boiling. Remove from the heat, stir in the couscous, cover and allow to rest for 2 minutes. Place saucepan over a low heat and stir with a fork to break up the grains.
    Mix yoghurt and honey together and refrigerate until required.
    To serve, heap couscous into bowls, spoon sweet yoghurt on top and scatter with almonds. Serves 4–6.

Porridge

Porridge is an essential winter breakfast at our place, and we don't mean the instant variety that is totally lacking in flavour and texture. What we're after is the real McCoy – delicious creamy porridge to keep us going until lunch. Personal taste will dictate whether or not you add salt; we never do.

150 g (5 oz) rolled oats
500 ml (1 pt) water
375 ml (12 fl oz) milk

Pinch of salt, optional
Milk and honey for serving

Place oats, water and milk in a heavy-based saucepan. Add salt if using. Bring to the boil, then reduce to a gentle simmer. Cook for 10–15 minutes, stirring occasionally. Serve immediately with milk and honey drizzled on top. Serves 4.

Sultana porridge
Add 60 g (2 oz) sultanas to the cooking porridge.

Apple porridge
Add 1 grated apple to the cooking porridge.

Stewed fruit porridge
Serve porridge with stewed fruit (quinces and rhubarb are our favourites), natural or vanilla yoghurt and brown sugar or maple syrup.

Summer fruit compote

This compote of fruit uses ripe stone fruit and fragrant passionfruit. The passionfruit adds a great tropical flavour, and you can also try adding a handful of grapes for the last 5 minutes of cooking.

3 nectarines, cut into thick wedges
6 plums, quartered
6 apricots, quartered
Pulp from 4 passionfruit

Pinch of saffron threads
90 ml (3 fl oz) water
90 ml (3 oz) caster sugar

Place the prepared fruit, saffron, water and sugar in a heavy-based saucepan and cook over a medium heat until the liquid comes to the boil. Reduce heat and simmer for 20 minutes, stirring occasionally. Allow to cool slightly.
    Serve at room temperature with natural yoghurt. Serves 4–6.

Grilled peaches with goat's curd and honey

A rather decadent breakfast – and it makes a great dessert too.

4 peaches, cut in half and stone removed
100 g (3½ oz) fresh goat's curd or ricotta
90 ml (3 oz) full-flavoured honey

Place peach halves skin side down on a grill tray. Cook under a hot grill until golden and slightly softened. Place peaches onto plates; divide goat's curd between halves and drizzle with honey. Serves 4.

Rhubarb and ricotta toast

This is a super-quick breakfast idea that is simple but seductive. If rhubarb is not in season try it with stone fruit, apples or cherries.

200 g rhubarb
250 ml (8 fl oz) water
125 g (4 oz) caster sugar
1 tsp vanilla extract

150 g (5 oz) fresh ricotta
4 slices sourdough
Honey for serving

Wash and cut rhubarb into 5 cm (2 in) lengths. Dissolve sugar in water, then bring to the boil. Reduce to a simmer, add rhubarb pieces and cook for 3–4 minutes until soft. Remove from the heat and set aside.

Toast the sourdough and spread with ricotta, add warm poached rhubarb pieces, drizzle with honey and serve immediately. Serves 4.

Fig and ricotta toast
Omit rhubarb. Allow 2 fresh figs per person, sprinkle with caster sugar and grill for 3–4 minutes under a hot grill; serve on top of ricotta.

Strawberry and ricotta toast
Poach strawberries instead of rhubarb, cooking for just 2–3 minutes.

Plum jam

Like many Australians we have a plum tree in our backyard. In a good season we get enough jam to keep us going through half the year.

2 kg (4 lb) plums
250 ml (8 fl oz) water

2 tbsp lemon juice
1.5 kg (3 lb) caster sugar

Quarter plums and remove stones. Place plums, water and lemon juice in a large heavy-based saucepan. Bring to the boil over medium heat and cook for 20 minutes, or until fruit is soft. Meanwhile warm sugar either by placing it in a heatproof bowl in the oven, or in the microwave. Add sugar to stewed fruit and stir well until sugar dissolves. Raise heat and cook for 15–20 minutes, stirring often.

Check to see whether jam has reached setting point by placing a teaspoon of mixture onto a chilled plate. Tip the plate; if the jam runs, cook for a further 5 minutes, then try again. Pour into sterilised jars while still hot. Makes 2½ litres (2⅔ pt).

Berry jam

A simple berry jam to enjoy on toast. You can make this with a mixture of berries – such as blackberries, raspberries and strawberries – or just make a straight jam, such as raspberry.

1 kg (2 lb) berries
40 ml (1⅓ fl oz) lemon juice

1 kg (2 lb) caster sugar

If using strawberries and a mixture of other berries, cut strawberries in half. Wash berries. Place fruit, lemon juice and sugar in a large heavy-based saucepan. Cook over a low heat until sugar dissolves, stirring often. Raise heat and cook at a boil for 15–20 minutes.

After 15 minutes check to see if jam has reached setting point by placing a teaspoon of mixture onto a chilled plate. Tip the plate; if the jam runs, cook for a further 5 minutes, then try again. Pour into sterilised jars while still hot. Makes 1 litre (1⅔ pt).

Orange marmalade

You can make this marmalade with any citrus fruit. Try blood oranges, tangelos, mandarins – or even cumquats, which are our all-time favourite.

1 kg (2 lb) oranges
600 g (1⅓ lb) caster sugar
60 ml (2 fl oz) Cointreau

Cover oranges with water, bring to the boil and cook until soft, about 1 hour. Remove oranges and reduce cooking liquid to about 80 ml (2¾ fl oz). When oranges have cooled, peel them, discard all the pips, then purée the flesh. Strain this purée and add it to the cooking liquid.

Finely shred the peel, aiming for 100 g (3½ oz); add to the cooking liquid with sugar. Bring to the boil, add Cointreau and reduce heat. Cook until a syrupy consistency, stirring frequently. Test for setting point by putting a teaspoon of marmalade on a chilled plate. Tip the plate, if the marmalade runs, cook for a further 5 minutes, then try again. Pour into sterilised jars while still hot and enjoy as soon as it's cool. Makes 750 ml (1¼ pt).

Lemon curd (lemon butter)

This is arm-breaking work but well worth the effort because it's a rich and yummy treat.

4 egg yolks
200 g (7 oz) caster sugar
200 g (7 oz) soft butter

Grated zest 2 lemons
80 ml (2¾ fl oz) lemon juice

Beat egg yolks and sugar in a large heat proof bowl until pale and creamy. Add butter, lemon zest and juice. Place over a simmering pot of water and whisk continuously until thickened, 20–30 minutes. Store in sterilised jars in the refrigerator for up to 3 weeks. Makes 500 ml (1 pt).

Passionfruit curd
Substitute 60 ml (2 fl oz) of passionfruit pulp for lemon juice.

Microwave lemon curd

Instead of the endless whisking over a hot pot, try this microwave version. It's so quick and easy.

125 g (4 oz) butter
Grated zest 3 lemons
125 ml (4 fl oz) lemon juice

250 g (8 oz) caster sugar
4 medium eggs

Place butter, grated zest and juice of lemons in a microwave-proof bowl. Cook on high for 3 minutes. Add sugar and cook for 2 minutes. Stir in eggs, one at a time. Cook on low until mixture thickens, about 12–15 minutes. Stir occasionally. Store in sterilised jars in the refrigerator for up to 3 weeks. Makes 500 ml (1 pt).

QUICK BRUNCH IDEAS

- Fill mini croissants with dark chocolate shavings and bake for 10 minutes in a preheated oven 180°C (350°F). Serve with a bowl (rather than a mug) of hot chocolate for the ultimate brunch indulgence.
- Make a fruit salad of in-season pineapple, watermelon, lychees, banana and apricots and serve with natural muesli and toasted coconut shavings.
- Mash banana with a fork and add natural yoghurt, then drizzle honey on top.
- Toast sourdough bread and top with real butter and strawberry jam.
- Serve soft-boiled eggs with toast fingers and dukkah, page 44.

Winter fruit compote

Winter is a great time to prepare dried fruits as delicious compote to serve with breakfast. The choice of fruits that can be used is quite extensive – anything from prunes, apricots and raisins to figs, dates and peaches. Simply choose the combination which appeals to you. You can also substitute orange juice for the sugar and water if you prefer.

220g (7⅔ oz/1 cup) caster sugar
500ml (16 fl oz/2 cups) water
1 vanilla pod
4 cardamom pods (spilt open)

2 cinnamon sticks
1kg (2 lb) dried fruit of your choosing, as mentioned above
Natural yoghurt to serve

Place sugar and water in a large heavy-based saucepan over medium heat. Dissolve sugar in water. Once dissolved add vanilla, cardamom and cinnamon sticks and bring to a gentle boil. Allow to simmer for 5 minutes.

Prepare dried fruits by removing stones from the prunes, if using. Then place all the fruits into the simmering syrup. Cook gently for 20 minutes, then allow fruit and syrup to cool.

Remove cardamom pods and cinnamon stick if preferred. Serve compote with a dollop of natural yoghurt on top and a drizzle of the poaching liquid. Serves 6–8

Seasonal winter fruit compote
The compote recipe can use in-season winter fruits instead of dried, try a similar quantity of apple and pear wedges, quince slices and chopped rhubarb instead. Cook as directed.

> **TIP**
> This compote can be served warm, simply simmer for 10 minutes to reheat. Serve with a pot of porridge on a cold winter's morning.

Chicken stock
Beef stock
Fish stock
Vegetable stock
Potato and leek soup
Sweet potato and ginger soup
Roast tomato soup
Asian-inspired pumpkin soup
Green pea soup
Broad bean soup
Parsnip, ginger and lemon soup
Chicken noodle soup
Wonton soup
Duck and macadamia wonton soup
Udon soup with shiitake and roast duck
Tom yum
Laksa
Duck and pine mushroom bread soup
French onion soup
Beetroot soup
Roasted vegetable gazpacho
Moroccan lentil broth
Vegetable and barley broth
Corn chowder
Fish and fennel chowder
Minestrone
Oxtail soup

Soups and stocks

BASIC STOCKS, VEGETABLE SOUPS, BROTHS AND HEARTY SOUPS

There is no doubting how nourishing a bowl of soup can be. The nutritious liquid seems to seep into every part of your body, bringing warmth and instant energy. It can be a simple broth or a meal in a bowl, a chilled soup on a hot summer's evening or a huge bowl packed with noodles, slices of chicken, tofu and aromatic Asian herbs. There's a soup, it seems, to suit every occasion.

Like in all cooking, the higher the quality of the raw ingredients, the better the soup. This means having good stock, fresh vegetables, quality meats, great noodles, and top-grade everything else to put into your pot.

The question of using stock always crops up in any discussion about soup. There is no doubt that stock is essential for most soups, and the best stock is homemade. Of course we don't all want to make our own stock, nor do we all have the time. There are plenty of alternatives nowadays, with many quality food stores selling stock; there are cartons of stock on supermarket shelves; and if you're really stuck a stock cube can do the job.

THINGS YOU NEED TO KNOW ABOUT SOUPS AND STOCKS

- If you make a large pot of stock you can reduce it until the flavour is very concentrated. Then freeze in small quantities, even ice-cube trays, and reconstitute it later in water.
- Virtually all soups freeze well, so you can usually make enough for more than one meal.
- We prefer to thicken our soups with potato where possible, rather than using flour and butter in a roux. Simply add a peeled and diced potato to soup that will be puréed to ensure a nice consistency, or add a very finely diced potato to broth soups that are to be served as they are.
- Don't forget to try barley, rice, pasta, noodles, lentils, borlotti beans, split peas, chickpeas and haricot beans in your soup.
- We cook dried beans in a separate saucepan until they are tender, then add them to the soup in the later stages. This ensures that they are completely tender and it stops the soup going cloudy.
- Stock and soup will keep well for 2–3 days in the refrigerator and up to 3 months in the freezer.
- Bay leaves are excellent for adding a background herb flavour to all stock. They are best fresh and are easy to grow if you have a sunny spot in the garden.
- Stock and soup recipes sometimes call for a bouquet garni. This is a bundle of fresh herbs that includes bay leaves, thyme, parsley and celery leaves, tied with string or wrapped in muslin. You add it while the stock is simmering and remove it during straining.
- It's best to add cream to soup after it has been taken from the heat. Boiling liquid can curdle the cream.
- Use chicken or vegetable stock at your discretion in vegetable soups. We prefer chicken for its fuller flavour, but vegetable stock is just as good.
- Take care when puréeing soups: hot soup will cause nasty burns if it splashes onto your skin.
- Deep bowls are perfect for serving soup: they keep the liquid hot as you enjoy every last spoonful.

Chicken stock

Chicken stock is excellent to have on hand for many uses besides soup; risotto, gravy, casseroles and curries also benefit from the addition of good quality stock.

1 kg (2 lb) chicken bones
1 onion, roughly chopped
1 leek, roughly chopped
2 carrots, roughly chopped
2 celery stalks, roughly chopped

A few whole black peppercorns
2 bay leaves
Parsley stalks
2–3 litres (3⅓–5 pt) water

Place bones in a large pot. Add vegetables, peppercorns, herbs and water, and bring to the boil. Remove any scum from the surface, reduce to a simmer and cook for 2–3 hours. Strain and press down hard on the ingredients to extract all the flavour. When stock has cooled slightly, refrigerate to allow fat to set on the surface. Skim fat off the surface and the stock is ready to use. Makes 1–2 litres.

Asian chicken stock
Add 3 cm (1 in) root ginger, sliced, 2 tbsp soy sauce, 1 sliced lemongrass stalk and, optionally, a sliced chilli or two.

Rich chicken stock
Place the bones in a baking tray and roast in a preheated oven at 180°C (350°F) for 30–40 minutes, turning once or twice until golden brown and draining excess oil off occasionally. The bones can then be added to the vegetables and herbs and cooked in the usual way.

Duck stock
Use the same quantities of duck bones as directed in the chicken stock recipe, and roast them as described for rich chicken stock. This stock can also be reduced to 250 ml (8 fl oz) for an amazing rich sticky duck sauce.

Turkey stock
Use the same quantities of turkey bones as for chicken stock, and roast them as directed for rich chicken stock. This stock can also be reduced to 250 ml (8 fl oz) for an amazing rich sticky turkey sauce.

Beef stock

Beef stock can be made with a mix of beef and veal bones. The beef lends a hearty flavour, while the veal will bring a hint of richness and a slight stickiness to the stock.

500 g (1 lb) veal bones, such as shanks
500 g (1 lb) beef bones, such as shin
1 onion, roughly chopped
1 leek, roughly chopped
2 carrots, roughly chopped

2 celery stalks, roughly chopped
A few whole black peppercorns
2 bay leaves
Parsley stalks
2–3 litres (3⅓–5 pt) water

Preheat oven to 180°C (350°F). Place the bones in a baking tray and roast for 30–40 minutes, turning once or twice until golden brown and draining excess oil off occasionally.

Place bones in a large pot. Add vegetables, pepper, herbs and water, and bring to the boil. Remove any scum from the surface, reduce to a simmer and cook for 2–3 hours. Strain and press down hard on the ingredients to extract all the flavour. Set aside. When stock has cooled slightly, refrigerate to allow fat to set on the surface. Skim fat off the surface and the stock is ready to use. Makes 1–2 litres.

Veal stock
Use only veal bones in the beef stock recipe in order to make a stock that can be reduced to a rich, almost sticky consistency for sauces and gravy.

Game stock
Prepare a mix of veal bones with bones from duck, venison or quail and prepare as directed to produce a more full flavoured stock. This, too, can be reduced to a rich, almost sticky consistency for sauces and gravy.

Fish stock

Fish bones needs only 20 minutes of cooking to produce a good flavoured stock; any more and the stock may turn bitter. It's best to use bones from white fish, not oily fish. It's also better to ladle fish stock into a sieve, rather than just tip out the contents of the stockpot as you can with other stocks.

1 kg (2 lb) fish bones
250 ml (8 fl oz) white wine
1 onion, roughly chopped
1 leek, roughly chopped
2 carrots, roughly chopped
2 celery stalks, roughly chopped

Top of 1 fennel bulb, if available
A few whole black peppercorns
2 bay leaves
Parsley stalks
2–3 litres (3⅓–5 pt) water

Heat a stockpot over a medium heat. Add the bones and white wine and cook for 2–3 minutes. Add the vegetables, pepper, herbs and water, and heat until almost boiling. Remove any scum from the surface, reduce to a simmer and cook for 20 minutes. Strain by ladling into a sieve and set aside. When stock has cooled slightly, refrigerate it. Makes 1–2 litres.

Shellfish stock
Substitute shells from prawns, crabs and lobster for fish bones.

Roasted vegetable gazpacho (recipe page 33)

Green pea soup (recipe page 26)

Udon soup with shiitake and roast duck (recipe page 30)

Vegetable stock (V)

Vegetable stock is perfect when you want a lightly flavoured base for your finished dish, or are cooking a strictly vegetarian meal. It's quick to prepare and is easily made as required.

2 tbsp olive oil
3 onions, roughly chopped
2 leeks, roughly chopped
3 carrots, roughly chopped
2 celery stalks, roughly chopped

2 tomatoes, chopped
A few whole black peppercorns
2 bay leaves
Parsley stalks
2–3 litres (3⅓–5 pt) water

Heat olive oil in a stockpot, add vegetables and stir for a few minutes. Add pepper, herbs and water, and bring to the boil. Remove any scum from the surface, reduce to a simmer and cook for 20 minutes. Strain and press down hard on the vegetables to extract all the flavour. Set aside. Makes 1–2 litres.

Roasted vegetable stock (V)
Place the vegetables in a baking tray and drizzle with a little olive oil. Roast in a preheated oven at 180°C (350°F) for 20–30 minutes, stirring once or twice until golden brown. The vegetables can then be added to the stockpot and cooked as described. This stock is great in full-flavoured dishes.

Potato and leek soup

Potato and leek soup is nutritious, tasty and easy to make. Everyone should learn how to make this soup before leaving home.

Olive oil for cooking
1 onion, diced
2 celery stalks, diced
2 leeks, sliced
4 potatoes, peeled and diced

1 garlic clove, crushed
1 litre (1⅔ pt) chicken or vegetable stock
Salt and freshly ground black pepper
Cream and fresh herbs to taste

Heat a heavy-based saucepan over a medium–high heat. Add a generous splash of oil, onion, celery and leek. Cook for 5–6 minutes, stirring often. Add potatoes and garlic and cook for a further 3–4 minutes. Add enough stock to just cover and a little salt and pepper, and bring to the boil. Reduce heat and simmer for 15 minutes, or until potatoes are tender.

Remove from heat, purée soup using a food processor and pass through a strainer back into a clean saucepan. To serve, bring soup back to the boil, check seasoning, and add cream if desired and chopped herbs to garnish. Serves 4.

Mushroom soup
Use only 1 leek. Add 300 g (10 oz) mushrooms with potatoes and continue as described.

Asparagus soup
Make as potato and leek soup, but use only 1 leek and add 300 g (10 oz) fresh asparagus tips to the soup just before puréeing.

Potato and watercress soup
Use only 1 leek and cook as described. Adding a few handfuls of freshly picked watercress to the soup as it is about to be puréed will give it a fresh green colour and a gutsy watercress flavour.

Sweet potato and ginger soup

Sweet potato is very similar to pumpkin in that it produces a soup with an excellent texture. The ginger gives it a lift too.

Olive oil for cooking
1 onion, diced
2 celery stalks, diced
1 leek, sliced
2 sweet potatoes, peeled and diced
3 cm (1 in) ginger, peeled and sliced
1 garlic clove, crushed
1 litre (1⅔ pt) chicken or vegetable stock
Salt and freshly ground black pepper
Cream and fresh herbs to taste

Heat a heavy-based saucepan over a medium–high heat. Add a generous splash of oil, onion, celery and leek. Cook for 5–6 minutes, stirring often. Add sweet potato, ginger and garlic and cook for a further 3–4 minutes. Add enough stock to just cover, and salt and pepper, and bring to the boil. Reduce heat and simmer for 15 minutes, or until sweet potato is tender.

Remove from heat, purée soup using food processor and pass through a strainer back into a clean saucepan. To serve, bring soup back to the boil, check seasoning, and add cream if desired and chopped herbs to garnish. Serves 4.

Pumpkin and coriander soup
Substitute ½ butternut pumpkin for sweet potatoes. Add a handful of chopped fresh coriander leaves just before serving. Leave ginger in or take out, according to your taste.

Spiced pumpkin and lentil soup
Remove ginger; substitute ½ butternut pumpkin for sweet potatoes. Add 1 tbsp curry paste and 60 g (2 oz) red lentils with the onion.

Carrot and coriander soup
Substitute 3–4 carrots for sweet potato, adding the juice of 1 orange as well.

Roast tomato soup ⓥ

Roasting tomatoes brings an extra intensity to this soup. Adding a dollop of pesto as you serve it takes it one step further.

1 red capsicum
500 g (1 lb) roma tomatoes
Olive oil for cooking
Freshly ground black pepper
1 onion, diced
1 garlic clove, crushed

1 small red chilli, halved
2 small celery sticks, chopped
1 carrot, sliced
2 potatoes, peeled and diced
1 litre (1⅔ pt) vegetable stock
Pesto to serve, optional

Preheat oven to 200°C (390°F).

Cut capsicum in half and remove seeds. Cut tomatoes in half and place on baking tray along with capsicum halves. Lightly drizzle with oil, sprinkle with ground pepper and cook in preheated oven for 30 minutes, or until tomatoes are soft and browned. Place capsicums in a plastic bag and seal to allow steam to lift skins. When tomatoes and capsicums have cooled, peel and discard skins.

Heat a large saucepan over a medium heat. Add a splash of oil, onion, garlic, chilli, celery and carrot. Cook for 5 minutes, stirring occasionally, until softened. Add potatoes, cook gently for another 5 minutes, then add peeled tomatoes and capsicum. Add vegetable stock and bring to the boil. Simmer gently for 20 minutes or until potatoes are soft. Purée and pass through a strainer into a clean saucepan.

Return soup to the boil, check seasoning and adjust consistency.

Add a dollop of pesto to each bowl of soup if desired. Serves 4.

Asian-inspired pumpkin soup

This soup came about when we got totally fed up with regular pumpkin soup. All we've done is add some Thai paste for flavour and coconut milk for creaminess. Now, it's anything but boring.

2 tbsp vegetable oil
2 tbsp Thai curry paste
1 onion, diced
1 celery stalk, diced
1 tomato, chopped

1 kg (2 lb) pumpkin, peeled and diced
Salt and freshly ground black pepper
1 litre (1⅔ pints) vegetable or chicken stock
400 ml (13 fl oz) coconut milk
Coriander leaves to garnish

Heat a large heavy-based saucepan over medium heat. Add oil and Thai paste and cook for 5 minutes, stirring often until fragrant. Add onion, celery, tomato, pumpkin and salt. Reduce heat and cook for 15 minutes, stirring often.

Add stock to the saucepan, raise the heat and bring to the boil. Reduce to a simmer, cover saucepan and cook for 20 minutes, or until pumpkin is tender. Purée soup and strain into a clean saucepan.

Return soup to the boil, whisk in the coconut milk and adjust seasoning. Serve with coriander leaves on top. Serves 6.

Green pea soup

Soup made with fresh green peas is a real taste sensation; it's also very easy to make. Here the peas are lightly cooked, then added to a simple potato base and puréed until smooth. A few fresh herbs, a splash of cream and it's ready.

3 tbsp butter
1 onion, diced
1 stick celery, sliced
1 leek, white only, washed and sliced
2 cloves garlic, crushed
3 medium potatoes, peeled and diced
Salt and freshly ground black pepper

500 ml (1 pt) light chicken stock
1 kg (2 lb) peas in the pod – 450–500 g (approx. 1 lb) podded peas
12 basil leaves, sliced
12 mint leaves, sliced
90 ml (3 fl oz) cream

Melt butter in a heavy saucepan over medium heat. Add onion, celery and leek; cook for 5 minutes, stirring often. Add garlic, potato, salt and pepper, cook for a further 3 minutes. Pour in stock. Bring to the boil; reduce heat and simmer until all ingredients are tender, about 10–15 minutes.

Bring a pot of water to the boil. Add a pinch of salt, then the podded peas and cook until vibrant green and tender, about 5 minutes. Pour into a colander; refresh by running under cold water. It is essential to cook the peas separately to avoid overcooking them and turning the soup grey-green.

Purée peas and stock together and pass through a fine sieve. Return to a clean saucepan. To serve, bring the soup to a gentle boil. Remove from the heat and add the chopped herbs and cream. Adjust the consistency with more stock if required, season to taste and serve. Serves 6.

Broad bean soup

Broad beans can be a delicious ingredient, especially when they are small and sweet. Avoid large beans – these are likely to be woody and bitter. It's best to pod them and also to remove the thin inner layer that encases each bean before use.

Olive oil for cooking
1 onion, diced
1 garlic clove, crushed
1 potato, diced
1 litre (1⅔ pt) chicken or vegetable stock

Sprig of sage
Salt and freshly ground black pepper
1 kg (2 lb) broad beans, podded
90 ml (3 fl oz) cream

Heat a large heavy-based saucepan over medium heat, add oil and onion. Cook for 5 minutes, stirring often until soft but not coloured. Add garlic and potato and cook for a further 2–3 minutes. Add stock, sage and a pinch of salt and bring to the boil. Cook for 15–20 minutes, or until potato is cooked. Add broad beans and cook for a further 5 minutes.

Remove soup from the heat, purée in a food processor and strain into a clean saucepan. Return to the boil, remove from the heat, whisk in the cream and adjust seasoning. Serves 4.

With crispy prosciutto
Heat a small pan over medium heat, add a splash of oil and cook 8 prosciutto slices until crisp. Remove and place on paper towel to drain excess oil. Chop roughly and sprinkle on top of each bowl of soup.

Parsnip, ginger and lemon soup

An unusual-sounding combination, but in fact the lemon and ginger really add a refreshing sharpness to the creamy parsnip flavour.

2 tbsp olive oil
1 onion, diced
1 leek, sliced
1 × 5 cm (2 in) piece ginger, peeled and chopped
1 garlic clove, crushed
1 celery stalk, chopped
1 carrot, diced
1 tomato, diced
4 parsnips, chopped
½ lemon
Salt
500–750 ml (1–1½ pt) vegetable or chicken stock
2 tbsp cream
Chopped parsley to garnish

Heat a heavy-based saucepan over medium heat. Add oil, onion, leek, ginger, garlic, celery and carrot. Cook for 5–7 minutes, stirring often, or until softened. Add tomato and parsnips, cook for a further 5 minutes. Add lemon, salt and enough stock to cover. Bring to the boil, reduce heat and simmer for 15–20 minutes or until all vegetables are cooked.

Remove lemon, purée soup and strain into a clean saucepan. Return soup to the boil, then remove from the heat. Add cream and adjust the seasoning.

Sprinkle chopped parsley on top to serve. Serves 4.

Chicken noodle soup

An easy soup to make and incredibly nourishing too. Those Jewish mothers really know a thing or two. Well ... any mother, come to that.

500 g (1 lb) chicken casserole pieces or thigh pieces
1 onion, roughly chopped
1 leek, roughly chopped
2 carrots, roughly chopped
2 celery stalks, roughly chopped
A few whole black peppercorns
2 bay leaves
Parsley stalks
2–3 litres ($3\frac{1}{3}$–5 pt) water
100 g ($3\frac{1}{2}$ oz) thin spaghetti, broken into 5 cm pieces
2 tbsp chopped parsley

Place chicken pieces in a large pot, add vegetables, peppercorns, herbs and water, and bring to the boil. Remove any scum from the surface, reduce to a simmer and cook for 2–3 hours. Remove chicken pieces and set aside to cool.

Strain liquid and press down hard on the ingredients to extract all the flavour. When stock has cooled slightly, refrigerate to allow fat to set on the surface. Skim fat off the surface and the stock is ready to use. You should have 1 litre ($1\frac{2}{3}$ pt). Add water if necessary.

Remove skin and bone from chicken pieces and dice the chicken meat. Bring reserved cooking liquid back to the boil. Add spaghetti and simmer for 10 minutes until pasta is cooked. Add chicken, return to the boil, check seasoning and add parsley to serve. Serves 4.

Chinese noodle soup
Instead of spaghetti use thin Chinese noodles, either fresh or dried, and season with soy sauce. Serve with sliced spring onions on top instead of parsley.

Vietnamese noodle soup
Flavour broth with grated ginger, sliced chilli, thinly sliced lemongrass and a few drops of fish sauce. Replace spaghetti with rice noodles and serve with coriander leaves, a handful of bean sprouts and some crispy fried shallots on top.

Chicken and corn soup
Add kernels from 2 cobs of corn (or a small tin of kernels) to the broth. Instead of spaghetti use thin Chinese noodles, either fresh or dried, and season with a little soy sauce. Just before serving, lightly whisk one egg and stir into the soup. Serve with sliced spring onions on top instead of parsley.

TIP
A table salad is the perfect accompaniment to the Vietnamese noodle soup. This consists of 200 g (7 oz) bean sprouts, 6 sliced spring onions, 2 sliced small red chillies, 2 limes cut into large wedges, plus a few sprigs of Vietnamese mint leaves, Thai basil leaves and coriander leaves. Wash all ingredients well, drain and place on a large platter to serve with the soup.

Wonton soup

We love this style of soup, where the simplicity of the broth is combined with the silky softness of delicate wontons. We think you will too.

150 g (5 oz) pork or chicken mince
2 spring onions, sliced
2 tsp grated ginger
1 tbsp soy sauce
1 tbsp chopped coriander

1 packet wonton wrappers
1 litre (1⅔ pt) chicken stock
Soy sauce as required
2 spring onions, sliced

Mix together mince, spring onion, ginger, soy sauce and chopped coriander. Lay 6–8 wonton wrappers out flat in front of you. Brush two edges of each wonton with water. Place one teaspoon of meat mixture in the centre of each wrapper. Fold each wonton in half, press edges together and hold firmly to seal. Repeat until all mince mixture is used.

Bring chicken stock to the boil, then reduce to a simmer. Carefully add the wontons to the simmering stock and cook for 3–4 minutes. Season to taste with soy sauce and serve with sliced spring onions Serves 4.

Duck and macadamia wonton soup

Roast duck is widely available from all Asian roast-house restaurants. They will often supply a little tub of cooking juices if requested. If they do, this will make a great addition to the cooking stock.

¼ roast duck
750 ml (1¼ pt) water
60 ml (2 fl oz) light soy sauce
1 × 5 cm (2 in) piece ginger, sliced
1 small red chilli, split

6 shallots, sliced
2 tbsp chopped coriander
60 g (2 oz) macadamia nuts, chopped
1 packet wonton wrappers
4 spring onions, chopped

Remove meat from duck. Thinly slice meat and set aside. Place duck bones, cooking juices (if available), water, soy sauce, ginger and chilli in a saucepan and bring to the boil. Reduce to a simmer and cook for 25 minutes, removing scum as it comes to the surface. Strain into a clean saucepan. You should have 1 litre (1⅔ pt). Add water if necessary.

Combine duck meat with shallots, coriander and macadamia nuts. Season to taste.

Lay 6–8 wonton wrappers out flat in front of you. Brush two edges of each wonton with water. Place one teaspoon of duck mixture in the centre of each wrapper. Fold each wonton in half, press edges together and hold firmly to seal. Repeat until all mixture is used.

To serve, bring stock to the boil. Add wontons and poach for 3–4 minutes. Divide wontons between bowls, ladle broth over and garnish with spring onions. Serves 4.

Udon soup with shiitake and roast duck

This is a Japanese-influenced soup and one that can be varied in many different ways to suit different moods and tastes. We like to adapt it by adding slices of Chinese duck and coriander to blend with the traditional Japanese flavours and textures. We love it as a late dinner.

1 litre (1⅔ pt) chicken stock
3 tbsp miso paste*
4 tbsp tamari*
250 g (8 oz) udon noodles
200 g (7 oz) broccoli, cut into 2 cm (¾ in) pieces
150 g (5 oz) shiitake mushrooms, sliced
½ roast duck, flesh removed from bone and sliced
2 spring onions, thinly sliced
½ cup coriander leaves

Bring chicken stock to the boil. Mix miso paste and tamari together and add to boiling stock. Allow to cook for 3–4 minutes. Add the noodles, mushrooms and broccoli, cook for 2 minutes. Add duck and spring onions. Return to the boil then remove from the heat. Add coriander leaves and check seasoning. Serves 4.

Udon soup with tofu
Replace roast duck with 300 g (10 oz) soft tofu. Dice this and add to the broth with coriander.

Tom yum

The ingredients and food of Thailand really opened up our palates to the possibilities of other Asian countries. For that we'll be forever thankful. This is a simple broth that uses many of the aromatic Thai ingredients we have come to know and love.

1 skinless chicken breast fillet, thinly sliced
2 tbsp tom yum paste*
500 ml (1 pt) chicken stock
500 ml (1 pt) water
2 kaffir lime leaves, shredded
3 spring onions, chopped
1 lemongrass stem, thinly sliced
4 shallots, sliced
4 coriander stems and roots, chopped
1 tbsp shaved palm sugar
2 tbsp fish sauce
2 tbsp lime juice
Coriander leaves to garnish
Sliced red chillies, optional

Marinate chicken in tom yum paste for 30 minutes.
   Place stock and water in a large saucepan. Add lime leaves, spring onions, lemongrass, shallots, coriander, palm sugar and fish sauce. Bring to the boil over a medium heat. Reduce to a simmer and cook for 20 minutes. Strain into a clean saucepan. Add chicken and lime juice, and simmer for 5 minutes. Check seasoning, adding more fish sauce if necessary. Serve with coriander leaves and chillies if desired. Serves 4.

Prawn and coconut tom yum
Marinate 500 g (1 lb) green (raw) peeled prawns in tom yum paste. Add them to the strained soup along with the lime juice and 125 ml (4 fl oz) coconut milk. Serve with coriander leaves and chillies.

Laksa

We were tossing up as to which chapter this dish should be in – is it a noodle dish, a curry or a soup? As you can see, the soup chapter won. But boy, oh boy, what a soup!

200 g (7 oz) dried vermicelli noodles
2 tbsp vegetable oil
2 tbsp laksa paste
500 ml (1 pt) chicken stock
250 ml (8 fl oz) water
400 ml (13 fl oz) coconut milk
2 tbsp fish sauce
2 tomatoes, diced, optional
½ red capsicum

12 green (raw) prawns, heads and shells removed
Handful of bean sprouts
100 g (3½ oz) deep fried beancurd, sliced
1 cup mixed herbs, to include Vietnamese mint, coriander, Thai basil
2 limes, cut into wedges
Crispy shallots* to serve

Place vermicelli noodles in a large bowl and cover with boiling water. Soak for 8–10 minutes, or until the noodles soften. Drain and set aside.

Heat a large saucepan or wok over a medium heat and add the vegetable oil. Add the paste and stir for 2–3 minutes, or until aromatic. Add chicken stock, water and coconut milk, and bring to the boil. Add fish sauce, tomato, capsicum and prawns. Simmer until prawns are cooked, about 3–4 minutes.

To serve, divide noodles between four bowls. Add bean sprouts and slices of bean curd. Ladle broth into bowls and top with a large handful of fresh herbs and shallots. Serve with lime wedges. Serves 4.

Chicken laksa
Substitute 1 sliced chicken fillet for prawns.

Duck and pine mushroom bread soup

This is a more complex version of bread and cheese soup. It's wonderful in early autumn, when pine mushrooms start to appear on market stalls, though any full-flavoured mushroom may be used.

1 litre (1⅔ pt) duck stock
Olive oil for cooking
2 duck breasts
1 garlic clove, crushed

200 g (7 oz) pine mushrooms, thinly sliced
250 ml (8 fl oz) light red wine
4 slices day-old sourdough bread
½ cup chopped flat-leaf parsley

Preheat oven to 180°C (350°F).

Place duck stock in a medium-sized saucepan and bring to the boil. Reduce to a gentle simmer. Heat a heavy-based frying pan over a medium–hot heat, add a splash of olive oil and cook duck breasts for 2–3 minutes on each side. Place in preheated oven for 10 minutes, or until cooked to medium–rare. Remove and allow to rest for 10 minutes.

Drain excess fat from pan, leaving just enough to cook mushrooms. Add garlic and mushrooms to hot pan and cook for 3–4 minutes until soft and fragrant. Add wine, stir well, then add this mixture to the simmering stock.

Cut duck breast into thin slices. Arrange a piece of bread in each bowl, top with parsley and duck slices. Divide hot broth and mushrooms over bread and duck. Serves 4.

French onion soup

Serve huge bowls of this intensely flavoured soup with a loaf of good bread, a wedge of full-flavoured cheese (such as English farmhouse cheddar) and a green salad. It will prove once and for all our theory of how satisfying the holy trinity of soup, bread and cheese can be.

2 tbsp butter
1 tbsp olive oil
6 onions, diced
2 garlic cloves, crushed
Salt and freshly ground black pepper

2 tbsp flour
1½ litres (2⅔ pints) beef stock
12–18 slices French bread
Grated cheese

Heat a heavy-based saucepan over a medium heat. Add butter and oil, allow to melt then add the onions and garlic. Cook and stir occasionally for 30 minutes, by which time the onions should develop a pale golden colour. Sprinkle in the flour and cook for 3–4 minutes, stirring often.

Add stock and bring to the boil, whisking occasionally to ensure that the flour is incorporated. Reduce to a simmer, cover the pot and cook for 45 minutes. By this stage it should have achieved a good gutsy flavour. Season to taste.

Top bread slices with grated cheese and cook under a hot grill until cheese melts. Pour soup into bowls and place cheese croutons on top. Serves 4–6.

Creamy onion soup
Add one diced potato to cooked onions, use chicken instead of beef stock and purée soup when cooked. Stir in a few tablespoons of cream just before serving. Sprinkle with chopped parsley and freshly grated black pepper.

Beetroot soup

This soup is rich, warming and restorative. It's also easy to prepare as it's a simple matter of cooking diced beetroot in an aromatic broth until tender. It's also a great use of beetroot, a vegetable that we happen to adore.

2 tbsp olive oil
1 onion, diced
1 celery stalk, diced
1 garlic clove, crushed
3 large beetroots, peeled and diced 1 cm (¼ in)

100 ml (3½ fl oz) orange juice
750 ml (1½ pt) chicken or beef stock
1 tbsp balsamic vinegar
Salt and freshly ground black pepper
Natural yoghurt or sour cream to serve

Heat a heavy-based saucepan over a medium heat. Add oil, onion and celery and cook for 4–5 minutes, stirring often. Add garlic and diced beetroot and cook for a further 5 minutes, stirring often. Add orange juice, stock and vinegar and bring to the boil. Lower heat and cook for 15–20 minutes, or until beetroot is tender.

Add lots of pepper, check seasoning and serve each bowl with a spoonful of yoghurt or sour cream. Serves 4.

Roasted vegetable gazpacho

This soup takes the classic gazpacho idea and combines it with roasted vegetables, which we find adds a terrific depth of flavour and richness. It's a soup that takes a little time to prepare and requires top-quality ingredients – the sort of thing we make on a lazy Sunday afternoon in summer.

The roasted vegetable purée
3 red capsicums
Olive oil for cooking
6 tomatoes

1 onion, peeled and quartered
1 small red chilli, halved
3 cloves garlic, peeled
Salt and freshly ground black pepper

Preheat oven to 200°C (390°F).

Rub capsicums with oil and place in a baking tray. Put tomatoes, onion, chilli and garlic in another baking tray and toss with oil, salt and pepper. Roast until capsicum skins blister and tomatoes become soft, about 30 minutes. Place capsicums in a plastic bag and seal to allow steam to lift skins.

Allow tomatoes and capsicums to cool, then set aside 2 capsicums for later use. Remove and discard seeds and skins from tomatoes and capsicum. Purée the tomato, capsicum, onion, garlic and chilli with cooking juices. Pass through a sieve and refrigerate.

The diced vegetables
1 Lebanese cucumber
3 tomatoes, blanched and skins removed
½ green capsicum
Salt and freshly ground black pepper

125 ml (4 fl oz) olive oil
3 tbsp chopped parsley
½ cup shredded basil
500 ml (1 pt) vegetable or chicken stock
Shredded basil to garnish

Remove the skin and seeds from the cucumber, dice finely and place in a colander with salt and set aside to drain.

Quarter tomatoes, remove seeds and dice remaining flesh finely. Dice green capsicum the same size. Take the reserved roasted capsicums, remove skins and seeds, and dice the flesh same size as the tomato. Rinse cucumber and pat dry.

Combining
In a large bowl mix the puréed roasted vegetables, the diced vegetables, the olive oil and herbs. Add enough stock to adjust the consistency, keeping in mind the soup will thicken as it chills. Check seasoning.

Place the soup and serving bowls in the refrigerator for one hour before serving.

Give chilled soup a final taste test, and then pour into bowls and garnish with the shredded basil. Serves 6.

Moroccan lentil broth v

There are times when you want a soup packed with the goodness of lentils and vegetables, without it being bland. If so, this soup certainly fits the bill. Every mouthful is flavoured with aromatic saffron, a hint of garlic and a little fiery harissa paste.

2 tbsp olive oil
1 onion, finely diced
1 leek, thinly sliced
2 celery stalks, finely diced
2 carrots, finely diced
2 garlic cloves, crushed

20 saffron stems
2 tsp harissa paste*
1 litre (1⅔ pt) vegetable stock
150 g (5 oz) red lentils
2 tbsp chopped parsley

Heat a medium-sized saucepan over a medium heat and add oil. Add onion, leek, celery and carrots and cook for 5 minutes or until beginning to soften, stirring often. Add garlic, saffron and harissa and cook for 2–3 minutes until fragrant. Add stock and bring to the boil.

Rinse lentils under cold running water, then add to the soup. Reduce heat and cook for 15–20 minutes, or until lentils are completely tender. Check seasoning, add parsley and serve. Serves 4.

Vegetable and barley broth

This style of soup can be altered to include virtually any combination of ingredients. The choice of vegetables below is our winter selection. In summer it would rely more heavily on tomatoes, capsicums, zucchini, sweet corn and celery.

60 g (2 oz) barley
1–2 tbsp olive oil
1 onion, finely diced
1 leek, thinly sliced
1 celery stalk, finely diced
1 carrot, finely diced
1 parsnip, finely diced

1 potato, finely diced
1 small swede or turnip, finely diced
2 garlic cloves, chopped
Salt and freshly ground black pepper
1250 ml (2½ pt) vegetable or chicken stock
Chopped parsley

Place barley in a small saucepan, cover with plenty of water and bring to the boil. Reduce heat and simmer for 30 minutes, or until barley is tender. You may need to skin the surface a little during cooking. Drain barley, rinse under cold water and set aside.

Heat a saucepan over a medium heat and add oil. Add the chopped vegetables, garlic and salt and pepper and cook for 10 minutes, stirring often. Add stock and bring to the boil. Reduce heat to a simmer, cover the saucepan and cook for 20 minutes, or until the vegetables are tender.

Add the barley and chopped parsley to soup, then adjust the consistency and seasoning. It should have quite a peppery tang. Serves 4–6.

Corn chowder

We have been making and enjoying this creamy, chunky corn soup forever. Make it once and it's sure to become a favourite of yours too. Remember to keep all the vegetables finely diced, as this soup is not puréed.

2–3 tbsp olive oil
1 onion, finely diced
2 garlic cloves, crushed
1 leek, chopped finely
2 celery sticks, chopped finely
1 zucchini, chopped finely
2 carrots, chopped finely
2 tbsp plain flour

1 litre (1⅔ pt) vegetable or chicken stock
2 corn cobs, kernels removed with a sharp knife
250 g (8 oz) creamed cottage cheese
2 tbsp sour cream
1 tbsp chopped parsley
1 tbsp chopped basil

Heat a heavy-based saucepan over medium heat. Add the oil, onion, garlic, leek, celery, zucchini and carrot. Cook for 7–8 minutes, stirring often. Stir in the flour. Lower the heat to allow the flour to cook completely. Pour in stock and return to the boil, whisking occasionally.

When boiling, add corn kernels, then simmer for 10 minutes. Remove from the heat, whisk in cheese and sour cream. Add the chopped parsley and basil then check seasoning. Serves 4.

Fish and fennel chowder

Chowder with seafood is yet another great favourite of ours. The flavour of the fish, the sweetness of corn and a tiny hint of chilli is a combination we really enjoy. Take care to choose a variety of fish that will keep its shape during cooking. Ask your fishmonger if you're not sure.

Olive oil for cooking
1 onion, finely diced
2 garlic clove, crushed
2 small red chillies, de-seeded and diced
1 fennel bulb, diced 1½ cm (⅔ in)
1 red capsicum, diced 1½ cm (⅔ in)
2 potatoes, diced 1½ cm (⅔ in)
2 tbsp plain flour

2 corn cobs, kernels removed with a sharp knife
1 litre (1⅔ pt) fish stock
500 g (1 lb) trevally fillets, skin removed and diced 2 cm (¾ in)
125 g (4 oz) crème fraîche
¼ cup torn basil leaves

Heat a large heavy-based saucepan over medium heat. Add oil, onion, garlic, chillies and fennel, stir and cook for 4–6 minutes until soft. Add capsicum and potato, and cook for a further 5 minutes. Reduce heat, add the flour, stir and cook for 2 minutes.

Add corn kernels and enough fish stock to just cover. Bring to the boil, stirring. Reduce to a simmer and cook for 5 minutes, ensuring potato is soft. Add fish and cook briefly. Remove from the heat, add crème fraîche and herbs, check the seasoning and adjust the consistency as required with remaining fish stock. Serves 4.

Shellfish chowder
Substitute peeled prawns, mussels or oysters for the white fish and proceed as described. Prawns will take 3–4 minutes to cook, mussels 2–3 minutes and oysters only 30 seconds to heat through. You can even add oysters after soup has been poured into bowls.

Minestrone

The ingredients list might look somewhat daunting, but don't be alarmed. You can use any or all of what we suggest, or even more, depending on what you have available. Sweet corn, peas, green beans, spinach leaves, chopped cabbage and cooked chickpeas are some of our other favourite ingredients to add. Be warned: minestrone seems to grow and grow.

Oil for cooking
1 onion, diced
1 celery stalk, diced
1 leek, thinly sliced
1 carrot, diced
½ red capsicum, diced
1 potato, diced

2 garlic cloves, crushed
250 ml (8 fl oz) tomato purée
750 ml (1½ pt) chicken or vegetable stock
Salt and freshly ground black pepper
60 g (2 oz) risoni
4 tbsp chopped parsley and basil or a dollop of pesto

Heat a large heavy-based saucepan over a medium–high heat. Add a generous splash of oil and add onion, celery, leek, carrot, capsicum and potato. Cook for 8–10 minutes, stirring often. Add garlic and cook for 1–2 minutes more. Add tomato purée, stock, salt and pepper and bring to the boil. Add risoni and reduce heat to a simmer. Cook for 10 minutes, check seasoning and add herbs to taste. Serves 4.

Oxtail soup

Oxtail soup is delicious and rich – perfect for a warming meal. It's a soup that requires a hefty 3–4 hours of simmering in order to draw out the best flavours. Oxtail soup was a constant in my winter diet as a child growing up in Ireland, so perhaps I still make it for nostalgic reasons. AC

1 kg (2 lb) oxtails, cut into 3–4 cm (1¼–1½ in) pieces
Seasoned flour
Olive oil for cooking
2 onions, diced
2 carrots, diced
3 celery stalks, diced
2 leeks, sliced

3 tbsp tomato paste
750 ml (1½ pt) red wine
1.5 litres (3 pt) beef stock
2–3 bay leaves
2–3 sprigs thyme
Salt and freshly ground black pepper
Chopped parsley

Coat each piece of oxtail with seasoned flour, shaking well to remove any excess.

Heat a large saucepan over a medium heat and add a generous splash of oil. Add onion, carrot, celery and leek, and cook for 5–10 minutes, stirring regularly. Remove vegetables from pan and set aside. Return pan to a medium–high heat, add more oil if needed and cook each piece of oxtail until brown.

Add tomato paste and cook briefly for 1–2 minutes, stirring occasionally. Return vegetables to pan and add red wine, stock, herbs and pinch of salt, and bring to the boil. Remove any scum as it rises to the surface and reduce heat to low. Allow soup to simmer for 3–4 hours.

Remove oxtail and set aside to cool. Purée soup and strain liquid into a clean saucepan. When oxtail is cool enough to handle, remove all meat from the bones and dice finely. When ready to serve bring soup to the boil; add oxtail meat, return to the boil and check seasoning. Add chopped parsley. Serves 6.

Platters
Baba ghanoush
Tzatziki
Hummus
Beetroot dip
Tapenade
Guacamole
White bean dip
Dukkah
Pita crisps
Crostini
Blinis
Tomato and fresh herb salsa
Chicken liver pâté
Smoked trout pâté
Pecorino and pancetta vine leaf parcels
Artichoke, prosciutto and buffalo mozzarella parcels
Pandan chicken parcels
Roast duck, chilli and coriander rolls
Spring rolls
Prawn rice paper rolls
Vietnamese dipping sauce
Thai fish balls
Onion bahjis
Boreks
Sushi rice
California rolls
Summer vegetable terrine
Goat's cheese soufflé

Nibbles and entrées

DIPS, PLATTERS AND SMALL THINGS

Having friends around is something we do most weekends. It could be anything from a sit-down dinner for four to a casual barbecue for ten or more, children included. Much of what we serve on such occasions is covered in this book, but this chapter is all about what we serve before the main meal begins.

This is our take on cocktail food for today: dips and nibbles to whet the appetite, crispy pastries, antipasto platters of flavoursome foods, plus delicious crunchy toasts and delicate blinis to accompany the glass or two of sparkling that is an essential part of every good occasion. Well, it is at our place – particularly if it's a bottle of sparkling red.

THINGS YOU NEED TO KNOW ABOUT NIBBLES AND ENTRÉES

- If you plan to stand up and eat nibbly food, make sure that it's suitable to be eaten with one hand.
- Remember to offer serviettes.
- For a full-on cocktail party experience, allow at least 7 items per person for the first hour and add 2 more for each hour after that.
- If you expect your guests to be drinking a lot of alcohol, up the food accordingly.
- Serve nibbles that are in keeping with the dishes and flavours you are serving for the main meal.
- Keep the dish fairly small; it's supposed to be a tasty beginning to the meal, rather than a filling one.
- Serve a dish that is suitable for the weather, too: rich dishes in cool weather and lighter food in the warmer months.

Platters

A mixed platter is an excellent way to provide tasty nibbles before a meal and can be made up well in advance so that you can enjoy the party too. Remember to arrange the components so that different-coloured and -flavoured foods are alongside each other to help make the platter more attractive to the eye.

Antipasto platter
The following can be considered for an antipasto platter: frittata wedges, black or green olives, bocconcini, sun-dried tomatoes, marinated artichoke hearts, diced feta cheese, strips of roasted red capsicum plus thinly sliced prosciutto, ham and salami. A bowl of tapenade is also good here.

Serve with plenty of sliced foccacia bread or grissini sticks.

Middle-Eastern platter
A Middle-Eastern platter might include small dolmades, felafel balls, black or green olives, marinated artichoke hearts and wedges of cucumber, capsicum and tomato. Thinly sliced bastourma (a spice-coated air-dried beef) and thinly sliced salami are also good, along with hummus, baba ghanoush and/or tzatziki. A bowl of dukkah (page 44) and olive oil are also a good match with these foods.

Serve with toasted crisp breads or pita bread.

Vegetable crudité platter
A typical crudité platter might include carrots, red capsicum, fennel and stalks of celery, all cut into long sticks; mushrooms, washed and quartered; cucumber cut into thin circles; tomatoes cut into wedges; and cherry tomatoes. Provide a few dips such as guacamole, beetroot dip or hummus.

Serve with grissini sticks, corn chips and crisp breads.

Baba ghanoush v

Baba ghanoush is a classic Middle-Eastern dip made with eggplants that have been cooked over a flame – best done over a gas stove or on a barbecue. It's this cooking that gives the dip its distinctive smoky flavour and aroma.

2 medium eggplants
½ tsp crushed garlic
1–2 tbsp lemon juice
3 tbsp tahini

90 g (3 oz) natural yoghurt
Pinch of ground allspice
White pepper and salt

Cook each eggplant over a gas flame until the skin is charred and the flesh is completely softened inside. If eggplants are not completely softened they can be finished in a 180°C (350°F) preheated oven. Allow to cool completely.

Peel away charred skin carefully and spoon flesh into a bowl. Mash with a fork until smooth. Stir in garlic, lemon juice, tahini and yoghurt along with allspice, white pepper and salt. Mix well and season to taste.

Serve with slices of Turkish pide bread or as part of a Middle-Eastern antipasto platter. Serves 6–8.

Tzatziki v

Tzatziki can be used as a dip with warm crusty bread or served with spicy curries or Middle-Eastern dishes to tone down the chilli heat. We're rarely without it in our refrigerator. Ewe's, goat's or buffalo milk yoghurt, instead of the more usual cow's milk, will add an extra flavour dimension.

350 g (12 oz) natural yoghurt
1 garlic clove, crushed
1 Lebanese cucumber, grated
Pinch of salt

Freshly ground black pepper
Pinch of dried mint
¼ cup chopped coriander leaves, roughly chopped

Mix all ingredients together and season to taste. Serves 8–10.

Basil tzatziki
Substitute basil leaves for coriander.

> **TIP**
> If your yoghurt is a bit runny, place a clean tea towel in a sieve, tip in yoghurt and drain over a bowl in the refrigerator for at least 2 hours or, better still, overnight. Discard the whey and then use the thick yoghurt.

Hummus (v)

Hummus is probably the most famous of all the Middle-Eastern dips. It's easy to make and the chickpeas give it a delicious nutty taste.

150 g (5 oz) chickpeas, soaked overnight
2 cloves garlic, chopped
90 ml (3 fl oz) tahini
2 tsp ground cumin
2 tsp ground coriander

2 tbsp lemon juice
3 tbsp olive oil
Salt and freshly ground black pepper
Sweet paprika

Drain chickpeas and place in a saucepan, cover with plenty of water and bring to the boil, reduce heat and cook for 30–40 minutes, or until chickpeas are soft. Drain and retain cooking liquid.

Place cooked chickpeas in a food processor and pulse until they are smooth. Add garlic, tahini, spices, lemon juice, oil, salt and pepper. Blend until all ingredients are smooth and well combined. If it's still thick add some of the cooking liquid. Adjust the seasoning by adding extra spices, lemon juice or salt and pepper.

Place the dip into a serving bowl. Drizzle a little olive oil on top, and sprinkle with sweet paprika. Serve with Lebanese bread. Serves 8–10.

Beetroot dip (v)

We were first introduced to beetroot dip many years ago in Turkey, where it is often called beetroot salad. Basically we love it, and we think you will too.

3 medium beetroots
1–2 tbsp red wine vinegar
3 tbsp olive oil

2 garlic cloves, crushed
1–2 tsp horseradish cream
Salt and freshly ground black pepper

Place beetroots in a saucepan, cover with plenty of water and bring to the boil over a medium heat. Once boiling, reduce heat, cover and cook for 30–40 minutes, until beetroots are tender.

Allow beetroots to cool, remove skins and chop flesh roughly. Place beetroot in food processor; add vinegar and oil and process until smooth. Add garlic, horseradish, and salt and pepper to taste.

Serve with pita crisps or slices of baguette. Serves 8–10.

Creamy beetroot dip
For a milder, creamier dip, add 125 g (4 fl oz) sour cream or natural yoghurt with garlic and horseradish.

Tapenade

Tapenade is a rich olive paste with a full-flavoured taste that comes from the addition of garlic, anchovies and capers. It's the type of thing we make in a fairly large quantity as it will keep refrigerated for 2–3 weeks with a layer of olive oil on top. We recommend hand chopping the ingredients to ensure a coarse texture, rather than the smooth paste that comes from a food processor.

100 g (3½ oz) salted capers
700 g (1 lb 7 oz) pitted kalamata olives
60 g (2 oz) anchovies, including oil
6 garlic cloves, crushed
2 tbsp chopped parsley
Freshly ground black pepper
250–350 ml (8–12 fl oz) olive oil

Soak capers in cold water for 10 minutes and rinse several times to remove excess salt. Drain well and chop finely. Coarsely chop the pitted olives and the anchovies. Stir capers, olives, anchovies (and their oil), garlic and parsley together in a large bowl. Season with freshly ground black pepper.

Add enough olive oil to make into a paste-like consistency. Place in an airtight container, cover with a layer of olive oil and refrigerate.

Serve with thick wedges of hot toast. Serves 10–12.

Guacamole v

This dip is famous all over the world, and when you taste a good'un, you realise why. It's tasty, fresh and completely more-ish. Here is our favourite variation, just one of many hundreds in the world.

2–3 ripe avocadoes
1 tbsp lemon or lime juice
1–2 green chillies, de-seeded and diced
2 tbsp chopped coriander
1 spring onion, sliced
1 tomato, finely diced
Salt and freshly ground black pepper
Tabasco, optional

Peel avocadoes and place flesh in a bowl. Mash to a coarse consistency with a fork. Add lemon juice, chilli, coriander, spring onion and tomato. Season with salt and pepper, adding a few drops of Tabasco if desired. Stir gently and taste, adding more citrus juice or chilli to suit.

Serve with toasted pita triangles or warmed corn chips. Serves 6–8.

White bean dip (v)

This light and tasty dip is made from haricot beans and flavoured with lashings of garlic, fresh herbs and freshly ground black pepper. Serve with a drizzle of your best olive oil on top.

200 g (7 oz) haricot beans, soaked overnight
2–3 garlic cloves, crushed
2 tbsp lemon juice
Salt and freshly ground black pepper
3 tbsp chopped flat-leaf parsley
Olive oil

Drain beans and place in a saucepan. Cover with plenty of water and bring to the boil, reduce heat and cook for 20–30 minutes, or until beans are soft. Drain well.

Place beans in food processor and purée until smooth. Add garlic and lemon juice, then season to taste with salt and pepper.

Place in a bowl and stir in chopped parsley. Drizzle olive oil on top before serving. Serves 6–8.

Dukkah (v)

Dukkah is an Egyptian spice blend that can be used in a myriad of ways. The simplest is to offer a bowl of olive oil and a bowl of dukkah with fresh bread. Dunk the bread into the oil, then into the dukkah. Delicious!

75 g (2⅔ oz) sesame seeds
50 g (1¾ oz) hazelnuts
30 g (1 oz) coriander seeds
50 g (1¾ oz) almonds
30 g (1 oz) cumin seeds
Sea salt flakes to taste

Toast all seeds and nuts separately until fragrant, either in a dry frying pan or on a baking tray in a preheated oven 180°C (350°F).

Allow to cool, then crush roughly in a mortar and pestle or use pulse on a food processor. Either way they should not be too finely ground. Add salt to taste. Serves 10–12.

Pita crisps (v)

1 × 450 g (15 oz) packet pita bread
Olive oil as required
Salt flakes
Poppyseed or toasted cumin seeds

Preheat oven to 180°C (350°F).

Using scissors cut around pita to produce 2 circles. Brush each pita bread circle (brown side) with olive oil, then sprinkle on salt and poppyseed. Lay the circles on top of each other as they are ready.

Cut each circle in half, then quarters, then each quarter into 3 triangles. Lay flat on baking trays and cook in preheated oven for 5–10 minutes or until crisp. Makes 80.

Lemon pepper pita crisps
Allan hates these, but that lemon and pepper mix you buy in the supermarket is perfect on pita crisps. MC

Cheese and sesame seed pita crisps
Brush pita bread with oil, then sprinkle on grated parmigiano and sesame seeds. Cut and cook.

Crostini

Crostini are slices of French stick that have are baked until they are crisp. They can be topped with a myriad of different ingredients or served with dips.

1 French stick
Olive oil as needed

Preheat oven to 160°C (320°F).

Slice bread into 1 cm (⅓ in) slices. Brush each slice with olive oil. Place onto flat baking trays and cook in preheated oven for 10–15 minutes or until crisp on top. Turn crostini slices over and continue cooking for 10 minutes more, or until golden. Makes 20–30.

Crisp breads
Thinly slice foccacia bread and brush with a little olive oil as directed in the crostini recipe.

Blinis

Blinis are small yeasty buckwheat pancakes that were traditionally served with caviar in Russia. Even if you're not serving caviar they make a great base for many other toppings.

1 sachet (7g) dried yeast
2 tbsp warm milk
200 ml (7 fl oz) milk
125 g (4 oz) buckwheat flour

2 medium eggs, separated
Pinch of salt
2 tbsp melted butter

Whisk together yeast and warm milk in a large bowl. Leave in a warm place until bubbles form on the surface. Whisk in milk, flour, egg yolks and salt. Cover and leave until bubbles again form on the surface.

Beat egg whites until stiff. Fold whites into the blini mixture.

Heat a heavy-based pan over a medium heat. Brush melted butter into pan, then spoon level tablespoons of blini mix into the pan. Allow to cook until bubbles appear on the surface, turn over and cook the other side for 1–2 minutes, until just golden brown.

Place cooked blinis on a flat tray to cool. Continue cooking until all mixture is used. When all blini are cooked, cover with cling film until you are ready to add the toppings. Makes 20–25.

Toppings for crostini and blini
Goat's curd and tapenade, page 43
Goat's curd and pesto, page 89
Pesto with roast capsicum and a dollop of ricotta
Sun-dried tomato with salami, feta and basil
Marinated artichoke with roast capsicum
Rocket leaves with pesto and goat's cheese
Thinly sliced ham with Dijon mustard
Salami with tapenade
Chicken liver pâté, page 46
Smoked salmon, sour cream, freshly ground black pepper and dill
Smoked salmon with sour cream and horseradish
Salmon caviar, crème fraîche and chives
Green olive salsa, page 143
Tomato and fresh herb salsa, page 46

Tomato and fresh herb salsa ⓥ

We use this salsa for a multitude of different things, including serving on top of crostini and blinis, as a fresh-tasting dip or spooned over barbecued chicken fillets.

4 ripe tomatoes
1 Lebanese cucumber
6 basil leaves, thinly sliced

Balsamic or sherry vinegar
Olive oil
Salt and freshly ground black pepper

Dice tomatoes and cucumber finely. Mix tomato, cucumber and basil together and season to taste with vinegar, olive oil, salt and pepper. Makes 250 ml (8 fl oz).

Chicken liver pâté

This pâté recipe is from our good friend Ruth Wirtz and is one of the smoothest, most delicious pâtés we've ever tasted. It is cooked at a fairly low temperature to retain its smooth texture and has a great flavour combination of bacon, onion, garlic and chicken livers. Make it just once and you too will be hooked.

250 g (8 oz) butter
2 onions, diced
2 garlic cloves, crushed
Salt and freshly ground black pepper

4 bacon slices, diced
500 g (1 lb) chicken livers, trimmed of any white sinew
1 tbsp brandy (optional)

Preheat oven to 160°C (320°F).

Heat a heavy-based pan over a medium heat. Melt 2 tbsp butter, add onion and garlic. Cook gently until onion begins to soften, about 6–7 minutes. Season well with salt and pepper. Add the bacon and livers to pan and continue to cook over a low heat for 5–6 minutes. Transfer ingredients to an ovenproof dish, cover and cook in preheated oven for 20 minutes. Melt remaining butter.

Allow livers to cool for 5 minutes, then place in a food processor. Purée until smooth, then add melted butter. Purée again until very smooth. Add brandy if using, then season to taste as required. Pour the mixture into a sieve and strain any remaining lumps. Spoon the pâté into a terrine dish or a few small bowls. Cover with cling film and chill overnight.

Serve with hot toast triangles or crackers. Makes 750 ml (1¼ pt).

Duck liver pâté
For a richer pâté replace chicken livers with duck livers, or any combination of pheasant, duck or even goose livers.

Other pâté flavours
This pâté can easily be varied by the addition of green peppercorns, port, Madeira, orange zest or cooked mushrooms.

Smoked trout pâté

We often use this recipe for smoked fish other than trout. Smoked mackerel is also excellent. However, it will need a little more lemon juice to cope with the oiliness of the fish.

200 g (7 oz) smoked trout
100 g (3½ oz) cream cheese
2 tsp horseradish cream

2–3 tbsp lemon juice
Salt and freshly ground black pepper

Remove the skin and all of the bones from the smoked trout. Flake the fish pieces and place in a food processor. Add the cream cheese and process until smooth. Add horseradish and enough lemon juice to get a good consistency, then season with salt and pepper. Serves 8–10.

Pecorino and pancetta vine leaf parcels

These little vine-leaf-wrapped parcels can be made 4–5 hours ahead of time and then cooked as guests are enjoying a drink. Cook them on a barbecue plate, in a frying pan or in the oven – they taste pretty much the same no matter which approach you take.

12 vine leaves
200 g (7 oz) pecorino cheese, sliced thinly

12 thin slices pancetta
Olive oil

Rinse vine leaves under cold running water, then lay out flat on paper towel. Place 1 slice of pancetta in the centre of each leaf and cover with shavings of pecorino. Fold vine leaves over to enclose ingredients.

Brush each parcel with a little olive oil to ensure they don't stick during cooking.

Cook each parcel for 2 minutes on each side on a barbecue plate, in a pan or for 4 minutes in a preheated oven 180°C (350°F). Makes 12.

Artichoke, prosciutto and buffalo mozzarella parcels

These parcels are an excellent pre-dinner snack with drinks. If you can't get buffalo mozzarella use regular cow's milk mozzarella.

12 slices prosciutto, not too thin
3 buffalo mozzarella, each cut into 3 slices
12 basil leaves

6 baby artichoke hearts, cut in half
Toothpicks

Lay prosciutto slices out flat. Lay a slice of mozzarella on top, followed by a basil leaf and an artichoke half. Roll up to encase the fillings and secure with a toothpick.

Cook each parcel for 6–8 minutes on a barbecue plate, in a pan or in a preheated oven 180°C (350°F). Makes 12.

Pandan chicken parcels

Pandan chicken parcels are pieces of black-bean-marinated chicken wrapped in an aromatic pandan leaf. They are easily cooked in the oven.

1 tbsp black beans*, soaked and drained
1 tsp chilli paste
1 tbsp kecap manis*

1 kg (2 lb) skinless chicken thigh fillets
20 pandan leaves*
Toothpicks

Finely chop black beans, then mix with chilli paste and kecap manis. Cut each thigh fillet into 4 evenly sized pieces. Marinate chicken in black bean mixture for 1 hour.

Preheat oven to 180°C (350°F).

Place one piece of chicken at one end of each pandanus leaf, then roll the pandanus leaf around chicken. Secure the pandanus leaf by putting a toothpick through it and the chicken.

Place parcels onto a baking tray and cook in preheated oven for 10–15 minutes, turning once. Serve them and advise guests to remove toothpick and pandan leaf before eating. Makes 20.

Roast duck, chilli and coriander rolls

Roast duck from an Asian roast house is one of our all-time favourite takeaway foods. It's crispy, it's full flavoured and it's ready to eat. Here it's rolled up in roti bread with sweet chilli, coriander leaves and fresh salad ingredients to create a real taste sensation. We love this for its simplicity.

1 roast duck
½ iceberg lettuce
2 Lebanese cucumbers
3 tomatoes

4 pieces roti bread or pita bread
3–4 tbsp sweet chilli sauce
1 cup coriander leaves

Preheat oven to 180°C (350°F).

Remove meat from roast duck, discarding any visible fat as you go. Cut the meat and crispy skin into thin shreds. Thinly slice the lettuce, cucumbers and tomatoes.

Heat bread in preheated oven for 3–4 minutes and remove. While still warm spread each with sweet chilli sauce, then scatter lettuce, cucumber, tomato and a few coriander leaves over the bread. Add a few strips of duck meat and roll the bread up, enclosing all ingredients. Cut into four equal-sized pieces and serve while still warm. Serves 8–10.

Spring rolls

We like to make tiny finger-sized spring rolls to serve before a meal, particularly if it's to be one with Asian flavours.

50 g (1¾ oz) vermicelli noodles
250 g (8 oz) pork mince
1 garlic clove, crushed
1 tsp grated ginger
½ red capsicum, finely diced
4 spring onions, green tops only, thinly sliced
1 tbsp kecap manis*

1 tbsp sweet chilli sauce
½ tbsp fish sauce
200 g (7 oz) packet small spring roll wrappers
1 medium egg, lightly beaten
Vegetable oil for deep-frying
90 ml (3 fl oz) soy sauce
2 small red chillies, chopped

Place noodles in a large bowl and cover completely with boiling water. Stand for 5 minutes to soften, then drain well.

Place noodles, pork mince, garlic, ginger, capsicum, spring onions, kecap manis, sweet chilli sauce and fish sauce together in a large bowl and mix well.

Peel a spring roll pastry wrapper off the stack and place in front of you with one corner facing downwards (like a diamond). Brush liberally with beaten egg. Place a teaspoon of the mixture near the bottom of the pastry; fold the bottom corner up over the filling, then fold the sides in. Roll up to the top and ensure wrapper seals well. Repeat with remaining ingredients.

Pour vegetable oil into a wok or a deep saucepan to a depth of 4 cm (1½ in) and heat. Deep-fry spring rolls 4 at a time until golden brown and allow to drain on a wok rack or kitchen paper.

Mix the soy and chilli together in a small bowl and serve as a dipping sauce with the spring rolls. Makes about 36.

Prawn rice paper rolls

Rice paper rolls are a firm favourite in our household, and with visitors too, it seems, if the speed with which they disappear is any indication. The soft, silky white wrappers usually encase fresh-tasting prawns, noodles, chopped peanuts and aromatic herbs. A lime-flavoured dipping sauce completes the picture. In a word, they're yum.

50 g (1¾ oz) cellophane noodles
6 cooked prawns, peeled, de-veined and
   thinly sliced
60 g (2 oz) roasted peanuts, chopped
2 tbsp chopped coriander

1 small carrot, finely grated
1 tbsp sweet chilli sauce
12 Vietnamese mint leaves, shredded
12 large rice paper wrappers

Place noodles in a large bowl and cover completely with boiling water. Stand for 5 minutes to soften, then drain well.

Place noodles, prawns, peanuts, coriander, carrot, chilli sauce and Vietnamese mint together in a large bowl and mix well. Season to taste.

Fill a large bowl with hot tap water; then soak the rice paper wrappers one at a time until softened. Remove carefully and drain on absorbent paper or a tea towel. Lay the wrappers out flat, then divide the filling on the bottom centre of each softened wrapper. Roll end up over filling, fold in sides and roll up to the top.

Serve with the Vietnamese dipping sauce described below. Makes 12.

Roast duck rice paper rolls
Instead of prawns, use ½ roast duck, meat removed and sliced.

Vietnamese dipping sauce

1 tbsp shaved palm sugar
2 tbsp lime juice
3 tbsp fish sauce

1 small red chilli, sliced
1 tbsp water

Dissolve sugar into the lime juice; add fish sauce, chilli and water. Allow flavours to infuse for 30 minutes before using.

Thai fish balls

The local fishmongers in Asian shopping streets sell fish mince topped with spring onions. This mince has been pounded until it has developed a texture that is springy. However 'regular' fish mince will work well with this recipe.

500 g (1 lb) fish mince
2 tbsp sweet chilli sauce
1 tbsp fish sauce
4 spring onions, thinly sliced
1 tbsp chopped coriander

1 medium egg
50 g (1¾ oz) dried breadcrumbs
Vegetable oil
Sweet chilli sauce for serving

Mix together fish mince, sweet chilli sauce, fish sauce, spring onions, coriander, egg and breadcrumbs until well combined. Roll into small balls about 2 cm (¾ in) across.

Heat a heavy-based pan over a medium heat. Add a thin layer of oil then cook the fish balls until golden brown all over.

Serve with sweet chilli sauce for dunking. Makes 20.

Onion bahjis v

Onion bahjis are deep-fried fritters of crisp onions and spices, but to many English people onion bahjis also mean a late-night Indian snack on the way home from the pub.

3 onions
150 g (5 oz) chickpea flour*
150 g (5 oz) plain flour
2 tsp baking powder
1 medium egg

1 tsp salt
3 tsp ground cumin
3 tsp ground coriander
Oil for deep-frying

Finely dice onions and blanch in a pot of boiling water. Drain onion well and reserve 250 ml (8 fl oz) of cooking liquid for batter mixture. Combine chickpea flour, plain flour, baking powder, egg, salt, ground cumin, ground coriander and reserved cooking liquid. Whisk until smooth. Add onion and mix well.

Pour vegetable oil into a wok or a deep saucepan to a depth of 4 cm (1½ in) and heat. Deep-fry spoonfuls of the onion bahji mix until golden brown and allow to drain on a wok rack or kitchen paper. Makes 20–24.

Boreks (v)

Boreks are a cheese pastry we learned to make in Turkey. In a way they are not unlike a spring roll, except the filling is cheese with a hint of garlic and mint.

250 g (8 oz) haloumi cheese, grated
125 g (4 oz) sheep's milk feta cheese, chopped
1 garlic clove, crushed
12 mint leaves, chopped
12 flat-leaf parsley leaves, chopped
Freshly ground black pepper
1 medium egg
250 g (8 oz) Turkish pastry (which can be hard to find), filo pastry or spring roll wrappers
Vegetable oil for deep-frying

Mix cheeses, garlic, mint and parsley with plenty of freshly ground black pepper. Taste the mix to ensure it has a good flavour. Stir egg into the mixture.

Cut pastry into 8 cm (3 in) squares. Lay out pastry squares and brush edges with cold water. Place a spoonful of the mixture onto the centre of each pastry (or spring roll wrapper).

Place a teaspoon of mixture near the bottom of the pastry; fold the bottom corner up over the filling, then fold the sides in. Roll up to the top and ensure wrapper seals well.

Pour vegetable oil into a wok or a deep saucepan to a depth of 4 cm (1½ in) and heat. Deep-fry boreks 4 at a time until golden brown, then allow to drain on kitchen paper. Makes 20–30.

Sushi rice

This is the rice that is used to make the ever-popular California rolls and sushi.

400 g (14 oz) medium-grain (sushi) rice
625 ml (20 fl oz) water
3 tbsp rice wine vinegar
1 tsp sugar
1 tsp salt

Place rice and water into a saucepan. Cover with a lid, bring to the boil, then reduce to a low simmer. It is important to keep covered with a lid, so as not to allow the steam to escape. This helps the rice to cook correctly.

It will take about 8–10 minutes for all the water to be absorbed. Allow the covered rice to stand covered for 5 minutes before using.

Warm rice wine vinegar in a small saucepan, add sugar and salt, stir until dissolved. Stir this into the rice while still hot. Allow rice to cool slightly before using to make sushi or California rolls.

California rolls

California rolls make perfect party food. However, they take a bit of practice to get just right. You'll need a bamboo mat to make the rolling easier, plus a few other Japanese ingredients, including wasabi and pickled ginger.

1 quantity sushi rice, previous page
1 packet nori sheets
Wasabi
1 carrot, cut into a thin julienne
1 cucumber, cut into a thin julienne

1 avocado, peeled and thinly sliced
Pickled ginger, as required
Seafood such as smoked salmon, cooked peeled prawns or crab meat, optional

Prepare sushi rice as directed. Lay out one nori sheet on your bamboo mat. Cover most of the nori with cooked rice, leaving the top 1 cm (⅓ in) free of rice.

Near the bottom spread a small layer of wasabi across the rice. Add a row of cucumber, carrot, avocado and pickled ginger. Add a layer of seafood if desired. Wet the top 1 cm of nori with a little pickled ginger juice. Roll nori around fillings, compressing tightly with the bamboo mat. Continue rolling until all rice and nori is used.

Chill rolls for 20 minutes before slicing each one into 10 pieces.

Serve with pickled ginger, wasabi and soy sauce. Makes 4–5 rolls (40–48 pieces).

Summer vegetable terrine ⓥ

Layers of our favourite summer vegetables sandwiched together with basil and goat's cheese equals totally yum. Although it takes a little bit of time to put together, come dinnertime it's just a matter of slicing and serving.

2 eggplants
Salt
3 small zucchinis
Olive oil
2 red capsicums
3 roma tomatoes
150 g (5 oz) firm goat's cheese

100 g rocket (3½ oz), washed and dried
⅓ cup basil leaves
Red wine vinegar
Freshly ground black pepper and salt
1 × log baking tin, 23.5 × 13.5 × 7 cm (9 × 5 × 2½ in)

Red wine dressing
3 tsp red wine vinegar
Salt and freshly ground black pepper
125 ml (4 fl oz) extra virgin olive oil

Preheat oven to 200°C (390°F)

Slice eggplants lengthways into ½ cm (¼ in) slices and sprinkle with salt; allow to drain in a colander for 30 minutes. Rinse under cold running water, then dry well. Slice the zucchini lengthways into ½ cm (¼ in) slices.

Heat a heavy-based pan over a medium–high heat. Add a splash of olive oil and cook eggplant, then zucchini slices, until tender and golden brown, then set aside.

Rub red capsicums over with olive oil and roast for 20–25 minutes until skins blister. Place capsicums in a plastic bag and seal to allow steam to lift skins. When cool, remove and discard the skins and seeds. Cut capsicums into thick strips. Slice the tomatoes and goat's cheese.

Line the baking tin with cling film lengthways and across, leaving plenty of overhang. Begin layering vegetables starting with one third of eggplant slices across the bottom. Sprinkle with a few drops of vinegar, olive oil, salt and pepper. Continue to sprinkle with vinegar, oil, salt and pepper between each layer.

Add a layer of zucchini slices, then half of the rocket, half of the capsicum, all the basil, tomato and goat's cheese, then another third of eggplant slices. Add remaining rocket, capsicums and finish with eggplant slices. Push down firmly when adding the rocket leaves.

Fold the overhanging cling film over the vegetables. Place filled baking tin on a baking tray to catch any overflowing juices. Cut a piece of thick cardboard to fit snugly in the top of the terrine. Weigh down with a heavy weight, around 4 kg in total is required to compress the ingredients together, such as 2 × 2 litre juice or milk cartons. Refrigerate overnight with the weights on top of the terrine.

To serve, remove weights and cardboard from terrine. Peel back the top layer of cling film and place a chopping board on top. Turn board and the tin over carefully. Remove tin and cling film from the pressed terrine. Wipe away any excess juices.

Make dressing by stirring together red wine vinegar with salt and pepper, then lightly whisk in oil. Evenly slice the terrine and carefully place onto serving plates, add a splash of the dressing and serve. Serves 6–8.

Goat's cheese soufflé v

Soufflés are rumoured to be tricky to make, but they are, in fact, quite easy. A fan-forced oven will help them to rise and it is important not to open the oven door during cooking, as a cold draught may make them collapse. It's a good idea to make sure everyone is seated in time to have the soufflés served straight from the oven.

350 ml (12 fl oz) milk
40 g (1⅓ oz) butter
40 g (1⅓ oz) plain flour
300 g (10½ oz) goat's cheese, mashed

3 medium eggs, separated
Salt and freshly ground black pepper
6 × 175 ml (6 fl oz) ramekins/soufflé dishes, buttered

Selection of dips, including, Baba ghanoush, Tzatziki, Hummus, Beetroot dip and Tapenade (recipes pages 41 – 43)

Roast duck, chilli and coriander rolls (recipe page 49)

Summer vegetable terrine (recipe page 53)

Preheat oven to 180°C (350°F).

Place milk in a small saucepan and bring to the boil. Melt butter in another pan over a low heat. Add flour to melted butter and cook for 2 minutes, stirring occasionally. Increase heat and add the hot milk, whisking well to avoid lumps. Cook for 2–3 minutes over low heat, stirring the thick sauce occasionally. Remove from the heat. Add goat's cheese and stir until melted. Stir egg yolks through and check seasoning.

Whisk egg whites until stiff and fold into warm cheese sauce. Divide mixture between buttered soufflé dishes and place immediately into preheated oven. Bake for 20–25 minutes, or until well risen and golden brown.

Serve immediately. Serves 6.

Pan-fried fish fillets
Pan-fried fish with coconut curry sauce
Seven-spice fish fillets
Deep-fried fish fillets in beer batter
Smoked trout and avocado toasts
Baked fish parcels with coconut milk and kaffir lime
Crispy skin fish with spring onions
Pan-fried swordfish with olive ratatouille
Poached salmon
Lemon butter sauce
Whole smoky salmon
Barbecued oysters
Steamed oysters with Asian flavours
Lemon mayonnaise
Malaysian curry prawns
Sizzlin' garlic prawns
Prawn cocktail
Lime and chilli mayonnaise
Steamed mussels with garlic
Mussels with Thai chilli broth
Spiced pipis with risoni
Crab cakes with Thai cucumber salad
Stir-fried crabs with black beans and ginger
Pan-fried calamari
Deep-fried Thai calamari
Seared calamari with chilli and balsamic dressing

Pan-fried fish with coconut curry sauce

Every now and again the curry craving takes over and we jazz our fish up like this.

500 g (1 lb) firm white fish fillets
Seasoned flour
Oil and butter for cooking

300 ml (10 fl oz) coconut milk
2 tbsp Thai curry paste

Cut fish into 10 cm (4 in) pieces. Coat with flour, shaking excess away. Heat a heavy-based frying pan over a medium–high heat. Add a splash of oil and a knob of butter (for flavour and browning). Cook fish for 3–4 minutes, or until golden brown. Turn over, add more oil and butter if needed and continue cooking for a further 2–3 minutes. Remove fish; keep warm in a preheated oven.

Tip excess oil away and return pan to the heat. Add coconut milk and Thai paste and bring to the boil, stirring occasionally. Once boiling, reduce heat and cook for 2–3 minutes. Serve the sauce on top of the fish. This fish and sauce combination is great over a bowl of noodles. Serves 4.

Seven-spice fish fillets

Here fish fillets are dusted with a flavoursome spice mixture and flour with great results. Who said cooking was difficult?

60 g (2 oz) plain flour
1 tsp sweet paprika
½ tsp ground ginger
½ tsp chilli powder
½ tsp ground coriander
¼ tsp ground cinnamon

¼ tsp ground cardamom
¼ tsp allspice
1 tsp salt
500 g (1 lb) firm white fish fillets
Oil for cooking
Lemon wedges to serve

Mix flour, spices and salt together. Cut fish onto 10 cm (4 in) pieces. Coat fish with spice mix, shaking excess away. Heat a heavy-based frying pan over a medium–high heat. Add a splash of oil. Add fish (you may need to cook in two batches). Cook fish for 3–4 minutes, or until golden brown. Turn over, add more oil if needed and continue cooking for a further 2–3 minutes. Serve with lemon wedges and couscous, page 134. Serves 4.

Creole fish fillets
Substitute Creole spice blend, page 111, for spice mix.

Deep-fried fish fillets in beer batter

This batter is guaranteed to be light and fluffy because of the yeast in the beer. Small fish fillets like flathead and strips of rockling are perfect to use.

300 ml (10 fl oz) beer
2 tbsp olive oil
1 medium egg
170 g (6 oz) plain flour
Pinch of salt
500 g (1 lb) firm white fish fillets
Seasoned flour
Oil for deep-frying

Whisk together beer, oil and egg. Sift flour and salt and add to beer, whisk until smooth. Add more beer if needed. Set aside for 30 minutes. Coat fish in seasoned flour, then batter, allowing excess to drip off.

Ease fish gently into hot oil and cook until golden, turning fish over once. Drain on absorbent paper, sprinkle with salt and serve with lemon wedges, lemon mayonnaise, page 66, and salad. Serves 4.

Smoked trout and avocado toasts

This dish is really a combination of a delicious salad on toasted Italian bread. We love it – firstly because the ingredients are readily available at delicatessens and supermarkets, and secondly because it's quick and easy to make.

1 whole smoked trout
500 g (1 lb) asparagus, ends trimmed off
200 g (7 oz) watercress sprigs, tips picked (or rocket)
18 basil leaves, torn roughly
100 ml (3½ fl oz) lemon mayonnaise, page 66
A little lemon juice
1 tsp Dijon mustard
6 thick slices crusty casalinga bread
1 ripe avocado, diced
150 g (5 oz) cherry tomatoes, halved
2 tbsp chives, finely chopped

Gently peel skin from fish. Remove flesh from the bones and flake into large pieces.

Cook asparagus in boiling water for 2 minutes, then refresh immediately under cold running water. Place asparagus in a bowl with watercress sprigs (or rocket) and basil leaves.

Mix mayonnaise with lemon juice and mustard to taste. It should be fairly runny so add a little boiling water if needed.

Lightly toast the sourdough and spread each with the mayonnaise. Place each slice of toast on a serving plate and top with asparagus and greens. Then divide the avocado, cherry tomatoes and smoked trout between each plate. Spoon more mayonnaise over the top and scatter with chopped chives. Serves 6.

Baked fish parcels with coconut milk and kaffir lime

We can't express how simple to make baked fish parcels are and how dramatic they look as you serve them.

1 carrot
8 choy sum stems
4 greaseproof paper squares
4 kaffir lime leaves
2 spring onions, sliced

1 lemongrass stalk, sliced
2 tbsp fish sauce
4 firm white fish fillets
60 ml (2 fl oz) coconut milk
Coriander sprigs

Preheat oven to 180°C (350°F).

Peel the carrot, then cut long strips from the carrot using the peeler. Cut choy sum into 6 cm (2 in) lengths. Lay four greaseproof paper squares out flat. Divide carrot and choy sum between paper squares and lay one kaffir lime leaf on top of each pile. Divide spring onions and lemongrass between piles. Sprinkle with fish sauce.

Place fish on top and pour coconut milk over. Fold paper ends in and pull remaining two edges up together. Roll over tightly to finish on top of the fish. Cook fish in preheated oven for 15 minutes. Serve with jasmine rice. Serves 4.

Crispy skin fish with spring onions

Choose either 1 large fish, such as snapper or perch, or 4 small individual fish such as barramundi or red snapper.

8 spring onions, thinly sliced
2 garlic cloves, crushed
2 tsp grated ginger
1 large fish (1 kg–2 lb) or 4 (250 g–8 oz) small ones, scaled and gutted

1 tbsp light soy sauce
Peanut oil for cooking
4 spring onions, sliced, green tops only for garnish
Soy sauce to serve

Preheat oven 180°C (350°F).

Mix spring onions with garlic, ginger and soy sauce and stuff into the cavity of the fish. With a sharp knife, make 3 slashes on each side of the fish through to the bone. Heat a heavy-based frypan, add enough peanut oil to cover the base of the pan and cook fish until golden brown on each side.

Place on a baking tray and bake in preheated oven (20 minutes for large fish, 10 minutes for small fish). Heat 100 ml (3–4 fl oz) of peanut oil over a high heat while fish is cooking (the oil must be very hot to get the fish skin to crackle). When the fish is removed from the oven, pour a small ladleful of the hot oil right over the entire fish. The skin will crackle instantly.

Garnish with green tops of spring onions and drizzle each fish with light soy sauce to serve. Serves 4.

Pan-fried swordfish with olive ratatouille

You can substitute the swordfish with any oily fish such as salmon, tuna or even marlin. Either way the olive ratatouille is a great match.

Olive oil for cooking
1 onion, finely diced
1 long thin eggplant, finely diced
1 small zucchini, finely diced
Freshly ground black pepper
2 garlic cloves, crushed

3 roma tomatoes, finely diced
90 g (3 oz) kalamata olives, pitted and roughly chopped
1 tbsp tomato paste
2 tbsp chopped basil leaves
4 × 200 g (7 oz) swordfish steaks

Heat 3 tablespoons of oil in a small saucepan over a medium–high heat. Add onion, eggplant, zucchini and pepper. Stir and cook for 5 minutes or until soft. Add garlic, stir well, then add tomatoes, olives, and tomato paste. Bring to the boil, reduce to a simmer, then cover and cook for 20 minutes, stirring occasionally.

Heat a heavy-based frying pan over a medium heat. Brush swordfish with olive oil and grind a little black pepper over each steak. Cook swordfish for 2–3 minutes on each side for medium–rare, or 4–5 minutes for medium.

Serve swordfish fillets on top of ratatouille. Serves 4.

Poached salmon

A perfect summer dish and exceptionally easy to prepare, although a fish kettle makes the cooking process easier.

1 whole salmon, about 2–3 kg (4–6 lb), cleaned
Water
500 ml (1 pt) white wine, optional
2 tsp salt
2 carrots, sliced

1 bay leaf
Parsley stalks
Juice of 2 lemons
6 peppercorns
1 onion, sliced
Handful of fresh dill

Place salmon in a large pot, preferably one with a heavy base. As said, a fish kettle is ideal, or a large stockpot. The salmon could be cut in half to cook, or the head removed, but then it doesn't make such a stunning impression.

Add enough liquid to cover – half water and half wine is ideal. Add remaining ingredients. Cover with a lid and bring to the boil. Remove pan from heat and leave fish to cool in cooking liquid. Overnight is best, but allow at least 1–2 hours.

Carefully remove the fish from the cooking liquid and serve with lemon mayonnaise, page 66, or lemon butter sauce, crusty bread and salad. Serves 10–12.

Lemon butter sauce

This is excellent with all manner of fish dishes, but our favourite way of serving it is with salmon and potato cakes page 177, pan-fried fish fillets, page 58, or poached salmon, page 62.

60 ml (2 fl oz) white wine
100 g (3½ oz) soft butter

2 tbsp lemon juice
Salt and freshly ground black pepper

Place white wine in a small saucepan and allow to reduce by half. Reduce heat and whisk butter in piece by piece. Finally, add lemon juice, season and keep sauce warm on the side of the stove. Serves 4–6.

Whole smoky salmon

Cooking a whole salmon in a kettle barbecue with smoking chips produces a moist, translucent fish with just a hint of smoky flavour. This could just be the perfect summer lunch dish.

200 g (7 oz) mesquite wood chips, soaked in water for 30 minutes

1 whole salmon or ocean trout, about 2–3 kg (4–6 lb), cleaned
Piece of foil 60 cm × 30 cm (24 in × 12 in)

Prepare kettle barbecue in the normal manner. When coals have turned to white ash, it is ready to cook in.

Drain the smoking chips well, then place them on top of the hot coals.

Lay whole fish onto foil. Turn up the edges a little to form a small lip. Place salmon in barbecue. Cover and cook for 1 hour or until the fish is just cooked through.

Excellent with lemon wedges, homemade lemon mayonnaise, page 66, good bread and a salad. Serves 10–12.

HOW TO OPEN OYSTERS

It's not *essential* to know how to open an oyster because any good fishmonger will open them for you, but it's a handy thing to know.

The main rule with opening oysters is to be careful. The special knife you'll need can do serious damage to unprotected hands and fingers. You will need to apply quite of bit of energy to get the oysters to open.

To open an oyster, first rinse under running water, scrubbing if necessary to remove sand. Place oyster on a firm surface with flat side uppermost. Wrap a tea towel around the hand that will hold the oyster, just in case, and insert oyster knife in between shells. Work knife into joint, twisting and levering until you feel muscle release. Carefully lift top shell away, taking care not to spill the oyster's delicious juices. Oysters are attached to the bottom shell by a small muscle that must be gently cut to release it.

Once opened, oysters are best eaten immediately – and certainly within 24 hours – to enjoy their sea-freshness. Unopened oysters will keep for 3–4 days in the crisper section of the refrigerator if wrapped in a damp cloth.

Just watch out for small bits of shell that may wander into the oyster's juices from opening. Oysters are often sat on a bed of coarse salt, in their shells, to prevent juices spilling, but crushed ice is good too.

Enjoy oysters as they are or serve a squeeze of lemon juice, or a drop or two of chilli sauce for simplicity. Oysters can be removed from their shells, mixed with a sauce and returned to their shells for serving. A simple method is to chop 1 small red chilli and mix with 3–4 tbsp of soy sauce. Mix oysters with soy sauce, then serve in the shell or just spoon a small amount over. A simple salsa, such as tomato and herb page 46, is also good.

In our house oysters are eaten simply as there are, cooked on the barbecue or steamed with Asian flavours.

Barbecued oysters

The oysters don't need to be pre-opened for this recipe as the heat from the barbecue grill will open their shells. Spoon on your preferred sauce and enjoy. This sauce will make enough for at least 2 dozen oysters.

125 ml (4 fl oz) rice wine vinegar
2 tbsp caster sugar
60 ml (2 fl oz) lime juice
2 tbsp fish sauce

1 small red chilli, de-seeded and finely diced
4 shallots, thinly sliced
2 dozen oysters, still closed in their shells

Place vinegar in a small saucepan and heat over a gently heat. Add sugar and stir until dissolved. When cool add lime juice, fish sauce, chilli and shallots.

Place unopened oysters on hot barbecue grill (they sit well on the bars). Cook for 3–4 minutes, or until the shells pop open. Using a small knife, pry shells off and place oysters on a platter. Spoon sauce into shells to serve. Makes 2 dozen.

Steamed oysters with Asian flavours

Lightly steaming oysters is a really great way of serving them if you're not too keen on them raw. It's also a good way of adding in new flavours such as the Asian marinade here. If you prefer your oysters raw, this same marinade is ideal as an accompaniment. Simply spoon it over freshly opened oysters and enjoy.

2 tbsp mirin*
1 tbsp sweet chilli sauce
2 tsp light soy sauce
½ tsp fish sauce

30 ml (1 fl oz) lime juice
2 spring onions, thinly sliced
6 Vietnamese mint leaves, thinly sliced
2 dozen oysters, freshly opened

Mix all of the marinade ingredients together in a bowl. Add the oysters, with their juices, to the bowl. Allow to marinate for 10 minutes.

Pour 10 cm (4 in) of water into a wok and bring to a gentle boil. Place the empty oyster shells into a bamboo steamer (you may need two decks to cook two dozen at the same time). Spoon an oyster into each shell with plenty of the marinade. Place over the steaming water and cover. Cook for 1½ minutes.

Gently place the bamboo steamer onto a large platter, taking care not to spill the delicious juices. Place on the dining table and allow your guests to pick the oysters out, one by one. Serves 4 as an entrée.

HOW TO COOK PRAWNS AND OTHER SHELLFISH

When I was a young girl my father would take my brother and me shrimping down at the local beach. With homemade nets and old ice-cream containers tied around our waists we would fish for dinner. Back home we would boil the prawns briefly, then gather around the draining board when it was covered with hot cooked prawns, lemon wedges, brown bread and butter and eat to our hearts' content. MC

Here's how we did it.
Bring a large pot of water to the boil. Add a generous pinch of salt. Add prawns and cook for 1–2 minutes or until water just comes back to the boil and prawns turn pink. Remove, refresh under cold water if eating them later; if not, serve straight away while still warm.

The same method applies to all shellfish; just adjust cooking times accordingly.

Crabs, lobsters and crayfish
Put to sleep first by placing in the freezer for 30 minutes before cooking. Cook in boiling salted water for 8 minutes per 500 g (1 lb).

Yabbies
Put to sleep first by placing in the freezer for 20–30 minutes before cooking. Cook in boiling salted water for 6–8 minutes.

Lemon mayonnaise

This is ideal for dipping warm prawns into, so if you've always wanted to make your own mayonnaise there's no time like the present. This can easily be done in a mixer, in a food processor, or by hand with a simple bowl and a whisk if you prefer (which doesn't take long at all).

2 egg yolks
Salt and freshly ground black pepper
½ tsp Dijon mustard

125 ml (4 fl oz) olive oil
1 tbsp lemon juice
1–2 tbsp boiling water

Place egg yolks, salt, pepper and mustard in food processor or bowl. Blend or whisk for 2–3 minutes or until white and creamy. Slowly drizzle in oil until a thick, creamy consistency is reached. If oil is added too fast the mayonnaise may separate. Add lemon juice and season if needed. If mayonnaise is too thick add a little boiling water to thin it.

Tartare sauce
Add 2 tsp soaked, chopped capers, 30 g (1 oz) chopped cornichons* and 1 tbsp chopped parsley at the end.

Malaysian curry prawns

Cooking curry paste and coconut milk to a thick sauce is a grand way of adding good flavours to barbecued food. Any type of curry paste can be used in this way; you can try a Thai or Indian paste for something different next time.

2 tbsp Malaysian curry paste
200 ml (7 fl oz) coconut cream
Salt

1 kg (2 lb) green (raw) prawns
30 skewers

Place curry paste and coconut cream in a small saucepan. Bring to the boil. Simmer for 2–3 minutes and add salt to taste.

Shell and de-vein prawns. Thread one prawn onto each skewer, through the centre lengthways. Brush with coconut curry sauce.

Place prawns on oiled barbecue plate. Cook for 2 minutes, basting often. Turn over and cook for a further 2 minutes, continuing to baste. Makes 30 skewers.

Sizzlin' garlic prawns

The combination of prawns and garlic is a classic that goes back a long, long way. Now you can try it yourself at home to see how good it can be.

500 g (1 lb) green (raw) prawns
2 tbsp olive oil
4 garlic cloves, crushed

1 small red chilli, de-seeded and finely diced
Pinch of saffron threads, soaked in 1 tbsp boiling water, optional

Shell and de-vein prawns. Heat small pan over medium–hot heat. Add oil, garlic and chilli. Cook briefly for 1–2 minutes until fragrant. Add prawns and cook for 2 minutes, then turn over. Add saffron water, if using, and cook for a further 2 minutes.
    Serves 2–4.

Prawn cocktail

For those of you who couldn't care less about food fashion, here is our take on this great dish: pan-fried juicy prawns tossed with fresh salad ingredients and topped with a lime and chilli mayonnaise.

1 iceberg lettuce
150 g (5 oz) rocket leaves
1 avocado
2 Lebanese cucumbers

1 punnet cherry tomatoes
Olive oil for cooking
1 kg (2 lb) green (raw) prawns, peeled and de-veined

Carefully remove 6 large outside leaves from lettuce to use as cups to hold salad. Break remaining lettuce into bite-sized pieces. Wash iceberg and rocket leaves, then dry using a salad spinner.
    Cut avocado in half, remove stone, peel and cut into thin slices. Slice cucumbers thinly. Cut tomatoes in half. Toss lettuce, avocado, cucumber and tomatoes together. Arrange salad in iceberg cups.
    Heat a large frying pan over a medium heat, add 1–2 tablespoons of oil and cook prawns for 1–2 minutes on each side. Arrange prawns on top of each salad cup. Top with a generous spoonful of lime and chilli mayonnaise. Serves 6.

Lime and chilli mayonnaise

This can easily be made in a mixer, in a food processor, or by hand with a simple bowl and a whisk if you prefer (which doesn't take long at all).

2 egg yolks
30 ml (1 fl oz) lime juice
Salt and freshly ground black pepper
1 garlic clove, peeled
1 tsp tomato paste

2 small red chillies, de-seeded and finely diced
½ tsp Dijon mustard
125 ml (4 fl oz) olive oil
1–2 tbsp boiling water

Place egg yolks, lime juice, salt, pepper, garlic, tomato paste, chilli and mustard into food processor or bowl. Blend or whisk for 2–3 minutes, or until pale and doubled in bulk.

Slowly drizzle in oil, taking care not to let egg yolks curdle. If they start to do so blend in a spoonful of boiling water. To adjust consistency, add boiling water as needed.

Steamed mussels with garlic

A bowl of garlicky mussels is a tasty start to a good meal; it's also a dish that takes only a few minutes to cook. Remember to purchase mussels with their shells closed and discard any that do not open during cooking.

2 tbsp olive oil
4 garlic cloves, crushed
125 ml (4 fl oz) dry white wine
1 kg (2 lb) mussels, shells scrubbed and beards removed

Pinch of saffron threads
Chopped parsley
Knob of butter
Salt and freshly ground black pepper

Heat a wok or large frying pan over high heat. Add a swirl of oil, then the garlic, and stir for 1 minute, or until fragrant. Add white wine and saffron. Allow liquid to come to the boil, then toss mussels in. Cover with a lid and leave to steam for 3–4 minutes.

Place four serving bowls near where you are cooking. Remove lid, shake pan well and remove cooked mussels as they open. Place them directly into the bowls.

Remove pan from heat and discard any that did not open during cooking. Add chopped parsley and butter to the cooking liquid and whisk through. Check seasoning and add salt and pepper if needed.

Pour cooking juices over the mussels and serve immediately. Serves 4.

Mussels with Thai chilli broth

This dish is great for lunch, or as a smart entrée for a dinner party. You have to believe us when we say mussels are easy to cook; they just sound, and look, terrifying.

3 tomatoes, quartered
2 small red chillies, halved
3 garlic cloves, bruised
1 × 5 cm (2 in) piece fresh ginger, sliced
2 sticks lemongrass, sliced
400 ml (13 fl oz) coconut cream
2 tbsp fish sauce

250 ml (8 fl oz) fish stock
1 bunch coriander
6 red shallots, sliced
½ red capsicum, sliced
250 g (8 oz) chow mein noodles
2 kg (4 lb) fresh mussels, cleaned

Place tomatoes, chillies, garlic, ginger and lemongrass in a heavy-based saucepan. Add coconut cream, fish sauce and stock.

Wash coriander well, roughly chop roots and stems, reserving leaves for later, and place in the saucepan. Bring to a gentle boil and allow to simmer for 20 minutes. Remove from the heat and strain infused coconut milk into a clean saucepan. With a ladle force any remaining liquid through the sieve and set aside until ready to serve.

Bring infused coconut milk to the boil. Add shallots and capsicum, and allow to simmer until needed.

Put a kettle of water on to boil. Pour boiling water over noodles and set aside. Heat wok, add 2 cm (¾ in) of boiling water and toss mussels in. Cover with a lid; allow to steam for 2 minutes. Remove mussels as they open and keep warm until remainder are opened. Drain noodles.

To serve, divide noodles into bowls, add 8 mussels per person for an entrée or 12 for a main course, discarding any that are not open. Add to sauce a handful of coriander leaves, pour over the noodles and serve.

Serves 6 as an entrée or 4 as a main course.

HOW TO CLEAN MUSSELS

Rinse under cold running water and pull sharply at beards to remove, discarding any open shells. Scrub shells if necessary. Place clean mussels under a damp cloth in the refrigerator until needed.

Spiced pipis with risoni

Risoni is pasta shaped like a grain of rice and pipis are small, silvery coloured shellfish. Together they make a delicious combination. If one were having a candle-lit supper this would be just the dish for the lady of the house to prepare.

500 g (1 lb) pipis
2 tbsp olive oil
1 onion, finely diced
1 carrot, finely diced
1 leek, thinly sliced
1 garlic clove, crushed
2 small red chilli, de-seeded and finely diced
1 tbsp tomato paste
1 litre (1⅔ pt) chicken stock
200 g (7 oz) risoni
1 tbsp chopped parsley
Salt and freshly ground black pepper

Rinse the pipis under cold water and discard any opened shells. Keep refrigerated until needed.

Heat a large saucepan over a medium heat. Add oil and onion, carrot and leek. Cook for 5 minutes, stirring often. Add garlic, chilli and tomato paste, cook for a further 2 minutes. Add stock and bring to the boil. Once boiling add a pinch of salt and risoni. Return to the boil, then lower the heat, cover with a lid and cook for 6 minutes.

Check risoni is *al dente*, add the pipis, cover again and cook for 2 minutes. Uncover and watch for pipis beginning to open. Remove pipis as they open and place in a warm bowl. Continue cooking until most of the pipis have opened, discard any which won't open. Add parsley to the risoni and check the seasoning.

Divide pipis and risoni evenly between 4 warmed soup bowls. Serve with crusty bread. Serves 4.

Crab cakes with Thai cucumber salad

These crab cakes were on the menu when we welcomed in the year 2000 with friends at home. It was a great start to a memorable meal. One large crab weighing about 1.5 kg (3 lb) will be perfect for this recipe, otherwise smaller crabs to the weight. Or even easier buy fresh crab meat from your local fishmonger. This recipe is just as delicious with lobster or crayfish meat.

Crab cakes
200 g (7 oz) fresh crab meat
1 medium egg
2 tbsp chopped coriander
15 ml (½ fl oz) lime juice
200 g (7 oz) fresh breadcrumbs
4 spring onions, very finely chopped
Salt
Tabasco sauce
Ghee or olive oil for cooking
2 limes, cut into wedges

Pan-fried swordfish with olive ratatouille (recipe page 62)

Mussels with Thai chilli broth (recipe page 69)

Lasagne using the Veal ragu (recipe page 90)

Place crabmeat, egg, coriander, lime juice, breadcrumbs and spring onions in a bowl and mix lightly. Add a pinch of salt and a few drops of Tabasco to season and combine. Divide mixture into 8 and pat into burger shapes. Refrigerate until needed.

To serve, heat a heavy-based frying pan over medium heat. Add 1–2 tablespoons of ghee (or olive oil), add crab cakes and cook for 5–8 minutes on each side until golden brown on the outside and hot in the middle. It is essential to cook crab cakes slowly over a medium heat to ensure they cook right through to the centre, without browning too much. You can pan-fry them until crispy on the outside and put them in a preheated oven 180°C (350°F) for 10 minutes if you prefer.

Meanwhile toss cucumber with dressing and divide between 4 plates. Place two crab cakes on each plate and serve with lime wedges. Serves 4.

Thai cucumber salad

This salad is also good with poached salmon, page 62.

2 cucumbers
½ cup coriander leaves
6 shallots, thinly sliced
1 small red chilli, de-seeded and finely diced
½ tbsp palm sugar

15 ml (½ fl oz) lime juice
1 tbsp fish sauce
Black freshly ground black pepper
2 tsp rice vinegar
2 tbsp peanut oil

Peel cucumbers, then, using the vegetable peeler, slice strips of cucumber from one end to the other, discarding centre seeds. Place cucumber strips in a colander and leave to drain for 30 minutes. Toss cucumber with coriander leaves, shallots and chilli and set aside until ready to serve.

Prepare dressing by dissolving palm sugar in lime juice and fish sauce. Add freshly ground black pepper to season and whisk in vinegar. Finally add the oil. Toss dressing with cucumber strips just before serving.

Stir-fried crabs with black beans and ginger

Never tried cooking crabs at home? It's so easy you'll kick yourself for not doing it earlier.

4 blue swimmer crabs, about 200–300 g (7–10 oz) each, preferably live
1 tbsp black beans*, soaked in cold water
2 tsp grated ginger
2 small red chillies, de-seeded and finely diced

2 garlic cloves, peeled and crushed
1 tbsp peanut oil
150 ml (5 fl oz) water
Coriander leaves to garnish
Steamed rice to serve

If using live crabs, freeze for 30 minutes to put them to sleep. Cut each crab into quarters, leaving claws attached. Rinse each piece under cold running water to remove innards. Drain well and refrigerate until needed.

Rinse black beans well and chop finely. Place in a small bowl with ginger, garlic and chillies. Mix well.

Place wok over high heat for 5 minutes without oil. The wok has to be really hot to cook the crabs quickly. Prepare yourself and get the range hood or extractor going full blast. Add the peanut oil, swirl to coat surface and add black bean mixture. Stir for 20 seconds, allowing the kitchen to fill with the fragrant aromas. Add crab pieces, and cook and stir for 2–3 minutes. Add the water. Cover with a lid and cook for 5 minutes, stirring occasionally.

Place crabs, liquid and all, on a hot platter and top with coriander leaves. Serve with steamed rice. Napkins and finger bowls of water are probably a good idea too. Serves 4 as an entrée.

Spicy pipis with black bean and ginger
Replace crab with 1 kg (2 lb) pipis (or mussels). Get the spice mix cooked and just throw the pipis in along with the water and cook until shells open.

Pan-fried calamari

'Roundy things' (calamari rings) according to our son Luke, are meant to be eaten at least once a week. This is how we do it at home.

500 g (1 lb) calamari rings (can be cut from tubes 1 cm (⅓ in) wide)
Seasoned flour
Oil for frying
Lemon wedges

Toss calamari with flour to coat, then shake well; a sieve does a good job of removing the excess flour.

Fill shallow frying pan with 1 cm (⅓ in) oil and place over a medium–high heat. Add calamari rings one by one, cooking as many as will fit into the pan without overlapping. Cook for 30 seconds, turn over and cook until golden brown. Drain on absorbent paper and serve with lemon wedges. Serves 4 as an entrée.

Deep-fried Thai calamari

We're usually so greedy that we eat these spicy calamari rings as they are ready, but they would probably be good with a salad too.

500 g (1 lb) calamari rings
1 tbsp Thai red curry paste
2 tbsp potato starch (or cornflour)

Peanut oil for cooking
Handful Thai basil leaves
Lime wedges to serve

Mix calamari with Thai paste and set aside to marinate for 30 minutes. When ready to cook, stir through potato starch to coat.

Heat peanut oil in a wok and deep-fry calamari rings, adding one by one to stop them sticking together and frying no more than 5–6 at a time. Cook for 30 seconds, turn over and cook until golden brown. Continue cooking until all calamari are ready, serve on a platter with basil leaves and lime wedges to garnish. Serves 4 as an entrée.

Seared calamari with chilli and balsamic dressing

This is the type of recipe where you need to get everything ready before you start cooking, as the actual cooking part takes only about 5 minutes.

4 calamari tubes, about 125 g (4 oz) each
Oil for cooking
2 small red chillies, de-seeded and finely diced
2 tsp grated ginger
1 tbsp balsamic vinegar

Salt and freshly ground black pepper
2 tbsp lemon or lime juice
2 tbsp chopped parsley
2–3 tbsp olive oil
250 g (8 oz) salad leaves

Slit the calamari along one side. Remove any loose skin. Using a sharp knife, score the inside skin on an angle to create a crosshatch pattern. Refrigerate until needed.

Place a large heavy-based frying pan, or preferably two, over high heat. Add a splash of oil to the pan and cook chilli and ginger briefly. Add calamari, cut side down. Cook for 2–3 minutes until calamari starts to turn opaque. Turn over and continue cooking for a further 2–3 minutes. Add 1–2 tablespoons of water and continue cooking until calamari forms a roll. Remove from the heat.

Add vinegar, salt, pepper, juice, parsley and oil to the pan. Divide salad leaves between plates. Add one piece of calamari to each plate and drizzle sauce over the top. Serve immediately. Serves 4.

Cooking pasta
Potato gnocchi
Semolina gnocchi
Tomato sauce # 1
Tomato sauce # 2
Roasted tomato and red capsicum sauce
Tomato, olive and anchovy pasta sauce
Caramelised onions, feta and rocket combo
Roast tomato, pancetta and sweet onions with gnocchi
Pasta with tuna and artichokes
Penne with prosciutto, peas and mint
Linguini with smoked chicken and peas
Spaghettini carbonara
Spaghetti with breadcrumbs, tuna, parsley and lemon
Spaghetti with seafood and tomato sauce
Macaroni cheese
Spaghetti and meatballs
Spaghetti with pesto
Pesto
Quick-and-easy bolognaise
Veal ragu
Roast vegetable and goat's cheese lasagne

Pasta

BASICS, SAUCES, LASAGNE AND GNOCCHI

It's hard to believe that only twenty years ago spaghetti bolognaise was considered an exotic dish. It was what your mother cooked, and as children we went 'Cor Mum, I didn't know you could cook Italian'. Back then it was a dish that symbolised foodie sophistication, which was pretty amazing as it was topped with dried parmesan and the pasta was stuck together like glue.

As 21st-century people we know that spaghetti bolognaise is not the most exciting pasta dish around. We're more likely to toss smoked chicken with a herb cream sauce or roasted eggplants, tomatoes, olives and fresh basil with our pasta than anything else.

Pasta – whether plain or sophisticated – offers a dinner on the table in 15 minutes, and something to keep all members of the family happy. Thanks to the variety of pasta shapes and sauces we now enjoy, we can mix and match to create an endless diversity of dishes.

The simplest pasta meal we know comprises a drizzle of extra virgin olive oil and a handful of chopped flat-leaf parsley and parmigiano tossed through a bowl of piping-hot spaghetti. Talk about fast food.

The cooking times for pasta in these recipes are for dried pasta because that is what we tend to cook most often. If you're cooking fresh pasta, simply reduce the cooking time from 8 minutes to 3–4, depending on the pasta.

P.S. Children still love their mum's spaghetti bolognaise!

THINGS YOU NEED TO KNOW ABOUT PASTA

- Always put a pot of water for the pasta on to boil, then start your sauce.
- Allow 100 g (3½ oz) dried pasta per person.
- Allow 150 g (5 oz) fresh pasta per person.
- Add a good pinch of salt to boiling water.
- Don't add oil to the water, it just floats on top.
- Cook pasta in plenty of gently boiling salted water.
- Always drain your pasta well.
- Toss pasta with the sauce before serving.
- Always serve pasta piping hot.
- Never overcook your pasta.

PASTA ESSENTIALS

Fresh or dried?
Fresh pasta produces a soft eating experience and is perfect for filled pastas such as ravioli, lasagne and cannelloni.

Dried pasta, which is an essential modern pantry item, is firmer to bite into than fresh pasta. Choose one that suits your taste and budget.

What shape?
It all comes down to personal taste. We always cook spaghetti for spaghetti bolognaise; it just doesn't seem right with anything else. Likewise it has to be macaroni in macaroni cheese, though at a pinch penne will do. However, if you want farfalle with bolognaise sauce, be our guest; it has to be said that younger members of any family love the different shapes, so it's well worth exploring.

Any pasta suggestions given here are a guide only; feel free to change the shape to suit your tastes or whatever is in the cupboard.

Parmigiano reggiano
Parmigiano reggiano (often labelled as parmesan) is a classic Italian hard cheese. For the best flavour buy it in large chunks rather than pre-grated and grate it as required. The true parmigiano reggiano is quite expensive, but the flavour is so good that only a little is needed. Serve a bowl of grated or shaved parmigiano with most pasta dishes. Seafood and rich cream sauces rarely need cheese.

A big pot
We're talking a 10-litre (2 gallon) pot here, especially made for cooking pasta. Inside each pasta pot is a large colander so you lift your cooked pasta from the boiling water, rather than pouring the boiling water over the cooked pasta. The drained pot is then perfect for tossing the pasta with its sauce.

Tomato sugo (purée)
Tomato sugo is simply a ready-to-use Italian tomato sauce. The best tasting sugos come from Italy and our kitchen is never without one of these. Having heated the sauce while your pasta is cooking, you can add chilli and olives, a few chunks of tuna, a spoonful of pesto – or nothing at all!

Depending on the acidity of the tomatoes, you may need to add a pinch of sugar to tomato sauce based recipes.

Olive oil
Good olive oil is an essential ingredient if you're to enjoy pasta at its best. It's essential in making pasta sauces: to toss with pasta so that the strands don't stick to each other; and for pan-cooking or oven-roasting vegetables to go with your dish.

Cooking pasta

Pretty basic stuff, but a quick refresher course for those who may need it.

You will need:

A large pot, preferably 10 litre (2 gallon) with a pasta colander and lid
Lots of water
Salt
Your pasta – 100 g (3½ oz) dried or 150 g (5 oz) fresh per person

Fill pot ¾ full with water and bring to the boil over a high heat. Add a good pinch of salt. Add pasta, and stir until water has returned to the boil, so that the pasta doesn't stick to the bottom or itself. Reduce heat, cover and cook at a fast simmer.

If using dried pasta cook for 8 minutes, or check packet instructions. Very thin pastas cook quickly, while handmade artisan pasta may take longer than 8 minutes. Fresh pasta will take only 3–4 minutes.

Try a piece of pasta to see whether it's cooked to your liking. 'Al dente' pasta – with a little firmness in the centre – is the ideal. If you look at the pasta where you have bitten it, you should be able to see a pinprick of firm, pale centre. Some say that you throw a piece of pasta against the wall to see whether it's cooked – if it's done, it sticks; if not, it will slide off. Good fun, but hardly practical.

Remove inner colander, draining water away. Some people like to add a small amount of the cooking water back to the pasta to keep it moist. Toss the hot pasta with the chosen sauce in the pasta pot and serve immediately.

> **TIP**
> If you want to cook pasta in advance, follow the method above, but when you drain the pasta, refresh it by running the pasta under cold water until pasta is cold. Toss with a small amount of olive oil to prevent it sticking and refrigerate until needed. Reheat by plunging cold pasta into salted boiling water for 1 minute. Drain, then serve.

Potato gnocchi v

Toolangi Delight or Bintje potatoes are the best for making gnocchi. Again a pasta pot with a large colander will enable you to lift your cooked gnocchi from the boiling water, rather than pouring the boiling water over the cooked gnocchi (which is quite fragile).

1 kg (2 lb) potatoes
75 g (2⅔ oz) butter
3 medium eggs
3 egg yolks

Pinch of nutmeg
300 g (10½ oz) flour
Salt and freshly ground black pepper
Additional flour for dusting

Peel potatoes, then boil or steam until tender and drain well. Mash them while they're still hot, then add butter, eggs, egg yolks, nutmeg, flour, salt and pepper and stir until mixed. Divide into four; roll each into 2 cm (¾ in) thick sausages on a floured bench top. Cut into 2 cm (¾ in) lengths.

Bring a large pot of water to the boil over a high heat. Add a good pinch of salt. Plunge the gnocchi into boiling water, allow them to rise to the surface and cook for a further two minutes. Remove, and serve straight away with hot sauce.

If desired gnocchi can be pre-cooked, set aside to cool and tossed gently with olive oil. Reheat by placing the gnocchi gently back into boiling water for 1 minute, or by reheating in a microwave. Serves 4.

Semolina gnocchi ⓥ

Semolina makes soft and tender gnocchi. It's perfect for these gnocchi discs, which are grilled then served with a simple tomato salsa.

1¼ litre (2 pt) milk
1 bay leaf
Pinch of grated nutmeg
6 black peppercorns
1 onion, peeled and roughly chopped
Pinch of salt

180 g (6 oz) semolina
150 g (5 oz) parmigiano, finely grated
150 g (5 oz) gruyère, finely grated
3 egg yolks
50 g (1¾ oz) soft butter

Place milk in a heavy-based pan with bay leaf, nutmeg, peppercorns, onion and salt. Bring to a gentle boil, reduce heat and allow flavours to infuse for 5 minutes.

Strain milk into a clean heavy-based pan and return to the boil. Sprinkle in semolina and stir constantly as the mixture thickens and starts to bubble. Reduce heat and cook gently for 5–10 minutes until very thick, stirring all the time.

Combine the two cheeses. Remove semolina from heat, stir in egg yolks, butter and half of the cheese. Check seasoning, adding salt and pepper to taste. Pour into a greased deep dish (such as a large baking tray) and smooth down the top; it should be around 1 cm (⅓ in) thick. Sprinkle remaining cheese on top. Allow to cool in the refrigerator until set firm.

When cool, cut gnocchi into 4 cm (1½ in) circles. Arrange circles in small buttered gratin dishes, 3 circles per person, or place them on one large tray.

To serve, place gnocchi under hot grill and cook until cheese melts and turns golden brown. If grilling on one large tray, divide gnocchi between warmed plates. Serve topped with a simple tomato and herb salsa, page 46. Serves 4.

Tomato sauce #1 ⓥ

This recipe is your classic, tasty tomato sauce for pasta of all types. Sergio de Pieri, musician brother of cook Stefano di Pieri, revealed the secret of this sauce when we discussed with him the idea for this book. We were amazed at the depth of flavour that comes from this simple method of cooking the garlic in olive oil before adding any tomatoes. (Sergio is also a keen exponent of the need for a 'big' pasta pot.)

4 tbsp olive oil
2–3 cloves of garlic, coarsely crushed
2 × 400 g (14 oz) tins chopped peeled tomatoes or 800 g (1 lb 10 oz) chopped fresh tomatoes

Salt and freshly ground black pepper
2 tbsp chopped parsley
Pasta of your choice, 100 g (3½ oz) dried per person

Heat a medium-sized saucepan over a low heat. Add oil and heat for 3–4 minutes. Add garlic and cook for 1–2 minutes, until light brown. Add chopped tomatoes, salt and pepper. Simmer sauce for 10 minutes.

Bring a large pot of water to a boil over a high heat. Add a good pinch of salt.

Add pasta to boiling water and stir until water has returned to the boil. Reduce heat, cover and cook pasta at a fast simmer for 8 minutes.

Check that pasta is cooked, drain and toss with the sauce. Serves 6–8.

Tomato sauce with basil Ⓥ
Add chopped basil to the sauce for a fresh taste.

Tomato sauce with capers Ⓥ
Add 1 tbsp capers, soaked in water and drained, to the sauce.

Tomato sauce with chilli Ⓥ
Add 2 de-seeded and finely diced red chillies with cooking onions.

Creamy tomato sauce Ⓥ
Add 90 ml (3 fl oz) of cream to the sauce at the end.

Tomato sauce with roasted capsicum Ⓥ
Add 1 diced roasted red capsicum with the tomatoes.

Tomato sauce with roasted eggplant Ⓥ
Add diced roasted eggplant with the tomatoes.

Tomato sauce with olives Ⓥ
Add 90 g (3 oz) pitted olives to the sauce.

Tomato sauce with tuna
Add 300 g (10 oz) tinned tuna chunks to the sauce.

Tomato sauce #2 Ⓥ

This recipe is dead simple, but pretty basic in taste. We would serve this with a filled tortellini or ravioli to add more flavour, or just over penne for an uncomplicated meal.

Olive oil for cooking
1 onion, diced
1 garlic clove, crushed
1 tbsp tomato paste
6 fresh tomatoes, diced, or 1 × 400 g
    (14 oz) can chopped tomatoes

Salt and freshly ground black pepper
Chopped fresh herbs, basil and flat-leaf
    parsley are both good
Pasta of your choice, 100 g (3½ oz) dried
    per person

Heat a medium-sized saucepan over a medium heat. Add oil and onion and cook for 3–4 minutes, stirring often until onion softens slightly. Add garlic and cook for a further 1–2 minutes or until garlic is fragrant. Add tomato paste and cook briefly before adding tomatoes. Bring to the boil, reduce heat and cook for 5–8 minutes, stirring often. When sauce has thickened to desired consistency, check seasoning and add fresh herbs to taste.

Bring a large pot of water to a boil over a high heat. Add a good pinch of salt.

Add pasta to boiling water and stir until water has returned to the boil. Reduce heat, cover and cook pasta at a fast simmer for 8 minutes.

Check that pasta is cooked, drain and toss with sauce. Serves 4.

Tomato sauce with bacon
Add 150 g (5 oz) diced bacon (or pancetta) after cooking the onion for 3–4 minutes and continue cooking for another 4–5 minutes. Or use salami instead of bacon.

Tomato sauce with mushroom Ⓥ
Add 100 g (3½ oz) sliced mushrooms after cooking the onion for 3–4 minutes.

Tomato sauce with pesto Ⓥ
Finish sauce with a spoonful of pesto per person.

Tomato sauce with spinach Ⓥ
Add 100 g (3½ oz) washed spinach leaves for the last 3–4 minutes of cooking.

Roasted tomato and red capsicum sauce Ⓥ

This sauce is rich and satisfying because the vegetables are oven-roasted, plus it has a hefty amount of garlic. We like it with gnocchi or filled pastas such as ravioli. It's also very good with grilled meats.

2 red capsicums, quartered
500 g (1 lb) roma tomatoes, halved
6 garlic cloves, peeled
2 small red chillies

Olive oil for cooking
Salt and freshly ground black pepper
Pasta of your choice, 100 g (3½ oz) dried per person

Preheat oven to 180°C (350°F).

Place capsicums, tomatoes, garlic and chillies in a deep baking tray. Drizzle with olive oil and sprinkle with salt and pepper. Roast for 30 minutes. Remove capsicums and place in a plastic bag to allow steam to lift skins.

Remove all skins and seeds from the capsicums and tomatoes when they are cool enough to touch. Purée all vegetables and strain through a sieve. Add olive oil to adjust consistency and check the seasoning.

Bring a large pot of water to a boil over a high heat. Add a good pinch of salt.

Add pasta to boiling water and stir until water has returned to the boil. Reduce heat, cover and cook pasta at a fast simmer for 8 minutes.

Reheat sauce in a saucepan. Check that pasta is cooked, drain and toss with sauce. Serves 4–6.

Tomato, olive and anchovy pasta sauce

Try this tomato-based pasta sauce, which has a few other goodies thrown in for good measure.

2 tbsp olive oil
1 onion, finely diced
1 garlic clove, crushed
500 g (1 lb) fresh tomatoes, chopped
2–3 anchovies, chopped
2 tbsp tiny salted capers, rinsed and chopped

100 g (3½ oz) pitted kalamata olives.
Salt and freshly ground black pepper
Fresh herbs, basil and parsley are excellent
Pasta of your choice, 100 g (3½ oz) dried per person

Heat a medium-sized saucepan over a medium heat. Add oil and onion and cook for 3–4 minutes, stirring often, until onion softens slightly. Add garlic and cook for a further 1–2 minutes or until garlic is fragrant. Add the tomatoes and allow to come to the boil. Reduce heat; add anchovies, capers and olives. Cook for 5–8 minutes until sauce reduces. Add fresh herbs and check seasoning.

Bring a large pot of water to a boil over a high heat. Add a good pinch of salt.

Add pasta to boiling water and stir until water has returned to the boil. Reduce heat, cover and cook pasta at a fast simmer for 8 minutes.

Check that pasta is cooked, drain and toss with sauce. Serves 4.

Caramelised onions, feta and rocket combo Ⓥ

This is another favourite combination of ours: rich caramelised onions, salty feta and peppery rocket leaves. It's excellent with penne or orecchiette.

4 tbsp olive oil
4 onions, sliced
2 garlic cloves, peeled
1 small red chilli, halved, optional
2 sprigs fresh thyme

Salt and freshly ground black pepper
125 g (4 oz) feta, crumbled
125 g (4 oz) rocket, washed and chopped
Pasta of your choice, 100 g (3½ oz) dried

Heat oil in saucepan, add onions, garlic, chilli (if using) and thyme. Season well. Cook for 20–30 minutes on low heat, stirring often until onions soften and turn a golden caramel colour.

Bring a large pot of water to a boil over a high heat. Add a good pinch of salt. Add pasta to boiling water and stir until water has returned to the boil. Reduce heat, cover and cook pasta at a fast simmer for 8 minutes.

Drain excess oil away from onions. Toss with feta, rocket and cooked drained pasta. Serve immediately. Serves 4.

Roast tomato, pancetta and sweet onions with gnocchi

You don't have to serve this chunky, rich sauce with gnocchi – but take it from us: it's a magic combination. This is usually a dinner for two of us.

4 tomatoes
Olive oil for cooking
Salt and freshly ground black pepper
Pinch of caster sugar
60 ml (2 fl oz) olive oil
2 onions, diced

2–3 sprigs thyme
150 g (5 oz) pancetta, diced
2 tbsp chopped parsley
2–3 tbsp shaved parmigiano
300 g (10 oz) gnocchi

Preheat oven to 180°C (350°F).

Cut tomatoes into quarters, lay on a baking tray, skin side down, drizzle with olive oil and season with salt, pepper and sugar. Roast in preheated oven for 30 minutes.

Heat 60 ml (2 fl oz) of oil in a heavy-based frying pan. Add onions, thyme, salt and pepper. Cook over a low heat for 20–30 minutes or until onions are soft and slightly coloured. Turn heat up, add pancetta. Cook for 3–4 minutes until pancetta is crispy. Add roasted tomatoes, parsley and parmigiano. Check seasoning.

Bring a large pot of water to a boil over a high heat. Add a good pinch of salt.

Plunge the gnocchi into boiling salted water, allow them to rise to the surface and cook for a further 2–3 minutes. Toss sauce with cooked gnocchi and serve. Serves 2.

Roast pumpkin, pancetta and sweet onions with gnocchi
Substitute 200 g (7 oz) diced pumpkin for tomatoes.

Pasta with tuna and artichokes

Nothing tricky here – simply a pan of ingredients like onion, artichokes, tuna, lemon and parsley being cooked together. Then you add the cooked pasta, do the hokey-pokey and shake it all about.

Olive oil for cooking	300 g (10 oz) tinned tuna, drained
1 onion, diced	2 tbsp chopped parsley
1 garlic clove, crushed	Squeeze of lemon juice
200 g (7 oz) marinated artichoke hearts, quartered	Salt and freshly ground black pepper
	400 g (14 oz) dried orecchietti

Bring a large pot of water to a boil over a high heat. Add a good pinch of salt. Add pasta to boiling water and stir until water has returned to the boil. Reduce heat, cover and cook pasta at a fast simmer for 8 minutes.

Heat a heavy-based pan over a medium–high heat. Add a splash of oil and onion and cook for 4–5 minutes, stirring often until onion begin to soften. Add garlic and artichokes, cook, stirring often for 2–3 minutes. Add tuna, parsley, a squeeze of lemon juice, and salt and pepper to taste. Toss well to combine all ingredients.

Add drained, cooked pasta to the pan, toss to combine ingredients well, then serve straight away. Serves 4.

Penne with prosciutto, peas and mint

With this type of dish it's easy to serve the sauce on the side for fussy eaters, then toss the rest of the sauce together for those with grown-up tastes.

400 g (14 oz) dried penne
3 tbsp olive oil
1 onion, chopped
1 garlic clove, crushed
90 g (3 oz) prosciutto, about 8 thin slices, chopped
250 ml (8 fl oz) chicken stock
250 g (8 oz) peas
2 tbsp butter
Salt and freshly ground black pepper
1 tbsp chopped fresh mint

Bring a large pot of water to a boil over a high heat. Add a good pinch of salt. Add pasta to boiling water and stir until water has returned to the boil. Reduce heat, cover and cook pasta at a fast simmer for 8 minutes.

Heat a large shallow pan over a medium heat. Add oil and onion and cook for 3–4 minutes, stirring often, until onion softens slightly. Add garlic and cook for a further 1–2 minutes or until fragrant, then add prosciutto. Cook until prosciutto begins to crisp, stirring often.

Add stock, bring to the boil, then reduce heat. Simmer for 5 minutes, allowing stock to reduce slightly. Add peas; cook for 3–4 minutes, turning heat up if necessary. Remove from heat; add butter, salt and loads of pepper. Whisk to incorporate butter, salt, pepper add herbs.

Drain pasta, toss with sauce and serve. Serves 4.

Broad bean and bacon pasta sauce
Substitute bacon for prosciutto, double-podded broad beans for peas and basil for mint.

Linguini with smoked chicken and peas

Love this sauce with linguini. The smoked chicken will contribute a salty flavour, so taste before adding salt, if any, just before serving.

2 tbsp olive oil
1 onion, diced
1 garlic clove, crushed
250 ml (8 fl oz) cream
1 smoked chicken breast fillet
200 g (7 oz) sugar snap peas
Freshly ground black pepper
Chopped parsley to taste
400 g (14 oz) dried linguini

Heat a shallow frying pan over a medium–high heat. Add oil and onion and cook for 3–4 minutes, stirring often, until onion softens slightly. Add garlic and cook for a further 1–2 minutes or until garlic is fragrant. Add cream, bring to the boil, reduce and simmer for 5 minutes. Remove any skin from chicken and slice thinly. Top and tail peas and set aside. When cream has reduced by half add chicken and allow to heat through. Add peas, turn heat up slightly and cook for 2 minutes, stirring often. Check seasoning, add parsley.

Bring a large pot of water to a boil over a high heat. Add a good pinch of salt. Add pasta and stir until water has returned to the boil. Reduce heat, cover and cook pasta at a fast simmer for 8 minutes.

Drain pasta and toss with hot sauce and serve. Serves 4.

Smoked trout and asparagus cream sauce
Swap smoked trout for smoked chicken, being sure to remove all bones, replace peas with asparagus.

Spaghettini carbonara

Spaghettini is a thin spaghetti, and it's perfect for a rich, creamy sauce such as this.

125 g (4 oz) bacon, thinly sliced
4 egg yolks
2 tbsp cream
2 tbsp parmigiano, grated

Salt and lots of freshly ground black pepper
2 tbsp chopped parsley
400 g (14 oz) dried spaghettini

Bring a large pot of water to a boil over a high heat. Add a good pinch of salt. Add pasta and stir until water has returned to the boil. Reduce heat, cover and cook pasta at a fast simmer for 8 minutes.

Heat a frying pan over a medium heat and cook bacon until crispy. Beat egg yolks, cream, cheese, salt and pepper together. The pepper needs to be plentiful, so that it predominates in the finished dish.

Drain pasta and toss with egg mix, bacon and parsley and serve. Serves 4.

Spaghetti with breadcrumbs, tuna, parsley and lemon

Spaghetti with breadcrumbs, tuna, parsley and lemon is without a doubt one of my favourite pasta dishes. I know it's supposed to serve four but when I'm around it would be lucky to serve two. Coarsely chop the fresh breadcrumbs for a nicer texture in the finished dish. A good sourdough bread is best as it has a strong, gutsy flavour. AC

Olive oil for cooking
175 g (6 oz) sourdough bread, chopped into coarse breadcrumbs
2 garlic cloves, crushed
8 tbsp chopped parsley

Chopped zest and juice of 1 lemon
125 g (4 oz) parmigiano, grated
350 g (13 oz) tinned tuna, drained
Salt and freshly ground black pepper
400 g (14 oz) dried spaghetti

Bring a large pot of water to a boil over a high heat. Add a good pinch of salt. Add pasta and stir until water has returned to the boil. Reduce heat, cover and cook pasta at a fast simmer for 8 minutes.

Heat a large heavy-based frypan over a medium–high heat. Add a very generous splash of oil and breadcrumbs and cook for 4–5 minutes, stirring often until breadcrumbs are golden and crunchy. Add garlic, parsley, lemon zest, juice, cheese, tuna, salt and pepper. Cook briefly.

Drain pasta and toss to coat well with tuna/breadcrumb mix and serve. Serves 4.

Spaghetti with seafood and tomato sauce

This dish has a few more ingredients and a longer cooking time than other sauces, resulting in a richer taste. We think of it as the BMW version.

60 ml (2 fl oz) olive oil
2 onions, finely diced
2 small red chillies, de-seeded and finely diced
2 garlic cloves, crushed
125 ml (4 fl oz) white wine
500 ml (1 pt) tomato purée
Salt and freshly ground black pepper

Additional olive oil for cooking
300 g (10 oz) firm white fish, cut into ½ cm (⅓ in) slices
500 g (1 lb) green (raw) prawns, shelled and de-veined
500 g (1 lb) pipis or small clams
2 tbsp chopped parsley
400 g (14 oz) dried spaghetti or linguini

Heat a large shallow pan over a medium heat. Add oil, onions and chillies and cook for 3–4 minutes, stirring often, until onions soften slightly. Add garlic and cook for a further 1–2 minutes or until garlic is fragrant. Turn up heat, add white wine and boil until reduced by half. Add tomato sauce, allow to come to the boil, then reduce heat and cook for 5–10 minutes.

Bring a large pot of water to a boil over a high heat. Add a good pinch of salt. Add pasta and stir until water has returned to the boil. Reduce heat, cover and cook pasta at a fast simmer for 8 minutes.

Spaghetti with breadcrumbs, tuna, parsley and lemon
(recipe page 86)

Tofu and ginger stir-fry (recipe page 103)

Steamed ginger chicken (recipe page 104)

Heat another pan over a medium heat; add a splash of oil and cook first the fish, then the prawns in a little olive oil. Remove and set aside.

Add pipis to cooking sauce, cover with a lid and simmer for 3–4 minutes, until most of the shells have opened. Add cooked seafood, check seasoning, add parsley.

Drain pasta and toss together well with sauce. Tip into a large warm bowl and serve. Serves 4.

Macaroni cheese v

A classic you just can't pass up. The littlies love it, especially when it's all crispy and yummy on top. Be sure to remove white sauce from the heat before adding cheese; otherwise the sauce may curdle.

400 g (14 oz) dried macaroni
50 g (1¾ oz) butter
50 g (1¾ oz) flour
750 ml (1½ pt) hot milk

1 tsp Dijon mustard
200 g (7 oz) grated cheese – mix of parmigiano and cheddar
Salt and freshly ground black pepper

Bring a large pot of water to a boil over a high heat. Add a good pinch of salt. Add pasta and stir until water has returned to the boil. Reduce heat, cover and cook pasta at a fast simmer for 8 minutes.

Place a medium saucepan over a medium heat and melt butter without browning. Add flour and stir well to incorporate. Reduce heat and 'cook' the roux for 2–3 minutes, stirring often. What you are really doing here is cooking the flour.

Raise heat under roux and add 1 ladleful of hot milk. Whisk in well, then continue to add milk, one ladleful at a time, until it's all incorporated. Add mustard, reduce heat and cook for 3–4 minutes, stirring often. Remove from the heat, add three quarters of the cheese and stir well until melted. Season well with salt and pepper.

Drain pasta and stir through the cheese sauce. Pour into an ovenproof dish. Sprinkle remaining cheese on top and place under a hot grill until golden brown. Serves 4.

Macaroni cheese with ham
Ask at the deli for 2 × 1 cm (⅓ in) thick slices of leg ham and dice it. Add to sauce with the cheese.

Macaroni cheese with corn v
Add 200 g (7 oz) corn kernels to the sauce with the cheese.

Spaghetti and meatballs

Minced veal really will add a fuller flavour than regular beef mince, so ask you butcher if they can prepare some for you. Most children prefer the meatballs on the side, rather than tossed together with the sauce.

Olive oil for cooking
1 onion, diced
2 garlic cloves, crushed
350 g (12⅓ oz) veal mince
2 tbsp chopped basil
1 medium egg

40 g (1⅓ oz) dried breadcrumbs
Salt and freshly ground black pepper
A batch of tomato sauce # 1 (page 79) or
 # 2 (page 80)
400 g (14 oz) dried spaghetti

Heat a heavy-based frying pan over a medium heat. Add a splash of oil and onion and cook for 3–4 minutes, stirring often, until onion softens slightly. Add garlic and cook for a further 1–2 minutes or until garlic is fragrant. Set aside to cool.

Mix mince, basil, egg, breadcrumbs, salt, pepper and cooked onion together. Shape into small meatballs, 2 cm (¾ in). Heat a heavy-based pan over a medium heat, add a splash of oil and cook meatballs, in batches, until well browned. Heat the tomato sauce in a saucepan and add the meatballs. Keep at a gentle simmer.

Bring a large pot of water to a boil over a high heat. Add a good pinch of salt. Add pasta to boiling water and stir until water has returned to the boil. Reduce heat, cover and cook pasta at a fast simmer for 8 minutes.

Drain pasta and serve with sauce and meatballs on top. Serves 4.

Spaghetti with pesto ⓥ

This is a traditional pasta dish which is also one of the easiest – you simply cook spaghetti and then toss it with pesto sauce. Nothing to it really.

400g (14 oz) dried spaghetti
Pesto as required

Bring a large pot of water to a boil over a high heat. Add a good pinch of salt. Add pasta to boiling water and stir until water has returned to the boil. Reduce heat, cover and cook pasta at a fast simmer for 8 minutes.

Drain cooked pasta and toss with as little or as much pesto as your heart desires. Serve immediately. Serves 4.

Pesto

Pesto is a classic of the modern Australian kitchen. It appeared with the interest in Italian food and has become a staple refrigerator ingredient for many people. It has many, many uses, other than with spaghetti.

2 cups basil leaves
3 garlic cloves
75g (2⅔ oz) pine nuts
125ml (4 fl oz–½ cup) olive oil
100g (3½ oz) parmigiano reggiano, grated

Place basil leaves, garlic and pine nuts in a food processor and process until smooth. Pour in the oil and blend together. Add parmigiano and set aside.

Use immediately or place in glass jar, cover with a layer of oil and keep in the refrigerator. It can be stored for 2 weeks. Makes 300ml (10 fl oz).

Coriander pesto
Varying the ingredients slightly can make a quite different paste. This pesto is excellent stirred through noodles or added to stir-fries. Substitute the basil for coriander leaves, and the pine nuts with roasted peanuts. Also add 1 chopped green chilli, 30ml (1 fl oz) lime juice, 20ml (⅔ fl oz) fish sauce and 1 tsp grated ginger. Do not add the parmigiano.

Quick-and-easy bolognaise

This is strictly no-fuss and no-frills. Make this, double it even, and stash some away in the freezer for those days when cooking is just too hard. Also use this sauce in cottage pie, tacos or lasagne.

When I was first learning to cook we used to make enormous pots of sauce like this. One thing we had to do was to put all the ingredients into a pot, then put our hands in and squash everything together. This meant the sauce came out incredibly smooth, and never had lumps. If you can cope with the messy hands it's worth giving it a try. AC

1 kg (2 lb) lean beef mince
2 onions, diced
2 garlic cloves, crushed
1 small red chilli, de-seeded and finely diced, optional
250 ml (8 fl oz) tomato purée
375 ml (12 fl oz) beef stock
150 g (5 oz) tomato paste
2 tbsp chopped fresh herbs – basil, thyme, parsley
Salt and freshly ground black pepper

Place all ingredients into a large saucepan. Cook over a high heat until mixture starts to bubble. Stir well to incorporate all ingredients and break mince up. Once boiling, reduce heat to a simmer and cook for 1 hour, stirring often. Check seasoning and consistency. Serves 4–6.

Spicy bolognaise sauce
Add 2 finely diced and de-seeded chillies along with onions.

Beef and mushroom bolognaise
Add 150 g (5 oz) sliced mushrooms.

Veal ragu

This is it: the king of pasta sauces. Rich, decadent and well worth the effort involved. Make this sauce, transform it into lasagne and you have perfect 'going-away-for-the-weekend' food.

Olive oil for cooking
1 onion, diced
2 celery stalks, diced
1 carrot, diced
1 garlic clove, crushed
125 g (4 oz) pancetta, diced
1 kg (2 lb) coarse ground veal; silverside is excellent

2 tbsp tomato paste
125 ml (4 fl oz) white wine
375 ml (13 fl oz) beef stock
250 ml (8 fl oz) tomato purée
Sprig rosemary
2–3 sprigs fresh thyme
Salt and freshly ground black pepper
2 tbsp chopped parsley

Heat a heavy-based saucepan over a medium heat. Add a splash of oil and the onion, celery and carrot. Cook for 5–6 minutes, stirring often. Add garlic and cook for a further 1–2 minutes or until garlic is fragrant. Add pancetta and veal and cook until well-browned, stirring well. Add tomato paste, lower heat and cook for 2–3 minutes. Raise heat then add wine, stock, tomato purée, rosemary and thyme.

Bring to the boil, then reduce heat and simmer for 1 hour, stirring often. Check seasoning, add parsley and serve. Serves 4–6.

Traditional lasagne
Make a batch of cheese sauce (from Macaroni cheese recipe, page 87). Put half of ragu into a lasagne dish. Top with lasagne sheets, then a layer of cheese sauce, another layer of lasagne sheets, the ragu, lasagne sheets and finally cheese sauce. Sprinkle with grated cheese and bake in a preheated oven 180°C (350°F) for 30–40 minutes.

Beef lasagne
A simpler dish made with quick-and-easy bolognaise, page 88.

Roast vegetable and goat's cheese lasagne

This dish takes a bit of preparing as eggplant, zucchini, capsicum and mushrooms need to be roasted before you start. But it's well worth every extra minute spent.

Olive oil for cooking
1 red capsicum
1 eggplant
Salt and freshly ground black pepper
2 zucchini

175 g (6 oz) mushrooms, quartered
6–8 instant lasagne sheets
1 batch of tomato and basil sauce, page 80
150 g (5 oz) goat's cheese
Parmigiano shavings

Preheat oven to 200°C (390°F).

Rub capsicum all over with oil and roast until blistered, around 30 minutes. Place in a plastic bag until cool, then skin, de-seed and slice.

Slice eggplant, sprinkle with salt and set side until juices bead, about 20 minutes. Rinse, pat dry and lay in baking tray. Brush with oil, season and cook in preheated oven until brown and cooked, about 20 minutes.

Slice zucchinis lengthways into 4 slices. Place on baking tray, drizzle with oil, season and roast until just soft, 15–20 minutes.

Quarter mushrooms, place in a tray, drizzle with oil, season and roast for 10–15 minutes, until just cooked.

To assemble take a lasagne dish and arrange half of the vegetables in the base, starting with the eggplant and finishing with the capsicum and mushrooms. Cover with a lasagne sheet. Spoon tomato sauce over pasta and crumble half of the goat's cheese on top. Repeat with another layer of everything.

Scatter parmigiano shavings over the top. Wrap dish with foil and cook in preheated oven for 40 minutes. Remove foil and cook for a further 10 minutes, until cheese browns slightly. Serves 4–6.

Chicken and bok choy stir-fry
Chicken and ginger noodles
Beef, black bean and cashew nut stir-fry
Chilli beef stir-fry
Sour beef with lemongrass
Calamari with soy and chilli glaze
San choy bau
Barbecue pork and bok choy stir-fry
Barbecue pork and noodle stir-fry
Nasi Goreng (stir-fried rice)
Pad Thai (Thai rice noodles)
Singapore noodles
Spicy Sichuan noodles
Chinese stir-fried vegetables with noodles
Tofu and ginger stir-fry
Wok-fried Asian greens
Ginger-steamed choy sum
Steamed ginger chicken
Sweet chilli and mirin steamed tofu

The wok

STIR-FRIES, NOODLES AND STEAMING

Is the wok our most loved kitchen cooking utensil? Without doubt. And for good reason. It's quick to cook in, it's versatile and the results are delicious. Woks, unlike other saucepans, seem to be better the cheaper they are. And at the rate we go through them, that's a good thing.

These wide pans with sloping sides are essential for all stir-frying, steaming and deep-frying. Always buy your wok with a lid; these fit just inside the rim and are essential for softening ingredients during the last moments of stir-frying.

The recipes in this chapter are all described as serving between 2 and 4 people, depending on the food itself, but this is only a rough guide. A recipe for 2 will easily feed 4 if you serve it with rice or noodles.

THINGS YOU NEED TO KNOW ABOUT THE WOK

- A new wok will come with an oily seal to ensure that it doesn't rust before use. This needs to be scrubbed away with hot water and a gentle cleaner. Then place the wok over a high heat and wipe dry with paper towels. Remove from the heat; rub with vegetable oil, reheat, and wipe dry. Repeat 4–5 times to 'season' your wok; it is then ready for use.

- After each use of your wok, scrub it clean with a wok brush and place on a high heat to dry it thoroughly and prevent rusting.

- A wok must be very hot before you add the oil or any other ingredients – and we mean really hot.

- Never overfill the wok, as this will reduce its heating capacity and begin to boil your food instead of stir-frying it.

- Stir-frying in a wok is part frying and part steaming. This is why the lid is essential. Ingredients are initially sealed in the hot oil, then liquid is added and covered with the lid so that the liquid steams and cooks the ingredients.

- Stock or water are the best liquids to use. Although water is perfectly fine, we choose to use stock as its adds that little something extra. You could try Chinese cooking wine, too. Soy or fish sauce, due to their salt content, tend to cause the greens to release their liquid, producing a swampy mess. Use these ingredients only to season the dish at the end of cooking.

- Wok rack. This is a semi-circular metal rack that is supported by the rim the wok. Be sure to buy a rack that fits your wok. They are absolutely invaluable for placing deep-fried items on after cooking to allow excess oil to drain back into the wok and to keep them warm. Once you have used one, you will wonder what you ever did without it.

- Wok spatula. A flat square-shaped tool that slides easily around the bottom and sides of the wok perfectly. Metal and wooden spatulas are available, personal preference on what you would prefer. The practical shape of the spatula allows you to move foods around quickly and efficiently. When deep-frying large objects, such as whole fish, two spatulas used together make light work of removing these awkward shaped objects without breaking them.

- Chillies or chilli paste – it's a matter of personal preference. Sometimes we use chilli paste to boost the flavour, especially if there are no fresh chillies in the refrigerator. Chilli sauce and sweet chilli sauce can be added to just about every wok-cooked dish for the chilli heads.

- Grated ginger. Grated ginger is fresh ginger, peeled and grated on a special ginger grater, available at every Asian store. These graters remove the fibrous stems. Depending on thickness, a 2 cm (¾ in) piece of fresh ginger will give about a teaspoon of grated ginger.

- Noodles. Endless noodles, endless uses. We tend to use fresh Hokkien and flat egg noodles, plus dried vermicelli and rice noodles, the most. When preparing noodles we usually put the kettle on to boil, then pour boiling water over the noodles and set aside. Hokkien and flat egg noodles are fresh noodles, so they need only to heat through, which takes 4–5 minutes. Vermicelli and rice noodles are dried noodles, so need 7–8 minutes to become tender.

- Spring onions. Green onions, shallots, scallions – call them what you will. To us spring onions are long, thin green onions with slender white bulbs.
- Oil for cooking. Everyone has their favourite. For the wok we tend to use either peanut oil for flavour and its ability to cope with the high cooking temperatures, or olive oil because it's sitting next to the stovetop.
- Mysterious ingredients. There are books to tell you more, if you need to know, about Asian ingredients and what are the best brands. It's well worth trying to track one of these down. It also pays to always read the ingredients list on bottles, jars and packet before purchasing. Check use-by dates and avoid MSG at all costs.

Chicken and bok choy stir-fry

This is your stock standard stir-fry of chicken and Asian greens, with a gutsy flavour base of garlic, ginger and chilli to spice it up.

375 g (13 oz) chow mein noodles
2 tbsp peanut oil
1 garlic clove, crushed
1 small red chilli, de-seeded and finely diced
1 tsp grated ginger

4 spring onions, sliced
2 skinless chicken breast fillets, sliced
Chicken stock or water
2–3 bok choy
Soy sauce to taste

Put the kettle on to boil, then pour boiling water over noodles and set aside.
    Place wok over high heat; add peanut oil, then garlic, chilli, ginger and spring onions. Cook for 1–2 minutes, stirring often to avoid burning, until fragrant. Add sliced chicken and cook for a further 2–3 minutes, until browned.
    Add a splash of stock or water, cover with lid and cook for 2 minutes. Remove lid, add bok choy, cover and cook for a further 1–2 minutes, or until bok choy is lightly steamed. Add more stock if necessary.
    Drain noodles and add to the wok with soy sauce to taste. Serve immediately. Serves 3–4.

Chicken and cashew nut stir-fry
Add 100 g (3½ oz) roasted cashew nuts with noodles.

Chicken and broccoli stir-fry
Substitute 100 g (3½ oz) broccolini or broccoli florets for bok choy.

Chicken and black bean stir-fry
Add 2 tbsp soaked and chopped black beans with chicken.

Chicken and oyster sauce stir-fry
Add 1 tbsp oyster sauce with noodles, omitting soy sauce.

Chicken and ginger noodles

The ginger in this dish does wonders for lifting your general well-being. Any type of Asian green could be substituted if preferred, try bok choy, choy sum, or even broccolini.

2 skinless chicken breast fillets
1 bunch Chinese broccoli
375 g (13 oz) Hokkien noodles
2 tbsp peanut oil
1 garlic clove, crushed

1 small red chilli, de-seeded and finely diced
2–3 tsp grated ginger
4 spring onions, sliced
Chicken stock or water
Soy sauce to taste

Preheat oven to 180°C (350°F).

Heat a heavy-based frying pan over medium heat, add oil and brown chicken well on both sides, then transfer to baking dish and cook in preheated oven for 5 minutes Set aside for 5 minutes, then slice thinly.

Wash broccoli well, remove tough outer leaves and slice stems and leaves on the angle into 2 cm (¾ in) slices. Put the kettle on to boil. Pour boiling water over noodles and set aside.

Place wok over high heat; add peanut oil, then garlic, chilli, ginger and spring onions. Cook for 1–2 minutes, stirring often to avoid burning, until fragrant. Take care not to burn. Add Chinese broccoli, cook briefly, then add a splash of stock or water, cover with lid and cook for 2 minutes. Drain noodles. Remove lid, add hot noodles, sliced cooked chicken and more stock if necessary, toss, still cooking for 2–3 minutes, until well combined.

Season with soy sauce to taste. Serve immediately. Serves 3–4.

Tofu and ginger noodles V
Substitute 300 g (10 oz) firm, diced tofu for chicken, take care not to overcook or move about as it will break up.

Chicken and sweet chilli noodles
Use just 1 tsp grated ginger and add 1–2 tbsp sweet chilli sauce (depending on your tastes) with noodles and chicken.

Chicken and coriander noodles
Add 1–2 handfuls of fresh coriander leaves with noodles and chicken.

Beef, black bean and cashew nut stir-fry

This is our spin on the beef and black bean flavour combination we're all very familiar with. Using steak, as we do here, guarantees the finished dish will be tender and delicious.

2 × 200 g (7 oz) porterhouse steaks
2 tbsp black beans*, soaked and chopped
2 tsp chilli paste
2 tbsp peanut oil
2–3 bok choy
375 g (13 oz) Hokkien noodles

1–2 tbsp peanut oil
½ red capsicum, sliced
4 spring onions, sliced
90 g (3 oz) roasted cashew nuts
Soy sauce to taste

Coat steaks with black beans and chilli paste and marinate for at least 30 minutes.

Preheat oven to 180°C (350°F).

Heat a heavy-based frying pan over medium heat, add oil and brown steak well, then transfer to baking dish and cook in preheated oven for 10 minutes until medium–rare. Allow steaks to rest, then slice.

Put the kettle on to boil, then pour boiling water over noodles and set aside.

Place wok over high heat; add peanut oil, then capsicum, spring onions and bok choy. Cook briefly until vegetables soften. Add cashew nuts, soy sauce to taste and sliced beef. Cook briefly, stirring occasionally to combine. Drain noodles and toss together

Serve immediately. Serves 4.

Chilli beef stir-fry

This is one of the quickest stir-fries around, and one of the tastiest. I like it because it's quick, spicy and great for a quick iron hit, not to mention the decadence of using eye fillet. All you'll need is a bowl of steamed rice or some noodles to serve with it. MC

400 g (14 oz) eye fillet
1 tbsp peanut oil
1 bunch baby bok choy, leaves separated and washed
4 tbsp sweet chilli sauce

4 tbsp soy sauce
3 spring onions, thinly chopped
100 g (3½ oz) roasted peanuts, optional
Steamed rice or hot noodles to serve

Cut eye fillet into 1 cm (⅓ in) slices, then cut each slice into 1 cm (⅓ in) strips.

Heat a wok over a high heat, add oil, swirl around wok and add beef. Toss and cook for 2–3 minutes, or until beef is well browned. Add bok choy, stir well, then add chilli sauce, soy sauce, spring onions and peanuts. Allow to heat through and serve immediately with steamed rice or hot noodles. Serves 4.

Sour beef with lemongrass

As the name suggests sour beef with lemongrass is a full-flavoured dish with the gutsy taste of tamarind, blended with the fresher fragrance of lemongrass and lime juice.

1 lemongrass stem, sliced thinly
2 green chillies, de-seeded and finely diced
1 onion, peeled and chopped
1–2 tbsp peanut oil
60 g (2 oz) tamarind*
125 ml (4 fl oz) boiling water
Oil for cooking

400 g (14 oz) scotch fillet
1 bunch snake beans, cut into 3 cm (1 in) lengths, optional
1 tbsp shaved palm sugar
1 tbsp fish sauce
Juice of 1 lime

Place lemongrass, chillies, onion and oil in food processor. Process until paste is smooth. Soak tamarind in boiling water for 15–20 minutes. Use your fingers to work pulp free from tamarind seeds, strain and reserve liquid. Cut steak into 1 cm (⅓ in) slices, then cut each slice into 1 cm (⅓ in) strips.

Place wok over a high heat, add oil, swirl around wok and add paste. Cook for 2–3 minutes, or until distinctly fragrant. Add beef. Toss and cook for 2–3 minutes, or until beef is well browned. Add beans if using, then pour tamarind liquid in. Add palm sugar and fish sauce. Toss, still cooking, for 2–3 minutes, until well combined. Season with lime juice to taste. Serve immediately with steamed rice. Serves 4.

Calamari with soy and chilli glaze

Calamari seems luxurious, but it's actually a very reasonably priced ingredient. This soy and chilli glaze is as good with calamari as it is with prawns or crabs.

I'd like to say that we keep some calamari frozen for emergency dinners, but I can't claim any such forward planning. Any calamari that is brought into the house gets cooked and eaten straight away. MC

3 tbsp soy sauce, light soy for preference
1 tsp grated ginger
2 small red chillies, de-seeded and finely diced
1 tbsp sweet chilli sauce

90 ml (3 fl oz) mirin*
1 tbsp peanut oil
500 g (1 lb) calamari rings
1 cup Thai basil or coriander leaves
Steamed rice to serve

Mix together soy sauce, ginger, chilli, sweet chilli sauce and mirin.

Place wok over high heat; add oil and calamari rings and cook, stirring with a chopstick for 2–3 minutes to ensure even cooking. When calamari changes from translucent to white, pour in soy–chilli glaze and add basil leaves. Allow to bubble, then remove from the heat and serve immediately with steamed rice. Serves 4.

San choy bau

San choy bau is a classic Asian dish, often made with minced quail though minced pork is easier to come by. You can add mushrooms, water chestnuts, bean sprouts, bamboo shoots or anything else that takes your fancy.

1 iceberg lettuce
1–2 tbsp peanut oil
2 garlic cloves, crushed
2 tsp grated ginger
2 small red chillies, de-seeded and finely diced

750 g (1½ lb) pork mince
2 tbsp Chinese rice wine*
Soy sauce to taste
4 spring onions, chopped
Fresh coriander leaves
Chilli sauce

Peel whole leaves away from lettuce, wash well and chill until needed.

Heat wok until hot; add peanut oil, garlic, ginger and chillies, then cook until fragrant. Add pork mince and cook, stirring often, until meat changes colour. Add Chinese rice wine and soy sauce to taste, along with spring onions and coriander leaves. Toss until combined.

Spoon pork mince into lettuce cups, add coriander and chilli sauce to taste, roll up and away you go. Serves 4.

Barbecue pork and bok choy stir-fry

Barbecue pork, or char siew or as it is sometimes called, can be bought at any Asian roast house.

200 g (7 oz) cellophane noodles
1 tbsp peanut oil
4 spring onions, thinly sliced
½ red capsicum, thinly sliced
250 g (8 oz) barbecue pork, thinly sliced

2 bunches bok choy, washed and sliced
Chicken stock or water
90 g (3 oz) bean sprouts
2 tbsp soy sauce
Crispy fried shallots* to garnish

Put the kettle on to boil, then pour boiling water over noodles and set aside.

Place wok over high heat; add peanut oil, then spring onions and capsicum. Cook for 1–2 minutes, stirring often. Add barbecue pork, bok choy and a splash of stock. Cover with lid and cook for 3–4 minutes.

Drain noodles and add to wok with bean sprouts and soy sauce. Stir until hot, top with crispy fried shallots and serve. Serves 3–4.

Barbecue pork and noodle stir-fry

This is a really flavoursome mix of barbecue pork, or char siew as it is also known, with noodles and greens. It can be easily whipped up for a quick dinner.

375 g (13 oz) hokkien noodles
1 bunch Chinese broccoli
2 tbsp peanut oil
1 garlic clove, crushed
1 small red chilli, de-seeded and finely diced

2–3 tsp grated ginger
4 spring onions, sliced
200 g (7 oz) barbecue pork, thinly sliced
Chicken stock or water
Soy sauce to taste

Put the kettle on to boil. Pour boiling water over noodles and set aside.

Wash Chinese broccoli well, remove tough outer leaves and slice stems and leaves on the angle into 2 cm (¾ in) slices.

Place wok over high heat; add peanut oil, then garlic, chilli, ginger and spring onions. Cook for 1–2 minutes, stirring often to avoid burning, until fragrant. Add pork and Chinese broccoli, cook briefly, then add a splash of stock or water, cover with lid and cook for 2 minutes.

Drain noodles. Add hot noodles to wok and more stock if necessary. Toss, still cooking, for 2–3 minutes, until well combined. Season with soy sauce to taste. Serve immediately. Serves 3–4.

Barbecue pork and sweet chilli noodles
Use just 1 tsp grated ginger and add 1–2 tbsp sweet chilli sauce (depending on your tastes) with noodles.

Barbecue duck and hokkien noodles
Substitute half a roast duck for pork. Remove flesh from bones, discarding excess fat; slice into 1 cm (⅓ in) pieces.

Nasi Goreng (stir-fried rice)

For those times when you have leftover rice, here's the perfect thing to do with it. You can add anything to this, any cooked meat or fish that is on hand.

2 medium eggs
Peanut oil for cooking
4 red or golden shallots, diced
1 small red chilli, de-seeded and finely diced
1 carrot, finely diced
½ chicken breast, diced finely

60 g (2 oz) bean sprouts
1 bunch bok choy, thinly sliced
2 tbsp soy sauce
3 cups cold cooked rice
Fried onions, optional
Coriander leaves to garnish

Beat eggs together lightly. Heat wok over a high heat, add a splash of oil, add eggs and swirl well to coat the sides of the wok with egg mix. Cook briefly, then lift one edge away from wok and roll omelette up. Tip onto a chopping board, allow to cool.

Return wok to the heat, add another splash of oil, then add shallots, chilli and carrot. Cook for 2–3 minutes, stirring often. Add chicken, bean sprouts and bok choy and cook for a further 2–3 minutes, stirring. Add soy sauce, then add rice, breaking up if needed. Continue cooking and stirring constantly until rice is coloured by the sauce and heated through.

Slice omelette thinly, add to the wok with fried onions if using and toss to combine. Serve immediately, topped with coriander. Serves 2.

Pad Thai (Thai rice noodles) ⓥ

What we really like about it is that we generally have most of these ingredients on hand, so it's become a cupboard-dinner stand-by.

100 g (3½ oz) thin rice stick noodles
Oil for cooking
3 spring onions, thinly sliced
1 garlic clove, crushed
2 small red chillies, de-seeded and finely diced, or 2 tsp chilli sauce
2 medium eggs, lightly beaten

2 tbsp fish sauce
1 tbsp shaved palm sugar
125 g (4 oz) bean sprouts
60 g (2 oz) roasted peanuts
Fresh coriander leaves
Lime wedges to serve

Put the kettle on to boil. Pour boiling water over noodles and set aside.

Place wok over high heat; add a splash of oil, then spring onions, garlic and chilli. Cook for 1–2 minutes, stirring often to avoid burning, until fragrant. Push to one side, add eggs, allow it to just set lightly, then scramble it by stirring well. Drain noodles and add to wok with fish sauce, palm sugar, bean sprouts and peanuts. Stir constantly until heated through, 3–4 minutes.

Serve immediately with coriander leaves and lime wedges. Serves 2–3.

Singapore noodles

Singapore noodles are great to make if you have left-over cooked chicken or pork, as either can easily be used in place of the chicken breast in the recipe.

375 g (13 oz) hokkien noodles
Oil for cooking
2 medium eggs
2 garlic cloves, crushed
1 tsp grated ginger
1 small red chilli, de-seeded and finely diced
1 skinless chicken breast fillet, thinly sliced
½ capsicum, finely diced
4 broccoli florets, chopped
1 carrot, peeled and thinly sliced
90 g (3 oz) sugar snap peas
¼ wonga bok (Chinese cabbage), thinly sliced
150 g (5 oz) cooked shrimp
Chicken stock or water
4 spring onions, thinly sliced
2–3 tbsp soy sauce
Fresh coriander leaves to garnish

Put the kettle on to boil. Pour boiling water over noodles and set aside.

Beat eggs together lightly. Heat wok over a high heat, add a splash of oil, add eggs and swirl well to coat the sides of the wok with egg mix. Cook briefly, then lift one edge away from wok and roll omelette up. Tip onto a chopping board and allow to cool.

Return wok to the heat. Add another splash of oil, then garlic, ginger and chilli, and cook briefly, stirring frequently, until fragrant. Add chicken and cook until browned, stirring often. Add capsicum, carrot, broccoli and sugar snap peas, cook briefly, tossing occasionally. Add wonga bok, shrimp (and cooked meat if using), stir briefly, then add stock (or water).

Cover wok with lid and cook for 2–3 minutes, stirring once or twice. Add more stock if necessary to prevent vegetables from catching. Drain noodles and add to wok with the spring onions and soy sauce. Cook briefly, then serve immediately with coriander leaves scattered on top. Serves 3–4.

Spicy Sichuan noodles

This is a traditional Asian dish which is often called Chinese spaghetti bolognaise. It does in fact look like bolognaise and it is served on noodles, but it cooks in a fraction of the time and has flavours of ginger, chilli and soy sauce.

375 g (13 oz) Hokkien noodles
1–2 tbsp peanut oil
2 garlic cloves, crushed
2 tsp grated ginger
2 small red chillies, de-seeded and finely diced
4 red or golden shallots, peeled and diced

500 g (1 lb) pork mince
2 tbsp Chinese rice wine*
2 tbsp soy sauce
125 ml (4 fl oz) chicken stock
1 tsp Sichuan peppercorns, roasted and ground

Put the kettle on to boil. Pour boiling water over noodles and set aside.

Heat wok until hot. Add a splash of oil, garlic, ginger, chillies and shallots, then cook until fragrant. Add pork mince and cook, stirring often, until colour changes. Add Chinese rice wine, soy sauce and enough chicken stock to just cover. Stir until well combined, then simmer for 5–6 minutes, lowering heat if necessary.

Check the seasoning of the pork. Drain noodles and serve immediately with sauce on top. Sprinkle with Sichuan pepper. Serves 3–4.

Chinese stir-fried vegetables with noodles ⓥ

There are times when it's vegetables and noodles that you crave and meat or seafood doesn't enter into the picture. This is just the thing to satisfy that need.

375 g (13 oz) hokkien noodles
Oil for cooking
1 garlic clove, crushed
1 tsp grated ginger
1 small red chilli, de-seeded and finely diced
4 spring onions, thinly sliced
½ capsicum, finely diced

1 carrot, peeled and thinly sliced
4 broccoli florets, chopped
90 g (3 oz) sugar snap peas
1 bunch Chinese broccoli, cut into 5 cm (2 in) chunks
Stock or water
2–3 tbsp soy sauce
Fresh coriander leaves to garnish

Put the kettle on to boil. Pour boiling water over noodles and set aside.

Place wok over a high heat, add a splash of oil, and garlic, ginger, chilli and spring onions, cook briefly, stirring frequently, until fragrant. Add capsicum, carrot, broccoli and sugar snap peas, add stock (or water). Cover wok with lid and cook for 2–3 minutes, stirring once or twice. Add Chinese broccoli and more stock if necessary, cover and cook for 1–2 minutes.

Remove lid, stir, add soy sauce to taste and serve immediately with coriander leaves scattered on top. Serves 3–4.

Chilli beef stir-fry (recipe page 97)

Tuna teriyaki skewers (recipe page 121)

Stir-fried vegetables and egg with noodles Ⓥ
Make an omelette using 2 medium eggs as in Singapore noodles. Add with Chinese broccoli.

Stir-fried vegetables with tofu with noodles Ⓥ
Add 300 g (10 oz) firm, diced tofu with the Chinese broccoli.

Chilli stir-fried vegetables with noodles Ⓥ
Add another chilli and a dash of sweet chilli sauce to taste.

Tofu and ginger stir-fry Ⓥ

Cleansing and refreshing, this dish always makes us feel better, especially if we've been over-indulging. Must be something to do with that ginger, so add as much as you like or need.

Oil for cooking
3 spring onions, sliced
1 small red chilli, de-seeded and finely diced
2–3 tsp grated ginger
1 bunch Chinese broccoli, chopped
Stock or water
100 g (3½ oz) snow peas
300 g (10 oz) tofu, cut into 1 cm (⅓ in) cubes
60 g (2 oz) bean sprouts
Soy sauce to season
Steamed rice or noodles to serve

Heat wok over high heat. Add a splash of oil and spring onions, chilli and ginger and cook for 1–2 minutes, stirring, until fragrant. Add broccoli, cook and stir briefly, then add a splash of water or stock. Cover with lid and steam for 2–3 minutes,
   Remove lid, add snow peas, plus more liquid if required, cover and steam for 1 minute. Add tofu and bean sprouts, cover and steam for a further 2 minutes. Toss to combine ingredients, but do so carefully so as not to break up the tofu.
   Serve immediately with steamed rice or noodles. Serves 2.

Wok-fried Asian greens Ⓥ

In this recipe any greens can be used, such as bok choy, Chinese broccoli, choy sum or water spinach. Adjust cooking times slightly for the larger greens.

2 tbsp peanut oil
2 tsp grated ginger
2 cloves garlic cloves, crushed
1–2 bunches Asian greens, washed
Chicken stock or water
½ tsp sesame oil

Heat wok over a high heat. Add oil, then ginger and garlic and cook for 1–2 minutes until fragrant, stirring often. Add greens and toss well to coat with ginger/garlic until just beginning to wilt. Add a splash of stock (or water), toss and cover wok with lid and allow to cook for 2–3 minutes.

Remove lid, allow any excess water to evaporate. Stir sesame oil through and serve immediately. Serves 4 as a side dish.

Ginger-steamed choy sum v

This is ideal as a side dish to complement strong-flavoured foods such as the calamari with soy and chilli glaze, page 98.

60 ml (2 fl oz) water
2 tbsp fish sauce
1 tsp grated ginger

1 tbsp peanut oil
1 bunch choy sum, washed and cut into 3–4 cm (1¼–1½ in) pieces

Mix together water, fish sauce and ginger. Heat wok, add oil and swirl to cover the sides. Throw in choy sum and toss quickly to coat with oil. Pour in ginger/fish sauce mixture. Toss again, then cover the wok with the lid. Allow to cook for 3–4 minutes, stirring occasionally. Serve immediately. Serves 4 as a side dish.

Steamed ginger chicken

Steaming may not be the first thing that springs to mind when deciding how to cook chicken, but this is a dish that should be tried by everyone. The result is an incredibly tender and amazing-flavoured meal. Go on, try it.

4 chicken breast fillets on the bone, or off the bone if it's easier for you
125 ml (4 fl oz) light soy sauce
2 garlic cloves, peeled and sliced
2 small red chillies, sliced
1 tbsp fish sauce

80 ml (2¾ fl oz) water
60 ml (2 fl oz) rice wine vinegar
2 tsp sesame oil
4 cm (1½ in) ginger, peeled and shredded
Steamed rice to serve

Place chicken in a deep bowl. Mix together soy sauce, garlic, chilli, fish sauce, water, rice wine vinegar and sesame oil. Pour over chicken and leave to marinate in refrigerator for 4 hours, turning chicken once.

Place wok over a high heat, add 6 cm (2 in) of water and bring to the boil. Rest a plate in the bottom of a bamboo steamer and place into the wok. Arrange chicken fillets on the plate and pour the marinade over. Spread ginger over the chicken, cover and steam or 20 minutes, or until chicken is just cooked. Remove and allow to rest for 5 minutes in a warm place.

Cut each piece of chicken into 4 and serve immediately with cooking juices and steamed rice. Serves 4.

Steamed ginger fish
Substitute four firm fish fillets or cutlets for chicken breasts. Reduce cooking time to 8–10 minutes, depending on thickness of fish.

Sweet chilli and mirin steamed tofu ⓥ

This is another steamed dish, this time using tofu flavoured with ginger, mirin, spring onion and sweet chilli sauce.

750 g (1½ lb) soft tofu
2 tsp grated ginger
60 ml (2 fl oz) mirin*

6 spring onions, thinly sliced
2 tbsp sweet chilli sauce

Cut tofu into 1 cm (⅓ in) chunks. Place on a plate. Mix remaining ingredients together. Pour over tofu. Place plate in bamboo steamer. Place steamer over wok filled with boiling water and cook for 5–6 minutes. Remove plate and serve immediately. Serves 4 as a side dish.

Spicy barbecue marinade
Basic wine marinade
Kashmiri marinade
Oriental marinade
Spicy Mexican marinade
Soy and garlic marinade
Caribbean fish marinade
Creole spice blend
Simple Moroccan blend
Sweet sticky marinade
Salt and pepper spice
Lime and chilli chicken wings
Chicken saltimbocca skewers
Chicken satay kebabs
Chicken tandoori in naan bread
Pomegranate and sumac glazed duck
Barbecue beef fillet with chilli and garlic marinade
Classic beef and mushroom kebabs
Beef burgers with roasted vegetables
Spiced beef balls in basil leaves
Rosemary lamb kebabs
Moroccan lamb cutlets
Indian tikka lamb kebabs
Greek leg of lamb
Barbecue pork ribs
Sichuan pepper and honey pork fillet
Barbecued whole fish
Soy and ginger salmon kebabs
Tuna teriyaki skewers
Barbecued chermoula prawns
Garlic mushrooms
Sweet paprika corn cobs
Barbecue onion rings
Mushrooms with fresh herbs
Sesame sweet potato wedges
Barbecue sauce

Barbecues

AUSTRALIAN CLASSICS FROM THE GRILL

The barbie at our place gets fired up almost every day during summer and quite a bit during the cooler months too. One of our all-time favourite meals is char-grilled steak with baked potatoes and a healthy salad, not to mention the complementary glass or two of red wine.

We have a gas-fired trolley barbecue, for its ease of use and quick heating time We use our kettle barbie frequently for cooking whole fish or joints of meat – in particular the turkey on Christmas day.

We always find that food tastes and looks better outside; the natural light allows the colour of the food to really shine and the aromas, as the food cooks, gets any appetite going.

Barbecues are also very flexible; you can cook everything from sausages, lamb cutlets and steak through to fish, oysters, whole chickens and vegetarian foods.

We also like the fact that everyone can have just what they want, so sometimes we'll cook fish or even quail for ourselves, sausages or burgers for the children and then have polenta wedges, cobs of corn and salads to share. Then everyone's happy.

Barbecues are also great because there is only the one grill to clean. And this only needs to be scrubbed with a wire brush and wiped over with kitchen towel after cooking. Washing up has never been easier.

THINGS YOU NEED TO KNOW ABOUT BARBECUES

- Get to know your barbecue's hot and cold spots, then you can move food around accordingly.
- Use meats that don't have too much fat on them, as this will cause flames to flare up and singe the food (forget the 'BBQ' lamb chops).
- Food will take longer to cook on a windy day as wind disturbs the heat.
- Never barbecue in bare feet (you could be burnt by falling embers).
- Bring meat to room temperature before cooking it, in order to reduce cooking time.
- If cooking food with bones, such as a whole fish, you can shorten the cooking time by covering with a lid such as a wok lid.
- Do not flip-flop the meat around. Instead place meat on barbecue, cook as recommended, then rotate 180 degrees. Turn over and rotate once more. (Turn over only once.)
- Always cook longer on the first side.
- Never cut into meat to see if it is cooked as the juices escape.
- Allow large cuts of meat to rest for 5 minutes before serving.
- Never sit raw meat in full sun.
- Always bring food from the kitchen just before cooking.
- Never put cooked meat back onto a platter that has had raw meat on it, as bacteria might be transferred to the cooked meat.
- Ensure meat is cooked to the usual level of 'doneness' – especially pork and chicken, which must be cooked through to kill any bacteria.
- You can cook poultry such as chicken or quail easily on a barbecue by 'spatchcocking' it – cutting through the backbone and pressing it out flat. To do this, place the bird breast side up on a chopping board. Insert knife into cavity and cut down pressing firmly through the bone with a sharp knife. Press on top of the bird to flatten it. Turn the bird skin side down and trim away bones as desired.
- The easier option is to get your butcher to do it, ring in advance and ask him nicely.
- A wok lid makes a great cover for your whole fish, if you don't have one try a deep baking tray or a few layers of foil. Either will work okay.

Spicy barbecue marinade

The ultimate barbecue marinade, perfect for pork, beef or chicken.

60 ml (2 fl oz) tomato ketchup
1 tbsp Worcestershire sauce
1 tbsp white vinegar
4 tsp brown sugar

2 tsp Dijon mustard
1 tsp chilli powder
Dash of Tabasco

Whisk all the ingredients together and brush onto meat as it is barbecuing.

Basic wine marinade

Use white wine for white meats and use red wine for red meats.

90 ml (3 fl oz) olive oil
90 ml (3 fl oz) wine of your choice
2 shallots, finely diced

2 garlic cloves, crushed
3 tsp chopped fresh herbs
Salt and freshly ground black pepper

Mix all the ingredients together and brush onto meat as it is barbecuing.

Kashmiri marinade

This marinade is an aromatic blend of yoghurt and spices and goes well with quail – one of our favourite barbecue meats.

90 g (3 oz) natural yoghurt
1 tsp grated ginger
1 garlic clove, crushed
2 tsp lemon juice
1 tsp ground cumin
¼ tsp ground white pepper

½ tsp ground turmeric
½ tsp chilli powder
½ tsp salt
¼ tsp ground cinnamon
2 tbsp olive oil

Mix yoghurt, ginger, garlic and lemon juice with spices, salt and oil.

Oriental marinade

This mix is particularly good on chicken and pork.

1 tbsp black beans*, soaked and drained
90 ml (3 fl oz) soy sauce
2 tbsp fish sauce
2 tsp chilli paste
1 tsp sesame oil
2 tsp grated ginger

Mash black beans with a fork, then add remaining ingredients. Brush this onto meat as it is barbecuing.

Spicy Mexican marinade

This one really packs a punch. It is great on chicken wings, drumettes and beef ribs.

1 garlic clove, crushed
½ tsp salt
½ tsp chilli powder
1 tsp sweet paprika
½ tsp ground coriander
½ tsp ground cumin
1 tsp mustard seeds, crushed
½ tsp freshly ground black pepper
2 tbsp olive oil

Mix all ingredients together and brush onto meat as it is barbecuing.

Soy and garlic marinade

This is a simple marinade that works wonders with chicken, fish and pork.

1½ tbsp rice vinegar
2 tbsp soy sauce
1 garlic clove, crushed
Pinch of five-spice powder
1 tsp caster sugar
A few drops of Tabasco

Mix all ingredients together and brush onto meat as it is barbecuing.

Caribbean fish marinade

This is really good with fish, particularly oily fish like garfish, sardines and salmon.

60 ml (2 fl oz) lime juice
1 tsp allspice
3 spring onions, thinly sliced
1 small red chilli, de-seeded and finely diced
½ tsp salt
2 tbsp olive oil

Mix all ingredients together and brush onto fish just before barbecuing.

Creole spice blend

This blend is an oldie but a goodie. We like it best on chicken and fish.

4½ tsp sweet paprika
3 tsp onion powder
3 tsp garlic powder
1½ tsp thyme leaves

1½ tsp ground oregano
1 tsp cayenne pepper
1 tsp white pepper
1 tsp freshly ground black pepper

Mix the spices together well and coat chicken or fish just before barbecuing.

Simple Moroccan blend

This blend can be added to just about any meat successfully, particularly lamb and quail.

1 tsp ground coriander
1 tsp ground cumin
1 tsp sweet paprika

½ tsp salt
1½ tbsp lemon juice
2 tbsp olive oil

Mix the ingredients together to form a smooth paste. Brush it onto lamb just before barbecuing.

Sweet sticky marinade

This marinade goes particularly well with pork neck which can be bought from any butcher's shop in an Asian shopping area.

250 ml (8 fl oz) dark soy sauce
125 ml (4 fl oz) rice vinegar
2 tbsp honey
1 tsp sesame oil

2 garlic cloves, crushed
2 tsp grated ginger
2 tbsp hot bean paste
½ tsp five spice powder

Mix all ingredients together. Marinate meat for 1–2 hours and drain excess marinade before cooking.

Serve with Asian noodle salad, page 212.

Salt and pepper spice

A classic spice mix that's good with oily fish, quail, chicken and prawns.

3 tsp Sichuan pepper
½ tsp salt
½ tsp five-spice

Place the pepper and salt in a dry pan and cook over a medium heat. Stir until the salt turns golden, about 3 minutes. Crush until very fine in a mortar and pestle. Sieve to remove husks and stir five-spice through.
    Sprinkle the mixture onto meat or seafood just before barbecuing.

Lime and chilli chicken wings

This one is finger lickin' good. Children wolf these wings down without even realising the chilli is in there.

125 ml (4 fl oz) lime juice
4 small red chillies, de-seeded and finely diced
½ tsp salt
1 tsp caster sugar
2 tbsp olive oil
1 kg (2 lb) chicken wings

Mix lime juice, chilli, salt, sugar and oil together. Marinate chicken wings for 1 hour. Drain off excess marinade and use for basting during cooking.
    Place chicken on oiled barbecue grill. Cook for 20 minutes, turning often. Serves 5–6.

Lime and chilli lamb cutlets
Substitute 12 lamb cutlets for chicken wings and cook for 4–5 minutes on each side.

Chicken saltimbocca skewers

Anything on a skewer is a great hit at a barbecue. We sometimes make mini versions of these and serve them as a pre-dinner nibble.

2 tbsp olive oil
2 tbsp chopped fresh sage
Salt and freshly ground black pepper
4 chicken breast fillets, skinless
12 thin slices prosciutto
24 skewers

Mix together oil, sage, salt and pepper. Cut each chicken fillet into 6 long strips. Mix sage oil and chicken together.

Cut prosciutto slices in half lengthways. Lay out one slice of prosciutto and place 1 strip of chicken on top. Thread prosciutto and chicken onto skewers.

Place skewers on oiled barbecue plate. Cook for 4 minutes on each side. Makes 24.

Chicken satay kebabs

These satay kebabs are ideal as a starter or as part of a larger spread of food.

500 g (1 lb) chicken fillets
1 small onion, diced
1 tbsp soy sauce
60 ml (2 fl oz) peanut oil
2 tsp ground coriander
1 tsp ground cumin
1 tsp ground turmeric
¼ tsp ground cinnamon
1 tsp salt
1 tsp sugar
60 g (2 oz) roasted peanuts
20 skewers

Cut chicken into 3 cm (1 in) chunks. Make satay by placing remaining ingredients in a food processor and blend until smooth. Marinate chicken in the satay for 1 hour. Thread 4–5 pieces of chicken onto each skewer.

Place chicken skewers on oiled barbecue grill. Cook for 10 minutes, turning 2–3 times. Makes 10.

Beef satay kebabs
Substitute beef fillet for chicken.

Chicken tandoori in naan bread

We eat this dish with alarming regularity. Sometimes we make our own naan bread, page 229, but usually we purchase naan bread from the supermarket or Indian take-away for convenience.

4 skinless chicken thigh fillets
250 g (8 oz) natural yoghurt
2 tbsp tandoori paste
1 tbsp lemon juice
12 skewers
2 tomatoes, finely diced
1 Lebanese cucumber, finely diced
2 spring onions, thinly sliced
1 tbsp chopped mint
1 tbsp lemon juice, additional
2 tbsp olive oil
4 naan
Natural yoghurt, additional

Dice chicken into 3 cm (1 in) chunks. Mix together yoghurt, tandoori paste and lemon juice. Marinate chicken for 1 hour. Thread 4 or 5 pieces of chicken onto each skewer. Place chicken on oiled barbecue plate. Cook for 12 minutes, turning 3 or 4 times.

Mix together tomato, cucumber, onion, mint, additional juice and oil. Place bread on oiled barbecue grill for 1–2 minutes before serving. Serve chicken in hot bread with salad over the top. Add additional natural yoghurt. Serves 4.

Pomegranate and sumac glazed duck

Duck fillets are versatile and can be marinated in just about any type of flavour. This recipe is dedicated to our good friend Phillippa Grogan, who has a bottle of pomegranate syrup that is just waiting for a dish like this to come along. And you never know when a bottle of pinot may turn up too.

4 tbsp pomegranate syrup*
2 tbsp olive oil
3 tsp sumac*

Salt and freshly ground black pepper
4 duck breast fillets

Combine syrup, oil, sumac, salt and pepper. Pour over duck fillets and marinate for 1 hour. Drain off excess marinade and set rest aside to use for basting during cooking.

Place duck fillets skin side down on oiled barbecue grill. Cook for 9–10 minutes, rotating once or twice. Turn over and cook for a further 8–9 minutes, rotating once or twice times. Rest for 5 minutes.

Slice thickly to serve. Serves 4.

Pomegranate and sumac glazed quail
Pour marinade over 4 spatchcocked quails and marinate for 30 minutes. Cook for 5 minutes on each side.

THE PERFECT STEAK

We prefer porterhouse steak for barbecuing because it's one of the more tender cuts available and offers a good balance between flavour and juiciness, with just a thin layer of fat across the top to keep it moist during cooking. If you're more of a scotch fillet or rump sort of person, this general cooking method still works fine.

Choose steaks about 2 cm (¾ in) thick. Brush with oil and season with salt and pepper.

Place steak on oiled barbecue grill. Cook for 6 minutes, rotating once. Juices should start to bead on top of the steak; this is your cue to turn steak over.

Turn over and cook for a further 4–5 minutes, rotating once. For medium–rare – and we are talking the perfect steak here – when juices again begin to bead on the top remove steaks and allow to rest in a warm place for 5 minutes. If you prefer your steak medium, cook for a further 2 minutes.

> **TIP**
> To tell if your steak is cooked you'll need to prod the meat with your finger. First of all feel it raw: it's almost like soft butter. Compare this with the stages of 'doneness':
> - At rare it's like a sponge.
> - At medium–rare it should feel like the fleshier base of your thumb.
> - At medium it will feel like the base of your middle finger.
> - At well done it can bounce; this is to be avoided at all costs.

Barbecue beef fillet with chilli and garlic marinade

We used to think of fillet steak as a special-occasion meat, due its high price. Then we cooked two huge fillets for a New Year's Eve dinner and fed almost 20 people, which was very good value indeed.

1 small red chilli, de-seeded and finely diced
2 garlic cloves, crushed
1 tsp freshly ground black pepper
½ tsp sea salt
125 ml (4 fl oz) olive oil
1 eye fillet, about 1.5 kg (3 lb)

Mix chilli, garlic, pepper, salt and oil together. Rub over fillet and marinate for 30 minutes. Drain well. Set aside remaining marinade for basting during cooking.

Place fillet on oiled barbecue grill. Sear for 8–10 minutes on each side, rolling fillet over as required.

After a cooking time of 30 minutes the fillet will be medium–rare. For medium, cook for a further 10 minutes. Rest for 15 minutes, then slice. Serves 8–10.

Classic beef and mushroom kebabs

We call these our 'classic' kebabs because everyone loves them, children and grown ups included. I've been making these kebabs since I was about sixteen, when I was training to be a chef. They are always a hit. MC

1 kg (2 lb) tender beef, such as fillet, porterhouse or rump
2 tsp Dijon mustard
2 tsp chopped fresh rosemary
2 tbsp olive oil
60 ml (2 fl oz) red wine
Salt and freshly ground black pepper
1 red capsicum
16 button mushrooms, about 200 g (7 oz)
14 skewers

Cut beef into 2 cm (¾ in) chunks. Mix mustard, rosemary, oil, red wine, salt and pepper together. Pour over beef chunks and marinate for 1 hour.

Cut capsicum in half, remove seeds and dice to 2 cm (¾ in). Wipe mushrooms clean and cut in half.

Drain excess marinade off beef and set aside for basting during cooking. Thread ingredients onto skewers.

Place kebabs on oiled barbecue grill. Cook for 12 minutes, turning 3–4 times. Makes 14 kebabs.

Beef burgers with roasted vegetables

The roasted vegetables in this mix add a great extra flavour to the burgers. If you haven't got time, simply make them with salt and pepper, and perhaps a bit of chopped parsley.

1 onion, diced
1 red capsicum, diced
1 zucchini, diced
1 eggplant, diced, salted and rinsed

60 ml (2 fl oz) olive oil
Salt and freshly ground black pepper
1 kg (2 lb) beef mince

Preheat oven to 180°C (350°F).

Place diced vegetables in a baking tray and toss with oil. Roast in a preheated oven for 30–40 minutes, stirring often. Set aside to cool.

Mix roasted vegetables with beef mince. Season with salt and pepper. Divide into 8 and form into burger shapes.

Place burgers on oiled barbecue grill. Cook for 4 minutes, rotating once. Turn over and cook for a further 3–4 minutes, rotating once. Check that burgers are cooked to your preference. For more than medium–rare, cook for another 2 minutes. Makes 8.

Baby burgers
Divide the mix into 16 and shape. Cook for 3 minutes on each side.

Burgers with the lot
Cook some bacon strips and onions alongside the burgers, toast round rolls on the barbecue grill and assemble all ingredients with lettuce, tomato and mild mustard.

Spiced beef balls in basil leaves

This is an interesting way of spicing up some minced beef and then skewering it so it's easy to cook and eat. These balls are great with watercress tabouleh, page 211, and a bowl of tzatziki, page 41.

500 g (1 lb) minced beef
½ tsp ground nutmeg
½ tsp ground cinnamon
1 tsp ground coriander
1 tsp ground cumin
1 tbsp chopped mint leaves

1 tbsp chopped coriander leaves
¼ tsp salt
¼ tsp freshly ground black pepper
50 large basil leaves
10 skewers

Mix beef, spices and chopped mint and coriander together with salt and pepper. Divide mix into 10 × 50 g (1¾ oz) portions. Divide each portion evenly into 5 and roll into balls. Wrap each ball in a basil leaf.

Thread 5 basil-wrapped meatballs onto each skewer. Cook on grill for 9–10 minutes, turning once or twice. Serves 4.

Rosemary lamb kebabs

This is a simple kebab recipe that makes the most of the classic combination of lamb and rosemary. Cook the lamb to medium only, to enjoy the kebabs at their juicy best.

8 lamb fillets
3 tbsp olive oil
1 tbsp lemon juice

2 tbsp chopped fresh rosemary
Salt and freshly ground black pepper
20 skewers

Dice lamb into 2 cm (¾ in) squares. Mix oil, lemon juice, rosemary, salt and pepper together. Pour over lamb and marinate for 2 hours.

Thread lamb onto skewers, about 6 pieces per skewer. Use remaining marinade for basting during cooking.

Place lamb on oiled barbecue plate. Cook for 8 minutes, turning 3–4 times. Makes 20 kebabs.

Moroccan lamb cutlets

We just adore this blending of Moroccan spices on juicy lamb cutlets. Whenever we have them we feel compelled to eat some Moroccan couscous salad, page 214, and a bowl of tzatziki, page 41.

1 tsp ground coriander
1 tsp ground cumin
1 tsp sweet paprika
½ tsp salt

1½ tbsp lemon juice
2 tbsp olive oil
16 trim lamb cutlets

Mix spices, salt, lemon juice and oil together to form a smooth paste. Brush onto lamb cutlets. Cook for 3–4 minutes on each side. Serves 4.

Indian tikka lamb kebabs

Tikka paste usually packs a bit more punch than tandoori and, naturally enough, matches lamb really well. Try serving these with pilaf, page 127, and a green salad, page 209.

500 g (1 lb) lamb loin
3 tbsp tikka curry paste
2 tbsp lemon juice

90 g (3 oz) natural yoghurt
12 skewers

Dice lamb into 2 cm (¾ in) chunks. Mix tikka paste, lemon juice and yoghurt together. Pour over lamb and marinate for 30 minutes.

Thread lamb onto skewers. Place skewers on oiled barbecue plate. Cook 8 minutes, turning 3–4 times. Makes 12 skewers.

Greek leg of lamb

A leg of lamb cooked on the grill with these flavours of lemon juice, garlic and fragrant herbs is a beautiful thing. Besides tasting great it's also a good way to feed a crowd.

I think I've already mentioned how much I like lamb, garlic and herbs. No surprises, then, that this is one of my favourite barbecue recipes. MC.

3 tbsp olive oil
80 ml (2¾ fl oz) lemon juice
3 garlic cloves, crushed
½ cup chopped basil, oregano and parsley leaves
Salt and freshly ground black pepper

1 leg of lamb, boned and pressed flat
2 garlic cloves, peeled
60 ml (2 fl oz) lemon juice
1 cup parsley leaves
½ cup basil leaves
125 ml (4 fl oz) olive oil

Prepare marinade by mixing together oil, lemon juice, garlic, herbs, salt and pepper. Place lamb in a deep baking tray. Pour marinade over and marinate for 1 hour.

Prepare dressing by putting garlic, lemon juice, parsley and basil in a food processor. Blend until smooth. Gradually add oil, then season to taste.

Place lamb on oiled barbecue plate. Cook for 10 minutes, rotating once. Reduce heat to low and turn lamb over. Cover and cook for 10 minutes. Remove cover, rotate and cook for a further 10 minutes. Rest the meat for 10 minutes.

Cut into thick slices. Pour dressing over lamb and serve with Greek salad, page 209. Serves 6.

Barbecue pork ribs

Our children love barbecue pork ribs, or crispy pork as they call it. We often cook these in the oven on a baking rack over a dish of water (to prevent burning) and serve them with rice. As Mia and Luke say, they're crunchy and sticky.

3 tbsp tomato sauce
2 tbsp sweet chilli sauce

2 tbsp soy sauce
1 kg (2 lb) pork ribs

Mix tomato sauce, sweet chilli and soy sauce together. Pour over pork and marinate for 3–4 hours (if time permits). Drain well before cooking.

Place pork on medium oiled barbecue grill. Brush regularly with marinade. Cook for 10–15 minutes, turning 4–5 times. Serves 4.

Sichuan pepper and honey pork fillet

This recipe shows how good pork fillet can be when it's treated to a gutsy marinade. Just be sure to cook it for 15 minutes only, and rest the meat before slicing.

1 tsp Sichuan pepper
2 tsp sesame oil
1 tsp five-spice powder
½ tsp hot chilli sauce

2 tbsp honey
Pinch of salt
750 g (1½ lb) pork fillet

Toast Sichuan pepper in a small pan until fragrant. Crush with a mortar and pestle. Mix with oil, five-spice, chilli sauce, honey and salt. Pour over pork fillet and marinate for 1 hour.

Drain the pork and set aside remaining marinade for basting during cooking.

Place pork on medium-heat oiled barbecue grill. Cook for 15 minutes, turning 2–3 times. Rest the meat for 5 minutes. Slice and serve. Serves 4.

Barbecued whole fish

Whole fish are best cooked in a kettle-style barbecue, but if you only have a trolley barbecue you can still do it by covering with a lid as directed.

This is one of those dishes we can't believe people don't cook more often. It's extremely simple and fish tastes moist and magnificent when it has been cooked on the bone.

2 limes, sliced
10 cm (4 in) ginger, peeled and sliced
4 × 400 g (14 oz) whole fish, cleaned

Olive oil
2 tsp salt
Freshly ground black pepper

Place lime and ginger slices inside the cavity of each fish. Slash sides of fish diagonally a couple of times. Brush fish with oil. Rub salt and pepper over skin and place fish on oiled barbecue grill.

Cover with lid and cook for 8 minutes, rotating once. Turn over, cover, and cook for 7 minutes, rotating once. Serves 4.

Seven-spice with whole fish
Rub fish with seven-spice mixture, page 59, and cook in the same way.

Soy and ginger salmon kebabs

Cook these soy and ginger marinated salmon kebabs to medium–rare and you may never go back to lamb chops again.

750 g (1½ lb) salmon fillet, skin removed
1 tsp grated ginger
1 small red chilli, de-seeded and finely diced

1 tbsp kecap manis*
60 ml (2 fl oz) soy sauce
60 ml (2 fl oz) peanut oil
10 skewers

Dice salmon into 2 cm (¾ in) chunks. Mix remaining ingredients together. Pour over salmon chunks and marinate for 1 hour, turning once.

Drain salmon well and reserve remaining marinade for basting.

Thread salmon onto skewers. Place skewers on oiled barbecue plate. Cook for 3 minutes, basting as required. Makes 10.

Seven-spice salmon kebabs
Cut 750 g (1½ lb) salmon fillets into 2 cm (¾ in) chunks. Mix with seven-spice mixture and cook for 3 minutes on each side.

Tuna teriyaki skewers

As with all oily fish, you should cook these tuna teriyaki skewers only to medium–rare to enjoy them at their best. Try them just once and they're sure to become a favourite, like they are for me. AC

750 g (1½ lb) tuna
80 ml (2¾ fl oz) shoyu*
2 tbsp mirin*
2 tsp grated ginger

1 tsp sesame oil
1 tsp caster sugar
12 skewers

Cut tuna into 2 cm (¾ in) chunks. Mix remaining ingredients together. Pour over tuna chunks and marinate for 30 minutes.

Thread 4 chunks onto each skewer. Set aside remaining marinade for basting during cooking.

Place tuna on oiled barbecue plate and cook for 2 minutes. Turn over and cook for a further 2 minutes. Makes 12 skewers.

Barbecued chermoula prawns

What's a barbie without a prawn on it? This chermoula paste is extremely versatile; as well as on prawns, we use it on roasted vegetables and to make tagines.

2 tsp sweet paprika
1 tsp ground ginger
1 tsp chilli powder
1 tsp ground cumin
1 tsp ground coriander
1 tsp ground white pepper
½ tsp ground cardamom

½ tsp ground cinnamon
½ tsp allspice
1 tsp salt
2 tbsp lemon juice
3 tbsp olive oil
1 kg (2 lb) green (raw) prawns
30 skewers

Mix spices and salt with lemon juice and olive oil to form a smooth paste. Shell and de-vein prawns. Coat prawns with chermoula paste and marinate for 30 minutes. Thread one prawn onto each skewer, through the centre lengthways.

Cook on an oiled barbecue plate for 2 minutes on each side and serve with tzatziki, page 41. Makes 30 skewers.

Garlic mushrooms ⓥ

Mushrooms cope really well with the heat of a barbecue, and taste especially good when they are drizzled with this lovely garlic oil.

12 Swiss brown or field mushrooms
3–4 tbsp olive oil

2 garlic cloves, crushed
Salt and freshly ground black pepper

Wipe mushrooms with a damp cloth. Mix oil with garlic, salt and pepper.
   Place mushrooms on barbecue plate, brush with oil. Cook for 4 minutes, brushing with oil, rotating once. Turn over and brush with oil. Cook for a further 4 minutes, rotating once. Serves 4–6.

Sweet paprika corn cobs ⓥ

This has got to be what barbecues are made for: tender corn cobs with a dusting of aromatic sweet paprika on the outside.

3 corn cobs
3 tbsp olive oil

2 tsp sweet paprika
Pinch of salt

Remove green husks and silky tassels from corn. Cut each cob into 6 slices.
   Mix oil, paprika and salt together. Toss corn with paprika oil.
   Place corn slices on oiled barbecue grill. Cook for 10 minutes, turning often. Serves 4.

Barbecue onion rings ⓥ

What better way to whet everyone's appetites than with the aromas of cooking onions?

1kg (2 lb) red onions, sliced into 1cm (½ in) rings
40ml (1¼ fl oz) olive oil

Sprigs of fresh thyme
Salt and freshly ground black pepper

Toss onions with oil, thyme, salt and pepper. Place onions on barbecue plate and spread out over the entire surface.
   Reduce heat to low and cook for 30 minutes, turning often. Add extra oil as required. The onion rings will come apart a little as they are turned. Excellent with steak and lamb cutlets. Serves 6–8

Mushrooms with fresh herbs ⓥ

A good mix of mushroom varieties as described below will ensure a great combination of flavours and textures.

150g (5 oz) Swiss brown mushrooms
150g (5 oz) oyster mushrooms
100g (3½ oz) button mushrooms

2 tbsp olive oil
½ cup chopped fresh herbs
Salt and freshly ground black pepper

Wipe mushrooms with a damp cloth if required to remove grit. Mix the oil, herbs, salt and pepper together. Toss oil and mushrooms together.

Place mushrooms on oiled barbecue plate. Cook mushrooms for 15 minutes, turning often. Add extra oil if required. Serves 4–6

Sesame sweet potato wedges ⓥ

Sweet potato is excellent for the barbecue as it cooks fairly quickly.

2 medium sweet potatoes
2 tbsp sesame oil or olive oil
Salt and freshly ground black pepper

Peel the sweet potatoes then cut in half lengthways. Then cut each half lengthways into 4 wedges. Mix oil with a little salt and pepper.

Place wedges on oiled barbecue grill, brush with oil and cook for 10 minutes in total, turning from time to time. Serves 4-6

Barbecue sauce

This is the ultimate in barbecue sauces. Use it with free abandon at every barbecue you attend.

100 ml (3½ fl oz) tomato paste or sauce
2 tbsp Worcestershire sauce
2 tbsp red wine vinegar
90 g (3 oz) brown sugar

4 tsp smooth mustard
2 garlic cloves, crushed
250 ml (8 fl oz) water

Place all ingredients in a saucepan and bring to the boil. Reduce to a simmer and cook for 15 minutes. Adjust seasoning and consistency if required.

Rice
Steamed rice
Onion pilaf
Pumpkin, chickpea and saffron pilaf
Chicken risotto
Spring risotto
Asparagus and prawn risotto
Roast pumpkin, feta and pine nut risotto
Mushroom risotto with truffle oil
Mushroom risotto cakes
Paella

Couscous
Quick couscous
Traditional couscous
Spicy chicken fillets with coriander couscous
Seven-spice lamb fillets with onion couscous

Pulses
Indian-spiced beans
Moroccan chickpea and pumpkin stew
Kidney bean and vegetable chilli
Lentil dhal
Barbecued pork sausage with spiced lentils
Caramelised onion and chickpea burgers
Lentil and ricotta burgers

Polenta
The best soft polenta
Grilled polenta with garlic vegetables
Green olive salsa

Rice, couscous, pulses and polenta

FROM GRAINS TO BEANS

Rice

It's said that more people throughout the world sit down to a meal that uses rice than to any other food. Not really surprising when you consider the fact that virtually every country has its favourite rice dishes. What would Italian food be without risotto, Japanese cooking without sushi, North Africa without pilaf or Spanish cooking without paella?

Both of our childhood experiences of rice were pretty basic in comparison. If we ate rice, it was likely to be either part of a Chinese takeaway, or as basic boiled rice, (and we mean swamped in lots of water) or as rice pudding. Luckily, we have all come a long way since then and extended our food horizons to see what the rest of the world does with this nutritious, versatile and delicious grain.

THINGS YOU NEED TO KNOW ABOUT RICE

- The best way to cook rice is by the absorption (steamed rice) method.
- Even better is a rice cooker that does all the work for you.
- Don't stir rice during cooking as this allows steam and heat to escape.
- Generally speaking rice doesn't have to be washed before cooking. Only wash rice if you want to get rid of the starch, but even this is not necessary for the absorption method.
- 1 cup of raw rice equals 3 cups of cooked rice.
- The addition of salt is up to personal taste.
- Different rices have different flavours and uses.

VARIETIES OF RICE

Sushi rice
Rice for sushi is usually labelled as sushi rice, which is a short-grain rice.

Calrose rice
Calrose rice is a medium grain rice, which means the grains are shorter and plumper than long grain. It is ideal to accompany Chinese dishes and for making sushi. It releases starch during cooking and the grains stick together slightly, making it easy to eat with chopsticks. Calrose rice is best cooked by the absorption method, but can be boiled in plenty of water if necessary, however, it should be washed first. This rice is commonplace at supermarkets, but you can purchase large bags at Asian grocery stores very cheaply.

Arborio rice
Most rice for making risotto is labelled as arborio or risotto rice. This is a medium grain rice which releases starch during cooking to bind the mixture together lightly and add a distinctive creaminess to the finished dish. It also absorbs liquid and the flavours that have been added to the risotto. Vialone Nano and Carnaroli are also rice varieties grown in Italy especially for making risotto, both are quite expensive due to a limited supply. Look for them in specialist food stores.

Long-grain rice
The most famous of the many varieties of long grain rice is without doubt Basmati and Jasmine rice. Both of them are subtly perfumed, fragrant grains which match well with hundreds of different dishes. This type of rice contains less starch than others and will remain separate during cooking. They are best cooked by the absorption method. Long grain rice can be flavoured with saffron strands, nuts and spices or cooked with stock to produce a more full flavoured dish.

Glutinous rice
Glutinous rice is available in both a black and white variety and is so called not because of any gluten, but rather because of its stickiness when cooked. It requires

soaking for at least 6 hours and thorough rinsing before being cooked, usually steamed. It can be steamed, then rolled into balls and served with coconut milk and fresh fruit, or wrapped in banana leaves, with either sweet and savoury fillings and eaten as a snack. Black glutinous rice turns a beautiful purple colour when cooked, particularly when coconut milk is added.

Steamed rice V

A rice cooker should take away the fear of cooking rice. If that doesn't work for you, practise this method until you have it down pat. It's one of the best things you can learn. Once cooked, rice will keep warm for up 20 minutes. Salt is optional; we rarely add it to plain rice.

400 g (14 oz) rice
625 ml (1 pt and 4 fl oz) water
Salt, optional

Place rice and water (and any salt) in a saucepan. Cover with a lid, bring to the boil and then reduce to a low simmer. It is important to keep covered with a lid, so as not to allow the steam to escape. It will take about 15–20 minutes for all the water to be absorbed. It is also beneficial to allow the covered rice to stand for 5–10 minutes, covered, at room temperature before using. Serves 4–6.

Coconut rice V
Substitute half of the water for coconut milk.

Saffron rice V
Add a pinch of saffron strands to the cooking water.

Spiced nut rice V
Cook 30 g (1 oz) each of almonds, pine nuts and pistachios in 1 tbsp of oil until golden brown. Add a pinch of ground turmeric, cinnamon and chilli. Then add dry rice and cook briefly together. Add water and continue as described.

Onion pilaf V

Pilafs are a touch more sophisticated than plain steamed rice and are perfect with any spiced dish, particularly Indian and Middle-Eastern food.
    They have a richer flavour due to the fact they have onion, garlic and saffron added, and usually use stock instead of water.

2 tbsp olive oil for cooking
2 onions, diced
1 garlic clove, crushed
Pinch of saffron, optional

400 g (14 oz) long grain rice
750 ml (1½ pt) chicken or vegetable stock
2 tbsp chopped parsley

Preheat oven to 180°C (350°F).

Heat a large heavy-based saucepan over a medium heat. Add oil, onions, garlic and saffron (if using) and cook for 4–5 minutes until fragrant and soft. Add the rice and stir for 1–2 minutes. Add stock and bring to the boil, stirring often. Reduce heat, cover and cook in preheated oven for 30 minutes, or until rice is tender and stock has been absorbed. Allow to stand for 5 minutes before serving.

Check seasoning, add parsley and serve. Serves 4.

Pine nut and saffron pilaf V
Add 90 g (3 oz) of pine nuts to the onions. Cook for an extra 2–3 minutes, or until nuts are golden brown.

Pumpkin, chickpea and saffron pilaf V

An extended variation on the onion pilaf, this makes a substantial dish, certainly good enough for dinner.

- 2 tbsp olive oil
- 2 onions, diced
- 1 garlic clove, crushed
- Pinch of saffron threads
- 70 g (2⅓ oz) vermicelli noodles, roughly broken
- 750 g (1½ lb) pumpkin diced into 2 cm (¾ in) chunks
- 400 g (14 oz) long grain rice
- 750 ml (1½ pt) vegetable stock
- 70 g (2⅓ oz) currants
- 100 g (3½ oz) chickpeas, soaked and cooked until tender
- 2 tbsp chopped parsley
- ½ cup coriander leaves

Preheat oven to 180°C (350°F).

Heat a large heavy-based saucepan over medium heat. Add oil, onions, garlic and saffron and cook for 4–5 minutes until fragrant and soft. Add noodles and cook until they just start to colour. Add rice and pumpkin, cook for 2–3 minutes, add stock, currants and cooked chickpeas. Bring to the boil, stirring often. Reduce heat, cover and cook in preheated oven for 30 minutes, or until rice is tender and stock has been absorbed.

Allow to stand for 5 minutes before serving. Check seasoning, then add parsley and coriander and serve. Serves 4–6.

Lamb, chickpea and saffron pilaf
Omit pumpkin. Brown 500 g (1 lb) lean diced lamb in oil, remove and set aside. Cook onions, etc; return lamb to the pot with stock.

Chicken, sultana and sweet spice pilaf
Omit pumpkin, add 500 g (1 lb) diced chicken to cooking onions and seal. Add ½ tsp each of cinnamon, allspice and cardamom. Cook until fragrant. Continue as directed by recipe, swapping currants for sultanas and chickpeas for a handful of toasted flaked almonds.

Chicken risotto

This is the base from which all good risottos are created. Try it once or twice and you'll be a risotto master for life.

2 tbsp olive oil
1 onion, diced
1 leek, thinly sliced, optional
1 carrot, finely diced, optional
1 garlic clove, crushed
2 skinless chicken thigh fillets, diced
500 g (1 lb) arborio rice

250 ml (8 fl oz) white wine
1.5 litres (2½ pt) hot chicken stock
90 g (3 oz) parmigiano, grated
90 g (3 oz) butter, diced
2 tbsp chopped parsley
Salt and freshly ground black pepper

Heat a large heavy-based saucepan over a medium heat. Add oil, onion, leek, carrot and garlic and cook for 3–4 minutes until fragrant and soft. Add chicken and cook for 3–4 minutes, or until beginning to brown. Add rice and stir to coat with oil, then cook briefly. Add wine and stir until it is absorbed.

Begin adding hot stock – at first just enough to cover the rice, then a ladleful at a time as the stock is absorbed. Stir well with each addition. Continue cooking until rice is just done but each grain is still slightly firm in the centre, about 15–20 minutes.

Remove from the heat. Add parmigiano, butter and parsley and stir until risotto is creamy and cheese has melted.

Check seasoning and serve. Serves 4–6.

Chicken and mushroom risotto
Add 120 g (4 oz) sliced mushrooms with the chicken.

Chicken and roasted sweet potato risotto
Peel and dice 1 sweet potato. Toss with oil and roast in preheated oven. Add roasted chunks to risotto just before the cheese and butter.

Chicken and spinach risotto
Add 90 g (3 oz) blanched and chopped spinach for the last 2–3 minutes of cooking.

Chicken and asparagus risotto
Prepare 300 g (10 oz) asparagus spears by snapping the woody ends off and cutting spears into 3 cm (1 in) pieces. Blanch in boiling water for 2–3 minutes, then refresh under cold running water. Add for the last 2–3 minutes of cooking.

Chicken and pea risotto
Add 125 g (4 oz) cooked fresh (or frozen) peas for the last 4–5 minutes of cooking.

Spring risotto v

We like to make this vegetable risotto with chicken stock because it creates a richer dish, but you can use vegetable stock if you prefer.

1 kg (2 lb) broad beans
500 g (1 lb) asparagus spears
2 tbsp olive oil
1 onion, finely diced
1 leek, thinly sliced
1 garlic clove, crushed
500 g (1 lb) arborio rice

250 ml (8 fl oz) white wine
1.5 litres (3 pt) hot vegetable stock
90 g (3 oz) parmigiano, grated
90 g (3 oz) butter, diced
2 tbsp chopped parsley
Salt and freshly ground black pepper

Bring a large pot of water to the boil. Pod broad beans and blanch for 2–3 minutes, then remove and refresh under cold running water. Remove and discard pale green skins from broad beans. Prepare asparagus by snapping the woody ends off and cut spears into 3 cm (1¼ in) pieces. Blanch in boiling water for 2–3 minutes, then refresh under cold running water.

Heat a large heavy-based pan over medium heat. Add oil and onion, leek and garlic and cook for 3–4 minutes until fragrant and soft. Add rice and stir to coat with oil. Pour in white wine and stir until it is absorbed. Begin adding the hot stock – at first just enough to cover the rice, then a ladleful at a time as the stock is absorbed. Stir well with each addition.

Continue cooking until the rice is done but each grain is still slightly firm in the centre, about 15–20 minutes. Add asparagus spears and broad beans and remove from the heat. Add cheese, butter and parsley and stir until risotto is creamy and cheese has melted. Check seasoning and serve. Serves 4–6.

Asparagus and prawn risotto

This dish is a must when spring arrives and asparagus comes into its own. If you have the time, a stock made with the prawn shells is best; otherwise use chicken or vegetable stock.

500 g (1 lb) asparagus spears
2 tbsp olive oil
1 onion, diced
1 leek, thinly sliced
1 carrot, finely diced
1 garlic clove, crushed
500 g (1 lb) arborio rice
250 ml (8 fl oz) white wine

1.5 litres (3 pt) hot seafood, chicken or vegetable stock
500 g (1 lb) green (raw) prawns, peeled and de-veined
90 g (3 oz) parmigiano, grated
90 g (3 oz) butter, diced
2 tbsp chopped parsley
Salt and freshly ground black pepper

Prepare asparagus by snapping the woody ends off and cut tips into 3 cm pieces on the angle. Blanch in boiling water for 1–2 minutes, then refresh under cold running water. Set aside.

Heat a large heavy-based saucepan over a medium heat. Add oil, onion, leek, carrot and garlic and cook for 3–4 minutes until fragrant and soft. Add rice and stir to coat with oil, then cook briefly. Add wine and stir until is absorbed. Begin adding hot stock – at first just enough to cover the rice, then a ladleful at a time as the stock is absorbed. Stir well with each addition. Continue cooking until rice is just done but each grain is still slightly firm in the centre, about 15–20 minutes. Add prawns and cook for 2 minutes. Add asparagus and cook for a further 2 minutes. Remove from the heat.

Add parmigiano, butter and parsley and stir until risotto is creamy and cheese has melted. Check seasoning and serve. Serves 4–6.

Roast pumpkin, feta and pine nut risotto ⓥ

This risotto is similar to the recipe with roasted sweet potato and pancetta. The feta adds a lovely salty hit to the rice, while the toasted pine nuts bring a nutty crunch.

200 g (7 oz) pumpkin, diced 2 cm (½ in)
2 tbsp olive oil
Salt and freshly ground black pepper
2 tbsp olive oil, additional
1 onion, diced
1 leek, thinly sliced, optional
1 carrot, finely diced, optional
1 garlic clove, crushed

500 g (1 lb) arborio rice
250 ml (8 fl oz) white wine
1.5 litres (3 pt) hot vegetable stock
60 g (2 oz) pine nuts, toasted
30 g (1 oz) parmigiano, grated
60 g (2 oz) feta, crumbled
90 g (3 oz) butter, diced
2 tbsp chopped parsley

Preheat oven to 180°C (350°F).

Toss pumpkin with oil, salt and pepper. Roast in preheated oven for 15–20 minutes, or until pumpkin is tender and golden. Set aside.

Heat a large heavy-based saucepan over a medium heat. Add additional oil, onion, leek, carrot and garlic and cook for 3–4 minutes until fragrant and soft. Add rice and stir to coat with oil, then cook briefly. Add wine and stir until it is absorbed.

Begin adding hot stock – at first just enough to cover the rice, then a ladleful at a time as the stock is absorbed. Stir well with each addition. Continue cooking until rice is just done, for about 15–20 minutes. Add pumpkin and pine nuts and stir through, then cook for 1–2 minutes. Remove from the heat. Add cheeses, butter and parsley and stir until risotto is creamy and cheese has melted. Check seasoning and serve. Serves 4–6.

Mushroom risotto with truffle oil

Being fairly rich, this risotto lends itself to small portions. We typically have it alongside things like roast chicken, pot-roasted veal or pan-fried steaks.

2 tbsp olive oil
1 onion, diced
1 leek, thinly sliced, optional
1 carrot, finely diced, optional
1 garlic clove, crushed
250 g (8 oz) Swiss brown mushrooms, sliced
500 g (1 lb) arborio rice
250 ml (8 fl oz) white wine
1.5 litres (2½ pt) stock, simmering in a saucepan
100 g (3½ oz) parmigiano, grated
100 g (3½ oz) butter, diced
2 tbsp chopped parsley
2–3 tsp truffle oil
Salt and freshly ground black pepper

Heat a large heavy-based saucepan over a medium heat. Add oil, onion, leek, carrot and garlic and cook for 3–4 minutes until fragrant and soft. Add mushrooms and cook for 3–4 minutes, or until soft. Add rice and stir to coat with oil, then cook briefly. Add wine and stir until it is absorbed.

    Begin adding hot stock – at first just enough to cover the rice, then a ladleful at a time as the stock is absorbed. Stir well with each addition. Continue cooking until rice is just done, for about 15–20 minutes. Remove from the heat. Add parmigiano, butter, parsley and truffle oil and stir until risotto is creamy and cheese has melted. Check seasoning and serve. Serves 4–6.

Risotto with porcini mushrooms
Use only half of the mushrooms. Soak 10 g (⅓ oz) dried porcini mushrooms in 90 ml (3 fl oz) of boiling water. Add this soaking liquid to the risotto, reducing the stock by the same amount, and combine porcini mushrooms with the other mushrooms.

Mushroom risotto cakes ⓥ

Risotto cakes are an easy way of enjoying the flavours of risotto in a patty that can be cooked on the barbecue or in a pan. We've yet to come across someone who doesn't like them. Try them with your favourite salad.

2 tbsp olive oil
1 onion, finely diced
½ small carrot, finely diced
1 garlic clove, crushed
90 g (3 oz) Swiss brown mushrooms, thinly sliced
200 g (7 oz) arborio rice
800 ml (1½ pt) hot vegetable or chicken stock
60 g (2 oz) parmigiano, grated
15 basil leaves, thinly sliced
1 medium egg
25 g (¾ oz) dry breadcrumbs
Salt and freshly ground black pepper
Additional dry breadcrumbs
Olive oil for cooking

Heat a large saucepan over a medium heat. Add oil, onion, carrot and garlic and cook for 2 minutes, stirring regularly. Add mushrooms and cook for 3–4 minutes. Add rice and cook for 1 minute, stirring well. Add stock to saucepan and simmer until liquid is absorbed, about 12 minutes. Allow to cool slightly, then stir in parmigiano, basil, egg and breadcrumbs. Season to taste.

Divide into 12 and pat into round cakes. Sprinkle each cake with additional breadcrumbs. Heat a heavy-based frying pan over a medium–high heat. Add a splash of oil and risotto cakes. Cook for 3–4 minutes on each side until golden brown. Makes 12.

Roasted eggplant risotto cakes
Dice, salt, rinse and roast 1 eggplant until soft. Omit mushrooms and add cooked eggplant to the rice for the last 2 minutes of cooking. Try this with any other vegetables, such as asparagus or pumpkin.

Paella

Paella is made with short-grain rice, or you can purchase special paella rice at most top quality food stores. A paella pan makes light work of keeping all the ingredients together.

1 red capsicum, roasted, peeled and de-seeded and cut into long strips
2 tbsp olive oil
2 onions, diced
6–8 small garlic cloves
Pinch of saffron threads
1 tsp smoked paprika
350 g (12⅓ oz) paella rice
1 litre (1⅔ pt) chicken stock
90 g (3 oz) pitted olives
500 g (1 lb) chicken drumettes, roasted until golden
500 g (1 lb) green (raw) prawns, peeled and de-veined
500 g (1 lb) mussels, de-bearded, page 69
2 tbsp chopped parsley

Place a large heavy-based frying pan over a medium heat. Heat oil, add onions, garlic and saffron and cook for 4–5 minutes, stirring often. Add paprika, cook for 1–2 minutes, then add rice and cook briefly for 2–3 minutes, stirring often. Add most of the stock and allow to come to the boil, stirring often.

Add olives, roasted chicken and capsicum. Reduce heat and allow to cook for 15 minutes, stirring often. You may need to add more stock. Check that the rice is nearly cooked, add prawns and mussels and cook until mussels open (discard any that do not) and prawns turn pink.

Serve immediately with chopped parsley. Serves 4.

Couscous

Couscous is well known as a staple food of many North African countries, including Algeria and Morocco, and traditionally accompanies tagines and flavoursome stews. It is made from semolina (the centre of wheat grains) milled until it's halfway between grain and flour. Couscous is the result of grinding this semolina and rolling the tiny pellets in fine flour.

THINGS YOU NEED TO KNOW ABOUT COUSCOUS

- True couscous comes in many grades and is available from Middle-Eastern stores or health food shops.
- Traditionally couscous is steamed above tagines and stews, so that it both cooks as well as absorbing flavour from the dish below.
- The secret to good couscous lies in getting enough steam to make it light and fluffy and not undercooking it. Undercooking results in gluggy couscous and indigestion.
- 'Instant' couscous is a modern-day marvel, requiring little cooking and no preparation.
- Most supermarket couscous is the quick-to-prepare 'instant' variety, which is perfect for quick dinners.
- Avoid boil-in-the-bag or pre-flavoured couscous, as couscous should be neither 'boiled' nor pre-flavoured.

Quick couscous ⓥ

We didn't create this method; it's simply how it is described on the packet! If kept covered, couscous will stay warm for 10 minutes after cooking.

250 ml (8 fl oz) water or stock
1 tbsp olive oil
Pinch of salt

250 g (8 oz) instant couscous
A small knob of butter

Place water or stock, olive oil and salt in a saucepan and bring to the boil. Remove from the heat, stir in the couscous, cover and allow to rest for 2 minutes. Add the butter to the soaked couscous and place over a low heat. Stir with a fork to break up the grains and mix the butter through. Serves 4.

Saffron couscous
Add a pinch of saffron strands to the boiling liquid.

Herb couscous
Add 2 tbsp chopped fresh herbs, such as parsley or coriander, as you stir the couscous.

Roast pumpkin, feta and pine nut risotto (recipe page 131)

Barbecued pork sausage with spiced lentils (recipe page 140)

Pot-roasted chicken with 40 cloves of garlic (recipe page 151)

Traditional couscous ⓥ

This method is much more involved than quick couscous and probably the only time we do it is for dinner parties, or if we're feeling particularly 'time rich'. The couscous fluffs up beautifully and is best served plain to take on the flavours of the main dish.

150 g (5 oz) couscous
Water as needed
1 tbsp olive oil

Spread couscous out in a flat tray. Sprinkle with cold water, about 200 ml (6–7 fl oz). Rub wet couscous between hands to separate the grains. Leave for 20 minutes. Get steamer ready by lining it with cloth, such as muslin or a clean tea towel. Place couscous in the cloth, cover and steam for 15–20 minutes, then remove. Allow to cool slightly so you can handle it comfortably.

Tip couscous back onto flat tray and rub with fingers to break up any lumps (you can use a fork for this). Return to steamer and cook for a further 15 minutes. Repeat cooling/rubbing process. Rub through olive oil and steam again for a final 15 minutes. Serve immediately. Serves 4.

Spicy chicken fillets with coriander couscous

The 3 Cs – chicken, couscous and coriander – all appear in generous quantities in this recipe. Beautiful combinations of flavours such as this have confirmed our love of North African and Middle-Eastern food. Try it and you may well fall head over heels too.

90 g (3 oz) plain flour
3 tsp ground cumin
3 tsp ground coriander
2 tsp chilli powder
1 tsp turmeric
Salt and freshly ground black pepper
6 skinless chicken breast fillets
Oil for cooking
1 onion, diced
2 garlic cloves, crushed

1 small red chilli, de-seeded and finely diced
1 tsp ground cumin
1 tsp ground coriander
500 g (1 lb) instant couscous
100 ml (3½ fl oz) orange juice
500 ml (1 pt) chicken or vegetable stock
Pinch of salt
1 cup coriander leaves, roughly chopped

Preheat oven to 180°C (350°F).

Mix together flour and spices. Lightly coat chicken fillets with spice mixture. Heat a heavy-based frying pan; add a splash of oil and chicken fillets and cook for 2–3 minutes on each side until well browned. Place chicken fillets in preheated oven and cook for 10 minutes. Remove and rest, covered, in a warm place for 5 minutes.

Heat a heavy-based saucepan over medium heat. Add oil, onion, garlic, chilli, cumin and coriander and cook for 5 minutes, until soft, stirring often. Add couscous and cook briefly, stirring to prevent catching. Add orange juice, stock and salt and bring to the boil.

Remove from the heat, cover and allow to rest for 5 minutes. Place the couscous over a low heat. Stir with a fork to break up the grains. Check seasoning and stir through coriander.

Slice fillets into 3–4 pieces and serve on top of couscous, with tzatziki, page 41. Serves 6.

Seven-spice lamb fillets with onion couscous

Lamb stands up well to a bit of spice, which is why it's such a classic combination. In this case there are seven spices, which makes it seven times better than normal.

1 tsp sweet paprika
½ tsp ground ginger
½ tsp chilli powder
½ tsp ground coriander
½ tsp ground cumin
¼ tsp ground cardamom
¼ tsp allspice
½ tsp salt
1 tbsp lemon juice

Olive oil for cooking
8 lamb fillets, trimmed and sinew removed
2 tbsp olive oil, additional
500 g (1 lb) instant couscous
500 ml (1 pt) chicken or vegetable stock
Pinch of salt
2 tbsp chopped coriander or parsley

Preheat oven to 180°C (350°F).

Mix spices with salt, lemon juice and oil to form a smooth paste. Coat lamb fillets with spice paste and set aside to marinate for 1 hour.

Heat a heavy-based frying pan, add a splash of oil and lamb and cook for 2–3 minutes on each side until well browned. Place lamb in preheated oven and continue to cook for 5–7 minutes. Remove and rest, covered, in a warm place for 5 minutes.

Heat a heavy-based saucepan over medium heat. Add a splash of oil and onions, cook for 5–10 minutes, until soft and turning golden brown, stirring often. Add couscous, cook briefly, for 1 minute, stirring to prevent catching. Add stock and salt and bring to the boil.

Remove from the heat, cover and allow to rest for 5 minutes. Place the couscous over a low heat. Stir with a fork to break up the grains. Check seasoning and stir through chopped herbs.

Slice fillets into 3–4 pieces and serve on top of couscous, with tzatziki, page 41. Serves 4.

Pulses

The world of pulses is vast and we can only scratch the surface here. Pulses are typically the edible seeds of pod-bearing plants, such as peas, beans, lentils and chickpeas, which have been dried, so they make an excellent store-cupboard ingredient.

The smaller types, such as lentils, borlotti beans and split peas, can be cooked as they are after rinsing. Larger types such as chickpeas, lima beans, broad beans, borlotti beans and kidney beans, need soaking overnight, or at least for a few hours so they can soak up the liquid they lost in the drying process.

Even if you don't want to make a straight chickpea dish, you can just as easily add a handful or two of cooked chickpeas (or another pulse) to a meat dish a few minutes before it's served.

THINGS YOU NEED TO KNOW ABOUT PULSES

- Always pick over pulses to discard discoloured ones and any small stones. Rinse well to remove dust.
- Soaking beans is important, allowing the 'oligosaccharides' that cause flatulence to be released. Discard this water.
- Soaking overnight is usually recommended, but even putting them in to soak at breakfast time is a good start for that night's dinner.
- Try cooking two or three different pulses on a Sunday morning while pottering around the house, then leave them in the refrigerator to use over the next few days.
- Always cook pulses in plenty (at least double the pulse depth) of fresh, cold water. Bring to the boil, and simmer until tender.
- Ensure pulses are properly cooked; undercooking cause flatulence and indigestion.
- Always cook pulses independently of their finished dish. Once added to acidic sauces such as tomato their cooking process is halted.
- Dried pulses will not keep forever. While they don't decay, the older they are, the longer they take to cook.
- To save time, cook extra beans and freeze them.
- Never add bicarbonate of soda. Rumoured to reduce cooking time and to remove the skins of pulses, it only destroys their vitamin C and folic acid content.

Indian-spiced beans v

This is the type of dish we have when we want a quick spice hit. Once the beans are cooked it only takes about 10 minutes to chop the ingredients and get it all simmering. It's even quicker than waiting in line at the local Indian for a takeaway.

200 g (7 oz) black-eye (or borlotti) beans, soaked overnight
2 tbsp olive oil
1 garlic clove, crushed
1 tsp grated fresh ginger
2 onions
2 tsp curry paste
250 ml (8 fl oz) vegetable or chicken stock
Salt
125 g (4 oz) natural yoghurt
½ cup coriander leaves

Place beans in a medium-sized saucepan, cover with water, and bring to the boil over a medium heat. Reduce heat to medium–low and cook until beans are soft, about 30–40 minutes. Drain, and set aside.

Heat oil in a medium-sized saucepan over medium–high heat and cook garlic, ginger and onion for 5 minutes or until soft. Add curry paste and cook for a further 3–4 minutes until aromatic, stirring occasionally. Add beans, stock and salt.

Allow to come to the boil, then reduce heat to medium–low and cook for 10–12 minutes, until liquid thickens.

Stir in the yoghurt, sprinkle with coriander leaves and serve with steamed rice. Serves 4.

Moroccan chickpea and pumpkin stew v

We seem to eat vegetable dishes like this more and more often. The natural sweetness of the pumpkin combines really well with the other spicy ingredients.

100 g (3½ oz) chickpeas, soaked overnight
2 tbsp olive oil
1 onion, diced
½ red capsicum, diced
500 g (1 lb) pumpkin, diced 1 cm (⅓ in)
1 tsp grated ginger
1 garlic clove, crushed
2 tsp ground cumin
2 tsp ground coriander
1 tsp sweet paprika
1 tbsp tomato paste
500 ml (1 pt) vegetable stock
Salt and freshly ground black pepper
Coriander leaves

Place chickpeas in a medium-sized saucepan, cover with water and bring to the boil over a medium heat. Reduce heat and cook until soft, about 30–40 minutes. Drain and set aside.

Heat oil in a medium-sized saucepan over medium–high heat and cook onion and capsicum for 5 minutes or until soft. Add pumpkin, ginger, garlic and spices and cook for a further 3–4 minutes until aromatic, stirring occasionally. Add tomato paste and cook for 1–2 minutes. Add chickpeas and stock, plus salt and pepper.

Allow to come to the boil, then reduce heat to a simmer and cook for 10–12 minutes, until liquid thickens and pumpkin is cooked.

Sprinkle with coriander leaves and serve with steamed rice. Serves 4.

Kidney bean and vegetable chilli ⓥ

This is one of our favourite quick meals when we're in need of a chilli hit.
Like most of the other pulse recipes it only takes 10–15 minutes to get it on the stove, after which it can be left alone to simmer gently.

125 g (4 oz) kidney beans, soaked overnight
2 tbsp olive oil
2 onions, diced
2 carrots, diced
1 red capsicum, diced
1 eggplants, diced, salted and rinsed
2 garlic cloves, crushed

2 small red chillies, de-seeded and finely diced
2 tsp ground turmeric
2 tsp sweet paprika
2 tbsp tomato paste
250 ml (8 fl oz) vegetable stock
Salt and freshly ground black pepper
1 tsp harissa paste*, optional

Place kidney beans in a medium-sized saucepan, cover with water and bring to the boil over a medium heat. Reduce heat to medium–low and cook until beans are soft, about 30–40 minutes. Drain and set aside.

Heat a medium saucepan over medium–high heat, add oil and cook onions, carrot, capsicum and eggplant for 6–8 minutes, or until softened. Add garlic, chillies and spices and cook for a further 3–4 minutes, until aromatic, stirring occasionally.

Add tomato paste and cook for a further minute. Add stock, salt and pepper, plus harissa if using, and bring to the boil. Reduce heat to a simmer and cook for 10–12 minutes, until liquid thickens and vegetables are tender.

Check seasoning. Serve with steamed rice. Serves 4.

Lentil dhal ⓥ

Dahl is one of the classic dishes of Indian cooking. We have adapted it by adding a finely diced onion and carrot, as well as adding a little curry paste. Serve with some steamed rice and a dollop of natural yoghurt for a flavoursome meal. We typically use whole green lentils as they keep their shape and texture. Red lentils will cook much faster and turn into a fine purée as they have had their outer layer removed.

300 g (10 oz) whole green lentils
Olive oil for cooking
1 onion, diced
1 carrot, finely diced

2 tbsp curry paste
500 ml (1 pt) vegetable or chicken stock
2 tbsp chopped parsley or coriander

Sort through lentils, discarding any brown ones and pieces of grit, then rinse well.

Heat a heavy-based pan over a medium heat. Add a splash of oil, then cook onion and carrot for 3–4 minutes, or until softened, stirring occasionally. Add curry paste and cook for 3–4 minutes, until aromatic. Add lentils, stir to coat well with curry mixture, then add enough stock to cover the lentils. Bring to the boil, reduce heat and cook at a simmer for 30–40 minutes, or until lentils are soft.

Add more stock as needed, but take care not to add too much near the end. Add herbs and serve with steamed rice. Serves 4.

Barbecued pork sausage with spiced lentils

If it's raining and we can't get to the barbecue, we cook the sausage slices for this dish in a pan before serving them on top of the spiced lentils. This means we can eat the dish all year round.

200 g (7 oz) green lentils
1 tbsp olive oil
1 onion, diced
1 garlic clove, crushed
2 carrots, peeled and finely diced
1 celery stick, finely diced

2 tbsp curry paste
500 ml (1 pt) vegetable or chicken stock
Salt and freshly ground black pepper
Chopped parsley
500 g (1 lb) Polish pork sausage
Olive oil for cooking

Sort through lentils, discarding any brown ones and pieces of grit, then rinse well.

Heat a heavy-based pan over a medium–high heat. Add oil, onion, garlic, carrots and celery and cook for 5–6 minutes until soft. Add curry paste and cook until fragrant. Add lentils and cook briefly for a few moments. Add enough stock to just cover and bring to the boil. Lower heat, season with salt and cook for 30–40 minutes, or until lentils are soft. Add more stock as necessary and stir frequently. Stir through parsley and check seasoning.

Slice pork sausage into ½ cm (¼ in) slices. Brush with olive oil and barbecue or grill for 3–4 minutes on each side, or until brown and crispy.

Spoon lentils onto platter, arrange slices of grilled sausage on top and serve. Serves 4–6.

Caramelised onion and chickpea burgers ⓥ

These burgers are a taste sensation. We love them cooked on the barbecue and served with a huge dollop of tomato relish on top. Even if you thought you didn't like chickpeas you will, after trying these.

250 g (8 oz) chickpeas, soaked overnight
75 ml (2½ fl oz) olive oil
4 onions, sliced
2 tsp ground cumin
2 tsp ground coriander
1 tsp sweet paprika
½ tsp chilli powder
150 g (5 oz) spinach leaves, chopped
1 medium egg
100–150 g (3–5 oz) breadcrumbs
½ cup coriander leaves
Salt and freshly ground black pepper
Oil for cooking

Cook chickpeas in boiling water until soft, about 30–40 minutes. Drain and mash roughly.

Heat oil in saucepan, add onion, cumin, coriander, paprika and chilli. Cook for 20 minutes on low heat, stirring often until onions soften. Add spinach and cook until soft. Mix onion/spinach with chickpeas. Add egg, breadcrumbs and coriander. Mix to combine and season to taste. Divide into 12 and form into burger shapes.

Heat a heavy-based frying pan over a medium heat, add a splash of oil and cook burgers for 5–6 minutes on each side, until golden brown. Makes 12.

Lentil and ricotta burgers ⓥ

These burgers are devilishly more-ish. Again, we often cook them on the barbecue, or make small-sized ones and serve with relish as pre-dinner nibbles. We like to use red lentils for these burgers as they cook quickly.

30 ml (1 fl oz) olive oil
1 onion, diced
1 tsp curry paste
200 g (7 oz) red lentils, washed
500 ml (1 pt) vegetable stock
2 tbsp chopped fresh herbs
125 g (4 oz) ricotta
100 g (3½ oz) dry breadcrumbs
Oil for cooking

Heat a medium-sized saucepan over a medium heat. Add oil and onion and cook for 3–4 minutes, until soft. Add curry paste and cook for 3–4 minutes, until aromatic. Add lentils, stir well, and add enough stock to cover. Bring to the boil, then reduce the heat. Cook for 15 minutes, adding more stock as necessary. Cook until lentils are tender and all liquid is absorbed.

Place cooked lentils in a bowl and add herbs, ricotta and breadcrumbs. Mix well, season to taste. Divide into 12 portions and form into burger shapes.

Heat a heavy-based frying pan over a medium heat, add a splash of oil and cook for 5–6 minutes on each side, until golden brown. Makes 12.

Polenta

Some people may be a little fed-up with polenta, mostly due to a period of over-exposure in the food media. We, however, are not; we love it passionately. We like soft polenta served straight from the pot with a delicious cheesy flavour and porridge-like consistency. And we love it set into a firm block, sliced and cooked on a barbecue plate or in an oven until it's crisp on the outside.

If you need something other than pasta, rice or potatoes to serve with dinner, polenta is your man. And what we are most thankful for is the fact that the children love it too. Halleluiah. There's not too much to the cooking of polenta: as long as you get the proportion of polenta to liquid right, and you remember to stir it occasionally, you're set.

THINGS YOU NEED TO KNOW ABOUT POLENTA

- Polenta is the grainy flour milled from maize.
- Polenta is a seductive accompaniment to all dishes. Because of its subtle flavour, it's a perfect base for cheese flavouring or for robust meat dishes that need some balance and for soaking up juices.
- To cook polenta, bring the liquid to the boil and sprinkle polenta in gradually to prevent lumps forming. A whisk is excellent for this. Bring back to the boil, then reduce the heat to the lowest possible. Stir with a wooden spoon as it cooks.
- A pot of polenta retains a lot of heat inside the mixture, which, because it's thick, will 'plop' (like porridge) while cooking. Watch out for the 'plops' because if they catch you on the hand, they will burn.
- Polenta takes only about 20 minutes to cook.

The best soft polenta ⓥ

Using half and half water and stock adds a real richness to the finished polenta. If you don't have stock available use all water.

500 ml (1 pt) water
500 ml (1 pt) chicken or vegetable stock
180 g (6 oz) polenta

60 g (2 oz) grated parmigiano
Salt to taste

Bring water and stock to the boil in a heavy-based saucepan. Sprinkle polenta over and stir constantly to prevent any lumps forming. Reduce to a low simmer and cook for 30 minutes, stirring often, until the mixture thickens. Take care, as the polenta can splutter and burn; a long-handled spoon is ideal.

Remove from heat and stir through cheese. Season to taste, then serve straight away. Serves 4.

Herb polenta
Add 1–2 tbsp chopped herbs, such as parsley, thyme, basil or rosemary to polenta when you add the cheese.

Crispy polenta wedges
Pour cooked polenta into a deep baking dish and allow to set, at least 4 hours. Cut into wedges or triangles. Arrange on an oiled baking tray and bake in a preheated oven at 180°C (350°F) for 20 minutes, until crispy and golden. Alternatively cook the wedges on a hot barbecue plate or in a frying pan.

Grilled polenta with garlic vegetables ⓥ

Polenta that is to be cooked on a barbecue plate or in a pan will need to be poured into a dish and left to set hard. It can then be cut into wedges or triangles and cooked to your liking.

1 quantity best soft polenta, page 142, left to set in a dish
2–3 tbsp olive oil
3 garlic cloves, crushed
Salt and freshly ground black pepper
2 zucchini, cut in half lengthways,

1 small eggplant, cut into 8 wedges, salted and rinsed
8 mushrooms
2 tomatoes, cut in half
Pesto, optional

Cut polenta into 8 wedges. Mix the oil, garlic, salt and pepper together in a bowl. Brush the vegetables with a little olive oil, then arrange them on a barbecue plate or in a hot pan, with polenta.

Cook for 10–15 minutes, turning as required. Baste the vegetables with garlic oil during cooking.

Serve the vegetables on top of the polenta wedges, then add a dollop of green olive salsa. Serves 4.

Green olive salsa

The salsa is best chopped by hand to retain some texture, but if you are short of time you can pulse it in a food processor.

200 g (7 oz) pitted green olives
2 tsp capers, soaked and rinsed
2 anchovies

½ cup chopped flat-leaf parsley
100 ml (3½ fl oz) extra virgin olive oil
Freshly ground black pepper

Finely chop olives, capers and anchovies. Add parsley, oil and pepper to season. Set aside until needed.

This salsa can be made 24 hours in advance, but allow it to come back to room temperature before serving.

Roast chicken
Allan's Gravy
Sage and onion stuffing
Chestnut stuffing
Middle-Eastern fruit and nut stuffing
Oriental roast chicken
Chinese crispy-skin chicken
Pot-roasted chicken with 40 cloves of garlic
Moroccan roast turkey
Stuffed turkey breast
Roast beef with Yorkshire puddings
Beef pot-roast
Herb and garlic roast lamb
Basil and pine nut stuffed lamb
Mint sauce
Lamb topsides with roasted ratatouille
Roast rack of pork
Braised red cabbage
Roast duck
Pot-roasted veal with pancetta and mushrooms
Nine-spiced roasted vegetables with chickpeas
Roasted root vegetable chips
Rosemary and garlic potatoes

Roasts

TRADITIONAL, POT-ROASTS AND OTHERWISE

There is an intensely satisfying feeling that can only come from a roast dinner. It begins as the aromas from the roasting meat waft from the oven and continues as the gravy bubbles on the stove. Then, finally, it's served with abundant vegetables. Even the pickiest family members can be coaxed to the table when there's meal like this on offer.

Next to the ideal roast joint is the perfect roast spud. Roast potatoes are best cooked completely in the oven, but to save a bit of time they can be boiled first, then finished in the oven.

To get the maximum flavour, cook your potatoes under your joint of meat. The fat dripping onto them adds that extra something. If space doesn't allow this, roast potatoes separately in a large baking dish with a good knob of goose fat (yeah, decadent, we know – but yummy) and with salt and pepper.

Another method is to toss potatoes with olive oil, salt and pepper and place them in a baking tray. Add just enough stock (chicken if roasting a chicken, beef stock for beef) to come halfway up the potatoes. Turn occasionally during cooking. The stock soaks into the potatoes, making them creamy inside while leaving them still firm on the outside.

No matter what your preferred method for roasting potatoes, a roast just wouldn't be the same without them.

THINGS YOU NEED TO KNOW ABOUT ROASTS

- Good roasts mean top-quality meat.
- The oven must be preheated before the meat goes in.
- Meat can be browned before roasting to create a delicious outside crust. This can be done by placing the joint in a very hot oven 220°C (425°F) for 10 minutes, then lowering the oven to 180°C (350°F) and cooking as required; or by browning in a hot pan all over before placing the roast in the oven. The only exception to this rule is poultry, in which case the high temperatures can cause the flesh to dry out.
- Poultry comes with its own rules. Stuff the bird, and it will repay you by taking up to an extra 30 minutes to cook. Start the bird off upside-down, this keeps the juices in the breast and prevents it drying out. Finish cooking by turning the bird right way up for the last 30 minutes to crisp the skin.
- A roast needs fat to keep it moist; no fat makes for a dry, tasteless roast.
- Roast your vegies! They're delish that way. Potatoes, obviously ... but also carrots, parsnips, cauliflower, zucchini – just about every root vegetable; but not green vegetables such as green beans, broccoli, and so on.
- Good gravy can make or break a roast. For this reason alone keep an Allan in the kitchen. Second best, use Allan's gravy recipe, page 148. MC
- Use trimmings such as mint sauce, bread sauce, mustards, horseradish, Yorkshire puddings and stuffing to suit your own tastes. These are all optional extras.
- If you learn nothing else in life, learn how to make a great roast. This will prevent divorce and starvation and keep you happy with the opposite sex – or the same sex if that's your inclination.
- A good heavy-based roasting dish is a fantastic asset – one that doesn't wobble or warp during cooking, one that fits the meat and the potatoes together and one that sits happily soaking in the sink while you enjoy the fruits of your labour.
- Don't forget to rest your roast once it's cooked. Allow at least 10 minutes. Remove from baking dish, wrap in foil, place on a plate and cover with a dry tea towel. Any juices that come out should be added to the gravy.
- Always carve across the grain of the meat.
- A free-range chicken has loads more flavour than an ordinary chook.
- Meat cooked on the bone, such as racks, ribs, shoulders and leg, will have much more juice and meaty flavour than a boned roast.

ROASTING TIMES

Beef and veal
No bone: 15 minutes per 500 g (1 lb) plus 15 minutes (medium–rare)
Add 5 minutes per 500 g (1 lb) (medium)
Add another 5 minutes per 500 g (1 lb) (well done)
Bone-in: 20 minutes per 500 g (1 lb) plus 15 minutes (medium-rare)
Add 5 minutes per 500 g (1 lb) (medium)
Add another 5 minutes per 500 g (1 lb) (well done)

Lamb
No-bone: 20 minutes per 500 g (1 lb) plus 15 minutes (medium-rare)
Add 5 minutes per 500 g (1 lb) (medium)
Add another 5 minutes per 500 g (1 lb) (well done)
Bone-in: 25 minutes per 500 g (1 lb) plus 20 minutes (medium-rare)
Add 5 minutes per 500 g (1 lb) (medium)
Add another 5 minutes per 500 g (1 lb) (well done)

Pork
No-bone: 25 minutes per 500 g (1 lb) plus 25 minutes – cooked through
Bone-in: 30 minutes per 500 g (1 lb) plus 25 minutes – cooked through

Poultry
Whole chicken: 20 minutes per 500 g (1 lb) plus 20 minutes – cooked through
Turkey: 20 minutes per 500 g (1 lb) plus 20 minutes – cooked through
Note: If roast is stuffed, allow at least an additional 20 minutes overall.

How to tell if a roast is cooked
The following is the best method we know of testing a roast to see if it is ready.

Insert a small knife into the meat as described below and leave it there for 5 seconds. Then test the temperature of the knife blade by placing it, cautiously, on the fleshy part of your thumb. (You may prefer to use a meat thermometer.)

Some juices also come to the surface and the colour of these juices indicates how well cooked the meat is. It takes a bit of getting used to, as well as some trial and error, but it really works.

- Poultry. Insert the knife in between the leg and the body. If the juices that come to the surface are pink, return the roast to the oven for 5–10 minutes more. If juices run clear (no sign of blood) the poultry is ready. No need to test for temperature.
- Beef and lamb. Insert a small kitchen knife into the centre of the roast. Count to five. If the knife is warm (tepid), the meat is rare. If it's bearably hot, the meat is medium, which is with some pink left but no rare bits. This is ideal.
- Pork and turkey. Insert the knife into the thickest part of the joint. Unless the knife is unbearably hot, indicating a high internal temperature, return the roast to the oven. These meats need to be thoroughly cooked through.

Roast chicken

One of life's simple pleasures is a proper roast chook. Get a free-range one if you can and serve it with all the trimmings.

1 size 16 (1.6 kg 3 lb) chicken, free-range if you can

Olive oil
Salt and freshly ground black pepper

Preheat oven to 180°C (350°F).
    Rub chicken all over with oil and sprinkle salt and pepper all over, including in the cavity. Place chicken upside-down in roasting tray, or better still a baking rack across baking tray. Add some water to the tray to stop fat burning and creating yukky smells.
    Cook in oven for 45–55 minutes until chicken bottom is crisp. Turn over and cook for a further 30 minutes, until skin is golden brown and crisp. Check whether chicken is cooked by inspecting juices for any sign of blood (pinkness).
    Allow to rest for 10 minutes before carving. Serves 4.

Roast chicken with lemon
Cut a lemon in half, rub all over chicken and place lemon halves inside cavity for cooking.

Roast chicken with herbs
Using herbs such as thyme, rosemary or sage, chop roughly and pat all over chicken; put some in the cavity for good measure.

Roast chicken with honey
Mix 2 tbsp oil and 2 tbsp warm honey together and rub all over the chicken.

Roast chicken with spices
Use spice mix from Moroccan roast turkey, page 152, and rub over chicken.

Different cuts
Use any of the ideas described and apply them to chicken drumettes, drumsticks or wings, such as honey-roasted drumsticks.

Roast chicken and vegetables
Simply add 3–4 potatoes, 2 carrots, 2 onions and perhaps 2–3 parsnips (all peeled and cut into quarters) to the roasting dish along with chicken. Add 3–4 thyme sprigs and 1–2 rosemary sprigs.

Allan's gravy

I can never understand why people go to the trouble of roasting meat and vegetables and then use 'instant' gravy mixes. Gravy takes only 5 minutes to get ready, then 15 to simmer gently. There's nothing hard about that. To get maximum flavour for your gravy, make it in the dish the meat was roasting in while the meat is resting. Or just make it in a saucepan from scratch. Vary stock and wine to suit your roast. AC

2 tbsp butter
2 tbsp plain flour
2 tbsp red or white wine

1 tbsp tomato paste
375 ml (12 fl oz) stock
Salt and freshly ground black pepper

If using the roasting dish, pour excess fat away. Place it over a medium–low heat, add butter and melt (if not using roasting dish use a small saucepan). Stir in flour and cook for 1–2 minutes, stirring often. Add wine, tomato paste and stock and bring to the boil, whisking often. Reduce heat and allow to simmer for 10–15 minutes, stirring often. Check seasoning, add juices that come from resting meat and serve in a warmed jug alongside roast. Serves 6–8.

Sage and onion stuffing

Sage and onion are the traditional flavourings for meat stuffing. Feel free to adapt or adjust them to your own tastes.

200 g (7 oz) day-old sourdough bread
2 tbsp butter
4 onions, sliced
2 tbsp chopped sage
1 tbsp chopped parsley
1 medium egg
Salt and freshly ground black pepper

Tear bread into large chunks and soak in cold water for 5–10 minutes. Squeeze well to remove all water and crumble bread into a bowl.

Heat a small saucepan over a medium heat. Add butter and onions and cook for 5–6 minutes, stirring often until onions soften. Add cooked onion, sage, parsley, egg and lots of salt and pepper to the bread. Mix well to combine.

Either stuff into bird and cook as directed or spoon into a small greased baking dish and cook alongside the roast for 30 minutes, or until crunchy on top.

Chestnut stuffing

Chestnuts can be tiresome to prepare, but this recipe is your hard-earned reward. Good with chicken, turkey (add 90 g (3 oz) raisins or cranberries at Christmas time) or pheasant.

250 g (8 oz) chestnuts
2 tbsp olive oil
1 onion, finely diced
2 garlic cloves, crushed
4 bacon slices, chopped
2 tbsp chopped parsley
75 g (2⅔ oz) dry breadcrumbs
1 medium egg
Salt and freshly ground black pepper

With a sharp knife make two slits in the chestnuts from top to bottom. Place in a saucepan, cover with water and bring to the boil. Reduce to a simmer and cook for 10 minutes. Allow to cool, then peel, removing both outside shell and inside skin. Chop roughly and place in a bowl.

Heat a small saucepan over medium heat; add olive oil, onion and garlic and cook until soft. Add bacon and cook lightly. Add this mixture to the chestnuts.

Add parsley, breadcrumbs, egg, salt, and pepper. Mix well.

Either stuff into bird and cook as directed or spoon into a small greased baking dish and cook alongside the roast for 30 minutes, or until crunchy on top. This recipe makes enough for two chickens, so we usually freeze half for another roast.

Middle-Eastern fruit and nut stuffing

This is an aromatic, sweet and nutty stuffing that is excellent in a big corn-fed chicken.

60 g (2 oz) butter
1 onion, diced
Pinch of saffron threads
60 g (2 oz) almonds

60 g (2 oz) pine nuts
125 ml (4 fl oz) white wine
75 g (2⅔ oz) sultanas
75 g (2⅔ oz) dry breadcrumbs

Heat a heavy-based frying pan over medium heat. Add butter and cook onion with saffron, almonds and pine nuts until onion is soft and nuts are brown. Add white wine and sultanas and cook until wine has evaporated.

Remove from heat. Stir onion mix into breadcrumbs. Spoon stuffing into chicken or other bird of your choice and cook as directed. Enough for two chickens.

Oriental roast chicken

This chicken recipe is, in a word, delicious. It first appeared in a book of ours called Tucker for Tots in 1996, and we still make it today. You can forget the traditional roast trimmings and just serve it with rice and greens, or noodles. If you can marinate it for 3 hours it will have a more pronounced flavour; if not, no worries. Children love this and it's perfect for picnics too.

90 ml (3 fl oz) soy sauce
½ tbsp fish sauce
2 tsp chilli paste
1 tsp sesame oil

1 tbsp black beans*, soaked and chopped, or 1 tbsp black bean sauce
2 tsp grated ginger
1 chicken, size 16 (1.6 kg/3 lb)

Mix soy sauce, fish sauce, chilli paste, sesame oil, black beans and ginger together. Rub all over chicken and, if time permits, marinate for 3 hours.

Preheat oven to 180°C (350°F).

Place chicken upside-down in roasting tray or, better still, on a baking rack across a baking tray, adding some water underneath to prevent burning. Place in the preheated oven and cook for 45 minutes until chicken bottom is crisp. Turn over and cook for a further 30 minutes, until skin is golden brown and crisp. Check that chicken is cooked by checking juices for any sign of blood (pinkness). Allow to rest for 10 minutes before carving.

Serve with rice and steamed greens. Serves 4.

Roast rack of pork (recipe page 156)

Thai red beef and bok choy curry
(recipe page 164)

Chinese crispy-skin chicken

Crispy skin chicken is a bit of an addiction with us; we can't go to a Chinese restaurant without ordering it. At home we rub the chicken with a pepper and salt marinade, fry it to give it a crispy skin, then roast it to finish cooking.

2 tbsp Sichuan pepper
½ tsp salt
1 size 16 (1.6 kg/3lb) chicken
3 tsp grated ginger
1½ tbsp rice wine vinegar

1½ tbsp soy sauce
1½ tbsp dry sherry
Vegetable oil for cooking
1 lemon, cut into wedges

Heat a pan over a medium heat. Add Sichuan pepper and salt and stir constantly for 1–2 minutes until the pepper emits a fragrant smoke. Crush in a mortar and pestle and store in an airtight jar.

Cut chicken in half through the backbone and trim away rib bones. Place together in a deep bowl 1 tsp of salt and pepper mix, ginger, vinegar, soy sauce and sherry. Mix well, then add chicken and rub marinade all over. Marinate chicken skin side down for 1–2 hours, if time permits.

Preheat oven to 200°C (390°F).

Heat a wok over a high heat and add 3–4 cm (1 in) of vegetable oil.

Remove chicken from marinade and pat dry on absorbent paper. Add chicken carefully to hot oil and cook skin side down until golden, about 3–4 minutes. Turn over and cook for a further 4–5 minutes. Place chicken skin side up on a baking tray and cook in the preheated oven for 15 minutes.

To serve, chop chicken into thick slices and sprinkle with some Chinese pepper and salt mix. Serve with plain steamed rice and lemon wedges. Serves 4.

Pot-roasted chicken with 40 cloves of garlic

Don't worry too much if you don't like fresh garlic; it transforms completely during the cooking process and becomes sweet and nutty. There's no way anyone would ever guess that there are 40 garlic cloves in there, which means you don't really have to count them – just chuck in a generous amount. Even if you don't add the garlic cloves, you'll still have a delicious pot roast to enjoy.

I adore this dish because it produces a roast chicken, yummy garlic cloves and a stunning sauce – all from the one pot. AC

1 lemon
1 chicken, size 16 (1.6 kg/3 lb)
2 tbsp olive oil
1 tsp thyme leaves

Salt and freshly ground black pepper
40 cloves of garlic (no need to peel)
300 ml (10 fl oz) chicken stock
250 ml (8 fl oz) white wine

Preheat oven to 180°C (350°F).

Cut lemon into quarters and stuff into the cavity of the chicken. Rub chicken with oil, thyme, salt and pepper. Place chicken, breast side up, in a heatproof casserole pot. Scatter garlic cloves around chicken. Pour the stock and wine around the chicken. Place the casserole over a medium heat and allow liquid to come to the boil. Place lid on the casserole and put into the preheated oven. Cook for 1 hour.

Remove lid and continue cooking chicken for a further 20–30 minutes or until chicken is golden brown. Remove chicken carefully to a serving platter and keep warm. Spoon the garlic cloves into a small serving dish. Strain the remaining liquid into a bowl. Spoon off the fat from the surface and pour liquid into a serving jug. Check the seasoning of the sauce then serve with the chicken.

At the table each person can squeeze the silky garlic purée from the cloves to eat with the chicken and the sauce. Serves 4.

Moroccan roast turkey

A turkey buffe is a turkey with the legs removed. It takes a shorter time to cook than a whole turkey and has white meat only.

We often prepare this dish for Christmas day and cook it in our kettle barbecue. It comes out moist, tender and full of flavour. You can, of course, cook the turkey without the spice mix if you prefer.

1 turkey buffe, 3½–4 kg (7–8 lb)	½ tsp ground cinnamon
4 tsp ground cumin	Pinch of ground cloves
4 tsp ground coriander	½ tsp salt
2 tsp ground ginger	¼ tsp freshly ground black pepper
2 pinches of saffron threads, about 20	50 ml (1¾ fl oz) olive oil

Preheat oven to 180°C (350°F)

Pat turkey dry. Mix spices, salt and pepper together with oil and brush over turkey skin. Place turkey in a large roasting tray, Roast in preheated oven for 1¼ hours. Turn over, baste well and cook for a further 45 minutes. Remove and rest for 20 minutes before carving. This is excellent with Moroccan couscous salad, page 214. Serves 10–12.

Stuffed turkey breast

Ask your butcher to even out the thickness of the breast if necessary. Better still, if you ask nicely and bring your stuffing with you, your poultry person will stuff and roll the fillet for you. Just don't forget to say please.

1 kg (2 lb) turkey breast	Olive oil
Stuffing of your choice, see pages 149–150	Salt and freshly ground black pepper

Preheat oven to 180°C (350°F).

Lay turkey on chopping board skin side down. Push to one side the underfillet (small fillet under the main part of the breast), keeping it attached. Lay stuffing down the centre and wrap turkey around stuffing.

Roll fillet carefully so skin is uppermost. Take a piece of string, about 30 cm (1 ft), and tie the thick part of the fillet tightly. Continue to wrap string around turkey 2 cm (¾ in) apart from first tie. Thread end of string under and pull tightly. Tie with a knot and repeat action until turkey is evenly rolled with string around.

Rub with oil; sprinkle with salt and pepper. Place in baking tray and cook in preheated oven for 1 hour and 20 minutes, or until turkey is cooked through. Remove from tray; wrap in foil and rest in a warm place for 10–15 minutes.

Carve and serve. Serves 4–6.

Roast beef with Yorkshire puddings

We always had trouble finding a small cut of beef for roasting – until we tried scotch fillet. Scotch is usually considered to be a steak cut, rather than a roast, but it's actually very good for roasting, particularly with Yorkshire pudding. Just make sure any excess fat is trimmed from the top, leaving a nice thin layer to baste the meat while it's in the oven.

Olive oil for cooking
Salt and freshly ground black pepper
1.5 kg (3 lb) scotch fillet, trimmed of excess fat

300 ml (10 fl oz) milk
2 tbsp olive oil
1 tsp salt
2 medium eggs

Preheat oven to 220°C (425°F).

Rub beef all over with oil, salt and pepper. Place beef on a baking rack over the baking tray and cook in preheated oven for 20 minutes. Lower temperature to 180°C (350°F) and cook for a further 1 hour, for medium–rare. Remove beef; wrap in foil and rest in a warm place.

While beef is cooking, whisk milk, oil, salt and eggs together until smooth. Allow to stand for 30 minutes. When beef is cooked and resting, raise oven temperature to 220°C (350°F). Brush muffin tins with oil and heat in oven for 5 minutes. Pour batter mix into hot tins and return to the oven for 15 to 20 minutes or until risen and golden brown.

Slice beef and serve with puddings and potatoes, and gravy in a warmed jug alongside. Serves 6.

Mustard roast beef
Rub beef with grain mustard.

Horseradish Yorkshire pudding
Add 2 tsp creamed horseradish to batter.

Roast rib of beef
Swap scotch fillet for 2 x 3 ribs (bones) of beef, about 1.5 kg (3 lb) per set. Cook beef in a fry pan over a medium heat until golden brown all over. Roast in preheated oven for 40 minutes (medium-rare, longer if so desired) and rest for 15–20 minutes before serving.

Beef pot-roast

This recipe is an absolute must for us to cook several times in the cooler months. The first sign of a cool night and we're into it. Simple method and ingredients combined with a long slow cooking time mean that you are still in good shape to enjoy it when it finally appears as a magnificent roast complete with its own gravy.

1.5 kg (3 lb) beef, fresh silverside or bolar blade
2 tbsp olive oil
125 ml (4 fl oz) beef stock
125 ml (4 fl oz) red wine
2 tbsp tomato paste
1 onion, diced
2 carrots, diced
1 garlic clove, crushed
1 bay leaf
2–3 sprigs of thyme
Salt and freshly ground black pepper

Preheat oven to 180°C (350°F).

Heat a large heavy-based saucepan or roasting dish over a medium heat. Rub the beef with oil and add it to the saucepan. Cook the meat on all sides until well browned all over, about 10 minutes.

Add stock, wine and tomato paste. Scatter the vegetables around the meat. Add fresh herbs along with a sprinkle of salt and pepper. Cover with a tightly fitting lid or with foil and place in the preheated oven.

Cook for 2½ hours, then check the meat for tenderness and adjust the seasoning of the sauce if required.

Cut into thick slices and serve with vegetables and the sauce. Serves 4–6.

Herb and garlic roast lamb

You can roast lamb just as it comes, or do as we do and add flavours like garlic, rosemary and basil. The water in the bottom of the roasting dish stops these ingredients burning and can be used to form the base of your gravy if so desired.

2 tbsp chopped rosemary
2 tbsp chopped basil
2 garlic cloves, crushed
2 tbsp lemon juice
2 tbsp olive oil
Salt and freshly ground black pepper
1 easy-carve leg of lamb

Preheat oven to 180°C (350°F).

Mix herbs, garlic, lemon juice, oil and salt and pepper together. Rub all over lamb. Place lamb in a deep baking dish. Add 2 cm (¾ in) water.

Cook in preheated oven for 1–1½ hours. Check occasionally to ensure water hasn't evaporated, add more if necessary.

Remove from the oven; rest for 20 minutes in a warm place before carving. Strain the liquid left in the bottom of the roasting pan and use it in your gravy. Serves 6.

Roast lamb with pesto
Smear 60 g (2 oz) pesto all over lamb and roast as described.

Roast lamb with mustard
Rub 2–3 tbsp grain mustard over lamb and roast as described.

Basil and pine nut stuffed lamb

Easy-carve legs of lamb are a twenty-first century revolution, they're easy to deal with and they carve beautifully. We often cook a leg of lamb this way, which involves simply untying the lamb, filling it with pesto, then re-tying it. Basil and pine nut stuffed lamb has never been easier.

I feel as Australian as Dame Edna Everage every time I have a mouthful of roast lamb. MC

90 g (3 oz) pine nuts
1 cup basil leaves
Salt and freshly ground black pepper

50 g (1¾ oz) parmigiano, grated
1 easy-carve leg of lamb
2 tbsp olive oil

Preheat oven to 180°C (350°F).

In the food processor, pulse pine nuts, basil, salt and pepper, leaving the mixture as chunky as possible. Add parmigiano and mix to incorporate. Untie the lamb, spread it with the pesto, then re-tie it.

Cook in preheated oven for 1–1½ hours. Remove from the oven; rest for 20 minutes in a warm place before carving. Serves 6.

Mint sauce

125 ml (4 fl oz) boiling water
2 cups fresh mint leaves, chopped
1 tbsp caster sugar

125 ml (4 fl oz) cider or white wine vinegar
Salt to taste

Pour boiling water over mint and sugar. Set aside to soak for 30 minutes. Add vinegar and salt to taste. Serve with lamb.

Lamb topsides with roasted ratatouille

Give ratatouille a modern day make-over with this delicious dish. Chop all the vegetables to a small dice, about 5 mm (¼ in).

1 kg (2 lb) small potatoes, halved
Olive oil for cooking
Salt and freshly ground black pepper
1 small eggplant, chopped, salted and rinsed
1 onion, chopped
2 small zucchini, chopped
1 red capsicum, chopped
1 tomato, coarsely chopped
1 garlic clove, crushed
1 tbsp chopped flat-leaf parsley
1 tbsp chopped thyme
2 lamb topsides, about 400 g (14 oz) each

Preheat oven to 190°C (375°F).

Place potatoes in a roasting pan, drizzle with olive oil and season to taste. Combine chopped eggplant, onion, zucchini, capsicum and tomato in another roasting dish. Scatter with garlic, herbs, salt and pepper and drizzle with olive oil.

Place lamb topsides on a baking rack over the vegetables. Place both roasting dishes into the preheated oven and cook for 40 minutes, stirring ratatouille occasionally. Remove lamb from roasting pan, cover with foil and rest in a warm place for 10 minutes. Continue cooking potatoes and vegetables until potatoes are golden and vegetables are tender.

Slice lamb and serve with potatoes and roasted ratatouille. Serves 4.

Roast rack of pork

We occasionally have a roast rack of pork for mid-year Christmas dinner. The tender slices of crackling-topped meat with creamy roast potatoes really hit the spot on a cold, winter's night.

2 kg (4 lb) rack of pork, trimmed and scored
2 tbsp olive oil
2 tbsp salt
Freshly ground black pepper
500 ml (1 pt) chicken stock
2 kg (4 lb) potatoes, peeled and sliced
60 g (2 oz) butter

Preheat oven to 220°C (425°F).

Rub the pork with oil, salt (yes, all of it) and pepper. Pour stock into a deep roasting dish, place a baking rack across the top and place pork on to top of that.

Cook in preheated oven for 20–30 minutes. The crackling should rise and become puffy. Lower oven temperature to 180°C (350°F) and cook for 40 minutes. Add sliced potatoes to stock, top with dobs of butter and sprinkle with salt and pepper.

Return to oven with pork still on top. Cook for a further 1 hour. Check that pork is cooked. Remove it; wrap in foil and rest in a warm place for 20 minutes. Return potatoes to oven and cook for a further 20 minutes until tender and stock is absorbed. Carve pork and serve with potatoes. Serves 6.

Braised red cabbage

This red cabbage has a flavoursome sweet and sour flavour, which comes from the red wine vinegar and redcurrant juice. It is excellent with roast pork, bratwurst sausages and pork chops.

I can't imagine eating roast pork without this red cabbage. It must be a throw-back to my Scandinavian roots as my mother is from Denmark and regularly cooked dishes such as this. MC

75 g (2⅔ oz) butter
1 red cabbage, sliced
100 ml (3½ fl oz) red wine vinegar
100 ml (3½ fl oz) redcurrant juice, or blackcurrant cordial

Heat a large heavy-based saucepan over medium heat. Melt butter, add cabbage and toss well. Stir in vinegar and redcurrant juice, cover and cook for 20–30 minutes, stirring often. Serves 6–8.

Roast duck

Most people put roasting a duck into the too hard basket, but essentially it's no different to roasting a chicken. Quite a bit of fat will come from the duck as it cooks, but all you need to do is pour this away from time to time.

1 duck, size 2–2.5 kg (4–5 lb)
Olive oil
Salt and freshly ground black pepper
1 orange

Preheat oven to 200°C (390°F).

Remove any giblets, neck and loose fat from duck. Wipe inside and out to remove moisture. Rub duck all over with oil and season inside and out with salt and pepper. Cut orange into quarters and stuff into cavity. Place duck upside-down in roasting dish.

Roast for 20 minutes; remove and tip excess fat away. Return to oven for a further 20 minutes; remove. Again tip excess fat off and turn duck breast side up. Return to oven for a further 30 minutes, checking once to see if more fat needs to be drained away. Check to see if duck is cooked by inserting knife between thigh and body, looking for clear juices.

Rest duck in a warm place for 15 minutes before carving. Serves 4.

Chinese roast duck
Use Sweet sticky marinade, page 111, on duck. Roast as described.

Sumac and pomegranate roast duck
Mix 80 ml (2¾ fl oz) pomegranate syrup, 30 ml (1 fl oz) olive oil and 3 tsp sumac. Rub over duck and marinate for 1 hour. Drain excess marinade away. Roast as described.

Pot-roasted veal with pancetta and mushrooms

Veal responds really well to pot-roasting as all the juices that come from the meat go directly into the sauce. This is great served with mashed potatoes or polenta.

1 kg (2 lb) veal nut
Olive oil
Salt and freshly ground black pepper
2 tbsp chopped fresh rosemary
150 g (5 oz) pancetta, diced 1 cm (⅓ in)

2–3 garlic cloves
125 ml (4 fl oz) white wine
125 ml (4 fl oz) chicken stock
180 g (6 oz) button mushrooms, halved

Preheat oven to 180°C (350°F).

Heat a heatproof casserole pot (such as Le Creuset) over a medium heat. Add a splash of oil and brown the veal all over. Remove saucepan from heat. Season veal with salt and pepper. Add rosemary, pancetta, garlic, wine and stock to the veal. Cover the casserole and cook in preheated oven for 1 hour. Turn veal over, add mushrooms, cover and continue cooking for 30 minutes.

Cook the veal uncovered for 15 minutes to brown the outside and reduce the sauce a little. Remove veal; rest for 5–10 minutes. Carve the veal, check seasoning of cooking liquid and serve together. Serves 4.

Nine-spiced roasted vegetables with chickpeas ⓥ

This is truly a memorable dish – lots of chunky vegetables covered in an aromatic spice paste and roasted to perfection. The long list of ingredients makes this recipe look much harder than it really is, so don't be put off by it.

150 g (5 oz) chickpeas, soaked overnight
1 tsp sweet paprika
½ tsp ground ginger
½ tsp chilli powder
½ tsp ground coriander
½ tsp ground white pepper
¼ tsp ground cardamom
¼ tsp ground cinnamon
¼ tsp allspice
1 tsp salt
Juice of 1 lemon

2 tbsp olive oil
4 potatoes, peeled
1 eggplant
2 zucchini
Olive oil for cooking
2 large carrots
2 parsnips
½ pumpkin
375 ml (12 fl oz) vegetable stock
Couscous, page 134, and tzatziki, page 41, to serve

Preheat oven to 180°C (350°F).

Place chickpeas in a medium-sized saucepan, cover with water and bring to the boil over a medium heat. Reduce heat and cook until soft, about 30–40 minutes. Drain and set aside.

Mix all of the spices together with the salt, lemon juice and oil to form a smooth paste. Cut potatoes and eggplants into thick wedges. Salt eggplant and stand for 30 minutes, until juices bead. Rinse well and dry. Cut zucchini in half lengthways, then halve again.

Heat a pan over a medium heat and cook eggplant and zucchini in a small amount of oil until golden brown. Peel carrots and parsnips. Cut as for zucchini. Cut pumpkin into thick fingers.

Rub the spice mix over all of the prepared vegetables.

Arrange potatoes, parsnips and carrots in a deep baking tray. Pour half of the stock over and bake in preheated oven for 30 minutes, turning occasionally.

Place eggplant, zucchini, pumpkin and chickpeas in another dish and pour remaining stock over. Cook for a further 20 minutes alongside potatoes.

Serve vegetables on top of couscous accompanied by tzatziki. Serves 4.

Roasted root vegetable chips

We're very keen on roasting vegetables in this way, as it gives them such a tasty golden coating. We eat them whether we're having a roast dinner or not.

3 medium swedes
3 large carrots
4 medium parsnips

6 large potatoes
Salt and freshly ground black pepper
Olive oil

Preheat oven to 180°C (350°F).

Peel swedes, carrots and parsnips and cut into long, fat, chip-shape pieces. Place in a bowl. Scrub potatoes and cut into 8 wedges each. Add potatoes to other vegetables, sprinkle salt and pepper over and toss with enough olive oil to coat.

Arrange in a single layer on baking tray(s) and cook on top shelf of preheated oven for 40 minutes or until golden brown and crispy. Serves 6.

Rosemary and garlic potatoes

1 kg (2 lb) potatoes
olive oil
salt and freshly ground black pepper

rosemary
20 cloves of garlic

Preheat oven to 180°C (350°F).

Chop your favourite roasting potatoes into 2 cm (¾ in) chunks. Toss in a deep baking tray with olive oil, salt, pepper, and loads of rosemary and at least 20 cloves of garlic. Roast for an hour, tossing occasionally, until potatoes are golden brown and crispy. Serves 4.

Thai red curry paste
Rendang curry paste
Thai green chicken curry
Thai red beef and bok choy curry
Red curry of duck
Beef rendang
Hot and sour beef curry
Malaysian fish curry
Indian chicken curry
Indian beef curry
Coconut chicken curry
Indian lamb, spinach and potato curry
Kashmiri lamb
Fragrant vegetable curry
Sweet potato and cashew nut curry

Curries

INDIAN, THAI, MALAYSIAN AND NEW CLASSICS

A beautiful rich curry, with enough spice to let you know it's there, with meat that melts in your mouth, a bowlful of steamed rice and a spoonful of natural yoghurt, is perhaps one of the most satisfying meals you can make.

Curry is a generic term applied to spicy food, usually from Asia, most commonly India. They are not called curries there. Nor do traditional chefs use pre-made curry pastes, sauces or spice mixes. Each dish is made up from selected spices, blended as they go into the pot, which is fine if you have plenty of time to spare, but most of us don't.

Our curries are a mixture of simple spice combinations, our own curry pastes or (more commonly) quick curries using pre-brought curry pastes. We tend to eat one of these curries at least once a week.

THINGS YOU NEED TO KNOW ABOUT CURRIES

- Curries don't require any special cooking pots or equipment.
- A heavy-based saucepan with a tightly fitting lid will cover just about every curry we know of.
- Curries make very inexpensive and flavoursome meals.
- When making a traditional curry you must have fresh spices, or it's not even worth starting.
- We also use curry pastes – they are convenient, easy and quick. You can add more or less to suit your tastes.
- We often use two pastes, such as Madras and Hot, to get a more complex flavour.
- Start off mild and build up to spicier curries over time.
- You can choose to make quick curries, using prime, tender cuts of meat, or there are slower curries, using cheap meat, cooked long and low to impart wonderful flavours and aromas.
- Virtually all recipes can have their meat component replaced with chunks of vegetables, only the cooking times will be shorter.
- A big bowl of yoghurt, or tzatziki, page 41, is wonderful with all Indian-style curries.
- Many people find spice addictive. Expect to find yourself adding more chilli and other spices as your tastebuds are won over.
- A rice cooker will help you make lots of perfectly steamed rice to accompany your curries.

Thai red curry paste

Before there was a plethora of excellent curry pastes on the market we had to make our own. We have included them here for the curry purists who like to make everything from scratch. We'll happily admit to using pre-brought curry pastes about 90 per cent of the time.

4 long red chillies, de-seeded and roughly chopped
1 onion, diced
⅓ bunch coriander, roots, stems and leaves, roughly chopped
2 cm (¾ in) galangal, thinly sliced and finely diced
1 lemongrass stem, thinly sliced and finely diced

2 garlic cloves, peeled and chopped
1 tbsp ground coriander
1 tbsp ground cumin
1 tsp ground turmeric
1 tsp paprika
2 tsp dried shrimp paste
1 tsp salt

Place chillies and onion in a food processor and blend to a fine paste (when done first, onions release their liquid, making it easier to blend the other ingredients without the need to add water, which can dilute the overall flavour).

Add coriander, galangal, lemongrass and garlic and purée until smooth, stopping occasionally to push down ingredients with a spatula. Add remaining spices, dried shrimp paste and salt, and blend until combined. Store in a clean, dry glass jar, and cover the surface with oil. This will keep in the refrigerator for up to 3–4 weeks or can be frozen.

Thai green curry paste
Omit paprika and use green chillies instead of red. It packs quite a punch, so approach with caution.

Rendang curry paste

Rendang is a famous Malaysian curry that is slowly cooked to tender, aromatic perfection.

1 onion, diced
1 lemongrass stem, chopped thinly
2 garlic cloves
5 cm (1¾ in) peeled ginger, chopped
1 tsp salt

2 tsp ground coriander
2 tsp ground cumin
45 g (1½ oz) desiccated coconut
2 dried red chillies, soaked in water
60 ml (2 fl oz) water

Place all ingredients in food processor and blend until smooth. Store in a clean, dry glass jar and cover surface with oil. This will keep in the refrigerator for up to 3–4 weeks.

Thai green chicken curry

The basic method for all Thai curries is much the same. Heat coconut cream until the natural oils appear on the surface, then add paste and cook the spices in the coconut oil. It sounds unusual, but this way produces a curry that's much more pungent and has fuller flavours than one produced by our conventional way of cooking the spices in oil, then adding coconut milk and meat.

1 tbsp peanut oil
500 g (1lb) skinless chicken thigh fillet, chopped
150 ml (5 oz) coconut cream
3 tsp Thai green curry paste
2 tbsp shaved palm sugar

2 tbsp fish sauce
400 ml (14 fl oz) coconut milk
400 g (14 oz) diced potato
½ cup coriander leaves
Jasmine rice to serve

Heat a large heavy-based saucepan over a medium heat. Add oil and chicken and cook until browned. Remove chicken from pot and set aside. Place coconut cream in the same saucepan and cook over medium–high heat until it separates and the oil floats on the surface. (This will take about 5 minutes.)

Add curry paste and allow to cook until fragrant, stirring constantly, about 5 minutes. Add palm sugar and cook briefly before adding fish sauce and coconut milk. Bring liquid to the boil, then return chicken to the pot along with diced potatoes. Reduce heat and simmer for 15–20 minutes, or until potatoes are cooked.

Add coriander leaves to taste, check seasoning and serve with jasmine rice. Serves 4.

Thai red chicken curry
Substitute red Thai paste for green.

Thai green chicken and spinach curry
In the last minutes of cooking add 90 g (3 oz) washed spinach leaves – or other vegetables such as peas, green beans or capsicum.

Thai red beef and bok choy curry

This is the same base recipe as for Thai curry, but it uses red curry paste. The beef is cooked separately to ensure that it remains tender. Then it is sliced and added to the sauce just before it is served. We have made it this way hundreds of times and it's always a success.

1 tbsp peanut oil
500 g (1 lb) scotch fillet
150 ml (5 oz) coconut cream
3 tsp Thai red curry paste
2 tbsp shaved palm sugar
2 tbsp fish sauce

400 ml (14 fl oz) coconut milk
1 bunch baby bok choy, washed and sliced
½ red capsicum, thinly sliced
100 g (3½ oz) roasted cashew nuts
½ cup coriander leaves
Jasmine rice to serve

Preheat oven to 180°C (350°F).

Heat a heavy-based ovenproof frying pan over high heat. Add oil and cook fillet until browned all over. Place beef in preheated oven for 15–20 minutes, or until cooked to medium–rare. Allow to cool. Slice into thick strips, discarding fat and gristle.

Place coconut cream in a heavy-based saucepan and cook over medium–high heat until it separates and the oil floats on the surface. (This will take about 5 minutes.)

Add curry paste and allow to cook until fragrant, stirring constantly, about 5 minutes. Add palm sugar and cook briefly before adding fish sauce and coconut milk. Bring liquid to the boil, then reduce heat and simmer for 8–10 minutes. Add bok choy and capsicum, and cook until slightly softened. Add beef and cashew nuts. Cook until heated through.

Add coriander leaves to taste, check seasoning and serve with jasmine rice. Serves 4.

Thai red fish curry
Swap beef for raw fish chunks. Add them with the bok choy and capsicum. Of course, vary the vegetables to suit your own tastes. Finish with a squeeze of fresh lime juice to add zest and lift all the flavours.

Red curry of duck

Another variation on the basic Thai curry theme, this time with different vegetables and herbs to get a slightly more complex result. This dish is full-on protein, which makes it smart enough for a dinner party, assuming you are serving side dishes with it. For a one-pot wonder, add vegetables such as Asian greens or bamboo shoots to balance the dish.

1 Chinese roast duck, available at any Asian roast house
500 ml (1 pt) coconut milk
4 tsp Thai red curry paste
2 tbsp shaved palm sugar
2 tbsp fish sauce
125 ml (4 fl oz) chicken stock
4 kaffir lime leaves, optional*
½ cup Thai basil leaves
Steamed rice to serve

Using a sharp knife remove all duck flesh from the carcass, taking care to leave duck in reasonably large pieces with skin intact. Discard bones and chop duck into 2 cm (¾ in) chunks, if necessary.

Place coconut milk, paste, sugar and fish sauce in a large heavy-based saucepan over a medium–high heat. Bring to the boil, reduce heat and simmer for 5–10 minutes. Add stock, duck meat and kaffir leaves if using. Continue to simmer for 5–10 minutes, allowing duck meat to be flavoured with the curry sauce. Take care not to boil or overcook as the duck pieces will start to break up.

Add basil leaves and serve immediately with steamed rice. Serves 4.

Red curry of quail
Substitute roast quail for roast duck.

Beef rendang

Rendang is perfect with the usual accompaniments of steamed rice and hot roti bread. Together with our friends Max and Sophie Allen we've discovered that a magnum of Chimay stout with this dish will pass a winter's night with considerable comfort.

Allan and I disagree on how we prefer our rendang cooked. I like it dry and falling apart in the traditional way, while Allan prefers his moister. Luckily this doesn't stop us eating rendang with alarming frequency. MC

1 tbsp peanut oil
200 g (7 oz) rendang paste, page 163
1 kg (2 lb) blade steak, diced
1 tbsp tamarind*
125 ml (4 fl oz) boiling water
250 ml (8 fl oz) coconut cream
1 star anise
1 cinnamon stick
Coriander leaves to garnish
2 tbsp toasted coconut, optional
Steamed rice and roti bread to serve

Heat a heavy-based saucepan over a medium–high heat. Add oil and paste and fry for 5–6 minutes or until fragrant, stirring often. Add beef and cook for 5–10 minutes, or until beef starts to colour, but before spices begin to burn. Soak tamarind in boiling water for 5–10 minutes. Use your fingers to work pulp free from tamarind seeds, strain reserving liquid. Add tamarind liquid, coconut milk, star anise and cinnamon to the pot. Allow to come to the boil, reduce to a simmer, cover with a lid and cook for 1 hour, stirring occasionally.

Remove lid and continue cooking rendang until beef is tender and most of the liquid has evaporated. Stir often to prevent sauce catching, this will take a further 30–45 minutes.

To serve sprinkle coriander leaves and coconut if using on top and serve alongside steamed rice and crisp roti bread. Serves 4.

Hot and sour beef curry

This is a very simple dish to make, yet it has a really interesting, complex flavour. It's packed with tender chunks of beef and potato in a sour tamarind and coconut sauce.

Olive oil for cooking
2 tsp chilli powder
2 tsp ground coriander
¼ tsp ground cardamom
1 tsp turmeric
2 garlic cloves, crushed
2 tsp grated ginger

1 kg (2 lb) blade steak, diced
1 tbsp tamarind*
125 ml (4 fl oz) boiling water
250 ml (8 fl oz) coconut cream
1 star anise
500 g (1 lb) potatoes, diced, optional

Heat a heavy-based casserole pot over a medium–high heat. Add oil and spices, garlic and ginger and fry for 5–6 minutes or until fragrant, stirring often. Add beef and cook for 5–10 minutes, or until beef starts to colour but before spices begin to burn. Soak tamarind in boiling water for 5–10 minutes. Use your fingers to work pulp free from tamarind seeds, then strain liquid and reserve.

Add tamarind liquid, coconut cream and star anise to the pot. Allow to come to the boil, reduce to a simmer, cover with a lid and cook for 1 hour, stirring occasionally.

Add potatoes and cook for a further 20–30 minutes or until beef and potatoes are tender. Check seasoning and serve. Serves 4–6.

Indian lamb, spinach and potato curry (recipe page 169) with naan bread (recipe page 229)

Thai chicken balls (recipe page 179)

Salmon and potato cakes (recipe page 177)

Malaysian fish curry

Curry pastes sound harder to make than they actually are, but after the first couple of attempts, they become obviously simple. A food processor cuts the work in half. Try doubling the paste and freezing half for next time. The fish in this dish can be left whole or diced, depending on how you like it.

- 50 g (1¾ oz) tamarind*
- 125 ml (4 fl oz) boiling water
- 1 lemongrass stalk, chopped
- 2 dried red chillies, soaked in boiling water and drained
- 2 garlic cloves, peeled
- 1 tbsp grated ginger
- 1 onion, chopped
- 2 tsp ground coriander
- 2 tsp ground cumin
- 1 tsp ground fennel, optional
- 1 tsp turmeric
- 1 tsp salt
- 60 ml (2 fl oz) vegetable oil
- 60 ml (2 fl oz) vegetable oil, additional
- 250 ml (8 fl oz) coconut milk
- 4 firm fish steaks or 750 g (1½ lb) diced white fish, such as ling, cod, flathead or trevally

Soak tamarind in boiling water for 15–20 minutes. Use your fingers to work pulp free from tamarind seeds, strain reserving liquid.

Place lemongrass, chillies, garlic, ginger and onion in food processor and blend until smooth (can be done in a mortar and pestle if you want to give your biceps a work out). Add spices, salt and oil and blend briefly until smooth.

Heat a large heavy-based saucepan over a medium–high heat. Add additional oil and paste and fry until fragrant. Add tamarind liquid and coconut milk, bring to the boil. Reduce to a simmer and cook for 10–15 minutes.

Remove skin from fish if needed and add fish. Simmer for a further 5–6 minutes, or until fish is just cooked. Serve with steamed rice. Serves 4.

Indian chicken curry

I've called this 'Indian' chicken curry to differentiate between it and the preceding curries. But to me it's just a basic curry that I cook all the time, varying the ingredients according to what I feel like – and whatever is in the refrigerator. I use a combination of both medium and hot curry pastes to alter the flavour; however, you can make your own, or of course make it hotter or milder to suit you. MC

- Olive oil for cooking
- 1 onion, diced
- 3 tbsp curry paste
- 500 g (1 lb) skinless chicken thigh fillets, diced
- 250 ml (8 fl oz) tomato purée
- 250 ml (8 fl oz) chicken stock
- Steamed rice to serve

Heat a large heavy-based saucepan over a medium–high heat. Add oil and onion and cook until onion just begins to soften. Add curry paste and cook for 5–10 minutes, until fragrant but not allowing spices to burn. Add chicken and cook briefly for 2–3 minutes, just browning the chicken. Add tomato purée and stock and bring to the boil. Reduce heat and simmer for 15–20 minutes, uncovered. Serve with steamed rice. Serves 4.

Indian chicken, potato and spinach curry
Add diced cooked potato and spinach leaves for the last 2–3 minutes of cooking.

Indian chickpea and spinach curry V
Omit chicken and add cooked chickpeas. Add spinach and coriander leaves for the last 2–3 minutes of cooking.

Indian vegetable curry V
Omit chicken. Add a selection of vegetables such as sliced zucchini, capsicum, broccoli, green beans, peas, sliced red cabbage or bok choy to vary the textures.

Indian beef curry

This is based on a Vindaloo recipe and it's quite fiery, so make sure there's plenty of thirst-quenching beer and a big bowl of natural yoghurt nearby.

2 tbsp vinegar
Pinch of salt
3–4 curry leaves
1 tbsp ground coriander
1 tbsp ground cumin
1 tsp chilli powder
½ tsp turmeric
250 g (8 oz) natural yoghurt
1 kg (2 lb) blade steak, diced
2 tbsp oil
2 onions, diced

2 tsp grated ginger
2 garlic cloves, crushed
3 tomatoes, diced
1 tsp cumin seeds
2–3 cloves
2–3 cardamom pods
1 cinnamon stick
250 ml (8 fl oz) beef stock
Coriander leaves to garnish
Steamed rice to serve

Mix vinegar, salt, curry leaves, coriander, cumin, chilli, turmeric and yoghurt together. Pour over beef and set aside to marinate for at least 2–3 hours, or ideally overnight. Stir once or twice if possible.

Heat a heavy-based saucepan over a medium heat. Add oil and onions, cook for 5–6 minutes or until onions are soft. Add ginger and garlic and cook for a further 1–2 minutes. Add marinated beef, tomatoes, cumin seeds, cloves, cardamom, cinnamon stick and stock and bring to the boil, stirring often. Cover with a lid, reduce heat and cook for 1–1½ hours. Check to see if beef is tender; if not, continue cooking. Serve curry with coriander leaves and steamed rice. Serves 4.

Coconut chicken curry

A similar method to that for the Indian chicken curry, but using chicken on the bone for a fuller, meatier flavour. Use your favourite paste here; it could be Thai, Burmese or even Madras.

1 kg (2 lb) skinless chicken casserole pieces
Seasoned flour
Oil for cooking
1 onion, diced
4 tbsp curry paste
250 ml (8 fl oz) chicken stock
250 ml (8 fl oz) coconut milk
Steamed rice to serve

Coat chicken pieces with flour, shaking well to remove excess (a sieve is best for doing this).
    Heat a heavy-based saucepan over a medium–high heat, add oil and cook chicken (in batches if necessary) until golden brown. Remove and set aside. Add onion, cook for 5–6 minutes, until slightly softened, then add curry paste. Cook for 8–10 minutes, until fragrant. Add stock, coconut milk and chicken pieces and bring to the boil. Reduce to a simmer and cover with a lid. Cook for 45 minutes, stirring occasionally.
    Serve with rice and steamed vegetables. Serves 4.

Indian lamb, spinach and potato curry

The long, slow cooking results in tender meat beautifully coated with a smooth rich curry sauce. Appealing, isn't it?

2 tsp ground coriander
2 tsp ground cumin
1 tsp ground turmeric
200 g (7 oz) natural yoghurt
2 tbsp lemon juice
1 kg (2 lb) diced lamb, such as leg
Oil for cooking
2 onions, diced
1 garlic clove, crushed
1 kg (2 lb) potatoes, peeled and diced
400 g (14 oz) crushed tomatoes
2 tbsp tomato paste
Salt and freshly ground black pepper
100 g (3½ oz) spinach leaves, washed
Steamed rice and naan bread to serve

Combine spices, yoghurt and lemon juice in a large bowl. Add lamb, mix well and set aside to marinate for at least 2–3 hours, or better still overnight.
    Place a large heavy-based saucepan over a medium–high heat. Add a splash of oil, the onions and garlic and cook for 5 minutes. Add lamb mixture, potatoes, tomatoes and tomato paste. Bring to the boil, season with salt and pepper, reduce heat and simmer uncovered for 1–1¼ hours or until lamb is tender. Check seasoning and add spinach. Cook for a further 2–3 minutes, or until spinach softens.
    Serve with steamed rice and naan bread. Serves 6.

Indian beef, spinach and potato curry
Substitute lamb for diced blade steak.

Kashmiri lamb

Diced leg of lamb will work nicely with this recipe, which features dried apricots and sultanas. However, diced mutton, if you can find it, is even better. Because it's a tougher meat, it takes longer to cook, so the flavours of the dish have even longer to develop. Ask you local butcher if they can get some in for you; it will be well worth the effort.

2 tbsp garam masala
2 tbsp Madras powder
1 tsp mixed spice
1 tbsp sweet paprika
1 tbsp ground ginger
Salt and freshly ground black pepper
125 g (4 oz) natural yoghurt

2 kg (4 lb) diced lamb or mutton
2 tbsp ghee
4 onions, diced
500–750 ml (1 pt–1¼ pt) chicken stock
125 g (4 oz) dried apricots, sliced
125 g (4 oz) sultanas
Basmati rice to serve

Mix all the spices, salt and pepper and yoghurt together. Mix with lamb and marinate overnight or at least 2–3 hours.

Heat a large, heavy-based casserole dish over a medium–high heat. Add ghee and onions and cook until golden in colour, 5–6 minutes, stirring often. Add marinated lamb and enough chicken stock to just cover.

Simmer uncovered for 1–1½ hours, until almost tender. If using mutton this could easily take an extra hour. Add apricots and sultanas and cook for a further 30–45 minutes, or until meat is tender.

Serve with basmati rice. Serves 6–8.

Fragrant vegetable curry ⓥ

The choice of vegetables here can be changed to suit personal tastes or to use what's best in season. During winter we use the mixture listed below; during the warmer months we use mostly capsicum, eggplant and zucchini.

Oil for cooking
1 tsp brown mustard seeds
½ tsp ground cumin
½ tsp ground coriander
½ tsp chilli powder
½ tsp ground turmeric
1 tsp curry powder
¼ tsp ground cardamom
¼ tsp ground cinnamon
1 onion, diced

1 potato, diced
1 parsnip, diced
1 carrot, diced
1 small swede, diced
1 small sweet potato, diced
Small wedge pumpkin, peeled and diced
250 ml (8 fl oz) vegetable stock
Salt and freshly ground black pepper
¼ cauliflower, cut into florets, optional
Steamed rice to serve

Heat a heavy-based saucepan over a medium–high heat. Add a generous splash of oil and all the spices, cook for 2–3 minutes until distinctly fragrant but not burning. Add diced vegetables and cook in aromatic spice mix for 1–2 minutes. Add enough stock to just cover, season with salt and pepper and bring to the boil. Reduce to a simmer, cook for 15–20 minutes, or until vegetables are just tender. Add cauliflower for last 3–4 minutes of cooking.

Check seasoning, add more stock or water if necessary to adjust consistency. Serve with steamed rice. Serves 4.

Sweet potato and cashew nut curry v

In this simple curry the sweetness of the potato is a perfect match for the spices, while the cashews add a nutty crunch. You may, of course, add other vegetables if so desired.

Oil for cooking
1 tsp brown mustard seeds
1 tsp ground coriander
1 tsp ground turmeric
2 garlic cloves, crushed
2 tsp grated ginger
2 medium sweet potatoes, peeled and diced
    2 cm (¾ in)

1 tbsp shaved palm sugar
250 ml (8 fl oz) coconut milk
250 ml (8 fl oz) vegetable stock, or water
90 g (3 oz) toasted cashew nuts
Handful of basil leaves, torn
1 tbsp fish sauce
Squeeze of lime juice
Steamed rice to serve

Heat a heavy-based saucepan over a medium–high heat. Add a splash of oil and mustard seeds. Cook for 2–3 minutes, or until seeds start to pop. Add coriander and turmeric and cook for a further 2–3 minutes. Add garlic and ginger and cook for another 2–3 minutes, stirring often. Add diced sweet potatoes, sugar, coconut milk and stock. Stir well and bring to the boil.

Reduce to a simmer and cook for 20 minutes, stirring often until potato is cooked. Add nuts, basil, fish sauce and a generous squeeze of lime juice.

Serve with steamed rice. Serves 4.

Chicken schnitzel
Parmigiano crumbed veal cutlets with caponata
Caponata
Salmon and potato cakes
Katsudon (Japanese crumbed pork)
Beef burgers with red wine and onion gravy
Savoury mince
Thai chicken balls
Chicken and veal polpettini
Birgit's frikadella
Lion's-head meatballs
Lamb kofta skewers
Moussaka
Veal, sage and onion meatloaf
Pan-fried steak with mushroom sauce
Steak with oven chips
Beef stroganoff
Pan-fried herb chicken fillets
Pan-fried chicken with mushroom sauce
Chicken saltimbocca
Lamb cutlets with red wine onions
Lamb steaks with oregano and spiced onions

The fry pan

STEAKS, CHOPS AND CRUMBED FOOD

For generations the frying pan has been the centre of many family meals. It has produced everything from the standard 'meat and three veg' through to schnitzel, savoury beef and even fried eggs to serve on toast.

The frypan gets a seriously good workout in our kitchen too – from homemade fish fingers and lamb cutlets with red wine onions to chicken saltimbocca and the perfect steak. Or it can even be the simplicity of sausages and onion gravy. There's something for every member of the family in our pan.

A good frypan is also where most sauces are made, often after meat has first been cooked in it so all the flavours are captured in the final dish. Finally, the frypan is our substitute barbecue when winter rain sets in and we can't cook outdoors any more. Take away our frypan and our eating experiences would be seriously depleted.

THINGS YOU NEED TO KNOW ABOUT THE FRY PAN

- You need a large heavy-based frypan such as Le Creuset – this is what we use all the time. We also have a smaller pan which is great for 2 chicken breasts or 2 steaks. But you'll need the biggie for a family of four.
- A grill pan is also fantastic for cooking just meats – steaks, chops and chicken – as it enables the flesh to cook on the hot metal ridges while most oil drains away.
- Traditionally clarified butter was used to cook meats. With a great taste and high burning point it's ideal. But now that we're concerned about animal fats many people have switched to oil: mono- or poly-unsaturated.
- You can use whatever oil you like in the frypan, particularly if you have a special dietary requirement. We use extra virgin olive oil. We buy this in a large tin and decant it into a clean dark wine bottle which we top with an oil pourer. This is the cheapest way to do it.
- Just how much oil you add depends largely on what you are cooking. Crumbed food will soak up a lot of oil, as does some meat, though generally 1–2 tbsp will do it.
- When we are feeling indulgent we cook with a splash of oil and a knob of butter. This adds the richness of butter to the high cooking temperature of oil. Butter makes the food turn a lovely golden brown (which doesn't always happen with oil) but if used alone it will burn at a high heat.

DEGLAZING AND REDUCING

Deglazing and reducing are the two basic principles for making a sauce.

Deglazing is the process of adding a liquid, usually alcohol such as wine, to a hot pan after meat has been browned and transferred to the oven to finish cooking. Tip any oil from the pan away and return to the heat. Always take care when adding alcohol as it may ignite. This is fine – really good, actually – but you don't want to have your hand in the way. When we're cooking for the family we just use stock. Okay, let the alcohol evaporate, but make sure some liquid stays in the base of the pan; remember that the pan is over a high heat. Then you add stock.

Reducing is adding stock to the remaining juices in the pan and boiling rapidly in order to evaporate the liquid. Usually the liquid is reduced by half; any more and it starts to get too strong. Once the stock is reduced by half, any finishing ingredients such as herbs or cream are added. Don't add the cream any earlier as it will curdle, but you want it to reduce a little to make the sauce thicker. A knob of butter whisked in at the end will thicken it slightly, as well as adding sheen and a lovely rich taste.

Chicken schnitzel

A classic and ever-popular dish. With schnitzel the variations are endless because you can change not only the meat but also breadcrumb additives. Serve schnitzel with lemon wedges, mashed potatoes and peas.

2–3 skinless chicken breast fillets
Seasoned flour
1 medium egg
150 ml (5 fl oz) milk

90 g (3 oz) dry breadcrumbs
Olive oil for cooking
Lemon wedges to serve

Cut the small fillet from underneath each larger fillet, then cut remaining piece into 3 or 4 pieces, depending on original size.

Using a meat hammer pat each piece of chicken gently 2–3 times on each side until flat and of an even thickness. The easiest way to do this is to lay a large square of cling film on a chopping board, put 1 or 2 pieces of chicken on it, fold half of cling film over the top and then pat gently; the cling film stops the chicken sticking to the hammer (as it does with all meats).

Put flour in a shallow bowl. Beat egg and milk together in another bowl and put breadcrumbs in another bowl. Dip chicken pieces into flour and shake off excess. Then dip into egg and finally into breadcrumbs, making sure each piece of chicken is well coated at each stage. If wanted, chicken can now be placed in refrigerator until you are ready to cook it.

You will need to cook the schnitzels in batches, so turn the oven to 140°C (280°F) to keep each batch warm while you keep cooking. Heat a large heavy-based frying pan over a medium–high heat. Add a generous splash of oil and 3–4 chicken pieces to the pan, making sure chicken doesn't overlap or else it will not cook properly. Cook for 2–3 minutes, until golden brown on one side. If pan becomes dry add more oil as needed. When brown on one side, turn over and cook for 2 minutes on other side, or until golden brown. Remove and place on a tray in warm oven. It's a good idea to line tray with clean brown paper or kitchen paper to absorb excess oil and keep food crisp.

Repeat process until all chicken is cooked. Serves 4–6.

Sesame schnitzel
Add 1–2 tbsp sesame seeds to the breadcrumbs.

Lemon and herb schnitzel
Add the grated zest of 1 lemon and 1 tbsp chopped parsley to breadcrumbs.

Cheesy schnitzel
Substitute 30 g (1 oz) of breadcrumbs for grated parmigiano.

Veal schnitzel
Use thin veal in place of chicken.

Indian spiced schnitzel
Add 2 tbsp curry powder to breadcrumbs.

Chicken nuggets
Chop chicken into 3 × 3 cm (1 × 1 in) chunks, then crumb as directed.

Crumbed lamb chops
Use trim lamb chops, allow 3 per person and crumb as directed. Serve with ratatouille.

Fish fingers
Cut 500 g (1 lb) of firm white fish fillets into finger shapes then crumb as directed.

Parmigiano crumbed veal cutlets with caponata

This is a very refined way of serving veal cutlets. They are coated with parmigiano flavoured breadcrumbs and then serving with a sweet–sour caponata sauce, which contrasts beautifully with the richness of the meat.

Seasoned flour*
1 medium egg
150 ml (5 fl oz) milk
90 g (3 oz) fresh breadcrumbs
60 g (2 oz) parmigiano, grated

1 tbsp finely chopped parsley
6 veal cutlets (one per person, or two if small)
Olive oil for cooking

Preheat oven to 180°C (350°F). Place flour in one bowl, beat egg and milk together in a second bowl and mix breadcrumbs, cheese and parsley in a third bowl. Take veal cutlets one by one and coat first in flour, then egg mix, then breadcrumbs.

    Place a heavy-based frying pan over high heat, add a generous splash of olive oil and cook veal cutlets for 3–4 minutes on each side until golden brown. Remove veal to a baking tray and cook in oven for a further 5–10 minutes (depending on size), or until just cooked. Remove from oven, cover, and allow to rest in a warm place for 5–10 minutes.

    To serve place a spoonful of caponata on each plate; add veal cutlets and serve. Serves 6.

Caponata

2 eggplants, cut into 1 cm (⅓ in) dice
Salt
200 ml (7 fl oz) olive oil, approximately
1 onion, diced
2 celery sticks, cut into 1 cm (⅓ in) dice
1 red capsicum, cut into 1 cm (⅓ in) dice

100 g (3½ oz) pitted green olives
2 tsp salted capers, soaked and rinsed
75 ml (2½ fl oz) white wine vinegar
2 tbsp caster sugar
Chopped basil and parsley
Salt and freshly ground black pepper

Place diced eggplant in a colander and sprinkle with salt. Leave until juices bead, about 20–30 minutes. Rinse well and pat dry.

    Place a large heavy-based frying pan over medium heat. Add enough olive oil to cover base of pan. Cook eggplant in batches until golden brown, adding more oil if necessary. Remove from pan and cook onion, celery and capsicum until soft. Return eggplant to pan, and add olives, capers, vinegar and sugar. Heat a little until sugar has dissolved, taking care not to overcook eggplant. Remove from heat and allow to cool at room temperature. Before serving, add herbs to taste, and salt and pepper if necessary. Serves 6.

Salmon and potato cakes

You can use any fish for this recipe, but the rich taste of Atlantic salmon works best for us every time. It's amazing how far 400 g (14 oz) of salmon can go and how good it can be. Just don't forget the lemon butter sauce.

750 g (1½ lb) potatoes
Knob of butter
Salt and freshly ground black pepper
1–2 tbsp olive oil
2 × 200 g (7 oz) pieces Atlantic salmon
1 tbsp chopped fresh dill, optional

Seasoned flour*
1 medium egg
150 ml (5 fl oz) milk
90 g (3 oz) dry breadcrumbs
Olive oil for cooking

Peel, boil and mash potatoes. Add butter, salt and pepper to taste. Heat a heavy-based frying pan over medium heat, add olive oil and cook salmon for 2 minutes on each side. Allow fish to cool slightly, then flake the flesh discarding skin and bones (if any). Add fish to mashed potato along with dill if using.

Divide mixture into 12 equal-sized pieces and pat into burger shapes. Put flour in a shallow bowl. Beat egg and milk together in another bowl and put breadcrumbs in a third bowl. Coat each fish cake in flour and shake excess off. Then coat with egg and finally bread crumbs, making sure each cake is well coated at each stage. Fish cakes can be refrigerated until needed.

Preheat oven to 180°C (350°F). Place a heavy-based frying pan over high heat, add a generous splash of olive oil and cook fish cakes for 3–4 minutes on each side until golden brown. You may have to do this in batches.

Place fish cakes on a baking tray and cook in preheated oven for a further 10 minutes. Serve with lemon butter sauce, page 63, or a squeeze of lemon juice. Makes 12.

Katsudon (Japanese crumbed pork)

This is a dish we've only recently begun cooking at home, although we've been eating it in Japanese restaurants for quite a while. It's essentially crumbed pork slices cooked in a pan with beaten egg and served on rice with dashi broth poured over it.

1 pork fillet, about 500 g (1 lb)
Seasoned flour*
1 medium egg
150 ml (5 fl oz) milk
90 g (3 oz) dry breadcrumbs (the coarse
  Japanese kind if you can find them)
1 onion, sliced

250 ml (8 fl oz) dashi*
60 ml (2 fl oz) soy sauce
90 ml (3 fl oz) mirin*
Olive oil for cooking
3 medium eggs, additional
Steamed rice for serving

Cut pork into slices. Using a meat hammer, pat each piece of pork gently 2–3 times on each side until flat and of an even thickness (cover pork with cling film to prevent pork from sticking to hammer). Lay between two sheets of cling film and pat gently with a meat hammer. Put flour in a shallow bowl. Beat egg and milk together in another bowl and put breadcrumbs in a third bowl. Coat pork in flour and shake off excess. Then coat with egg and finally breadcrumbs, making sure each piece of pork is well coated at each stage. If you want, you can now placed pork in refrigerator until you are ready to cook it.

Make your broth by combining onion, dashi, soy and mirin in a small saucepan. Bring to the boil over a medium heat, reduce to a simmer and cook for 10 minutes.

Heat a large heavy-based frying pan over a medium–high heat. Add a generous splash of oil and enough pork pieces to fit into the pan, making sure pork doesn't overlap or else it will not cook properly. Cook for 2–3 minutes until golden brown on one side. If pan becomes dry add more oil as needed. When brown on one side, turn over and cook for 2 minutes on other side, or until golden brown.

Beat additional eggs together and pour into pan around pork pieces. (If cooking in batches, pour half egg in and keep remaining beaten eggs for second batch). Cook for 1–2 minutes until egg sets. Serve pork over rice with a spoonful of the hot broth. Serves 4.

Beef burgers with red wine and onion gravy

Beef burgers are a perennial favourite at our table. We'll bet they are at your place too. They are absolutely delish with mashed potatoes and green beans.

1 kg (2 lb) beef mince	2 onions, sliced
Salt and freshly ground black pepper	250 ml (8 fl oz) red wine
Olive oil for cooking	250 ml (8 fl oz) beef stock

Preheat oven to 180°C (350°F).

Mix mince with salt and pepper and form into 8 burger shapes. Heat a heavy-based frying pan over a medium–high heat. Add a splash of oil and cook burger for 3–4 minutes on each side until brown. Remove from the pan to a baking tray and place in hot oven to continue cooking. Return pan to heat, add onions and cook for 4–5 minutes, until soft, stirring often. Add red wine and bring to the boil. Allow to reduce by half, then add stock. Lower heat and allow to simmer for 3–4 minutes.

Serve burgers with red wine and onion sauce over them. Serves 4.

Sausages with onion gravy
Substitute burgers with sausages. Make sauce with stock only, leave out the wine.

Ginger-chicken burgers with satay sauce
Substitute minced beef for minced chicken, adding 2 tsp each of grated ginger, sweet chilli sauce, kecap manis* and dry breadcrumbs. Mix well then divide and cook as directed. Combine 200 g (7 oz) satay sauce with 150 ml (5 fl oz) coconut milk in a small saucepan over a medium heat. Stir well until boiling. Serve together.

Savoury mince

Savoury mince doesn't sound very exciting but we cook this a lot and transform it into something else. It's good in baked potatoes, made into cottage pie, spiced up as chilli con carne or spooned into taco shells.

Olive oil for cooking
2 onions, diced
1 kg (2 lb) lean beef mince
2 garlic cloves, crushed
150 g (5 oz) tomato paste
250 ml (8 fl oz) tomato purée
500 ml (1 pt) beef stock
Salt and freshly ground black pepper
2 tbsp chopped parsley

Heat a large heavy-based saucepan over a medium–high heat. Add a splash of oil and onions and cook for 5–6 minutes, until soft, stirring often. Add beef and garlic and cook until beef has changed colour. Add tomato paste, stir well and cook for 1–2 minutes. Add tomato purée, stock, salt and pepper and bring to the boil. Reduce heat and cook at a simmer for 25–30 minutes, or until stock has reduced. Check seasoning and add parsley. Serves 4–6.

Cottage pie
Place cooked mince in a deep baking dish. Cover with mashed potato and bake in preheated oven for 30–40 minutes until top is golden brown.

Chilli con carne
Add 2–3 tsp chilli paste with beef and cook as described. When cooked add 90 g (3 oz) soaked, drained and cooked red kidney beans. Serve with rice and sour cream.

Mexican mince
Add 2 tsp ground cumin, 2 tsp ground coriander, 2 tsp sweet paprika and 1 tsp chilli powder after the onions are cooked. Cook for 1–2 minutes, until fragrant. Add beef and continue with recipe.

Tacos
Serve savoury mince with taco shells, grated cheese, tomato salsa and shredded lettuce. Add 2 tsp of chilli paste to beef for a spicy version.

Thai chicken balls

The old trick of hiding vegetables in minced meat always works. Sometimes we add even more, or sometimes none at all to suit our tastes. These chicken balls are also good as nibbles with a bowl of sweet chilli sauce.

500 g (1 lb) chicken mince
½ red capsicum, diced
3 spring onions, thinly sliced
1 carrot, grated
1 medium egg
1 tbsp soy sauce
1 tbsp sweet chilli sauce
2 tbsp chopped coriander
90 g (3 oz) dry breadcrumbs
Olive oil for cooking
Rice to serve

Mix chicken with all ingredients, adding enough breadcrumbs to bring mixture together. Roll into small balls. Heat a heavy-based frying pan over a medium–high heat, add a splash of oil and cook chicken until golden brown all over.

Serve with rice and extra sweet chilli sauce. Serves 4.

Thai fish balls
Substitute fish mince for chicken mince.

Chicken and veal polpettini

These are a fairly adult type of meatball, which is not to say that children don't eat them like they're going out of fashion.

100 g (3½ oz) day-old bread
250 ml (8 fl oz) milk
300 g (10 oz) veal mince
300 g (10 oz) chicken mince
Salt and freshly ground black pepper
3 tbsp chopped parsley

2 garlic cloves, crushed
Zest of 1 lemon
60 g (2 oz) parmigiano, grated
Flour for dusting
Olive oil for cooking
2 lemons, cut into wedges

Tear bread into small pieces. Soak in milk for 10–15 minutes. Squeeze well to remove excess liquid. Place bread in a bowl, add mince, salt, pepper, parsley, garlic, lemon and parmigiano. Mix well.

Roll mixture into small balls, about 3 cm (1 in) in diameter. Roll each ball lightly in flour. When ready heat a heavy-based pan over a medium–high heat. Add a splash of oil. Cook polpettini in batches for 5–6 minutes, shaking often until polpettini are golden brown all over. Remove and keep warm in preheated oven 140°C (280°F) until all are cooked. Serve with lemon wedges. Serves 4–6.

Birgit's frikadella

Frikadella are probably the simplest burgers you'll ever come across. The mix is easy to make and just plonk the burgers into the pan as they come without forming them into patties,.

This is a standard family meal in Denmark where my mum, Birgit, comes from. I'm still trying to get the rest of my family to love it as much as I do, but I guess you just had to be there. MC

60 g (2 oz) rolled oats
500 g (1 lb) veal or pork mince (or a mix of the two if available)
Salt and freshly ground black pepper

Milk, as needed
Olive oil for cooking
Pickles to serve

Place rolled oats in food processor and whiz until they are very fine. Add the mince, plus salt and pepper, and whiz until smooth and combined. Add a splash of milk if the mix is very thick.

Heat a heavy-based frypan over a medium–high heat and add a generous amount of oil. Drop spoonfuls of mix into oil and cook for 10 minutes, turning occasionally. Each frikadella should be golden brown all over.

Serve with pickles. Serves 4.

Lion's-head meatballs

Lion's-head meatballs are an easy peasant dish, but they taste as if you've gone to a lot of trouble. Serve them with Wok-fried Asian greens, page 103.

500 g (1 lb) pork mince
6 shiitake mushrooms, finely chopped
90 g (3 oz) water chestnuts, finely chopped
1 egg white
4 spring onions, thinly sliced
2 tsp grated ginger
3 tsp cornflour
30 ml (1 fl oz) Chinese rice wine*

½ tsp salt
100 g (3½ oz) vermicelli noodles
½ Chinese cabbage
Extra cornflour
Olive oil for cooking
500 ml (1 pt) chicken stock
3 tbsp soy sauce
2 tbsp Chinese rice wine*

Mix together pork, mushrooms, water chestnuts, egg white, spring onions, ginger, cornflour, rice wine and salt until well combined. Divide mixture into 16 portions and roll into balls with extra cornflour if too wet.

Preheat oven to 180°C (350°F). Pour boiling water over noodles and set aside to soften, then drain. Chop cabbage into 3 cm (1 in) chunks. Lay cabbage, then noodles, into the bottom of a deep baking tray.

Coat meatballs with extra cornflour. Heat a large heavy-based frypan over a medium–high heat. Add a splash of oil and cook meat balls for 3–4 minutes, or until brown all over. Place meatballs on top of noodles. Mix together stock, soy sauce and rice wine and pour over meatballs and other ingredients. Cover tray with foil and cook in preheated oven for 45 minutes. Serve with steamed rice. Serves 4.

Lamb kofta skewers

Minced lamb is becoming more widely available nowadays so making these kofta skewers is now easy. They are also very good barbecued.

1 kg (2lb) finely minced lamb
1 onion, finely diced
3 tsp ground coriander
4 tsp ground cumin
½ tsp ground cinnamon
½ tsp ground allspice
½ tsp ground white pepper

2 tsp oregano leaves, chopped
2 tsp harissa paste*
1 tsp salt
90 g (3 oz) burghul
12 skewers
Olive oil for cooking

Place lamb, onion, ground spices, oregano, harissa and salt in a large bowl. Knead well by hand for five minutes. Refrigerate for 1 hour so flavours can develop.

Soak burghul in plenty of cold water for 20 minutes. Drain well.

Divide kofta mixture into 12 equal pieces and shape into thick fingers. Scatter burghul onto a plate and roll lamb until coated. Thread skewers through the centre of each kofta.

Heat a heavy-based frying pan over a high heat, add a splash of oil and cook lamb for 12–15 minutes, turning frequently. Serve with tzatziki, page 41; green salad, page 209; and Turkish pide bread. Makes 12.

Moussaka

Our family remains divided on who likes this dish and who doesn't, but it's such a classic we just had to include it. Make sure your lamb mince is lean or there'll be oil everywhere. Here speaks the voice of experience.

2 tbsp olive oil
1 onion, diced
1 garlic clove, crushed
750 g (1½ lb) lean lamb mince
400 ml (14 fl oz) tomato purée
2 tbsp tomato paste

½ tsp ground cinnamon
Salt and freshly ground black pepper
2 eggplants
Olive oil for cooking
6 potatoes, boiled and sliced
1 quantity cheese sauce, page 87

Heat a heavy-based pan over a medium–high heat. Add oil and onion and cook for 4–5 minutes, until soft, stirring often. Add garlic and lamb and cook, stirring often, until lamb changes colour. Add tomato purée, paste, cinnamon, salt and pepper. Bring to the boil, reduce heat and simmer for 45 minutes. Check seasoning.

Slice eggplants, sprinkle with salt and set aside until juices bead. Rinse and pat dry. Place on a flat tray, drizzle with oil and grill until tender.

Preheat oven to 180°C (350°F). Lay potatoes in the base of a deep baking dish, such as

Steak with oven chips (recipe page 184)

Hungarian chicken casserole (recipe page 192)

a lasagne dish. Spoon lamb mince on top. Lay eggplant slices on top and cover with cheese sauce. Bake in preheated oven for 40 minutes, until golden brown and heated through. Serve with green or Greek salad, page 209. Serves 4–6.

Veal, sage and onion meatloaf

Meatloaves are out of fashion. Sad, but true. But half of my wardrobe is out of fashion, too, and that doesn't stop me wearing it. In fact, it'll probably all be back in again next year, just like meatloaf. MC

Olive oil for cooking
2 onions, diced
4 slices bacon, chopped
1 garlic clove, crushed

1 kg (2 lb) veal mince
2 tbsp chopped sage leaves
90 g (3 oz) dry breadcrumbs
1 medium egg

Heat a frypan over a medium–high heat. Add a splash of oil and cook onions for 3–4 minutes, stirring often. Add bacon and cook for a further 3–4 minutes until cooked. Add garlic and cook for 1–2 minutes. Remove from heat and allow to cool.

Preheat oven to 180°C (350°F).

In a large bowl mix veal, onion/bacon mix, sage, breadcrumbs and egg together. Place into a greased loaf pan and bake for 40 minutes.

To test whether the meatloaf is cooked insert a small knife into it. If juices run clear the meatloaf is ready.

Allow to cool in the tin before slicing. Serves 4–6.

Pan-fried steak with mushroom sauce

A simple but stylish steak dish with a tasty sauce. It is excellent served with baked potatoes.

4 × 250 g (8 oz) porterhouse steaks
Olive oil for cooking
1 onion, finely diced
250 g (8 oz) Swiss brown mushrooms, cut into wedges

250 ml (8 fl oz) beef stock
90 ml (3 fl oz) cream
Salt and freshly ground black pepper

Preheat oven to 180°C (350°F).

Heat a heavy-based pan over a medium–high heat. Brush steaks with oil and cook for 3 minutes on each side, until well browned. Place steaks on a tray and cook in preheated oven for 5 minutes (medium–rare).

Return pan to the heat, add more oil if required, onion and mushrooms. Cook for 5–6 minutes, until onion and mushrooms are well softened. Stir occasionally. Add the stock, bring to the boil and reduce by half. Add cream to the sauce and simmer for a further 2–3 minutes. Season well, adding lots of pepper. Serve steaks with sauce on top. Serves 4.

Steak with oven chips

The oven chips included here are wicked. Seeing that they are so easy to make we can't understand why anyone buys those frozen ones. It's these or nothing as far as we are concerned.

1.5 kg (3 lb) Desiree potatoes
Olive oil for cooking
2 tbsp rosemary leaves
1 tbsp chopped parsley
Salt and freshly ground black pepper
4 × 200 g (7 oz) fillet or porterhouse steaks

Preheat oven to 200°C (390°F).

Cut potatoes into thick wedges. Place oil, herbs, salt and pepper in a large bowl. Add potato wedges and toss well. Place wedges onto a large baking tray, skin side down, and cook in preheated oven for 45–55 minutes, turning tray occasionally. Potatoes will be golden brown when ready.

Heat a heavy-based frypan over a medium–high heat and add a splash of oil. Add steaks and cook for 4–5 minutes on both sides. Rest briefly in a warm place, then serve with lots of potato wedges and perhaps a green salad. Serves 4.

Beef stroganoff

This is a really speedy meal that is cooked entirely in one pan, yet it comes complete with a creamy sauce. Try it with rice or noodles.

500 g (1 lb) beef fillet
Olive oil for cooking
1 onion, diced
150 g (5 oz) mushrooms, sliced
250 g (8 fl oz) sour cream
2 tsp Dijon mustard
Salt and freshly ground black pepper

Cut beef into thin strips and set aside.

Heat a large heavy-based pan over a medium–high heat. Add a splash of oil, onion and mushrooms. Cook for 5–6 minutes, until both onion and mushrooms are soft. Remove from the pan and set aside. Add more oil if needed, add beef strips and cook briefly, browning beef but without adding too much colour. Return onion and mushrooms to the pan. Add cream, mustard and salt and pepper. Allow to heat through, simmering but not boiling or else cream will separate. Serves 4.

Pan-fried herb chicken fillets

A chicken fillet coated lightly with fresh herbs is a great-tasting mix. If anyone partaking of this meal has a problem with herbs leave a fillet or two plain. This dish is good with soft polenta or mashed potato.

Handful of chopped herbs: parsley, thyme, rosemary, oregano
Salt and freshly ground black pepper
2 tbsp olive oil
4 small chicken breast fillets

Mix herbs, salt, pepper and oil together. Rub over chicken fillets and leave to marinate, at least 10 minutes or up to 3 hours if time permits.

Preheat oven to 180°C (350°F).

Heat a heavy-based frying pan over a medium–high heat; add oil and chicken and cook for 2–3 minutes on each side until well browned. Place in preheated oven and continue to cook for 10 minutes. Remove and rest, covered, in a warm place for 5 minutes before serving. Serves 4.

Pan-fried chicken with mushroom sauce

This dish is the equivalent to the pan-fried steak with mushroom sauce. It too is excellent served with baked potatoes.

Olive oil for cooking
4 skinless chicken breast fillets
1 onion, diced
150 g (5 oz) mushrooms, sliced
250 ml (8 fl oz) chicken stock
90 ml (3 fl oz) cream
Salt and freshly ground black pepper
2 tbsp chopped parsley

Preheat oven to 180°C (350°F).

Heat a heavy-based frying pan over a medium–high heat, add oil and chicken fillets and cook for 2–3 minutes on each side until well browned. Place chicken fillets in preheated oven and continue to cook for 10 minutes.

Return pan to the heat and add more oil if needed. Add onion and mushrooms and cook for 5–6 minutes, stirring often, until softened. Add stock, bring to the boil and reduce by half. Add cream and allow to simmer for 1–2 minutes. Check seasoning, add parsley and serve sauce over chicken. Serves 4.

Chicken saltimbocca

This is a chicken version of veal saltimbocca. What you end up with is thin slices of chicken with prosciutto wrapped around each one and sage leaves in the centre. They are beautiful with a simple mushroom risotto.

4 skinless chicken breast fillets
Sage leaves
8 slices prosciutto
Salt and freshly ground black pepper
Olive oil for cooking

250 ml (8 fl oz) white wine
250 ml (8 fl oz) chicken stock
90 g (3 oz) butter
2 tbsp chopped parsley

Cut chicken fillets in half. Take each piece of chicken and use a meat hammer to pat gently 2–3 times on each side until they are flat and have an even thickness. (Lay a large square of cling film on a chopping board, put 1–2 pieces of chicken inside, fold half of cling film over the top and then pat gently; the cling film prevents the meat sticking to the hammer.)

Lay 3–4 sage leaves on each piece of chicken. Season lightly with salt and pepper and wrap 1 piece of prosciutto around each piece of chicken. Pat with meat hammer to bond prosciutto to the chicken.

Heat a heavy-based frypan over a medium–high heat. Add a splash of oil and brown chicken pieces, in batches if necessary, until golden brown on each side. Place cooked chicken in a warm oven while you prepare the sauce.

Tip any oil from pan and return to high heat. Add wine and reduce by half. Add stock and again reduce by half. Remove from heat and whisk in butter in small amounts. Check seasoning and add parsley.

Serve 2 chicken pieces per person, drizzle with sauce and serve with mushroom risotto or polenta. Serves 4.

Lamb cutlets with red wine onions

Just looking at all these recipes in this chapter has made us realise how much we eat pan-fried meat with some sort of sauce. Yikes.

2 tbsp olive oil
3 onions, sliced
1 tbsp chopped thyme leaves
1 tbsp Dijon mustard
½ tsp caster sugar

375 ml (13 fl oz) red wine
1 kg (about 16) small, trimmed lamb cutlets
1 tbsp olive oil
Salt and freshly ground black pepper

Preheat oven to 180°C (350°F).

Heat a heavy-based saucepan over a medium–high heat. Add oil, onions and thyme. Cook for 8–10 minutes, stirring often until onions are soft. Add mustard, sugar and wine, bring to the boil, then reduce heat. Simmer until wine has evaporated and onions are a pale pink colour, about 15 minutes. Season to taste and keep warm until lamb is cooked.

Heat a large heavy-based frypan over a high heat. Add a splash of oil and cook lamb cutlets for 2 minutes on each side, a few at a time. Place on a baking tray as they are ready and cook remaining cutlets. When all cutlets are done, place in preheated oven and cook for 5 minutes. Serve a spoonful of the red wine onions with lamb cutlets on top. Serves 4.

Lamb steaks with oregano and spiced onions

Lamb, onions and spices are a great combination. Here the spices and onion are slow-cooked to melting perfection, then served under thin slices of tender lamb.

60 ml (2 fl oz) olive oil
3–4 tbsp of oregano leaves
2 tbsp ground coriander
1 tbsp ground cumin
¼ tsp each salt and freshly ground black pepper
1 small red chilli, de-seeded and finely diced

1 garlic clove, crushed
1 tbsp tomato paste
4 onions, thinly sliced
1 red capsicum, thinly sliced
Olive oil for cooking
4 lamb topside steaks

Heat a heavy-based saucepan over medium heat. Add oil, oregano leaves, coriander, cumin, salt and pepper. Stir and cook for 2 minutes. Add chilli, garlic, tomato paste, onions and capsicum. Stir until well combined and the onions begin to soften. Cover, reduce the heat to low and cook for about 40 minutes, stirring every 5 minutes. When ready the onions will be totally softened, rich and aromatic.

Preheat oven to 180°C (350°F).

Heat a heavy-based frying pan over medium–high heat. Add a splash of olive oil, and cook lamb until well browned on all sides. Place in preheated oven and cook for a further 10 minutes or until medium–rare. Remove, put on a plate and cover with foil to rest for 10 minutes. Cut each lamb topside into ½ cm (¼ in) slices.

Divide the hot onions between the plates and top with slices of lamb. Serves 4–6.

Simple chicken casserole
Mediterranean chicken casserole
Hungarian chicken casserole
Moroccan chicken with tomatoes and olives
Soy-braised chicken
Moroccan chicken pie
Chicken and mushroom pie
Braised steak and onions
Basic beef stew
Dumplings
Mashed potato
Beef and Guinness pie
Beef and prune tagine
Corned beef (silverside)
Parsley sauce
Sour and spicy beef braise
Lamb tagine
Spanish lamb stew
Lamb hot pot
Tunisian lamb shanks
The pork dish
Osso buco
Pot-roasted veal shanks
Rabbit casserole
Aromatic vegetable tagine

Casseroles

STEWS, BRAISES AND TAGINES

There's no doubting that casseroles, stews or braises — whatever you want to call them — are a convenience food. And we're not talking about using the packets of powdered sauces on supermarket shelves, either. We're talking about the real thing here: fresh meat and vegetables combined with top quality seasonings in a pot.

Don't be put off by the long cooking time in a recipe. You'll only spend 30 minutes or so dicing, chopping and frying before putting the whole thing in the oven. Then you leave it well alone for $1\frac{1}{2} - 2$ hours. That gives you enough time to run down to footy practice, put the washing away, tidy up the bedroom, or put your feet up and have a long, well-deserved drink before dinner.

It's also very easy to transform any casserole into a pie. Simply cook as described until the meat is just tender. Transfer to a pie dish, cover with puff pastry, brush with egg wash and put it into a preheated oven for 30–40 minutes or until the pastry is crisp and golden brown.

THINGS YOU NEED TO KNOW ABOUT CASSEROLES

- The beauty of casseroles is that they only work if you use the cheaper cuts. You are never going to get a tender beef stew from topside or sirloin; it's always going to be chuck or blade steak. Likewise, with lamb: go for diced leg; with chicken, choose thigh fillets … You get the picture.

- Casseroles only work with long slow cooking – you can't cheat and turn the oven up and hope it does its thing in 45 minutes – but they are well worth the wait.

- Flour is used to thicken most casseroles – to get that stick-to-your-ribs sensation that we love so much – and there are two ways this can be added. You can either lightly cook the meat, then add 1–2 tbsp of flour before adding any liquid; or you can toss the meat in the flour before cooking it.

- You can put the meat and flour in a plastic bag and shake well to coat, or simply put the flour in a bowl, add the meat, then stir well. It's worth putting the flour-covered meat into a sieve and shaking well to ensure that any excess flour is removed; otherwise you will end up with a thicker-than-normal stew. Try the different options, then decide which method suits you best. Always remember to add a little salt and pepper to the flour before use; this is then called seasoned flour.

- An important stage in most dishes of this type is cooking the meat until it is lightly browned. This provides a depth of flavour as the dish cooks, as well as good colour. The vegetables are often lightly cooked too. There are even some recipes that skip this step altogether. Be sure to deglaze the base of the pan with wine or stock to make sure all the flavour goes into the finished dish.

- We use a variety of cookware for our casseroles. Most often we use a large oval Le Creuset pot which is made from enamelled cast iron. The thick metal base is perfect for the initial cooking of the ingredients, and the casserole can then be covered and popped straight into the oven for 1–2 hours. We know these pots are expensive – that's why we only have one; but one is usually enough and they tend to last a lifetime.

- Sometimes we cook the meat and vegetables in a frypan, and transfer them to a casserole dish as they are ready. For this we have Spanish terracotta pots. A terracotta or earthenware dish is perfect for casseroles, stews and braises. The materials from which they are made are excellent conductors of heat in the oven and present well at the table. These seem to be on sale everywhere now and are much cheaper than other casserole dishes. Terracotta dishes must be soaked in water for 24 hours, then dried in the oven, before their first use.

- Try to use skinless chicken pieces because during the cooking process the fat in the skin breaks down and floats to the top of the casserole, producing a layer of chicken fat.

- For casseroles such as The Pork Dish, page 202, where everything is just put in the pot without browning or frying first, these terracotta pots are a godsend as they go straight from oven to table.
- Casseroles can be cooked either over a low heat on the stovetop (a simmer pad is excellent to make sure the heat is spread over the base of the saucepan), or in the oven. It doesn't make any difference to the finished dish, though we fancy that cooking a casserole in the oven lessens the chances of catching or burning. If you have a crock pot lurking in the back of the cupboard, take advantage of it: these are ideal for cooking all casseroles, stews and braised dishes.

Simple chicken casserole

There are two main ways to make a chicken casserole: one with diced chicken, thigh fillets for preference, and the other with chicken on the bone. These cuts are often sold as casserole pieces. Again, leg portions are better, and you could make a casserole solely with skinless chicken drumsticks or thigh pieces. Another option is to purchase a whole chicken and cut it into 8 or 10 pieces, or better still get your butcher to do this.

1 kg (2 lb) skinless chicken casserole pieces
Seasoned flour
Olive oil for cooking
1 onion, diced
1 carrot, finely diced

1 garlic clove, crushed
1 tbsp tomato paste
750 ml (1½ pt) chicken stock
Chopped parsley to serve

Toss chicken pieces in flour and shake off excess. Heat a heavy-based saucepan over a medium heat, add a generous splash of olive oil and cook chicken pieces all over until golden brown. Remove chicken from the saucepan and set aside. Return saucepan to the heat and add more oil if necessary.

Cook onion, carrot and garlic until soft. Add tomato paste, cook briefly, then add stock and bring to the boil. Reduce heat to a simmer, return chicken to the saucepan, cover with a lid and cook for 1 hour, or until chicken is tender.

Check seasoning and when the casserole is ready to serve, sprinkle parsley on top. Serve with mashed potato. Serves 4.

Chicken casserole with wine
Substitute either white or red wine for half of the stock.

Chicken casserole with mushrooms
Add 100 g (3½ oz) sliced mushrooms with onion and carrot.

Chicken casserole with red capsicum
Add 1 diced red capsicum with the onion and carrot. Try adding 1–2 tsp chilli powder to add a touch of warmth.

Mediterranean chicken casserole

This takes the simple chicken casserole recipe and introduces a few more ingredients, such as mushrooms and olives, to add more complexity and body to the dish.

1 kg (2 lb) skinless chicken casserole pieces
Seasoned flour
Olive oil for cooking
1 onion, diced
1 carrot, finely diced
1 garlic clove, crushed

100 g (3½ oz) mushrooms, sliced
1 tbsp tomato paste
250 ml (8 fl oz) white wine
500 ml (1 pt) chicken stock
100 g (3½ oz) pitted kalamata olives
Chopped parsley to serve

Toss chicken pieces in flour and shake off excess. Heat a heavy-based saucepan over a medium heat, add a generous splash of olive oil and cook chicken pieces all over until golden brown. Remove pieces from the saucepan and set aside. Return saucepan to the heat and add more oil if necessary.

Cook onion, carrot and garlic until soft. Add mushrooms and cook for a further 3–4 minutes. Add tomato paste and cook briefly, then add wine and stock and bring to the boil. Reduce heat to a simmer, return the chicken to the saucepan, cover with a lid and cook for 1 hour, or until chicken is tender.

Add olives, check seasoning and, when ready to serve, sprinkle parsley on top. Serve with mashed potato. Serves 4.

Hungarian chicken casserole

Hungarian cooking is renowned for its use of aromatic paprika, which brings a deep, rich flavour to whatever it's used in. Use sweet paprika for a mild flavour or a hot paprika if you like a bit of heat in this casserole. AC

1 tbsp butter
Olive oil for cooking
1 kg (2 lb) skinless chicken thigh pieces
3 onions, thinly sliced
2 cloves garlic, chopped

2 tbsp sweet or hot paprika
2 tbsp flour
750 ml (1½ pints) chicken stock
Salt and freshly ground black pepper
Sour cream, optional

Preheat oven to 180°C (350°F).

Heat a heavy-based frying pan over a medium heat. Add butter and a tablespoon of olive oil. Cook chicken pieces until golden all over. Set chicken pieces aside in an ovenproof casserole dish. Add additional oil to the pan, if needed, with the onions and garlic and cook until they begin to soften, about 5–6 minutes. Sprinkle the paprika and flour over the onions and stir well for 1–2 minutes. Add stock and stir until it comes to the boil. Season to taste with salt and pepper.

Pour onions and sauce over chicken, cover dish and place in the preheated oven. Cook for 1½ hours, by which stage chicken will be tender. Uncover the dish and cook for 30 minutes more to reduce the sauce and intensify the flavour.

Serve with noodles or mashed potatoes, and sour cream if using. Serves 4.

Moroccan chicken with tomatoes and olives

This shows how the simple casseroling method can be adapted and transformed to include spices, preserved lemon and aromatic saffron. Serve it with pilaf or couscous.

1½ kg (3 lb) skinless chicken casserole pieces
Seasoned flour
Olive oil for cooking
1 onion, sliced
2 tsp ground cumin
2 tsp ground coriander
1 tsp sweet paprika
½ tsp allspice
Pinch of saffron threads
6 roma tomatoes, diced or 1 × 300 g (10 oz) can tomatoes
500 ml (1 pt) chicken stock
½ preserved lemon, soaked for 30 minutes, then diced
200 g (7 oz) green olives, pitted
Fresh parsley and coriander leaves

Toss chicken pieces in seasoned flour and shake off excess using a sieve.

Heat a heavy-based casserole pot or saucepan over a medium heat, add a generous splash of olive oil and cook chicken pieces all over until golden brown. Remove chicken pieces from the pot and set aside. Return pot to the heat and add more oil if necessary.

Cook onion and spices until fragrant. Add tomatoes and stock and bring to the boil.

Return chicken to the pot, add preserved lemon, cover and cook over a low heat for 1½ hours. Add olives for the final 15 minutes of cooking.

Check seasoning and add fresh herbs. Serves 6.

Soy-braised chicken

You're going to love this: only a handful of ingredients, no chopping – and it tastes fantastic. I feel like chicken tonight, at its best. MC

1 × 1.6 kg (3 lb) chicken
250 ml (8 fl oz) soy sauce
250 ml (8 fl oz) Chinese rice wine*
250 ml (8 fl oz) chicken stock
250 ml (8 fl oz) water
3 whole star anise
200 g (7 oz) caster sugar
Steamed rice and stir-fried greens to serve

Place chicken, breast side up, in a saucepan that will fit it snugly and that comes a lid. Add all the other ingredients and place over a medium heat. Bring to the boil, then reduce heat, cover with a lid and cook for 30 minutes. Remove lid, turn chicken over, cover and cook for a further 15 minutes. Remove from heat and allow to stand, covered, for 15–20 minutes before serving.

Chop the chicken into 10–12 pieces and serve with steamed rice and stir-fried greens. Serves 4–6.

Moroccan chicken pie

This will produce a rich-tasting pie that needs only a green salad to go with it. If you want it a bit spicier add 1 tsp chilli powder and 1 extra tsp of both coriander and cumin.

1 kg (2 lb) skinless chicken thigh fillets, diced
Seasoned flour
Olive oil for cooking
1 onion, diced
2 tsp ground cumin
2 tsp ground coriander
1 tsp sweet paprika
½ tsp allspice
½ tsp ground ginger
500 ml (1 pt) chicken stock
Salt and freshly ground black pepper
1 tbsp pomegranate syrup, optional*
Handful of coriander leaves
3 small zucchini, halved and cut into 1 cm slices
6–8 sheets filo pastry
Melted butter
Sesame seeds

Toss chicken with flour and shake well to remove excess. Heat a heavy-based casserole pot over a medium heat. Add oil and cook chicken in batches until golden brown. Set aside.

Using the same pot, cook onion and spices until fragrant. Return chicken to the pot and add stock, salt and pepper. Bring to the boil; reduce heat and simmer, uncovered, until chicken is tender, about 45 minutes. Check seasoning, add coriander, zucchini, and pomegranate syrup if using. Remove from heat.

Preheat oven to 180°C (350°F). Grease a 20 cm (8 in) springform cake tin. Brush butter on 6–8 sheets of filo and arrange them in cake tin, allowing excess to hang over the side. Spoon chicken filling into pastry and arrange excess pastry over the top, adding extra pastry if needed to enclose filling. Brush the top with butter and sprinkle with sesame seeds.

Bake in a preheated oven for 30 minutes, or until pastry is crisp and golden brown. Serves 4–6.

Chicken and mushroom pie

There's something special about serving a pie at the table. It always look as if you've gone to a lot of trouble, whereas in fact it's just a casserole with pastry on the top – but don't tell anyone.

1 kg (2 lb) skinless chicken thigh fillets, diced
Seasoned flour
Olive oil for cooking
6 bacon slices, cut into strips
200 g (7 oz) mushrooms, sliced
150 ml (5 fl oz) white wine
150–200 ml (5–7 fl oz) chicken stock
1 tsp fresh thyme leaves
1 tbsp chopped parsley
Salt and freshly ground black pepper
½ quantity puff pastry, page 248
Egg wash*

Toss chicken with flour and shake well to remove excess. Heat a heavy-based casserole pot or saucepan over a medium heat. Add oil and cook chicken in batches until golden brown. Set aside. Using the same pot, cook bacon and mushrooms until softened and beginning to colour. Add white wine and allow to come to the boil.

Return chicken to pot and add enough stock to just cover. Add herbs and season to taste, then reduce heat and allow to cook for 30–45 minutes.

Preheat oven to 180°C (350°F).

Spoon hot chicken mix into pie dish, cover with puff pastry, trim edges and brush with egg wash. Place in preheated oven and bake for 20–30 minutes, or until pastry is cooked and golden brown. Remove and serve. Serves 4.

Braised steak and onions

Braised steak and onions is a dish that everyone should learn how to make. It's perfect during the cooler months, when you need some gutsy, rib-sticking food. Serve with mashed potatoes and lots of vegetables.

Olive oil for cooking
4 onions, sliced
4 × 150 g (5 oz) pieces blade steak
250 ml (8 fl oz) red wine
250 ml (8 fl oz) beef stock
1–2 tbsp chopped fresh herbs
250 ml (8 fl oz) tomato purée
Salt and freshly ground black pepper

Preheat oven to 180°C (350°F).

Heat a heavy-based saucepan over a medium heat. Add oil and onions and cook until soft. Add steak, red wine, stock, herbs, tomato purée and salt and pepper. Cover with a lid and cook in a preheated oven for 1½ to 2 hours, or until tender. Serves 4–6.

Basic beef stew

A traditional dish with classic flavours cooked on top of the stove, this will fill your home with hearty, appetite-inducing aromas. Master it, then adapt it with other flavours and ingredients that you love.

Olive oil for cooking
6 slices bacon, cut into strips
16 shallots, peeled, or 2 onions, sliced
1 kg (2 lb) diced chuck or blade steak
Seasoned flour

500 ml (1 pt) red wine
250 ml (8 fl oz) beef stock
Bouquet garni
2 garlic cloves, crushed
Salt and freshly ground black pepper

Preheat oven to 180°C (350°F).

Heat a large heavy-based casserole pot or saucepan over medium–high heat, add 1 tablespoon of oil. Add bacon and cook for 2–3 minutes, until it begins to brown. Remove with a slotted spoon and set aside. Add shallots, or onions, and more oil if needed, and cook until beginning to brown. Remove with slotted spoon and set aside with bacon.

Coat beef with seasoned flour and shake in a sieve to remove excess. Brown in batches, using more oil as needed. Tip off excess fat and return beef, bacon and shallots to pot with red wine and stock. Bring to the boil, stirring often, then reduce heat and add bouquet garni, garlic and a pinch of salt.

Cover with lid, and cook for 2 hours on minimum heat or in a preheated oven 180°C (350°F). Check to ensure beef is tender. If not, continue cooking for a further 15–20 minutes before checking again. When ready adjust seasoning if needed and serve with mashed potatoes and steamed vegetables. Serves 4.

With dumplings
Add dumplings for the last 45 minutes to 1 hour of cooking.

With mushrooms
Add 100 g (3½ oz) sliced mushrooms with shallots/onions and cook for 2–3 more minutes.

Dumplings

Make these simple dumplings and add them with abandon to your favourite beef and chicken casserole for the last hour of cooking.

80 g (2¾ oz) dried breadcrumbs
150 g (5 oz) self-raising flour
75 g (2⅔ oz) soft butter, diced
Salt and freshly ground black pepper

1 tbsp chopped parsley
1 medium egg
50 ml (1⅔ fl oz) milk

Combine breadcrumbs and flour in a bowl. Rub butter through to form a sandy texture. Add salt, pepper and parsley and stir to combine. Add egg and enough milk to bring the mixture together. Knead to form a smooth dough. Roll into 3 cm (1¼ in) balls. Add to casseroles and stews during the last hour of cooking.

Horseradish dumplings
Add 50 g (1⅔ oz) finely grated fresh horseradish (use 2 tsp creamed horseradish if you can't find fresh) with salt and pepper to add more flavour.

Mashed potato

1 kg (2 lb) Desiree potatoes, peeled
2 tbsp butter
Salt and freshly ground black pepper
2 tbsp chopped parsley, optional
2 tbsp chopped chives, optional

Place potatoes in a saucepan and cover with cold water. Add a pinch of salt and bring to the boil. Simmer until potatoes are tender, about 10–15 minutes. Drain well and return potatoes to saucepan. Mash completely then add butter, salt, pepper and chopped herbs. Keep covered until required. Serves 4.

Beef and Guinness pie

This is a luscious, rich pie whose heart-warming power will be most appreciated on a really cold winter's night.

1.5 kg (3 lb) diced skirt steak
Seasoned flour
Olive oil for cooking
500 ml (1 pt) Guinness
500 ml (1 pt) beef stock
2 garlic cloves, crushed
150 ml (5 fl oz) cold water
250 g (8 oz) shallots, peeled and cut into quarters
100 g (3½ oz) butter
1 tsp salt
300 g (10½ oz) self-raising flour
Egg wash*

Coat beef with seasoned flour and shake excess off using a sieve. Heat a large heavy-based saucepan over medium heat, add a splash of olive oil and cook beef in small batches until golden brown, adding more oil if needed. Add Guinness, stock, garlic and shallots and bring to the boil. Season lightly, reduce heat to low, cover and cook for 1½–2 hours. Check seasoning. When beef is tender it's time to prepare the pastry.

Preheat oven to 180°C (350°F).

Combine water, butter and salt in a saucepan and place over medium heat until butter melts. Remove from heat, add flour and stir to combine quickly. Tip dough onto a floured board and knead quickly until smooth. Divide dough in two. Roll out a piece to fit into a

2 litre (3¼ pint) pie dish. Grease pie dish and line with pastry. Spoon hot pie filling into dish. Roll remaining pastry and cover the pie, trim edges and brush with egg wash. Bake in preheated oven until golden brown, about 15–20 minutes. Serves 4–6.

Beef and prune tagine

The casseroles and stews of the Middle East and North Africa are generally known as tagines. They typically include dried fruit, which produces a beautiful sweetness to complement the meats, vegetables and spices.

1½ tsp sweet paprika
1½ tsp chilli powder
2 tsp ground cumin
2 tsp ground coriander
1 tsp ground white pepper
1 tsp salt

2 tbsp lemon juice
3 tbsp olive oil
1 kg diced beef, blade or skirt
750 ml (1½ pt) beef stock
250 g (8 oz) pitted prunes
Coriander leaves

Mix spices, salt, lemon juice and oil to form a smooth paste. Coat diced beef with spice mixture and leave to marinate for at least 4 hours or overnight.

Preheat oven to 180°C (350°F).

Place marinated beef in a casserole dish with a tight fitting lid, add stock and cook for 1 hour. Remove lid, add prunes and return to the oven for a further 45 minutes. Check to see if beef is nearly cooked. If so, remove lid and finish cooking for the final 30 minutes with the lid off to reduce liquid.

Sprinkle with coriander leaves and serve with pilaf, page 127–8. Serves 4–6.

Corned beef (silverside)

Corned beef is regarded as an old-fashioned type of dish, but that doesn't mean we should underestimate it as a meal. Silverside should be soaked in cold water overnight to remove excess salt before cooking.

Adding oranges, lemon, peppercorns and chopped vegetables to the poaching water dramatically boosts the final flavour.

1.3 kg (2 lb 10 oz) silverside
1 bouquet garni
1 lemon, sliced
1 orange, sliced

10 peppercorns
2 onions, sliced
2 carrots, peeled and chopped

Classic beef pie using the Basic beef stew (recipe page 196)

Tunisian lamb shanks (recipe page 202)

Place silverside in a large pot/saucepan, add cold water to cover. Bring to the boil, discard water. Again add enough cold water to cover and add remaining ingredients and bring to the boil. Reduce to a simmer, skimming the surface if required. Cover with a lid and cook for 1 hour.

Remove pot from heat and allow to stand for 10–15 minutes. Remove silverside and slice. Serve with boiled potatoes and parsley sauce. Serves 4–6.

Parsley sauce

Parsley sauce is the classic accompaniment to corned beef.

30 g (1 oz) butter
30 g (1 oz) plain flour
500 ml (1 pt) boiling milk
2–3 tbsp chopped parsley
Salt and freshly ground black pepper

Heat a small saucepan over a medium heat and melt butter. Reduce heat to low, add flour, stir to form a roux and allow to 'cook out' for 1–2 minutes. Raise heat, add milk and whisk until a smooth sauce forms. Add parsley and season to taste.

Sour and spicy beef braise

Anyone who tastes sour and spicy beef braise would swear that whoever had made it had been slaving over a hot stove for hours. Truth be known, it takes about 15–20 minutes – tops – to get it cooking.

100 g (3½ oz) tamarind*
250 ml (8 fl oz) boiling water
1 kg (2 lb) blade steak
4 small red chillies, spilt
8 red shallots, peeled and halved
2–3 kaffir lime leaves
3 cm ginger, sliced
2 lemongrass stems, sliced
250 ml (8 fl oz) beef stock
60 g (2 oz) shaved palm sugar
60 ml (2 fl oz) fish sauce
Coriander leaves to serve

Soak tamarind in boiling water for 15–20 minutes. Use fingers to separate pulp from pips, then strain the liquid and discard the seeds.

Cut steaks into about 6 cm (2 in) pieces. Place beef, tamarind liquid, chillies, shallots, lime leaves, ginger, lemongrass, stock, sugar and fish sauce into a heavy-based saucepan. Bring to the boil, reduce heat, cover with a lid and cook for 1½ hours.

Try beef to see if it's tender yet; it could require up to 2 hours' cooking. If not, return lid and continue cooking until meat is tender.

Sprinkle with coriander to serve. Serves 4.

Lamb tagine

This is one of my favourite lamb dishes. Extremely simple and impressive, this recipe can be doubled or even trebled if you are feeding lots of people. MC

2 tsp sweet paprika	1 tsp salt
1 tsp ground ginger	2 tbsp lemon juice
1 tsp chilli powder	3 tbsp olive oil
1 tsp ground cumin	1 kg (2 lb) diced lamb
1 tsp ground coriander	Juice of 1 orange
1 tsp ground white pepper	500 ml (1 pt) chicken stock
½ tsp ground cardamom	90 g (3 oz) dried apricots, diced
½ tsp ground cinnamon	90 g (3 oz) sultanas
½ tsp allspice	Fresh coriander to serve

Mix spices, salt, lemon juice and oil to form a smooth paste. Coat diced lamb with spice mixture and leave to marinate for 4 hours or overnight.

Preheat oven to 180°C (350°F). Place lamb in a heavy-based saucepan that has a well-fitting lid, add orange juice and stock. Cook for 1 hour in oven, with lid on, stirring occasionally.

Remove lid, add apricots and sultanas and return to the oven for a further 30–60 minutes, or until lamb is tender. Serve with coriander leaves and pine nut pilaf, page 128; and tzatziki, page 41. Serves 4.

Spanish lamb stew

The slow cooking of lamb with delicious Spanish ingredients is a flavour combination that is hard to beat. Australian friend and food queen Phillippa Grogan introduced us to this dish one evening and we knew it had to be included here. It's deceptively simple to make and requires virtually no effort. AC

Olive oil for cooking	400 g (14 oz) tin chopped peeled tomatoes
1 kg (2 lb) diced lamb, shoulder for preference	Salt and freshly ground black pepper
1 onion, diced	750 ml (1½ pt) chicken stock
1 garlic clove, crushed	Small handful flat-leaf parsley, roughly chopped
2 roasted red capsicums, peeled, seeded and diced 1 cm (¾ in)	1 bay leaf

Preheat oven to 180°C (350°F).

Heat a large heavy-based saucepan over medium heat, add a splash of olive oil and cook lamb in small batches until golden brown, adding more oil if needed. Set aside. Add onions and garlic to the pan and cook until they begin to soften, around 5–6 minutes, stirring occasionally.

Return lamb to the saucepan along with diced red capsicum, tomatoes, salt and pepper. Add enough stock to cover, allow to come to the boil, then add parsley and bay leaf.

Cover dish and cook in the preheated oven for 1½ to 2 hours. Add more stock if required. The lamb is ready when it's deliciously tender and flavoursome. Serve with pilaf, page 127–8. Serves 4.

Lamb hot pot

A piping-hot lamb hot pot is the perfect meal on a cold winter's night. It's an all-in-one meal with a delicious mix of diced lamb and vegetables in a light sauce, all under a crust of golden potato slices. The traditional version utilises lamb chops. If you prefer, use them in this recipe, but we choose to use diced lamb. AC

Olive oil for cooking
1 kg (2 lb) diced lamb, shoulder for preference
1 onion, diced
1 garlic clove, crushed
1 carrot, diced
2 celery sticks, diced
1 tbsp flour

750 ml (1½ pt) chicken or beef stock
400 g (14 oz) tin chopped tomatoes
1 tbsp tomato paste
1 tbsp thyme leaves
Salt and freshly ground black pepper
1 kg (2 lb) potatoes
2 tbsp melted butter

Preheat oven to 180°C (350°F).

Heat a large heavy-based frypan over medium–high heat, add a splash of olive oil and cook lamb in small batches until golden brown, adding more oil if needed. Set aside lamb in an ovenproof casserole dish.

Add extra oil to the pan if needed. Reduce heat, add onion, garlic, carrot and celery and cook for 5–6 minutes until vegetables soften, stirring often. Sprinkle flour over vegetables and stir in, then cook for 3–4 minutes. Add stock, tomatoes, tomato paste and thyme. Bring to the boil, reduce heat and simmer for 10 minutes. Season to taste. Pour sauce over lamb.

Peel potatoes and slice into rounds. Arrange the potatoes on top of the lamb. Melt the butter and brush over the layer of potato. Place the hot pot into the preheated oven, uncovered, and cook for 2½ hours. Brush the potato slices with some of the casserole juices every half hour. Serves 4.

Tunisian lamb shanks

Another variation of our lamb tagine – just a bit more up-market. I like to serve the shanks standing upright with a spoonful of sauce drizzled over, just like in a restaurant. My butcher tells me that shanks from the forelegs are better quality than rear legs and so far this has been proven true. MC

Olive oil for cooking
2 onions, diced
2 carrots, diced
1½ tsp sweet paprika
1½ tsp chilli powder
2 tsp ground cumin
2 tsp ground coriander
1 tsp ground white pepper
1 tsp salt

4–6 lamb shanks
2 tbsp lemon juice
750 ml (1¼ pt) chicken stock
60 g (2 oz) dried apricots
90 g (3 oz) sultanas
½ preserved lemon, soaked and diced (or zest of 1 lemon)
60 g (2 oz) flaked almonds
Coriander leaves

Heat a large ovenproof casserole pot or saucepan over a medium–high heat. Add oil, onions and carrots and cook for 5–6 minutes, stirring often, until softened. Add spices and salt, then cook for a further 3–4 minutes. Add shanks to the pot and cook briefly. Add lemon juice, stock, apricots and sultanas. Bring to the boil. Cover with a lid, reduce heat and cook for 2 hours.

Check to see whether lamb is tender. If not, return to oven for a further 15–20 minutes and try again. Add preserved lemon (or zest), almonds and coriander leaves and serve with couscous, page 134. Serves 4–6.

The pork dish

Cook pork long and slow with these Asian flavours and it transforms into a wondrous dish. It's called 'the pork dish' simply because no other words can describe it. Try it: you'll see what I mean. MC

1 kg (2 lb) belly pork
3 spring onions, chopped
4 cm ginger, sliced
2 tbsp soy sauce
2 tbsp Chinese cooking wine
2 tbsp fish sauce

2 star anise
1 tsp Sichuan peppercorns, crushed
1 tsp black peppercorns, crushed
2 small red chillies, spilt in half
Water

Preheat oven to 180°C (350°F).

Place pork in casserole pot with a tight-fitting lid. Add all other ingredients and enough water to just cover. Put lid on and cook in preheated oven for 2 hours.

Remove pork and cut into 2 cm (¾ in) slices. Return to casserole and cook for a further 45–60 minutes, until pork is meltingly tender.

Serve with rice and Asian greens. Serves 4–6.

Osso buco

A classic veal casserole that is delicious served with mounds of mashed potato or soft polenta to soak up all the lovely tasty juices.

1 kg (2 lb) veal osso buco
Seasoned flour
Olive oil for cooking
1 onion, diced
2 celery stalks, diced
2 carrots, finely diced
2 garlic cloves, crushed
250 ml (8 fl oz) white wine

250 ml (8 fl oz) tomato purée
350–500 ml (12 fl oz–1 pt) chicken stock
Salt and freshly ground black pepper
1 garlic clove, crushed, additional
Zest of 1 lemon, chopped
3 tbsp chopped parsley
2 anchovy fillets, chopped

Dust osso buco with flour, shaking well to remove excess. Place a large heavy-based casserole dish or saucepan over a medium heat. Add a splash of oil and brown osso buco well on both sides, in batches if necessary. Remove veal and set aside. Add more oil if required and cook onion, celery and carrots for 6–8 minutes, stirring often, until soft. Add garlic and cook for a further minute.

Return veal to pan, add white wine, bring to the boil and reduce by half. Add tomato purée and enough stock to cover veal. Season with salt and pepper. Bring to the boil, reduce to a simmer, cover with lid and cook for 1 hour. Check to see whether veal is tender. If not, cook for a further 10 minutes and try again.

Mix additional garlic, lemon zest, parsley and anchovy together. Sprinkle over veal to serve. Serves 4.

Pot-roasted veal shanks

As veal is not always available, some retailers sell beef labelled as veal. To make sure your shanks really are veal, buy them from a butcher who specialises in European cuts; and take the extra precaution of ordering a few days ahead to make sure you don't miss out.

Olive oil for cooking
4 veal shanks
2 garlic cloves, crushed
1 onion, finely diced
1 carrot, finely diced
1 small turnip, finely diced
1 small swede, finely diced
1 celery stick, finely diced

2 tbsp plain flour
250 ml (8 fl oz) red wine
1 tbsp tomato paste
Salt and freshly ground black pepper
1 bouquet garni of bay leaf, thyme and parsley
Chopped parsley

Heat a heavy-based saucepan over a medium heat, add a dash of olive oil and brown the shanks all over. Remove shanks from the pan. Add vegetables and cook until soft, stirring often, about 10 minutes. Sprinkle with flour, stir, lower heat and allow to cook for 2 minutes.

Increase heat; add wine and stir vigorously to remove any sediment from the base of the pan. Simmer for 3–4 minutes. Add tomato paste and a pinch of salt. Place the shanks back in the pan and add enough water to just cover. Add bouquet garni and bring the liquid to the boil. Remove the scum as it rises to the surface. Lower heat; cover with a lid and cook for 1½ hours. Every 15 minutes, turn the shanks to allow even cooking. When tender, check seasoning and add chopped parsley.

Serve with mashed potatoes. Serves 4.

Rabbit casserole

This is the type of dish we usually get to eat only once each winter, so we always search out some top-quality farmed rabbits. It takes a bit of work to get it cooking. But, like all good casseroles, once it's in the oven your work is done. AC

125 g (4 oz) pancetta or streaky bacon
100 ml (3½ fl oz) verjuice*, or white wine
20 shallots or small pickling onions, peeled
2 garlic cloves, peeled
2 rabbits, skinned, cleaned and jointed
Seasoned flour for dusting
Olive oil for cooking
1 carrot, finely diced
2 leeks, thinly sliced
2 celery stalks, diced

1–2 bay leaves
2–3 thyme sprigs
250 ml (8 fl oz) white wine
500 ml (1 pt) chicken stock
20 button mushrooms
90 g (3 oz) sultanas
Salt and freshly ground black pepper
90 g (3 oz) pine nuts, toasted
Chopped parsley to serve

Preheat oven to 180°C (350°F).

Heat a large heavy-based casserole dish or saucepan over a medium–high heat. Cook pancetta in dry pan until golden. Add verjuice, shallots and garlic, cook until verjuice has evaporated and shallots begin to colour. Set aside.

Dust rabbit pieces with seasoned flour. Add a splash of oil to pot and cook rabbit pieces, in batches if necessary, until golden. Remove and set aside. Add more oil if required and cook carrot, leeks and celery until soft, about 6–8 minutes.

Return rear legs and saddle pieces to the pot along with herbs, wine and stock. Cover the casserole and cook in preheated oven for 40 minutes. Remove casserole from the oven and add the pre-prepared verjuice, shallots and garlic mixture, along with the mushrooms, sultanas and remaining rabbit pieces. Season to taste, cover and return to the oven for a further 30 minutes.

Check to see whether rabbit is tender. If not, cook for a further 10 minutes and check again. Check seasoning, add pine nuts and parsley and serve. Serves 6.

Aromatic vegetable tagine ⓥ

You can add just about any vegetable you like to this dish: capsicum, eggplant, pumpkin, okra, cauliflower or even mushrooms, just to name a few.

Olive oil for cooking
1 onion, diced
1½ tsp sweet paprika
1½ tsp chilli powder
2 tsp ground cumin
2 tsp ground coriander
1 tsp ground white pepper
2 carrots, cut into 3 cm (1 in) chunks

8 small potatoes, peeled and cut in half
2 parsnips, cut into quarters
1 sweet potato, cut into 3 cm (1 in) chunks
2 tbsp lemon juice
750 ml (1¼ pt) vegetable stock
Salt
2 zucchini, cut into quarters
Coriander leaves

Preheat oven to 180°C (350°F).

Heat a large heavy-based saucepan or ovenproof casserole pot over a medium–high heat. Add oil, onions and spices and cook for 5–6 minutes, stirring often, until softened. Add carrots, potatoes, parsnips and sweet potato. Cook for a further 3–4 minutes, stirring often. Add lemon juice, stock, season with salt. Bring to the boil.

Cover with a lid, reduce heat and cook (or, better still, cook in preheated oven 180°C (350°F)) for 45 minutes. Check to see whether vegetables are tender. Add zucchini; cook for a further 5 minutes, check seasoning and serve with coriander leaves. Serves 4–6.

Green salad
Greek salad
Tomato and white bean salad
Potato salad
Mayonnaise
Middle-Eastern carrot salad
Watercress tabouleh
Green bean, almond and feta salad
Asian coleslaw
Asian noodle salad
Mirin dressing
Simple bok choy salad
Barbecued vegetable salad
Moroccan couscous salad
Yoghurt dressing
Tomato and roast capsicum salad
Beetroot salad
Salad of fennel, walnuts and parmigiano
Blood orange and fennel salad
Beetroot fattouche
Caesar salad
Tuna Niçoise à la our house
Anchovy dressing
Thai chicken salad
Vietnamese beef noodle salad
Spice-crusted quail salad with pomegranate dressing
Moroccan chicken salad
Moroccan mussel and fennel salad

Salads

SIDE SALADS, LUNCH DISHES AND SMALL COURSES

Salads play a pretty large part in our meals, particularly in the warmer months. They can be an unassuming side dish that follows the main course or wondrous creations that are meals in their own right.

The simplest salads are just good, fresh leaves, in which case all you need to do is toss them in a bowl with vinegar and extra virgin olive oil and they're ready to go. But of course salads go well beyond tossing leaves together. They can contain raw or cooked vegetables, olives, feta and other firm cheeses, and even meats.

We enjoy numerous main course salads such as Niçoise, Thai noodle and Caesar. And others, we find ideal as entrées, offering a perfect blend of good flavours but not being too filling; these include Moroccan mussel and fennel salad; our fennel, walnut, onion and parmigiano salad; and the blood orange and fennel salad.

We even grow a few different lettuce types at home, including rocket, so we can enjoy a just-picked salad experience right through summer. Maybe you could find a sunny patch to plant a few yourself.

THINGS YOU NEED TO KNOW ABOUT SALADS

- All lettuces must be washed. Some lettuces, such as spinach and frisee, usually need two attempts to remove all grit.
- Lettuce must be dried well. This keeps it crunchy and ensures that the dressing will coat it.
- A salad spinner is an essential tool to make sure your lettuce leaves are perfectly dry.
- The only other utensils you'll need are a large bowl for salads that will be tossed and a couple of good platters and bowls for serving.
- Most salad dressings are a ratio of 3 parts oil to one part vinegar (acid).
- Add your seasoning to the acid, vinegar or juice to dissolve it. You cannot successfully season dressing once the oil is added.
- We usually make a small batch of dressing in a jar and keep it in the cupboard. Then all we have to do is shake and drizzle.
- Different flavoured vinegars will add variation to your salads; we generally alternate between red wine, sherry and balsamic vinegar.
- Likewise, your oil will make a difference; this is where a good quality extra virgin oil shines. We usually have a fruity extra virgin olive oil and a peppery extra virgin olive oil that we vary to suit the salad.
- We also use mustard oil, walnut or almond oil, and peanut oil for Asian-influenced salads.
- Some of our recipes have a separate dressing while in others the dressing is a part of the salad itself.
- To get slivers or shavings of vegetables, use a vegetable peeler. The long thin strips are much easier to eat in salads than chunky diced or sliced vegetables.
- Roasted and barbecued vegetables are also excellent in salads as they bring in a variety of different flavours and textures that you can't get from raw ingredients.
- We like to soak raw onion slices in hot tap water to remove the worst of the onion's powerful taste. Don't to let onion soak too long or it will lose its crispiness.

Green salad

Green salad doesn't mean all the leaves have to be green. You could just as easily add some bitter radicchio leaves for a striking contrast in both taste and colour.

250 g (8 oz) salad leaves, washed
1 Lebanese cucumber, peeled and thinly sliced
1 tbsp red wine vinegar

½ tsp Dijon mustard
Salt and freshly ground black pepper
3 tbsp extra virgin olive oil

Toss salad leaves and cucumber together.
    Mix together vinegar, mustard, salt and pepper. Add oil and whisk well. Toss dressing through salad. Serves 6.

Greek salad

Greek salad is known around the world as a simple yet satisfying combination of cucumber, feta cheese, tomatoes, lettuce and olives with a lemon dressing. It makes regular appearances on our table throughout summer.

1 Lebanese cucumber
½ red capsicum
200 g (7 oz) feta
3 ripe tomatoes
½ red onion, thinly sliced
1 cos lettuce, washed

90 g (3 oz) kalamata olives
2 tbsp chopped parsley
1½ tbsp lemon juice
Salt and freshly ground black pepper
3 tbsp extra virgin olive oil

Peel cucumber and remove seeds. Slice thinly. Dice capsicum and feta into 1 cm (½ in) squares. Cut tomatoes into wedges.
    Mix cucumber, capsicum, feta and tomatoes, onion, lettuce, olives and parsley in a bowl.
    Whisk lemon juice, salt and pepper together. Add oil and whisk well. Toss dressing through salad. Serves 6.

Tomato and white bean salad

This simple salad is a refreshing mix of ripe tomatoes, crisp cucumbers and tender white beans.

100 g (3½ oz) white beans (cannellini), soaked overnight
3 ripe tomatoes, diced
2 Lebanese cucumbers, diced
2 spring onions, thinly sliced

1 tbsp chopped mint leaves
2 tbsp lemon juice
2 tbsp extra virgin olive oil
Salt and freshly ground black pepper

Drain soaked beans and rinse under cold running water. Cook in boiling water under tender, about 30 minutes. Drain and cool.

    Mix beans with other salad ingredients and season to taste. Serves 6.

Potato salad

Potato salad is an essential summer experience. In fact, we often serve it in the cooler months, too, with pan-fried sausages or frikadella, page 180.

1.5 kg (3 lb) waxy potatoes, washed (peeled if preferred)
3 tsp salted capers, soaked, rinsed and drained

10 cornichons*, chopped
3 tbsp chopped flat-leaf parsley

Boil potatoes until just cooked. Drain and allow to cool. Cut into 1 cm (½ in) slices, or dice if preferred. Arrange on a platter.

    Chop capers and scatter over potatoes with cornichons and parsley. Drizzle mayonnaise over potato slices. Grind fresh black pepper over to serve. Serves 6.

Mayonnaise

If you're going to make your own salads you might as well make your own mayonnaise too. This can easily be done in a mixer, in a food processor, or by hand if you prefer. In fact making mayonnaise by hand with a simple bowl and a whisk doesn't take as long as you might imagine.

2 egg yolks
Salt and freshly ground black pepper
½ tsp Dijon mustard

100 ml (3½ fl oz) extra virgin olive oil
1 tbsp lemon juice

Combine egg yolks, salt, pepper and mustard together. Beat until white and creamy. Slowly add oil, whisking each addition. Finish with lemon juice. Keeps refrigerated for 2 weeks.

Middle-Eastern carrot salad

Carrots prepared in this way are good as part of a Middle-Eastern mezze plate or as a side dish to dinner. Their inherent sweetness seems to make them a natural match with the spices and lemon juice.

4 carrots
Olive oil for cooking
2 tsp cumin seeds

1 tsp sweet paprika
Juice of ½ lemon, to serve

Preheat oven to 180°C (350°F).

Peel carrots and cut into slices. Heat a heavy-based frying pan over medium heat. Add enough oil to cover base of pan, add cumin seeds and carrot slices. Cook until golden and the carrots are beginning to become tender. Sprinkle in the sweet paprika, then cook in preheated oven until tender, about 10–15 minutes.

Squeeze lemon juice over to serve. Serves 4.

Watercress tabouleh

Tabouleh really gets a lift by using watercress instead of parsley. We often serve this salad with Moroccan turkey at Christmas lunch and on any other salad-friendly days.

150 g (5 oz) burghul
1 bunch watercress, picked and washed
½ red onion, finely diced
500 g (1 lb) firm ripe tomatoes, diced

2 tbsp lemon juice
3 tbsp extra virgin olive oil
Salt and freshly ground black pepper

Soak burghul in cold water for 20 minutes, drain well. Chop watercress roughly. Place burghul, watercress, onion and tomatoes in a bowl. Mix well. Add lemon juice and olive oil. Season to taste with salt and pepper. Serves 6.

Rocket
Swap watercress for 100 g (3½ oz) washed and chopped rocket.

Green bean, almond and feta salad

This salad has become a modern classic for many people. It was introduced to us by our friend Sue Sloan, to whom we are eternally grateful.

500 g (1 lb) green beans, ends trimmed
100 g (3½ oz) flaked almonds, toasted
100 g (3½ oz) feta, crumbled
2 tbsp chopped parsley leaves

1 tbsp red wine vinegar
Salt and freshly ground black pepper
3 tbsp extra virgin olive oil

Cook beans in boiling water for 2 minutes. Refresh under cold water immediately. Cut beans in half and place on a platter.

Top with toasted almonds, feta and parsley. Whisk vinegar, salt and pepper together. Add oil and whisk well. Drizzle dressing over salad. Serves 6.

Asparagus
Substitute green beans for asparagus spears.

Asian coleslaw

This salad is good if you're having a large group over. It is excellent just as it is, or you can top it with roast beef, roast duck or barbecue chicken pieces.

½ wonga bok (Chinese cabbage), sliced
2 carrots, shredded
6 spring onions, thinly sliced
½ cup coriander leaves
1 tbsp shaved palm sugar

2 tbsp fish sauce
3 tbsp lime juice
Freshly ground black pepper
3 tbsp peanut oil

Toss wonga bok, carrot, spring onions and coriander together. Dissolve palm sugar in fish sauce and lime juice. Add pepper and whisk in oil. Toss vegetables with dressing and pile onto a platter. Serves 6.

Asian noodle salad

A salad such as this is virtually a dish in its own right thanks to the delicious soba noodles that form its base.

125 g (4 oz) soba noodles
100 g (3½ oz) snow peas
½ red capsicum, finely diced
1 carrot, shredded

2 Lebanese cucumbers, thinly sliced
4 red shallots, thinly sliced
20 Vietnamese leaves, shredded

Cook soba noodles in plenty of boiling water for 6–8 minutes. Refresh under cold water. Cook snow peas in boiling water for 2 minutes. Refresh under cold water and slice thinly.

Toss all ingredients together. To serve, mix salad with mirin dressing and pile onto a large platter. Serves 6.

Mirin dressing

1 tbsp shaved palm sugar
2 tbsp lime juice
1 tbsp fish sauce
2 tbsp mirin*
Freshly ground black pepper
2 tbsp chopped coriander leaves
3 tbsp peanut oil

Dissolve palm sugar in lime juice, fish sauce and mirin. Add pepper, coriander and oil. Whisk together well.

Simple bok choy salad

A salad such as this is excellent with meats from the barbecue or as part of any good feast with food-loving friends.

150 g (5 oz) baby bok choy, washed
½ cup coriander leaves
½ red capsicum, thinly sliced
6 spring onions, thinly sliced
4 red shallots, thinly sliced
2 tbsp lime juice
½ tsp soy sauce
Salt and freshly ground black pepper
3 tbsp peanut oil

Toss bok choy, coriander, capsicum, spring onions and shallots together. Place in a serving bowl.

Whisk lime juice, soy sauce, salt, pepper and oil together. Pour dressing over salad. Serves 6.

Spinach salad
Substitute bok choy for 125 g (4 oz) baby spinach leaves.

Barbecued vegetable salad

This salad is a beauty because it shows once and for all that the barbecue can do much more than just cook steaks and chops.

1 eggplant, cut into 8 wedges, salted and rinsed
2 small zucchini, cut into quarters
1 red capsicum, cut in 6 wedges, seeds removed
100 g (3½ oz) small mushrooms
3 tbsp olive oil
1 tbsp sherry vinegar
Salt and freshly ground black pepper
3 tbsp olive oil, additional
1 tbsp sherry vinegar, additional
20 basil leaves, thinly sliced

Toss all vegetables with oil, vinegar, salt and pepper. Place vegetables on oiled barbecue grill. Cook for 20–30 minutes. Turn regularly and brush with more oil if needed

Place vegetables on a platter. Drizzle with additional oil and vinegar. Sprinkle basil on top. Serves 6–8.

Moroccan couscous salad

This recipe involves a quite a few different steps but it's well worth the effort.

2 tbsp extra virgin olive oil
200 g (7 oz) instant couscous
200 ml (8 fl oz) water
Pinch of salt
100 g (3½ oz) chickpeas, soaked and cooked
200 g (7 oz) pumpkin, diced 5mm (¼ in) and roasted
½ red capsicum, diced into 5mm (¼ in) chunks
90 g (3 oz) toasted pine nuts
½ cup chopped coriander leaves
Salt and freshly ground black pepper

Heat oil in a saucepan. Add couscous; stir to coat with oil. Add water and salt and bring to the boil. Remove from the heat, cover and leave to soak for 5 minutes.

Use a fork to break up the grains, then tip the couscous into a bowl and allow to cool.

Mix couscous with remaining ingredients. Season to taste. Drizzle yoghurt dressing over the top. Serves 6.

Yoghurt dressing

150 g (5 oz) natural yoghurt
2 tsp chopped fresh mint
Freshly ground black pepper
2 tbsp lemon juice

Whisk all ingredients together.

Tomato and roast capsicum salad

The flavours of the sun are evident in every bite of this delicious salad.

1 red capsicum
2 tbsp olive oil
4 sun-ripened tomatoes
Fresh basil leaves, torn
Salt and freshly ground black pepper
1 tbsp sherry vinegar
3 tbsp olive oil, additional

Preheat oven to 200°C (390°F).

Rub capsicum all over with olive oil and place in a baking tray. Cook for 20–30 minutes, turning occasionally until blistered. Place capsicum in a plastic bag and seal. The steam created will lift the skins away from the flesh. Allow to cool, then remove all skin and seeds

Thai chicken salad (recipe page 218)

Barbecued vegetable salad (recipe page 213)

Salad of fennel, walnuts and parmigiano (recipe page 215)

and slice into thin strips.

Cut eyes from tomatoes. Cut in half, then into thin wedges. Mix tomato with capsicum, basil leaves, salt, freshly ground pepper, vinegar and oil. Allow to stand for at least 30 minutes at room temperature, then serve. Serves 4.

Beetroot salad

It's rare that we're without beetroot in our kitchen as it is so easy to prepare. Try this salad to find out for yourself.

1 bunch baby beetroots, or 3 large
1 tbsp red wine vinegar
Salt and freshly ground black pepper

2 tbsp mustard seed oil
1 tbsp chopped chives

Remove and discard leaves from beetroots. Place beetroot in a saucepan and cover with water. Bring to the boil, reduce to a simmer and cook until tender, about 30 minutes. Drain and allow to cool. When cool remove skins, cut flesh into evenly sized wedges and place in a bowl.

Whisk together vinegar, salt and pepper and oil. Pour over beetroots and top with chopped chives. Serves 4.

With tomato and mozzarella
Add 2 tomatoes, cut into wedges, torn basil leaves and slices of fresh mozzarella – buffalo mozzarella if you can get it.

Salad of fennel, walnuts and parmigiano

This is the type of salad that needs no accompaniment; it's simply perfect in its own right. We would serve a salad like this as its own course, after mains but before cheese, on a big dinner party night.

1 red onion, sliced
1 fennel bulb
90 g (3 oz) walnuts, toasted
60 g (2 oz) shaved parmigiano
A handful each of radicchio leaves and
   baby spinach leaves

1 tbsp sherry vinegar
Salt and freshly ground black pepper
3 tbsp extra virgin olive oil

Pour hot tap water onto onion and allow to stand for 2 minutes before draining.

Remove tough outer skin layer of fennel. Cut in half, remove core and slice fennel thinly. Roughly chop walnuts and toss with onion, fennel, parmigiano and salad leaves.

Whisk vinegar and salt and pepper together. Whisk in oil. Dress salad when ready to serve. Serves 4.

Blood orange and fennel salad

The amazing tang of blood oranges and the freshness of fennel are a winning combination in this brilliant salad.

1 red onion, sliced
2 fennel bulbs
4 blood oranges
90 g (3 oz) baby spinach leaves, washed
90 g (3 oz) kalamata olives

Generous handful of flat-leaf parsley
1 tbsp sherry vinegar
Salt and freshly ground black pepper
3 tbsp olive oil

Pour hot tap water onto onion and allow to stand for 2 minutes before draining. Place in a large bowl. Remove tough outer layer from fennel bulbs. Cut in half, remove core and slice fennel thinly. Add this to the onions.

Using a sharp knife remove all the peel and pith from oranges. Then remove the segments from the membrane, so that each segment is free from any pith or seeds. Squeeze any excess juice from orange membrane into a bowl and set aside for the dressing. Add blood orange segments to the fennel, along with the spinach leaves, olives and parsley.

Add the salt and pepper to blood orange juice and whisk together. Add oil. Drizzle dressing over salad and toss together gently. Serves 4.

Beetroot fattouche

You may well have noticed our obsession with beetroot, but feel free to make this salad with other vegetables such as tomato, asparagus, green beans or artichokes.

1 bunch baby beetroots, or 3 large
1 red onion, sliced
1 tsp sumac*
125 g (4 oz) pide bread, or foccacia
Extra virgin olive oil for cooking
1 baby cos, washed

1 Lebanese cucumber, halved and sliced
Generous handful of flat-leaf parsley leaves
2 tbsp lemon juice
Salt and freshly ground black pepper
3 tbsp olive oil

Remove and discard leaves from beetroots. Place in a saucepan and cover with water. Bring to the boil, reduce to a simmer and cook until tender, about 30 minutes. Drain and allow to cool. When cool remove skins, cut flesh into evenly sized wedges and place in a bowl.

Pour hot tap water onto onion and allow to stand for 2 minutes before draining. When cool toss onion slices with sumac.

Dice pide bread into 1 cm (⅓ in) chunks. Heat a heavy-based pan over a medium heat, then add a generous splash of olive oil and the bread chunks. Stir until bread becomes quite toasty, about 6–8 minutes. Mix beetroot with onion, bread chunks, lettuce, cucumber and parsley. Whisk lemon juice, salt and pepper together, then whisk in oil. Dress salad when ready to serve. Serves 4.

Caesar salad

There are many hundreds of ways to prepare this famous salad. This is how we do it. The dressing will make enough for 2 salads and will keep for 2 weeks in the refrigerator.

3 medium eggs
2 anchovies, optional
2 tsp Dijon mustard
2 tbsp red wine vinegar
Salt and freshly ground black pepper
125 ml (4 fl oz) olive oil
4 slices bacon

125 g (4 oz) day-old bread, diced 1 cm (½ in)
Oil for cooking
1 cos lettuce
90 g (3 oz) shaved parmigiano
1 tbsp chopped parsley

Place eggs in a small saucepan, bring to the boil and cook for 3 minutes. Refresh under cold water. When cool, peel shells and place soft-boiled eggs in food processor. Add anchovies if using, mustard, vinegar, salt and pepper. Whiz until creamy. Drizzle in oil until all incorporated. If too thick add 1–2 tbsp boiling water.

Cut bacon into chunks. Heat a frypan over a medium–high heat and cook until crispy. Remove from pan and set aside. Return pan to heat, add a generous splash of oil and cook bread until golden brown.

Wash lettuce and tear leaves into bite-sized pieces. Combine lettuce, bacon, croutons and half of the cheese in a bowl. Pour over just enough dressing to coat each piece. Toss to combine and serve with remaining cheese and parsley on top. Serves 4.

Tuna Niçoise à la our house

When we have had one of those days and it's all too much, we put the children to bed early and make a massive bowl of tuna Niçoise, open a bottle of wine and relax. Somehow the worries of the day seem to slip away as we talk, eat and drink together.

1 baby cos, washed and torn into bite-sized pieces
4 potatoes, diced and boiled
500 g (1 lb) green beans, blanched
2 tomatoes, cut into wedges

4 boiled eggs, cut into wedges
100 g (3½ oz) kalamata olives
300 g (10 oz) tinned tuna (in oil)
Chopped parsley to garnish

In a large platter put down first a layer of lettuce, then a second layer comprising potatoes, beans, tomato, egg and olives. Drain tuna and scatter it over the other ingredients. Drizzle the anchovy dressing over and serve with crusty bread and the aforementioned bottle of wine.

Serves 4 (or us 2).

Anchovy dressing

6 anchovy fillets, finely chopped
1 garlic clove, crushed
1 tbsp lemon juice
3 tbsp olive oil
Freshly ground black pepper

Prepare dressing by whisking all ingredients together.

Fresh tuna Niçoise
Grill 4 × 200 g (7 oz) tuna steaks and serve them on top of the salad in place of the tinned tuna.

Salmon Niçoise
Grill 4 × 200 g (7 oz) salmon steaks and serve then on top of the salad in place of the tinned tuna.

Thai chicken salad

This is another firm Campion–Curtis favourite, particularly when matched with a glass of lightly chilled riesling on a hot summer's night.

2 chicken breast fillets, skin removed
250 ml (8 fl oz) coconut milk
1 lemongrass stem, thinly sliced
2 small red chillies, halved
1 iceberg lettuce, washed and broken into bite-sized pieces
1 cucumber, skinned, halved and sliced
Handful of bean sprouts
6 shallots, sliced
1 cup coriander sprigs
150 g (5 oz) roasted peanuts
1 tbsp shaved palm sugar
2 tbsp lime juice
1 tbsp fish sauce
1 small red chilli, de-seeded and diced
Freshly ground black pepper
3 tbsp olive oil

Place chicken in a small saucepan and cover with coconut milk. Add lemongrass and chillies. Bring to the boil, lower heat and cook, covered, for 5 minutes. Turn chicken over and cook for a further 5 minutes. Check that chicken is cooked through. Allow to cool completely in coconut milk, then drain and slice thinly. Discard cooking liquid.

Combine lettuce, cucumber, bean sprouts, shallots, coriander, peanuts and cooked sliced chicken.

Prepare salad dressing by dissolving palm sugar in lime juice. Then stir in fish sauce, chilli and black pepper and whisk in olive oil. Toss dressing through salad and arrange on a large platter. Serves 4.

Coconut chicken and noodle salad
Combine cooked chicken with Asian noodle salad, page 212, instead of as described.

Thai prawn salad
Substitute 500 g (1 lb) cooked peeled prawns for chicken.

Vietnamese beef noodle salad

Lots of zingy flavours and great textures make this dish ideal for a light lunch or entrée.

500 g (1 lb) beef – girello or scotch fillet
2 tbsp fish sauce
1 tbsp peanut oil
200 g (7 oz) rice vermicelli noodles
60 ml (2 fl oz) lime juice
1 tbsp chilli paste
2 tbsp fish sauce, additional
1 tbsp shaved palm sugar
12 Vietnamese mint leaves, shredded
Freshly ground black pepper
3 tbsp peanut oil, additional
100 g (3½ oz) snow peas, blanched and thinly sliced
½ red capsicum, thinly sliced
100 g (3½ oz) shiitake mushrooms, finely diced
90 g (3 oz) cashew nuts, toasted
90 g (3 oz) bean sprouts
60 g (2 oz) crispy fried shallots*

Preheat oven to 190°C (375°F).

Rub beef all over with fish sauce and peanut oil and marinate for 30 minutes. Heat a heavy-based pan over a high heat. Add beef and brown all over. Place on a baking tray and cook in oven for 30 minutes or until medium-rare. Remove and leave to cool.

Put the kettle on to boil. Pour boiling water over noodles. Allow to stand for at least 5 minutes, then drain.

Mix together lime juice, chilli paste, additional fish sauce, palm sugar, mint and pepper. Whisk in additional peanut oil. Thinly slice beef, then shred thinly. Place beef into a bowl with any cooking juices and the dressing. Stir until beef is coated and allow to marinate for 30 minutes.

Toss noodles with snow peas, red capsicum, mushrooms, cashew nuts and bean sprouts. Pile high on a platter, spoon the beef and dressing on top and scatter crispy fried shallots over. Serves 4–6.

Spice-crusted quail salad with pomegranate dressing

We cook with quail quite a lot and our favourite ways of serving it typically include spices and other bold flavours. If fresh pomegranates are in-season, add a scattering of the jewel-like seeds over the salad.

4 quails, about 160 g (5½ oz) each, spatchcocked
1 tbsp ground coriander
1 tbsp ground cumin
1 tbsp sweet paprika
Salt and freshly ground black pepper
90 g (3 oz) butter lettuce, washed
60 g (2 oz) frisée leaves, washed
2 roma tomatoes, sliced into wedges
½ red capsicum, finely diced
Olive oil
3 tsp pomegranate syrup*
Large pinch of caster sugar
60 g (2 oz) pine nuts, toasted

Prepare the quail by placing the bird breast side up on a chopping board. Insert knife into cavity and cut down through breast bone with a sharp knife. Press on top of bird to flatten. Turn bird skin side down and trim away bones as desired. Mix together the coriander, cumin, paprika, salt and pepper. Sprinkle spice mix over quails. Leave to marinate for 1 hour.

Divide butter leaves between four plates and top with frisee, tomato wedges and red capsicum.

Heat a heavy-based pan over a medium–high heat. Add a splash of oil. Cook quails for 4–5 minutes on each side. Remove and rest, covered, in a warm place for 5 minutes.

Whisk together pomegranate syrup, sugar and 3 tablespoons of olive oil. Cut quails in half, arrange on top of salad, scatter with toasted pine nuts and drizzle with pomegranate dressing. Serves 4.

Moroccan chicken salad

We love to combine spicy flavours with meat such as chicken, then serve it atop masses of salad ingredients and chickpeas.

90 g (3 oz) plain flour
3 tsp ground cumin
3 tsp ground coriander
2 tsp chilli powder
1 tsp turmeric
Salt and freshly ground black pepper
Olive oil for cooking
4 skinless chicken breast fillets
250 g (8 oz) salad leaves, washed

Handful of coriander leaves
90 g (3 oz) chickpeas, soaked and cooked
1 Lebanese cucumber, peeled and thinly sliced
1 avocado, peeled and sliced
1 tbsp sherry vinegar
Salt and freshly ground black pepper
3 tbsp olive oil

Preheat oven to 180°C (350°F).

Mix together flour and spices. Lightly coat chicken fillets with spice mixture. Heat a heavy-based frying pan over a medium heat. Add a splash of oil and the chicken. Cook for 2–3 minutes on each side until well browned. Place on tray and cook in preheated oven for 5–6 minutes, or until cooked. Set aside.

Mix together salad leaves, coriander, chickpeas, cucumber and avocado. Whisk vinegar, salt and pepper together, then slowly whisk in oil. Toss dressing with salad and divide between four plates.

Cut chicken into thick wedges and serve on top of salad. Serves 6.

Moroccan mussel and fennel salad

This is perfect entrée food. Light but full of interesting textures and flavours.

1 kg (2 lb) mussels, shells scrubbed and beards removed
Water for cooking
1 red onion, sliced
1 tsp sumac*
½ tsp allspice
1 fennel bulb
2 tbsp lemon juice
1 garlic clove, crushed
Generous handful of flat-leaf parsley leaves
Salt and freshly ground black pepper
3 tbsp extra virgin olive oil
90 g (3 oz) rocket

Heat wok over high heat, add about 2 cm (¾ in) water and bring to the boil. Toss in mussels. Cover with a lid and leave to steam for 3–4 minutes. Remove lid, shake pan well and remove cooked mussels as they open. Discard any that do not open. Remove cooked mussels from shells and place in a small bowl.

Pour hot tap water onto onion and allow to stand for 2 minutes. Drain, then toss onion slices with sumac and allspice. Remove tough outer layer from fennel bulbs. Cut in half, remove core and slice fennel thinly (a mandolin is perfect for this if you have one).

Whisk lemon juice, garlic, chopped parsley, salt and pepper together, then whisk in oil.

Combine onion, fennel, rocket and parsley leaves and toss with salad dressing. Divide salad between six plates, or one large platter. Surround salad with mussels and serve. Serves 6.

Soda bread
Bread rolls
A great crusty loaf
Fruit bread
Polenta bread
Foccacia
Naan bread
Pizza dough
Pissaladière
Roasted vegetable calzone
Simple brioche
Sticky currant buns
Sugar syrup
Chelsea buns
Sticky cinnamon buns
Doughnuts

Bread, pizza, and sweet doughs

YEAST GOODS COVERING ALL TASTES

The world of bread, pizza and sweet doughs offers a huge range of wonderful things to eat. It's also an area of cooking that's quick and easy to learn if you consider the following two points:
- The base of virtually every recipe uses the same ingredients; namely flour, salt, water and yeast.
- Once you've mastered the method of making the simplest bread dough, then you'll know how to make everything else, as the method changes only slightly.

Most of the recipes here are for fairly rustic breads – the type that we make at home – and are quite easy to execute. What you won't find here are recipes of sourdough bread (which can take a day or two to make), tricky French baguettes and intricate croissants.

Our recipes don't necessarily follow traditional methods; rather they are recipes that are perfect for the home kitchen. Bread makers are a recent introduction to the kitchen and many people swear by them. We're not convinced that they are that easy, or that the bread is all that good. Many of them seem to require specially purchased ingredients and the ones we've tried all produce a square loaf with a hole in one end where it was cooked. If we could teach everyone how easy to it is to make a simple loaf of bread they would soon find their bread machine was unnecessary. However, if you love your bread maker and it stops you buying fluffy white square loaves from the supermarket, don't let us stop you.

THINGS YOU NEED TO KNOW ABOUT BREAD, PIZZA AND SWEET DOUGHS

- Yeast is available in two main forms: fresh and dried. Fresh is perfect if you do baking on a daily basis; sachets of dried yeast are better for infrequent use as these keep for many months in the cupboard.
- Yeast is usually mixed with a little warm water and a pinch of sugar in order to bring it to life.
- 7 g of dried yeast is equal to one sachet. If using fresh yeast, double quantities.
- Use plain unbleached flour, unless otherwise stated. If you have a supply of baker's or strong flour, use that in preference.
- Kneading dough is an essential part of making any yeast product. To knead, sprinkle a little plain flour onto a smooth surface. Place the dough in front of you and grab the far edge of the dough with your fingertips and bring it in to the centre. Then press it down with the heel of your hand. Repeat this until the dough takes on a smooth, almost silky feel. This can be anywhere from 5 to10 minutes. This is wonderful therapy for getting any grievances out of the way. It's also much better for everyone in the house if you take your bad thoughts out on the dough rather than them.
- Kneading can be done in a large mixer by using a dough hook attachment, if you have one, and running on the lowest speed.
- All doughs need a warm place in which to rise, which is not that easy on a cool day. Here are a few tricks to try:
  - Place the covered dough on top of a warm heater
  - Float the covered dough in a sink of warm water
  - Keep the covered dough on top of the stove with the oven on below
  - Warm the oven for 5 minutes then turn it off and use this as a warm place for your dough to rise
  - On hot days you can set your dough to prove in a sunny spot in the garden.
- Flat baking trays are best for baking bread and pizza. If you're really enthusiastic you can also purchase a ceramic or terracotta tray. These hold the heat well and will create nice crusty bottoms on your baked goods.

- A light brushing of butter or olive oil is enough to stop bread and pizza sticking to trays. We often add a light sprinkle of fine polenta or semolina too, a little of which sticks to the finished bread, adding a nice texture and crunch. Baking paper can also be used if you don't want to deal with greasing trays; this will leave your baking tray much cleaner.
- Scrolls, scones and loaves of bread can also be made in cake tins, log tins and even large muffin tins. Never feel you need to spend a lot of money on special baking trays or other accessories.
- The breads and sweet doughs you make at home don't keep as well as shop-bought products, which is all the more reason for eating them as soon as they come from the oven.

Soda bread

Soda bread is perfect for those who want a quick and easy loaf. This old-fashioned Irish recipe uses bicarbonate of soda and baking powder for rising and the dough is simply stirred together, shaped and baked until golden.

I have been eating this bread all my life, as it's what my mother whips up at the drop of a hat. It's excellent served warm with butter and jam. AC

375 g (13 oz) wholemeal self-raising flour
375 g (13 oz) self-raising flour
2 tsp baking powder
1 tsp bicarbonate of soda

1 tsp salt
500 ml (1 pt) buttermilk, or milk soured with lemon juice
Additional buttermilk for brushing

Preheat oven to 210°C (410°F).

Sift together the flours, baking powder, baking soda and salt. Stir in buttermilk and mix until combined to a firm dough. Shape the dough into a round about 4 cm (1½ in) high on a lined baking tray. Slash a deep cross into the top of the bread, then brush it with additional buttermilk.

Bake in preheated oven for 20 minutes. Remove from oven and brush with additional buttermilk. Reduce oven to 180°C (350°F) and cook bread for a further 40 minutes. A perfectly cooked loaf will sound hollow when tapped on the bottom. Wrap in a dry tea towel as it cools; this will help keep moisture in. Makes 1 loaf.

Fruity soda bread
Add 250 g (8 oz) of dried fruit to the dough; try a mix of raisins, apricots, currants and sultanas. ½ tsp of cinnamon, mixed spice or nutmeg goes well with the fruit.

Bread rolls

This bread roll recipe is so easy that absolutely everybody should try it. Have a go today.

1 sachet (7 g) dried yeast
1 tsp sugar
100 ml (3½ fl oz) warm water
450 g (15 oz) unbleached plain flour

60 g (2 oz) soft butter
1 tsp salt
175 ml (6 fl oz) water, additional
Egg wash*

Mix dried yeast with sugar and warm water. Leave in a warm place until mixture bubbles. In a large bowl rub the butter into the flour and salt. Add yeast and additional water. Mix together well, then place onto a floured surface.

Knead until smooth and no longer sticky, around 6–8 minutes. Place dough in a large bowl and cover with cling film. Prove in a warm place until dough doubles in size, 1–2 hours.

Preheat oven to 200°C (390°F).

Take proved dough and knead for 1–2 minutes. Divide dough into 12 evenly sized pieces. Shape into balls and place on greased baking tray. Cover with a cloth and leave to prove in a warm place for 20 minutes.

Brush rolls with egg wash and bake in preheated oven for 10–12 minutes, or until golden brown. Makes 12 rolls.

Sesame seed rolls
When rolls are proved, brush with egg wash* and sprinkle with sesame seeds, then bake as described.

Poppyseed rolls
When rolls are proved, brush with egg wash and sprinkle with poppyseeds, then bake as described.

Knot rolls
Take divided dough and roll each piece into a long snake-like shape about 15 cm (6 in) in length. Tie each piece into a knot, then prove and bake as directed.

A great crusty loaf

We find that this loaf is best on the day it is made, after which we usually slice it and use it for toast.

500 g (1 lb) unbleached flour
2 tsp salt
60 g (2 oz) soft butter

1 sachet (7g) dried yeast
250–300 ml (8–10 fl oz) warm water
Egg wash*

Sift flour and salt into a large bowl. Rub in butter. Add yeast and mix briefly. Add water – 250 ml (8 fl oz) should do it, but you may need more. Mix with a wooden spoon until mixture comes together. Tip onto a floured surface.

Knead until smooth and no longer sticky, around 6–8 minutes. Place dough in a large bowl and cover with cling film. Prove in a warm place until dough doubles in size, 1–2 hours.

Preheat oven to 200°C (390°F).

Take proved dough and knead for 1–2 minutes. Make into a loaf shape and either place on a greased and lined baking tray, or into a greased and lined loaf tin 23.5 × 13.5 × 7 cm (9 × 5 × 2½ in). Cover loosely with a tea towel and set aside to prove in a warm place for 30 minutes. Brush top with egg wash and slash the top 3–4 times with a small knife.

Bake in preheated oven for 25–30 minutes, or until well risen and golden brown and base sounds hollow when tapped. Makes 1 loaf.

Fruit bread

Everyone seems to love fruit bread, our family included. This loaf is excellent served warm from the oven with a decent smear of butter on top.

125 g (4 oz) dried apricots
60 g (2 oz) currants
125 g (4 oz) sultanas
Boiling water
2 sachets (14 g) dried yeast
1 tsp caster sugar

60 ml (2 fl oz) warm water
500 g (1 lb) unbleached plain flour
1 tsp mixed spice
175 ml (6 fl oz) milk
1 medium egg
Egg wash*

Place dried fruit in a bowl, pour boiling water over to cover. Allow to stand for 10 minutes, the drain, discarding water. Set aside.

Mix yeast with sugar and tepid water. Leave in a warm place until mixture bubbles. Sift flour and spice together. Add yeast, fruit, milk and egg, mix briefly, then tip dough onto a lightly floured surface. Knead until smooth and no longer sticky, around 6–8 minutes. Place dough in a large bowl and cover with cling film. Prove in a warm place until dough doubles in size, 1–2 hours.

Preheat oven to 210°C (410°F).

Take proved dough and knead for 1–2 minutes. Divide dough into 2 equal-sized pieces. Shape into loaves and place on greased baking tray. Cover with a cloth and leave to prove in a warm place for 20 minutes.

Brush with egg wash, slash tops 3–4 times and bake in preheated oven for 15–20 minutes, or until golden brown and bottom sounds hollow when tapped. Makes 2 loaves.

Polenta bread

Adding polenta to bread dough introduces a delightful yellow colour, and robust flavour and texture, to the finished loaf. It is good used to make sandwiches with fillings of roasted vegetables, goat's cheese and pesto.

2 sachets (14 g) dried yeast
1 tsp caster sugar
275 ml (9 fl oz) warm water
500 g (1 lb) unbleached plain flour

250 g (8 oz) polenta
1 tsp salt
2 medium eggs, lightly beaten
Egg wash*

Mix yeast with sugar and warm water. Leave in a warm place until mixture bubbles. In a large bowl sift together flour, polenta and salt. Add yeast and eggs. Mix together well, then place onto a floured surface.

Knead until smooth and no longer sticky, around 6–8 minutes. Place dough in a large bowl and cover with cling film. Prove in a warm place until dough doubles in size, 1–2 hours.

Preheat oven to 200°C (390°F).

Take proved dough and knead for 1–2 minutes. Divide dough into 2 equal-sized pieces. Shape into loaves and place on greased baking tray. Cover with a cloth and leave to prove in a warm place for 20 minutes.

Brush with egg wash and bake in preheated oven for 15–20 minutes, or until golden brown and bottom sounds hollow when tapped. Makes 2 loaves.

Rosemary polenta bread
Add 1 tsp chopped fresh rosemary to the polenta.

Foccacia

Foccacia is one of the easiest styles of bread to make. It's just the usual blend of yeast, water, salt, and flour with a little olive oil added. It's also easy to work with and can be made into virtually any shape you prefer: a huge oval loaf, a couple of thin round ones or even small individual ones.

1 sachet (7 g) dried yeast
Pinch of sugar
80 ml (2¾ fl oz) tepid water
1 tsp salt
250 ml (8 fl oz) tepid water, additional

60 ml (2 fl oz) olive oil
500 g (1 lb) unbleached plain flour
Additional olive oil
Salt flakes

Mix dried yeast with sugar and tepid water. Leave in a warm place until mixture bubbles. Stir in salt, additional water and oil. Stir in flour until combined. Place on a lightly floured surface. Knead until smooth and no longer sticky, around 6–8 minutes. Place dough in a large bowl, cover with cling film. Prove in a warm place until dough doubles in size, 1–2 hours.

Preheat oven to 200°C (390°F).

Take proved dough and knead for 1–2 minutes. Shape into 2 × 25 cm (10 in) rounds about 2 cm (¾ in) thick, or another size if you prefer. Place on greased baking trays and allow to prove for 15 minutes. Brush bread with olive oil and sprinkle with salt flakes.

Bake in preheated oven for 10–12 minutes, or until golden brown. Makes 2 foccacias.

Olive foccacia
Press 125 g (4 oz) pitted kalamata olives into proved loaves, then brush with oil and sprinkle salt over.

Rosemary foccacia
Roughly chop a few rosemary leaves and spread them onto the dough after the olive oil and salt.

Garlic foccacia
Slice 4 or 5 large peeled garlic cloves and press them into the dough after the olive oil and salt.

Naan bread

Naan bread is loved by one and all at our place, so we were determined to master it ourselves. This recipe follows a similar principle to other doughs, with the addition of a few other simple ingredients. When it's ready it can be cooked in a hot pan or, even better, outside on the barbecue hot plate.

2 sachets (14 g) dried yeast
1 tsp caster sugar
50 ml (1¾ fl oz) warm water
3 tsp caster sugar, additional
1 medium egg
1 tsp salt

125 ml (4 fl oz) natural yoghurt
125 ml (4 fl oz) milk
125 ml (4 fl oz) water
50 g (1¾ oz) melted butter
700 g (1¼ lb) unbleached plain flour
Olive oil for cooking

Mix yeast with sugar and water. Leave in a warm place until mixture bubbles. Stir in additional sugar, egg, salt, yoghurt, milk, water and melted butter. Add flour, mix briefly, then tip dough onto a lightly floured surface. Knead until smooth and no longer sticky, around 6–8 minutes. Place dough in a large bowl and cover with cling film. Allow to prove in a warm place until dough doubles in size, 1–2 hours.

Take proved dough and knead for 1–2 minutes. Divide into 16 × 80 g (2¾ oz) portions, and roll into balls.

Using a rolling pin or your fingers, make each bread 20 cm (8 in) across. Place a tight layer of cling film on a dinner plate and lay bread on it. Cover with more plastic and repeat until all portions are flattened.

Heat a flat barbecue plate or a heavy-based pan over a medium–high heat. Brush with a thin layer of olive oil, then cook naan until golden on each side, about 2 minutes each side. Makes 16 naan.

Garlic naan
Brush both sides of each naan with melted garlic butter as it finishes cooking.

Spice naan
Add 3 tsp of spice, such as ground cardamom, cumin and coriander to the dough.

Pizza dough

No matter what your favourite topping is, your enjoyment of pizza can only be improved by making your own base. This recipe makes a thick and chewy pizza base and is the sort of thing we make on weekends so the children can get involved in the mixing and kneading. They also love putting on their favourite toppings. We can't think of a better way to get another generation interested in cooking.

1 sachet (7g) dried yeast
Pinch of caster sugar
80 ml (2¾ fl oz) tepid water
80 ml (2¾ fl oz) olive oil

250 ml (8 fl oz) tepid water, additional
500 g (1 lb) unbleached plain flour
1 tsp salt

Mix dried yeast with sugar and tepid water. Leave in a warm place until mixture bubbles. Stir in oil and additional water. Add flour and salt, mix briefly, then tip dough onto a lightly floured surface. Knead until smooth and no longer sticky, around 6–8 minutes. Place dough in a large bowl and cover with cling film. Allow to prove in a warm place until dough doubles in size, 1–2 hours.

Preheat oven to 190°C (375°F).

Take proved dough and knead for 1–2 minutes. Divide into 2 equal pieces and roll each into a ball. Place on oiled baking trays and use fingers to press out until 20 cm (8 in) across and 2 cm (¾ in) thick. Cover and prove for 20 minutes.

Add toppings of your choice and bake in preheated oven for 10–15 minutes, or until pizza base is dry and golden underneath. Makes 2 pizzas.

Thin and crispy pizza
Use only half the yeast in the recipe to get
a thin and crispy pizza base.

PIZZA RULES

- The only rules for pizza are to use the flavours and foods you like, just don't use too many at once.
- In terms of number of toppings our advice is to stop at 2–3 on each pizza so you can really enjoy them.
- You should always begin with a good flavoured tomato purée or tomato sugo on your base. Ensure it is seasoned with salt and pepper or even a little chopped basil.
- Next up should be the main ingredients – this may be sliced ham or salami or even roasted vegetables.
- Its then time to add secondary flavours like olives, anchovies, sun-dried tomato or basil leaves.
- Cheese should be the final ingredient on your pizza, try a little mozzarella, parmigano or feta.

Some of our favourite combinations include:

- Salami, tomato and olives
- Salami, tapenade and mozzarella
- Ham and mozzarella with pan-fried eggplant
- Ham, olives and parmigano
- Roasted capsicum, basil and goat's cheese
- Roasted capsicum, olives and feta cheese
- Artichokes, eggplant and bocconcini cheese
- Artichoke, pesto and parmigano cheese
- Thinly sliced garlic, oregano and parmigano cheese
- Tapenade, tomato and goat's cheese
- Pesto, eggplant and goat's cheese
- Pesto, rocket leaves and parmigiano

Pissaladière

Pissaladière is a pizza topped with caramelised onions, anchovies and olives. As you can imagine, it is for those, like us, who enjoy robust, concentrated flavours on their pizza.

4 tbsp olive oil
4 onions, sliced
2 garlic cloves, peeled
1 small red chilli, halved
2 sprigs fresh thyme

Salt and freshly ground black pepper
½ quantity pizza dough, page 230
Anchovies as required, halved lengthways
Pitted kalamata olives as required

Heat oil in saucepan, then add onions, garlic, chilli and thyme. Add salt and freshly ground black pepper. Cook for 20–30 minutes on medium–low heat, stirring often until onions soften.

Roll dough to a rough rectangle shape 30 × 15 cm (12 × 6 in). Spread onions on top. Arrange anchovy halves in a diamond lattice formation and stud each diamond centre with an olive.

Preheat oven to 190°C (375°F).

Set aside to prove in a warm place for 15 minutes. Bake in preheated oven for 15–20 minutes, or until risen and golden brown. Makes 1 pizza.

Roasted vegetable calzone

Calzone is basically an enclosed pizza parcel, so anything you can put on pizza you can put into a calzone. Unlike pizza, though, calzone can be cooked with a sweet filling as well.

1 eggplant, diced 1 cm (⅓ in) chunks, salted and rinsed
1 zucchini, halved and cut 1 cm (⅓ in) slices
1 onion, diced
¼ pumpkin, peeled and diced
1 red capsicum, diced
Olive oil
Salt and freshly ground black pepper
3–4 oregano sprigs
1 quantity pizza dough, page 230
125 ml (4 fl oz) tomato purée
125 g (4 oz) mozzarella
Egg wash*

Preheat oven to 200°C (390°F).

Toss together eggplant, zucchini, onion, pumpkin, capsicum, oil, salt, pepper and oregano. Place in a deep baking tray and cook in a preheated oven for 40 minutes, until soft and cooked. Set aside to cool.

Divide dough into 6 × 150 g (5 oz) pieces. Roll each piece of dough into an oval 20 cm (8 in) long. Toss roasted vegetables with tomato purée and cheese. Divide vegetables between each dough oval, placing on lower half. Brush around vegetables with egg wash. Fold dough over and press edges together firmly. Transfer to greased baking dishes sprinkled with polenta. Brush the top of each calzone with egg wash. Set aside to prove in a warm place for 15 minutes.

Bake in a preheated oven for 20 minutes, or until golden brown. Makes 6 calzone.

Simple brioche

Brioche is a yeast loaf that is usually served at breakfast in France. This recipe is for one large brioche, although they are often made small, as an individual serving. Brioche is scrumptious toasted and served with butter and jam and it makes the most amazing bread-and-butter pudding.

2 sachets (14 g) dried yeast
1 tsp sugar
2 tbsp warm water
200 g (7 oz) plain flour
1 tsp salt
2 medium eggs, beaten
60 g (2 oz) melted butter

Mix yeast with sugar and warm water and set aside until yeast bubbles. Sift flour and salt together. Add yeast, eggs and butter to the flour. Mix briefly, then tip dough onto a lightly floured surface. Knead until smooth and no longer sticky, around 6–8 minutes. Place dough in a large bowl and cover with cling film. Allow to prove in a warm place until dough doubles in size, 1–2 hours.

Preheat oven to 190°C (375°F).

Take proved dough and knead for 1–2 minutes. Shape dough into a loaf and place in a greased loaf tin 23.5 × 13.5 × 7 cm (9 × 5 × 2½ in). Cover with a cloth and leave to prove in a warm place for 20 minutes.

Bake in preheated oven for 15–20 minutes, or until golden brown and bottom sounds hollow when tapped. Makes 1 large brioche.

Orange brioche
Add the chopped zest of 1 orange to flour.

Sticky currant buns

I adore currant buns and it has to be said that my only disappointment with Australia, and it's only this small one, is that there aren't enough currant buns in the baker's shops. MC

400 g (14 oz) plain flour
1 tsp mixed spice
2 sachets (14 g) dried yeast
60 g (2 oz) caster sugar
Pinch of salt

100 g (3½ oz) butter
2 medium eggs, lightly beaten
125 ml (4 fl oz) milk
90 g (3 oz) currants
Sugar syrup

Sift flour and spice together into a large bowl. Add yeast, sugar and salt, and mix briefly. Melt butter and mix with beaten eggs and milk. Pour onto flour, mix briefly with a wooden spoon, then tip out onto a floured bench. Knead for 4–5 minutes or until dough is smooth and silky. Place dough in a bowl, cover with cling film and set aside in a warm place to prove until doubled in bulk, about 1 hour.

When proved, tip dough onto floured surface, add currants and knead well to mix in fruit. Divide dough into 12 equal-sized pieces. Roll each one into a small bun shape and place all on a greased and lined baking tray. Cover tray with a tea towel and prove in a warm place for 20 minutes.

Preheat oven to 200°C (390°F).

Place buns in oven and bake for 15–20 minutes, or until risen and golden brown. When buns are cooked brush liberally with sugar syrup and allow to cool slightly before eating them warm. Makes 12 buns.

Sugar syrup

90 g (3 oz) caster sugar
3 tbsp water

Dissolve sugar in water over a low heat. Then raise the heat and cook for 5–6 minutes, or until it reduces to a light syrup.

Chelsea buns

Chelsea buns are a touch more complicated to make than currant buns, but the end result is well worth the effort.

400 g (14 oz) plain flour
2 sachets (14 g) dried yeast
60 g (2 oz) caster sugar
Pinch of salt
100 g (3½ oz) melted butter
2 medium eggs, lightly beaten

125 ml (4 fl oz) milk
60 g (2 oz) melted butter, additional
60 g (2 oz) caster sugar, additional
30 g (1 oz) currants
60 g (2 oz) sultanas
Sugar syrup, page 233

Sift flour into a large bowl. Add yeast, sugar and salt and mix briefly. Mix melted butter with beaten eggs and milk. Pour onto flour, mix briefly with a wooden spoon, then tip out onto a floured bench. Knead for 4–5 minutes or until dough is smooth and silky. Place dough in a bowl, cover with cling film and set aside in a warm place to prove until doubled in bulk, about 1–2 hours.

Tip dough onto floured surface and knead well. Roll out to a large square, about 30 cm (12 in). Brush with additional melted butter, then sprinkle liberally with additional caster sugar. Sprinkle with dried fruits. Roll up from one end to form a large Swiss roll shape. Cut into 2 cm (¾ in) slices. Place slices, cut side up, onto a lined baking tray. Cover tray with a tea towel and prove in a warm place for 20 minutes.

Preheat oven to 200°C (390°F).

Place proved buns in oven and bake for 15–20 minutes, or until risen and golden brown. When buns are cooked brush liberally with sugar syrup and allow to cool slightly before eating them warm. Makes 12 buns.

Swiss buns
Drizzle cooked buns with basic icing, page 299.

Jam swirls
Omit butter, sugar and fruit and spread dough with jam instead.

Cheat's hot cross buns
Add 60 g (2 oz) of chopped candied orange peel or mixed peel to bun dough. Slash tops with a knife to form cross shapes.

Sticky cinnamon buns

These cinnamon buns are rich, sticky and very more-ish. They're guaranteed to make your morning tea better than ever.

400 g (14 oz) plain unbleached flour
60 g (2 oz) caster sugar
½ tsp salt
2 sachets (14 g) dried yeast
50 g (1¾ oz) butter
1 medium egg

200 ml (7 fl oz) milk
75 g (2½ oz) soft butter
75 g (2½ oz) caster sugar
1 tsp ground cinnamon
Egg wash*

Sift flour, sugar, salt and yeast together into a large bowl. Melt butter and mix with egg and milk. Pour onto flour, mix briefly with a wooden spoon, then tip out onto a floured bench. Knead for 4–5 minutes or until dough is smooth and silky. Place dough in a bowl, cover with cling film and set aside in a warm place to prove until doubled in bulk, about 1–2 hours.

Tip dough onto floured surface and knead well. Roll dough out to a large square about 30 cm (12 in). Mix soft butter, sugar and cinnamon together and spread liberally over dough. Roll up from one end to form a large Swiss roll shape. Cut into 2 cm (¾ in) slices. Place slices, cut side up into a lined deep baking tray. Cover tray with a tea towel and prove in a warm place for 20 minutes.

Preheat oven to 200°C (390°F).

Brush with egg wash. Place proved buns in oven and bake for 15–20 minutes, or until risen and golden brown. Best eaten warm. Makes 12 buns.

Doughnuts

Believe it or not, we don't make these every day. But we're always glad when we do. You can pipe a dollop of jam or custard into the centre when the doughnuts have cooled—if they last that long.

Pinch salt
60 g (2 oz) caster sugar
1 sachet (7g) dry yeast
2 tbsp tepid water
300 g (10½ oz) unbleached plain flour

150 g (5 oz) soft butter, diced
3 medium eggs
Oil for frying
Caster sugar, additional
A little ground cinnamon

Mix salt, sugar, yeast and water. Leave in a warm place until mixture bubbles. Place flour in a large bowl, add butter and rub in until a breadcrumb texture is achieved. Make a small well in the centre, add proven yeast and mix lightly. Add eggs one by one, mixing well in between. Then turn dough onto a floured surface. Knead until smooth and no longer sticky, around 6–8 minutes. Place dough in a bowl, cover with cling film and set aside in a warm place to prove until doubled in bulk, about 1 hour.

Tip dough onto floured surface and knead well for 1–2 minutes. Divide dough into 10 evenly sized pieces. Shape into balls and place on greased baking tray. Cover with a cloth and leave to prove in a warm place for 20 minutes.

Heat oil to 175°C (345°F) or until a cube of bread turns golden.

Cook doughnuts in batches until golden-brown, turning once. Drain briefly; then roll in caster sugar and cinnamon mix while still warm. Makes 10 doughnuts.

Shortcrust pastry
Quiche Lorraine
Tomato and anchovy tart
Cheese and potato pies
Sweetcrust pastry
Almond sweetcrust pastry
Rich sweetcrust pastry
Ricotta tart
Apricot and frangipane tart
Raspberry and mascarpone tart
Passionfruit tart
Lemon tart
Lemon meringue pie
Apple tart
Almond pear tart
Bitter chocolate tarts
Apple and rhubarb pie
Free-form fruit pie
Fruit mince pies
Puff pastry
Rough puff pastry
Sausage rolls
Egg and bacon pie
Tarte tatin
Choux pastry
Profiteroles
Cheesy choux puffs
Hot water pastry
Vegetable pasties
Greek cheese pastries or spanakopita
Egyptian bread and butter pudding
Pistachio, almond and orange blossom baklava

Pastry

QUICHES AND TARTS

Pastry-making isn't an art; it's about having the knack. Some people just have that knack and others don't, but fortunately it can also be learned. Making pastry is one of those steadfast cooking methods that never changes; it's been made one way for generations, and probably will be so for generations to come. So why not learn it and pass it on?

In addition, pastry-making is simple chemistry. A mixture of flour, butter and water is always the basis; it's what you do with these ingredients that makes the difference.

Here we cover how to make basic pastries, such as shortcrust and sweetcrust, and give instructions for puff pastry, choux pastry and hot water pastry.

Many people swear by food processor pastry recipes and if you have one that works well for you, congratulations. We've never been that keen on the food processor way, so we stick to the tried-and-tested rubbing in method. Which, we have to point out, takes the same time as the food processor but with less washing up, so why bother?

Good pastry takes a bit of time and there are no shortcuts: it needs to be rested for at least 20 minutes every time it has been worked, or it will shrink during cooking.

THINGS YOU NEED TO KNOW ABOUT PASTRY

- Don't be afraid of pastry. We reckon that pastry, like dogs, can sense fear and will play up to it.
- Making pastry is like riding a bike: make it right once and you'll have the knack forever.
- Climate will affect pastry. If you live in a small, stuffy space where the average temperature on any given day in summer exceeds 30°C, you're not going to have too much luck. Keep ingredients and your work area as cool as possible.
- Practise making pastry; after all, practice makes perfect.
- Always dust your work surface and rolling pin with flour to stop the pastry sticking. Try to keep this dusting light, though; too much flour will affect the quality of the pastry.
- Try not to roll pastry too thin; 3 mm (⅛ in) is perfect.
- To check that you have rolled your pastry to the right width, place your tin on top of the pastry and allow an extra 2–3 cm (1 in) for the sides.
- To line a pastry tin, place your rolling pin on top of pastry at the edge closest to you. Pick up the edge of the pastry and roll the pin, bringing the pastry with it. Transfer the rolling pin to the edge of the tin and unroll pastry onto tin. Push pastry down into tin. Lastly, work your fingers around the side of the tin, making sure the pastry is pushed down into the corners. Trim any excess off the top using a small knife.
- Pastry is usually cooked in the oven before any filling is added. This is known as blind-baking.
- While all of this may sound like a lot of work, there is nothing – and we mean nothing – that even comes close to the taste and texture of homemade pastry.

Shortcrust pastry

This is the basic pastry that is used for all savoury tarts. It can be used for sweet tarts, too, if the filling is very sweet.

300 g (10½ oz) plain flour
Pinch of salt

150 g (5 oz) butter, diced
3–4 tbsp cold water

Sift flour with salt; rub in the butter to produce a breadcrumb texture. Add enough water to bring pastry together and knead briefly. Wrap in cling film and chill for 30 minutes.

Preheat oven to 180°C (350°F).

Roll pastry onto a lightly floured board to a 3 mm (⅛ in) thickness and line a greased 25 cm (10 in) flan tin. Work fingers around the side of the tin making sure pastry is pushed down into corners. Trim any excess off the top using a small knife.

Prick base with fork and rest for 30 minutes. Line pastry with greaseproof paper, then baking beans, pastry weights or rice and bake blind for 15 minutes in preheated oven. Remove paper weights, and bake for a further 5 minutes to crisp the pastry. Baked pastry shell is now ready to use as required.

Quiche Lorraine

Quiche Lorraine is the type of quiche that most people know of, with a filling that includes lots of cooked onion and bacon. No wonder it's so popular.

1 shortcrust pastry shell, page 238
2 tbsp olive oil
1 onion, diced
4 slices bacon, cut into strips
6 medium eggs

250 ml (8 fl oz) cream
Salt and freshly ground black pepper
2 tbsp chopped parsley
125 g (4 oz) parmigiano, grated

Preheat oven to 180°C (350°F).

Heat a heavy-based frypan over a medium heat, add oil and onions and cook for 4–5 minutes, stirring often until onion softens but doesn't colour. Add bacon and cook for a further 3–4 minutes. Remove from heat and allow to cool.

Beat eggs with cream, salt, pepper, parsley and cheese. Spoon onion and bacon mix into cooked pastry shell. Pour egg mix into baked pastry shell and bake in preheated oven for 30 minutes until golden brown and set. Serves 8.

Leek and goat's cheese quiche
Substitute 2 thinly sliced leeks for onion and goat's cheese for 60 g (2 oz) parmigiano.

Caramelised onion quiche
Cook 4 sliced onions in 60 ml (2 fl oz) olive oil with salt, freshly ground black pepper and a sprig or two of fresh thyme for 30 minutes. Stir often. The onions will turn dark brown and gloriously rich. Drain and allow to cool before placing in cooked pastry shell. Also delicious with goat's cheese rather than parmigiano.

Asparagus quiche
Cook onion until soft, add the bacon if you want to. Place blanched, chopped asparagus spears in pastry shell along with onion before egg mix.

Mushroom quiche
Add 125 g (4 oz) sliced mushrooms to pan while cooking onions. Cook for a further 5–6 minutes, or until mushrooms are softened. Allow to cool, then add to the pastry shell before egg mix.

Olive and spinach quiche
Cook onion until soft, remove and allow to cool. Add 90 g (3 oz) of black olive halves with 100 g (3½ oz) blanched, chopped spinach, then complete as described.

Tomato and anchovy tart

This tart is perfect for those of you who love the salty combination of anchovies and olives.

1 shortcrust pastry shell, page 238
Olive oil
1 onion, diced
1 garlic clove, crushed
6 tomatoes, diced

2 tbsp tomato paste
2 medium eggs
Salt and freshly ground black pepper
12 anchovy fillets
12 black olives

Preheat oven to 180°C (350°F).

Heat a heavy-based frying pan over medium heat, add a splash of olive oil and cook onion and garlic until soft. Add tomatoes and tomato paste and continue to cook until soft, about 10 minutes. Remove from heat and allow to cool. Add eggs and season to taste.

Pour into cooked pastry shell. Cut anchovy fillets in half lengthways, remove stones from olives and cut in half. Lay the anchovy strips over the tomato in a diamond lattice formation and put one olive half in each diamond.

Bake in preheated oven for 40 minutes, or until tomato filling is set and lightly brown. Serves 8.

Cheese and potato pies ⓥ

Scrumptious for lunch or afternoon tea or to pack into the picnic basket for a day at the beach.

1 quantity shortcrust pastry, page 238
500 g (1 lb) potatoes, diced 1 cm (⅓ in)
    and cooked until tender
150 g (5 oz) tasty cheese, grated

2 tbsp sour cream
1 tbsp chopped parsley
Salt and freshly ground black pepper
Egg wash*

Preheat oven to 180°C (350°F).

Roll pastry out to 3 mm (⅛ in) thickness. Cut 8 × 15 cm (6 in) circles. Combine potatoes, cheese, sour cream, parsley, salt and pepper. Spoon the mixture onto the bottom half of each pastry circle. Brush top half of pastry with egg wash. Fold pastry over to enclose filling. Crimp edges together and place on lined baking tray. Set aside to rest for 30 minutes.

Brush pies with egg wash and bake in preheated oven for 15–20 minutes, or until golden brown. Makes 8.

Sweetcrust pastry

Sweetcrust pastry is much easier to work with than shortcrust because of the sugar in it. This breaks down the protein in the flour and makes the pastry more supple. Use this for sweet tarts.

300 g (10½ oz) plain flour
150 g (5 oz) soft butter, diced
Pinch of salt

1 medium egg
50 g (1¾ oz) caster sugar

Place flour, butter and salt in a bowl and rub together until the mixture resembles fine breadcrumbs. Break egg into a separate bowl, add sugar and mix lightly. Add to flour mixture and mix until pastry comes together. Wrap in cling film and chill for 30 minutes.

Preheat oven to 180°C (350°F).

Roll pastry on a lightly floured board to 3 mm (⅛ in) thickness and line a greased 25 cm (10 in) flan tin. Work fingers around the side of the tin, pushing pastry down into corners. Trim any excess off the top using a small knife.

Prick base with a fork and rest for 30 minutes. Line pastry with greaseproof paper, then baking beans or rice and bake blind for 15 minutes in preheated oven. Remove paper and beans, bake for a further 5 minutes to crisp pastry. Baked sweetcrust pastry shell is now ready to use.

Almond sweetcrust pastry

Here almonds have replaced some of the flour, which introduces a lovely nutty flavour to the pastry.

200 g (7 oz) plain flour
100 g (3½ oz) ground almonds
Pinch of salt

150 g (5 oz) soft butter, diced
2 egg yolks
60 g (2 oz) caster sugar

Rub flour, almonds, salt and butter together until it resembles fine breadcrumbs. Lightly beat egg yolks and dissolve sugar in them. Make a well in the centre of flour mix, pour in egg and sugar and knead lightly to form a ball. Wrap in cling film and chill for 30 minutes.

Preheat oven to 180°C (350°F).

Roll pastry on a lightly floured board to 3 mm (⅛ in) thickness and line a greased 25 cm (10 in) flan tin. Work fingers around the side of the tin making sure pastry is pushed down into corners. Trim any excess off the top using a small knife.

Line pastry with greaseproof paper, then baking beans or rice and bake blind for 15 minutes in preheated oven. Remove paper and beans, bake for a further 5 minutes to crisp pastry. Baked almond sweetcrust pastry shell is now ready to use.

Rich sweetcrust pastry

Pastry with a high butter content is often describes as short pastry. It produces a stunning eating experience but can be difficult to roll in one piece. If this happens simply push pieces together to line the flan tin.

225 g (7¾ oz) plain flour
175 g (6 oz) soft butter, diced
Pinch of salt

1 egg yolk
60 g (2 oz) caster sugar

Place flour, butter and salt in a bowl and rub together until the mixture resembles fine breadcrumbs. Place egg yolk into a separate bowl, add sugar and mix lightly. Add to flour mixture and mix until pastry comes together. Wrap in cling film and chill for 30 minutes.

Preheat oven to 180°C (350°F).

Roll pastry on a lightly floured board to 3 mm (⅛ in) thickness and line a greased 25 cm (10 in) flan tin. If the pastry proves difficult to roll, simply push pieces together to line the flan tin. Work fingers around the side of the tin making sure pastry is pushed down into corners. Trim any excess off the top using a small knife.

Prick base with fork and rest for 30 minutes. Line pastry with greaseproof paper, then baking beans, pastry weights or rice and bake blind for 15 minutes in preheated oven. Remove paper and weights, and bake for a further 5 minutes to crisp pastry. Rich sweetcrust pastry shell is now ready to use.

Ricotta tart

A simple and easy tart to make, and one that can be adapted in many ways. The list of variations below should keep most tart lovers happy for a long time.

1 sweetcrust pastry shell, page 241
250 g (8 oz) ricotta
125 g (4 oz) caster sugar
3 medium eggs
1 tsp vanilla extract

125 ml (4 fl oz) cream
2 tbsp plain flour
Grated zest of 1 lemon
2 tbsp lemon juice
Ground cinnamon

Preheat oven to 180°C (350°F).

In a bowl, whisk together ricotta, caster sugar, eggs, vanilla, cream and flour with the grated zest and lemon juice. Spoon ricotta mix into cooked pastry shell. Sprinkle with cinnamon and bake in preheated oven for 40 minutes, or until firm. Serves 8.

Quince and ricotta tart
Slice 2 cooked quinces. Add to cooked pastry shell, then pour ricotta mix over.

Port-soaked prune and ricotta tart
Soak 300 g (10½ oz) pitted prunes in 2 tbsp port for 20 minutes. Add to cooked pastry shell, then pour ricotta mix over.

Date and orange ricotta tart
Substitute orange for lemon juice and zest. Add 300 g (10½ oz) fresh dates to cooked pastry shell, then pour ricotta mix over.

Optional extras
Add any fruit you like, such as raspberries, pear slices, or roasted nectarine wedges. You can also swap the ricotta for fresh goat's curd, mascarpone or fromage frais.

Apricot and frangipane tart

Frangipane is a gorgeous almond tart filling that is delicious on its own and even better when you pour it over roasted apricots. Tempting isn't it?

1 sweetcrust pastry shell page 241
8 ripe apricots
3 tbsp caster sugar
100 g (3½ oz) soft butter

110 g (3¾ oz) caster sugar, additional
2 medium eggs
100 g (3½ oz) ground almonds
1 tbsp plain flour

Preheat oven to 180°C (350°F).

Cut apricots in half and discard stones. Place on a baking tray skin side down. Sprinkle with sugar and roast in preheated oven for 20–30 minutes, until apricots soften and brown slightly.

Prepare frangipane by creaming butter and additional sugar until white. Add eggs and combine. Add ground almonds and flour and stir until well combined.

Place roasted apricot halves skin side down in baked shell. Spoon frangipane over them and bake for 30 minutes, until frangipane is set and golden brown. Serves 8.

Pear frangipane tart
Substitute poached pear slices for apricot halves.

Other fruits
As for the ricotta tart, the variations could go on forever. Add any fruit you like, such as raspberries, or roasted nectarine or peach wedges.

Raspberry and mascarpone tart

Raspberries are among our favourite fruits and we especially love them in tarts, where their acidic taste adds a lovely contrast. Use either basic sweetcrust pastry, page 241, or almond sweetcrust pastry.

1 almond sweetcrust pastry shell, page 241
250 g (8 oz) mascarpone
2 medium eggs
1 tsp vanilla extract

3 tbsp tokay or port
60 g (2 oz) caster sugar
250 g (8 oz) raspberries
Icing sugar to serve

Preheat oven to 180°C (350°F).

Lightly beat together mascarpone, eggs, vanilla, tokay or port and sugar until combined. Scatter raspberries over the cooked pastry base and pour mascarpone mix over. Bake in preheated oven for 20 minutes, or until set and golden brown.

Dust with icing sugar to serve. Serves 8.

Passionfruit tart

If we offer to bring a dessert to a friend's house, more often than not it's our passionfruit tart they'll ask for. It combines the exquisite tropical flavour of passionfruit and the creamy richness of mascarpone. In this recipe it's best to pour the filling directly into the still-warm just-baked pastry shell.

1 rich sweetcrust pastry shell, page 242
6 medium eggs
125 g (4 oz) mascarpone
200 g (7 oz) caster sugar

250 ml (8 fl oz) passionfruit pulp, from about 12–15 passionfruit
Grated zest of 2 lemons
80 ml (2¾ fl oz) lemon juice

Preheat oven to 180°C (350°F).

Beat eggs, mascarpone, sugar, passionfruit pulp and lemon zest and juice together. Allow to stand for 30 minutes before straining to remove passionfruit seeds. Pour strained filling into still-warm blind-baked pastry shell.

Reduce oven to 140°C (280°F). Place tart in oven and cook for 30 minutes if using a fan-forced oven (a non fan-forced oven will take 5–10 minutes longer). By this stage the filling will be just set on top. This is the time to remove it from the oven for a perfect consistency. Allow to cool, during which time it will finish setting. Serves 8.

Lemon tart

Few people can say no to a classic lemon tart, especially when it's as delectable as this.

1 sweetcrust pastry shell, page 241
4 medium eggs
220 g (7⅔ oz) caster sugar
Grated zest of 2 lemons

80 ml (2¾ fl oz) lemon juice
250 g (8 oz) melted butter
125 g (4 oz) ground almonds
Cream to serve

Preheat oven to 180°C (350°F).

Beat eggs and sugar until light and doubled in bulk, about 10 minutes. Add lemon zest and juice, butter and almonds, then mix to incorporate.

Pour into blind-baked tart shell. Bake in preheated oven for about 40 minutes, or until golden brown and set.

Serve at room temperature with cream. Serves 8.

Lemon meringue pie

A masterpiece of different flavour combinations. It's worth learning how to make sweet-crust pastry just to make this pie alone.

1 sweetcrust pastry shell, page 241
1 quanity lemon curd, page 16

4 egg whites
200 g (7 oz) caster sugar

Preheat oven to 220°C (425°F).

Spoon lemon curd into baked pastry shell and refrigerate.

Beat egg whites until stiff. Gradually add caster sugar until thick and glossy. Spoon meringue on top of set lemon curd, leaving big peaks.

Place in preheated oven and cook until golden brown, about 5–10 minutes. Serves 8.

Apple tart

We make this tart only when good-quality apples are in season, which is mostly throughout autumn and winter.

1 sweetcrust pastry shell, page 241
30 g (1 oz) butter
6 Granny Smith apples, peeled, cored and thinly sliced

3 tbsp brown sugar
1 tsp ground cinnamon
3 tbsp apricot jam
1 tbsp water

Preheat oven to 180°C (350°F).

Heat a heavy-based saucepan over a medium heat. Melt butter, then add apples, sugar and cinnamon. Cook briefly until apples just begin to soften, stirring carefully.

Place jam in small saucepan over a low heat with water. Bring to the boil and stir well. Brush pastry shell with apricot glaze. Arrange apple slices in the base of the baked pastry shell. Brush top apple slices with apricot glaze, then bake in preheated oven for 20 minutes or until golden brown and crisp. Serve with pure cream. Serves 8.

Almond pear tart

This tart has quarters of poached pear topped with a creamy almond and ricotta filling. Resistance is useless.

1 sweetcrust pastry shell, page 241
220 g (7⅔ oz) caster sugar
200 ml (7 fl oz) water
3 pears
3 medium eggs

110 g (3¾ oz) caster sugar, additional
½ tsp vanilla extract
100 g (3½ oz) ground almonds
250 g (8 oz) ricotta
Pure cream to serve

Preheat oven to 180°C (350°F).

To make sugar syrup place sugar and water in small saucepan and dissolve sugar over low heat. Bring to the boil, then simmer for 5 minutes. Peel, quarter and core pears and poach in sugar syrup until soft, 5–10 minutes. Remove pears from the syrup, drain and set aside.

Beat eggs, additionial sugar, vanilla, almonds and ricotta until combined. Place pear quarters in baked pastry shell and spoon almond mixture over.

Bake in preheated oven for 20–25 minutes, or until golden brown and set.

Serve warm with pure cream. Serves 8.

Bitter chocolate tarts

These tiny chocolate tarts are incredibly decadent, especially if you can source some gold leaf to decorate the tops with. Make them in mini tart shell trays or mini muffin tins and serve with coffee at the end of a meal.

1 quantity sweetcrust pastry, page 241
150 ml (5 fl oz) cream
150 g (5 oz) dark chocolate, chopped

1 tsp tokay or brandy
2 egg yolks
Gold leaf, optional

Preheat oven to 180°C (350°F).

Roll pastry out on a lightly floured board. Cut out 7.5 cm (3 in) circles. Lightly butter mini tart shells or mini muffin tins and place a pastry circle in each. Press circles down gently with fingers. Prick pastry with a fork.

Cook in preheated oven for 6–8 minutes, or until pastry is dry and just beginning to colour. Allow pastry shells to cool.

Place cream in a saucepan and bring to the boil. Remove from the heat and add chocolate. Whisk until chocolate is completely melted. Set aside to cool, whisking occasionally. Whisk in tokay or brandy and egg yolk. Spoon chocolate mixture into tart shells. Allow to cool completely. Decorate with a tiny sprinkle of gold leaf to serve. Makes 18 tarts.

Fruit bread (recipe page 227)

Free-form fruit pie (recipe page 247)

Apple and rhubarb pie

This is a proper winter dessert that begs to be served with hot custard. The pastry shell for the pie is baked as normal, then the apple filling is added. A raw pastry top is laid over the apple and the whole thing is then baked again.

Double quantity sweetcrust pastry, page 241
30 g (1 oz) butter
3 tbsp brown sugar
½ tsp ground cinnamon
6 Granny Smith apples, peeled, cored and sliced

1 bunch rhubarb, trimmed of green leaves and sliced
Egg wash*
Caster sugar, additional

Preheat oven to 180°C (350°F).

Roll out half of the sweetcrust pastry and line a 23 cm (9 in) flan tin. Rest for 30 minutes and bake blind (page 239). Roll out remaining pastry to 25 cm (10 in) across.

Heat a heavy-based saucepan over a medium–high heat. Add the butter, sugar and cinnamon and stir until melted. Add sliced apples and rhubarb, stir and cook for 5 minutes. Pile fruit immediately into blind baked pastry shell and cover with remaining sweetcrust pastry, pushing down and crimping the edges. Trim excess pastry. Make a small cross in centre of the pastry to allow steam to escape. Brush pastry with egg wash and sprinkle liberally with caster sugar.

Bake in preheated oven for 20 minutes or until golden brown. Allow to cool for 20 minutes before serving. Serves 8.

Apple and raspberry pie
Omit rhubarb. Cook apple on its own. Place cooked apple slices on cooked pastry base. Arrange 250 g (8 oz) fresh raspberries on top. Cover with pastry and continue.

Apple and rhubarb crumble tart
Forget the pastry top, cover with crumble mix, page 262, and bake for 15–20 minutes, or until golden brown and crunchy.

Free-form fruit pie

This is a rustic, handmade-looking tart. Make this with your choice of berries or whatever is in season. I love it with raspberries and blackberries, or just gooseberries. But most of all I love it with lashings of runny cream. MC

200 g (7 oz) plain flour
Pinch of salt
125 g (4 oz) soft butter, diced
Cold water as needed

800 g (1lb 10 oz) fresh or frozen berries
90 g (3 oz) caster sugar
Egg wash*

Sift flour with salt, then rub in the butter to produce a breadcrumb texture. Add enough water to bring pastry together, then knead briefly. Wrap in cling film and chill for 30 minutes.

Preheat oven to 200°C (390°F).

Roll pastry to a rough circle about 5 mm (¼ in) thickness. Place on largish flat greased baking tray. Arrange berries in the middle, sprinkle berries with sugar and pinch pastry up to overlap and form sides (don't expect them to meet in the middle). Brush pastry edges with egg wash and scatter with some more sugar.

Bake in preheated oven for 30–35 minutes, or until pastry is cooked and golden brown. Some juices may seep through pastry edges, but don't worry. Just serve it as it comes. Serves 4–6.

Fruit mince pies

What would Christmas celebrations be without a few mince pies to munch on?

75 g (2½ oz) currants
90 g (3 oz) sultanas
½ apple, grated
40 g (1⅓ oz) blanched almonds
40 g (1⅓ oz) brown sugar
½ tsp ground cinnamon
Zest of 1 lemon, chopped

Zest of 1 orange, chopped
1 tbsp lemon juice
1 tbsp orange juice
1 tbsp brandy or rum, optional
1 quantity shortcrust pastry, page 238
Egg wash*
2–3 tbsp caster sugar, additional

Preheat oven to 180°C (350°F).

Combine fruits, nuts, sugar, spice, citrus zest and juice and alcohol if using. Stir well and set aside to macerate for 2 hours.

Roll two-thirds of the pastry out on a lightly floured board. Cut out 7.5 cm circles. Lightly butter mini tart shells or mini muffin tins and place a pastry circle in each. Press circles down gently with fingers. Prick pastry with a fork. Cook in the preheated oven for 6–8 minutes, or until pastry is dry and just beginning to colour. Allow pastry shells to cool.

Fill shells with fruit mince. Roll remaining pastry out and cut into 5 cm (2 in) circles or stars and place on top of fruit mince. Brush with egg wash and sprinkle with additional sugar. Bake in preheated oven for 6–8 minutes, or until pastry tops are cooked. Makes 18.

Puff pastry

Puff pastry is usually thought best left to the experts, whereas in fact it's quite easy. It takes a few hours because of all the resting time, so you can do plenty of other things at the same time.

250 g (8 oz) plain flour
Pinch of salt
Squeeze of lemon juice

5–6 tbsp iced water
250 g (8 oz) butter

Sift flour and salt together in a large bowl. Add lemon juice and enough water to bring the pastry together. Tip onto a floured bench and roll pastry into a 20 cm (8 in) square. Wrap in foil and chill for 30 minutes.

Remove butter from the refrigerator 30 minutes before next stage and cut into thick slices. It is essential that the butter and the pastry are of a similar temperature and softness for rolling, so that the butter will be thoroughly incorporated.

Place chilled pastry on a floured bench and roll out to a 30 cm (12 in) square, leaving a thick centre that is about twice as thick as ends. Place butter slices in the centre of the pastry and press all over with fingertips to soften a little more. Fold in all edges, ensuring that the butter is completely encased in the pastry.

Turn over; dust with flour and roll into a long rectangle about 50–60 cm (20–24 in) long. Fold bottom third of the pastry up over the centre and fold top third down to cover it, like a letter. Make a single indentation with your finger on top of the pastry to signify the first fold. Wrap in foil and chill for 30 minutes.

Remove, turn 90° (quarter turn) and roll again into a long rectangle. Again fold into three, like a letter, and mark 2 indentations. Cover and chill for 30 minutes. Repeat until a total of 6 folds are completed. Remember to mark them as you go. After the last fold, roll pastry as required and allow to rest 30 minutes before baking.

If not using pastry immediately, divide and freeze.

Makes 500 g (1 lb) puff pastry, or enough for 2 pie tops.

Rough puff pastry

This is the 'quick' version of puff pastry. It's perfect when time is tight and you need a top for your pie. What you're doing here is three folds in one go, rather than six folds with resting time in between, as for true puff pastry.

250 g (8 oz) plain flour
Pinch of salt
250 g butter, diced

Squeeze of lemon juice
5–6 tbsp iced water

Place flour and salt in food processor. Add butter to the flour. Pulse 3–4 times. Don't try to make the butter disappear; it should still be nice and lumpy. Turn into a large bowl, add lemon juice and enough iced water, then knead lightly to bring the pastry together; don't over-knead. Wrap in cling film and rest in the refrigerator for 30 minutes.

Turn over, dust with flour and roll into a long rectangle about 50–60 cm (20–24 in) long. Fold bottom third of the pastry up over the centre and top third down to cover it, like a letter. Turn 90° (quarter turn) and roll again into a long rectangle. Again fold into three and turn 90°. Roll one last time (so three in total) into a long rectangle, fold into three, wrap in cling film and pop back in the refrigerator for 30 minutes before using as directed by the recipe.

Makes 500 g (1 lb) rough puff pastry, or enough for 2 pie tops.

> You can use either puff or rough puff pastry in any of the following recipes. Choose one that suits you. Or just buy some puff pastry from the shop.

Sausage rolls

The sausage meat typically offered for sausage rolls is not something we're all that keen to eat. We buy really good sausages and use them instead; then we know exactly what's in there.

500 g (1 lb) puff pastry, page 248
20 small skinless frankfurter sausages or baby bratwurst
Dijon or grain mustard, optional
Egg wash*

Roll pastry out to 3 mm (⅛ in) thickness – either a square or a rectangle will do. Use one sausage as a guide to cut out 20 evenly sized rectangles. They should be wide enough to wrap completely around the sausage 1½ times.

Spread a small amount of mustard onto the lower half of each rectangle. Place 1 sausage on top and brush the top half of the pastry with egg wash. Roll the sausage up in the pastry.

Preheat oven to 200°C (390°F).

Place sausage rolls on lined baking tray with the pastry join underneath. Brush with egg wash, slash each top with a knife in a few places to expose sausage. Rest for 30 minutes.

Bake sausage rolls for 15–20 minutes, or until pastry is cooked and golden brown. Makes 20.

Egg and bacon pie

A good egg and bacon pie is a beautiful thing and makes an excellent Saturday lunch.

500 g (1 lb) rough puff pastry, page 249
2 tbsp olive oil
2 onions, finely diced
400 g (14 oz) bacon slices, cut into strips
Freshly ground black pepper
2 tbsp chopped parsley
4 medium eggs
Egg wash*

Preheat oven to 190°C (375°F).

Divide pastry in half and roll each piece out to 3 mm thickness. Line 25 cm (10 in) pie dish with one piece of pastry.

Heat a heavy-based frypan over a medium heat. Add oil and onions and cook for 5–6 minutes, stirring often until onions soften. Add bacon and cook for a further 5–6 minutes, stirring often to stop bacon catching. Remove from heat and allow to cool. Season well with pepper. Add parsley and eggs and stir well to combine.

Spoon filling into lined pie dish. Brush edge on bottom piece of pastry with egg wash. Cover with remaining pastry piece. Crimp edges to join pastry pieces together.

Brush pastry top with egg wash and bake in preheated oven for 30 minutes or until pastry is risen and golden brown. Serves 8.

Tarte tatin

This is without a doubt the most incredible upside-down apple pie experience you're ever likely to have. Ideally you need a 22 cm (8½ in) Le Creuset or deep-sided cast iron pan for this recipe. If you have neither of these, cook apples in a heavy-based frying pan, then tip them into a similar-sized pie dish and top with pastry.

½ quantity rough puff pastry, page 249
75 g (2⅔ oz) butter
150 g (5 oz) caster sugar

4 granny smiths apples, peeled, cored and cut into eighths
Egg wash*

Preheat oven to 190°C (375°F).

Roll out pastry to 5 mm (¼ in) thickness and set aside to rest for 30 minutes.

Heat pan over a medium–high heat, add butter and sugar and cook for 8–10 minutes, stirring constantly. Cook until sugar and butter have cooked to a golden caramel colour. Carefully add the apple pieces, watch out for splashes and cook for just 2–3 minutes, stirring or tossing the pan to coat apples with caramel. The apples will begin to release their juice and stop the caramel overcooking.

Set the pan aside to cool a little. Either leave apple in the pan you cooked them in or transfer to a 22 cm pie dish. Place pastry over apples and tuck down the sides to completely cover apples, then trim excess away. Brush pastry with egg wash and place in preheated oven. Cook for 20–25 minutes, or until pastry is risen, golden brown and cooked. Remove from oven.

To serve, place a large plate or platter over pan or pie dish. Then, using oven gloves or tea towels, tip pan over and remove it, leaving apples on top and pastry on the bottom. Take care, as this is very hot. Serve immediately with thick cream.

Serves 6, or in our house the 4 of us.

Choux pastry

Choux pastry is what you need to make delectable things like profiteroles, éclairs and cheesy puffs.

125 ml (4 fl oz) water
125 ml (4 fl oz) milk
Pinch of salt
100 g (3½ oz) butter

150 g (5 oz) plain flour
5 medium eggs
Egg wash*

Place water, milk, salt and butter in a saucepan and bring to the boil. Tip in flour, stir and return to a low heat. Cook for 2–3 minutes, stirring constantly, until mixture begins to come away from saucepan side.

Tip contents into mixer. Break eggs into a jug and beat lightly. Start to add egg mix to pastry mixture, ensuring that eggs are well incorporated before adding more. Continue adding eggs until the pastry is of a dropping consistency – not too runny. You may not need to add all the eggs; it tends to vary a bit from batch to batch. Use choux pastry as directed in the recipe.

Profiteroles

I believe I must hold the world record for the most profiteroles eaten at one sitting – or I did when I was 10. I still love 'em. MC.

1 quantity choux pastry, page 251
1 quantity thick custard, page 274
1 quantity chocolate ganache, page 299

Preheat oven to 200°C (390°C).

Spoon teaspoonfuls of choux pastry onto lined baking trays. Place trays in the oven at the same time. With choux pastry it is important not to open the door in the first 10 minutes of cooking, as cold drafts will make the pastry sink.

Cook for 10 minutes, then turn oven temperature down to 180°C (350°F). Cook for another 10 minutes, then try one. They should be quite brown (more than golden-brown) and relatively dry inside. Resist the urge to pull them out too soon, because you will not fit enough cream into them if they are doughy inside. When ready, set aside to cool.

Take cold thick custard. Spoon into a piping bag if you have one, then poke piping nozzle into choux pastry base and squeeze to fill with custard. If not using a piping bag, slit profiteroles with a knife, then spoon custard into pastry. Set aside until ready to serve.

To serve, arrange 3–4 profiteroles on each plate (piled if you wish), or the entire batch on a large platter. Warm the ganache until it melts, then drizzle it over the profiteroles. Makes 30.

Éclairs
Pipe choux pastry into 8 cm (3 in) lengths to make éclairs. Bake as directed, then split them down one side. Fill them with pastry cream and drizzle melted ganache over the tops.

Passionfruit profiteroles
Fill pastry balls with passionfruit curd, page 16, and drizzle with lemon icing, page 299.

Cheesy choux puffs

These are ideal as a nibble before dinner. We find their light cheese flavour perfect with a glass or two of sparkling wine.

1 quantity choux pastry, page 251
90 g (3oz) gruyère or parmigiano, grated

Preheat oven to 200°C (390°C).

Add cheese to choux pastry mixture. Spoon teaspoonfuls of choux pastry onto lined baking trays. Place trays in the oven at the same time. With choux pastry it is important not to open the door in the first 10 minutes of cooking, as cold drafts will make the pastry sink.

Cook for 10 minutes, then turn oven temperature down to 180°C (350°F). Cook for another 10 minutes, then try one. They should be quite brown (more than golden-brown) and relatively dry inside. Resist the urge to pull them out too soon, as they will be doughy inside. When ready, set aside to cool. Makes 30.

Hot water pastry

This quick pastry is just what you need for making delicious pasties.

150 ml (5 fl oz) water
100 g (3½ oz) butter
1 tsp salt
300 g (10½ oz) self-raising flour

Place the water, butter and salt in a saucepan over a medium heat until butter has completely melted. Remove from heat, rapidly stir in flour and mix until dough forms a ball.

Place dough on a lightly floured board. Allow to cool for a few minutes, dust hands with flour and knead gently for thirty seconds. Divide dough as required and cover with a tea towel to keep warm. Use dough while still warm, as it becomes firm when cold. Use as directed in recipes.

Vegetable pasties v

These are great for lunches and picnics, or they can be made into small cocktail-sized party food and served with tomato relish.

2 tbsp olive oil
1 onion, finely diced
½ red capsicum, finely diced
2 medium potatoes, finely diced
2 tomatoes, roughly chopped
200 g (7 oz) piece of pumpkin, peeled and cut into 2mm dice
1 small carrot, finely diced

1 garlic clove, finely crushed
1 tbsp tomato paste
1 tsp curry paste
250 ml (8 fl oz) cold water
2 tbsp chopped parsley
1 quantity hot water pastry, above
1 medium egg, lightly beaten

Heat olive oil in a saucepan over a medium–low heat. Add prepared vegetables, tomato paste and curry paste. Stir together and cook for 5 minutes. Add water, bring to a simmer, cover and cook for 10 minutes. Uncover saucepan, raise heat to high and stir until liquid has evaporated, about 6–7 minutes. Stir in chopped parsley, season to taste and allow to cool.

Preheat oven to 180°C (350°F).

Divide hot water pastry into 6 equal pieces and keep warm. Roll out each pastry to a rough circle about 18 cm (6 in) across. Brush generously with beaten egg. Place one-sixth of vegetable mix in the centre of each pastry circle in a heaped oval. Raise the two sides together and press to seal on top of vegetable mix. Crimp edges to give a decorative look. Continue until all six pasties are made. Place on a greased baking tray and brush with beaten egg.

Cook for 30 minutes or until golden brown. Makes 6.

Greek cheese pastries or spanakopita ⓥ

The classic Greek spanakopita (cheese pie) is a winning light meal in our books. It can also be can be made into small cocktail-sized party food.

150 g (5 oz) spinach leaves
125 g (4 oz) ricotta
1 medium egg
150 g (5 oz) mashed feta
Pinch of nutmeg

Freshly ground black pepper
2 tbsp chopped parsley
6 sheets filo pastry
100 g (3½ oz) melted butter

Preheat oven to 180°C (350°F).

Blanch spinach leaves in boiling water. Refresh immediately under cold running water, squeeze excess water out and chop finely. Mix spinach with ricotta, egg, feta, nutmeg, pepper and chopped parsley until smooth.

Brush 1 sheet of filo pastry with melted butter, lay another sheet of filo pastry on top, brush again with butter and repeat until you have 6 sheets of filo pastry buttered together. Lay filo pastry layers in a 23 cm (9 in) flan tin. Spoon in spinach/ricotta mix. Fold pastry ends over to enclose filling completely. Brush top with melted butter.

Bake in preheated oven for 30 minutes, or until golden brown and slightly puffy. Serves 4–6.

Egyptian bread and butter pudding

Nothing is original, it seems. We've been playing around with this recipe since spotting it in an old cookbook. Recently we've seen two or three other variations on the same theme. Such is life.

100 g (3½ oz) filo pastry, 8–10 sheets
50 g (1¾ oz) melted butter
60 g (2 oz) dried apricots, diced
60 g (2 oz) sultanas
30 g (1 oz) flaked almonds, toasted
30 g (1 oz) shelled pistachios, toasted

30 g (1 oz) pine nuts, toasted
500 ml (1 pt) milk
150 ml (5 fl oz) thick cream
60 g (2 oz) caster sugar
2 tbsp pomegranate syrup*
Whole nutmeg

Preheat oven to 160°C (320°F).

Brush each sheet of filo with butter, crumple loosely and arrange on two baking trays. Bake in preheated oven for 20 minutes, or until crisp and golden.

Turn oven up to 220°C (425°F).

Butter a 20 cm (8 in) pie dish. Crumple filo sheets, retaining some largish pieces. Mix together dried fruit and nuts and layer alternatively with filo pastry in the pie dish. Place milk, cream and sugar in a saucepan and bring to the boil. Pour boiling milk over the pastry and fruit, drizzle with pomegranate syrup and grate fresh nutmeg over.

Bake in preheated oven for 15–20 minutes. Serves 6–8.

Pistachio, almond and orange blossom baklava

This recipe is inspired by Claudia Roden's A New Book of Middle-Eastern Food. *This book is well worth checking out if you're at all interested in food of the Middle East.*

200 g (7 oz) caster sugar
125 ml (4 fl oz) water
60 ml (2 fl oz) lemon juice
1 tbsp orange blossom water
330 g (11 oz) ground almonds
100 g (3½ oz) ground pistachios
½ tsp ground coriander
125 g (4 oz) melted butter
8 filo pastry sheets, cut in half

Preheat oven to 170°C (340°F).

Place sugar, water and lemon juice in a saucepan. Simmer until sugar has dissolved. Allow to cool completely, then stir in the orange blossom water. Mix together the almonds, pistachios and ground coriander.

Brush a 24 cm × 22 cm (9½ × 8½ in) baking dish with melted butter. Lay two sheets of filo in the bottom. Sprinkle a thin layer of nuts on top, fold hanging edges over. Place two sheets filo on top and brush with melted butter. Continue adding layers of nuts and filo until all ingredients are used. Brush top with plenty of butter.

With a sharp knife cut baklava into small diamond shapes and bake in preheated oven for 45 minutes.

When the baklava comes from the oven pour the orange blossom syrup over and allow to cool completely. To serve, run a knife along the lines previously cut. Serves 12.

Vanilla poached fruit
Poached quinces
Spiced poached pears
Sugar-roasted stone fruit with fresh cheese and honey
Caramel oranges
Caramel sauce
Rhubarb crumble
Cherry clafouti
Summer pudding
Raspberry sauce
Chocolate mousse
Lemon mousse
Coffee and cardamom mousse
Chocolate soufflé
Vanilla panna cotta
Caroline's (vodka and blood orange) jelly
Steamed lemon pudding
Sticky date pudding
Chocolate self-saucing pudding
Butterscotch pecan self-saucing pudding
Lemon delicious pudding
Christmas pudding
Bread and butter pudding
Rice pudding
Sago plum pudding
Thin custard
Thick custard
Crème caramel
Baked passionfruit custard
Zabaglione
Tiramisu
Pavlova
Meringues
Chocolate sauce
Pancakes
Vanilla ice-cream
Coffee semifreddo
Frozen nougat
Raspberry and Campari sorbet
Praline

Desserts

PUDDINGS, ICE-CREAMS, MOUSSES AND SWEET THINGS

There's no doubt about it: desserts are an essential food in our household. Everyone has their particular favourites, but it's usually time that dictates which dessert, if any, we make.

The simplest weekday desserts take only a few minutes to prepare, then we leave them to bake or simmer away while dinner is being eaten. These include steamed puddings, rice pudding, poached fruit or a pot of custard to serve with sliced bananas or stewed fruit.

It's on weekends that more complicated desserts have a chance to feature, especially if we're having friends over. Then we're likely to make ice-cream, a panna cotta or a decadent chocolate mousse. What we're serving takes into consideration the meal we are having, the weather and which fruits are in season; it's difficult, for example, to really enjoy a hot pudding after a summer's lunch, especially if that lunch has been a barbecue; or to really appreciate a cold summer pudding on a chilly winter's night, even if we *could* obtain tasty berries.

The individual ideas here can also be mixed and matched to make amazing flavour combinations. Poached tangelos could be served with a steamed ginger pudding and muscat custard, or try the coconut custards with a spoonful of poached pineapple alongside and some of the syrup drizzled over the top. There are also plenty of ideas for dessert in the cake and pastry chapters.

THINGS YOU NEED TO KNOW ABOUT DESSERTS

- Tackle the more complicated desserts only when time permits.
- Don't be afraid to try something new.
- Sheet gelatine is miles better than powdered, which often doesn't dissolve easily and has a funny taste.
- A tub of ice-cream in the freezer can be your stand-by dessert if you have a complete failure.
- Melt some chocolate and cream together to serve over the top of your ice-cream for an instant dessert.
- Family members and dinner guests love dessert – guaranteed!

Vanilla poached fruit

Poaching fruit is extremely easy – it's nothing more than heating water and sugar in a saucepan, adding a few aromatic spices if you feel like it, and simmering the fruit of your choice until it's tender. This will take anything from 5 minutes for berries up to 1½ hours for quinces. Poached fruit retains its shape during cooking; that's why we prefer it to stewed fruit, which disintegrates during cooking. Try berries, cherries, apricots, rhubarb, pineapple, peaches, pears or plums.

500 ml (1 pt) water
200 g (7 oz) caster sugar
Juice of 1 lemon

1 vanilla pod
500 g (1 lb) fruit

Place water, sugar, lemon juice and vanilla pod in a large heavy-based saucepan over medium heat. Stir until sugar is dissolved. Bring to a gentle boil. Allow to simmer for 15 minutes. Cut fruit if needed, place in poaching syrup and cook until just softened. Remove and either serve warm with some poaching liquid or allow to cool and serve in poaching liquid.

Spiced poached fruit
Add cardamom pods, cinnamon sticks, star anise, sliced fresh ginger or even chillies to add a touch of spice.

Dessert wine poached fruit
Substitute half of the water with dessert wine and reduce sugar by half.

USE POACHED FRUIT WITH
- with ice-cream, custard or alongside a simple cake
- on pancakes with a little of the syrup over the top
- in clafouti, tarts, steamed puddings and cakes
- with rice pudding
- under a rich layer of crème brûlée
- in crumbles, tarts and mousses.

Poached quinces

The bright yellow quince is one of our favourite autumn fruits – not only because their perfume will scent a room for weeks but also because of the incredible transformation they undergo during cooking. Virtually rock hard and inedible when ripe, they develop a deep ruby-red colour with an intense, glorious flavour as a result of poaching.

1 litre (1⅔ pt) water
220 g (7⅔ oz) caster sugar
1 vanilla pod
1 lemon, cut in half

2 cloves
4–6 quinces
Cream or vanilla ice-cream to serve

Prepare poaching liquid by placing water, sugar, vanilla, lemon and cloves in a large heavy-based saucepan. Bring liquid to a rolling boil.

Peel, quarter and core the fruit, adding quinces immediately to poaching liquid to prevent discolouration. Reduce to a simmer and cook for about 1½ hours, or until the quinces are tender and ruby red.

Serve quinces with a little of the warm syrup along with cream or vanilla ice-cream. Serves 6.

Spiced poached pears

Pears are one of the most popular fruits for poaching, and they match really well with aromatic spices such as cinnamon, vanilla and cloves.

400 g (14 oz) caster sugar
1 litre (1⅔ pt) water
1 star anise
1 cinnamon stick
2 cardamom pods

2 whole cloves
1 vanilla pod, spilt
Pinch of saffron threads
5 cm (1¾ in) fresh ginger, sliced
6 pears, peeled

Place sugar and water in a large saucepan, one that will fit the pears snugly, and dissolve sugar over a low heat. Add the star anise, cinnamon, cardamom, cloves, vanilla and saffron. Bring to the boil, reduce heat and simmer gently for 10 minutes.

Add peeled pears to simmering liquid. Cover saucepan and cook until fruit is soft. (Expect anything from 20 to 40 minutes, depending on pear variety.)

Test softness of pears by inserting a skewer into them; if not ready, continue cooking for a few minutes more.

Serve pears with a little of the warm syrup and cream or vanilla ice-cream. Serves 6.

Poached pear and almond pudding
Poach 6 peeled pears and retain liquid. Trim bottoms so fruit can stand upright in a buttered 2-litre (4 pt) ovenproof dish. Whisk together 250 ml (8 fl oz) milk, 4 medium eggs, 2 tbsp caster sugar, 60 g (2 oz) ground almonds and 2 tbsp self-raising flour. Pour the almond pudding mix around the pears and cook in preheated oven 180°C (350°F) for 30 minutes, or until puffed and golden brown. Dust with icing sugar and serve warm poaching liquid alongside with cream.

Sugar-roasted stone fruit with fresh cheese and honey

This is one of our favourite easy-to-prepare desserts. Roasting the stone fruit with a little sugar on top intensifies all the natural flavours. It is best done in summer when stone fruit is at its best; ripe nectarines, plums, peaches or apricots will all work a treat.

8 nectarines or peaches or 16 apricots or small plums
60 g (2 oz) caster sugar

100 g (3½ oz) ricotta or goat's curd
Full flavoured honey

Preheat oven to 200°C (390°F).

Cut fruit in half and remove the stones. Place the fruit halves, flesh side up, on a baking tray. Sprinkle sugar on top. Place into preheated oven and cook for 20–30 minutes, or until they are beginning to brown on top.

Place sugar-roasted fruit on a platter, spoon a dollop of ricotta or curd into the centre of each, then drizzle with honey. Serves 4–6.

Spiced roasted stone fruit
Sprinkle ground cinnamon, nutmeg, allspice, cardamom or ginger on to fruit before cooking.

Sugar-grilled stone fruit
Cook stone fruit under a hot grill for 3–4 minutes.

Caramel oranges

Caramel oranges are a classic 1970s dinner party dessert. Now, call us old-fashioned if you will but this is a classic match of flavours that should still be enjoyed today, regardless of trends.

6 oranges, or other citrus fruit
60 g (2 oz) shaved coconut, lightly toasted, optional

Cream to serve

Use a sharp knife to remove skin from oranges and slice the fruit thickly, discarding any pips. Place orange slices into a serving bowl and pour caramel sauce over. Allow to marinate for 2–3 hours before serving.
   Serve fruit and syrup with toasted coconut and cream. Serves 6.

Caramel sauce

90 g (3 oz) caster sugar
60 ml (2 fl oz) water

150 ml (5 fl oz) water, additional

Place sugar and water into a saucepan. Cook over a low heat until sugar dissolves. Raise heat and boil liquid. Stop stirring once liquid is clear; otherwise mixture will caramelise. Cook for 12–15 minutes, until liquid begins to colour; the desired colour is a lovely mix of gold and caramel, not dark brown. If needed, carefully swirl the saucepan to mix the caramel.
   Remove from heat and carefully add additional water; it will probably spit and spurt quite a bit at this stage, so take care. Stir well to make sure all caramel comes from the bottom of saucepan.

Butterscotch sauce
Butterscotch sauce is fantastic on steamed puddings, over ice-cream and with chocolate cake. Instead of adding the additional water, carefully add 60 g (2 oz) butter and 90 g (3 oz) brown sugar. Return to the heat and simmer until smooth. Stir in 125 ml (4 fl oz) cream and whisk until combined. If sauce cools, it will thicken; simply melt it over a low heat until runny again.

Rhubarb crumble

Rhubarb crumble, along with apple, is probably the most popular of all crumbles. Crumbles are a great thing for teenagers to try if they show an interest in cooking, as they are virtually no-fail.

2 bunches of rhubarb
60 g (2 oz) caster sugar
2 tbsp water

150 g (5 oz) soft butter, diced
250 g (8 oz) plain flour
150 g (5 oz) soft brown sugar

Trim off the leaves and root ends from the rhubarb and cut into 2 cm (¾ inch) chunks. Heat a heavy-based pot over medium heat. Add rhubarb, sugar and water. Reduce the heat to low, cover with a lid and cook for 5–10 minutes, stirring often. Remove from the heat and allow to cool.

Preheat oven to 180°C (350°F).

Rub together soft butter, flour and brown sugar until they resemble fine breadcrumbs. Place stewed rhubarb into a baking dish, top with crumble mixture and bake in preheated oven for 20 minutes, or until golden brown. Serve with cream or custard. Serves 4–6.

Nutty rhubarb crumble
Add 60 g (2 oz) of flaked almonds or chopped hazelnuts to the crumble mix.

Rhubarb oat crumble
Substitute 60 g (2 oz) of flour with rolled oats.

Cinnamon rhubarb crumble
Add 1 tsp ground cinnamon to the crumble mixture.

Cherry clafouti

Clafouti is a really simple dessert – a sweet batter poured over fruit and baked in the oven. This French dessert is traditionally made with cherries, but try it with peaches, figs, berries, nectarines or even plums.

3 medium eggs
80 g (2¾ oz) caster sugar
250 g (8 oz) natural yoghurt
250 ml (8 fl oz) milk

2 tbsp self-raising flour
1 tsp vanilla extract
500 g (1 lb) pitted cherries

Preheat oven to 180°C (350°F).

To make clafouti batter beat eggs in a bowl together with sugar, yoghurt, milk, flour and vanilla extract.

Lightly butter an ovenproof dish, then scatter the cherries (or other fruit) into it. Pour mixture over fruit and bake in preheated oven for 45 minutes. When ready, the clafouti will be puffed and golden. Serves 4.

Tomato and anchovy tart (recipe page 240)

Vanilla panna cottas and variations
(recipes page 266)

Caroline's (vodka and blood orange) jelly
(recipe page 267)

Summer pudding

Summer pudding is an old-fashioned English dessert; it's the sort of thing we serve when we're having a large group over on a hot summer's day.

10–15 slices day-old white bread, crusts removed
500 g (1 lb) strawberries
200 g (7 oz) raspberries
200 g (7 oz) blackberries
200 g (7 oz) redcurrants
200 g (7 oz) loganberries
500 ml (1 pt) water
220 g (7⅔ oz) caster sugar
Clotted cream for serving

Line a 1-litre (1⅔ pt) pudding bowl with day-old sliced white bread.

Sort berries and remove any stalks. Bring water and sugar to the boil. Place berries and currants in the hot syrup and allow to heat through for 1 minute. Drain immediately, reserving the liquid.

Return cooking liquid to the saucepan and boil until reduced by half. Allow berries and syrup to cool completely before gently mixing the two together again.

Spoon fruit into bread-lined bowl. Add enough cooking liquid to cover, then top with more bread. Place a small plate onto the top of the pudding (one which fits inside the rim of the bowl) and put a heavy weight on it. Refrigerate overnight.

To serve, remove pudding from bowl by placing a plate over the top of the bowl, turning it upside down and shaking gently. Serve with clotted cream. Serves 6–8.

Cherry berry pudding
Replace the strawberries with 500 g (1 lb) of pitted cherries and cook them for 1 minute before adding the remaining fruit. The cherries add a great richness to the pudding.

Raspberry sauce

Raspberry sauce is great to serve with so many sweet things – over Peach Melba or ice-cream, or alongside chocolate cake, for instance. You can also add this to fruit mousses or ice-cream in place of puréed fruit.

125 ml (4 fl oz) water
90 g (3 oz) caster sugar
250 g (8 oz) raspberries, stalks removed

Place water and sugar in a medium-sized saucepan over low heat and stir until sugar dissolves. Raise heat and bring to boil. Add raspberries, cook for 1 minute then remove from heat. Purée in a food processor and pass through a strainer to remove seeds.

Makes 250 ml (8 fl oz).

Strawberry sauce
Replace the raspberries with an equal quantity of strawberries. Or try blackberries or loganberries.

Chocolate mousse

A good chocolate mousse is a joy to behold, and to eat of course. This is our favourite chocolate mousse because it tastes brilliant, it's incredibly simple to make and it can easily have lots of other flavours added.

200 g (7 oz) dark chocolate, chopped
3 medium eggs, separated
250 ml (8 fl oz) whipping cream

Melt chocolate by placing it in a bowl over a pot of simmering water or in microwave on low for 1–2 minutes.
    Whip egg whites until soft peaks form. Whip cream until soft peaks form.
    Gently whisk egg yolks into cool melted chocolate. Add a spoonful of cream and egg whites and stir in; this will allow you to fold remaining egg whites and cream in without losing their 'air'.
    Gently fold in remaining egg whites and cream. Spoon into serving bowls. Refrigerate until set, about 3–4 hours, or overnight. Yummy served with fresh raspberries and cream. Serves 4–6.

Chocolate coffee mousse
Add 2 tbsp strong black coffee to melted chocolate with the egg yolks.

Chocolate brandy mousse
Add 2 tbsp brandy with egg yolks.

Jaffa mousse
Add chopped zest of 2 oranges to melted chocolate.

Frozen chocolate mousse
Line a log tin with plenty of cling film, leaving lots of overhang. Spoon mousse into tin and smooth the top. Completely cover with cling film and freeze overnight. Cut thin slices to serve.

Lemon mousse

Fruit mousses are seen by most people as fairly old-fashioned – the sort of thing Granny used to serve up. This is a pity, as a mousse is easy to make and lasts for a couple of days refrigerated. Mousses can be made with virtually any fruit and are as 'light as air' to eat, which is perfect in warmer weather or after a big meal.

Zest of 2 lemons, chopped
150 ml (5 fl oz) lemon juice
10 g gelatine* sheets

3 medium eggs, separated
125 g (4 oz) caster sugar
250 ml (8 fl oz) whipping cream

Place lemon zest and juice in a small saucepan and bring to the boil over a medium heat. Remove from heat, add gelatine and stir until dissolved.

Whisk egg yolks and sugar until pale and creamy. Fold lemon mixture into egg yolks. Beat egg whites until stiff. Whip cream until soft peaks form.

Add a spoonful of cream and egg whites to lemon base. Stir in until well combined; this will allow you to fold remaining egg whites and cream in without losing their 'air'. Gently fold in remaining egg whites and cream.

Spoon into serving bowl(s). Refrigerate until set, about 3–4 hours, or overnight. Serves 4–6.

Passionfruit mousse
Reduce lemon zest to 1 and substitute strained passionfruit pulp for lemon juice.

Birgit's easy mousse
This is my Mum's easy mousse, made with just two ingredients: a pack of lemon jelly crystals and a tin of evaporated milk. It's easy to make and it's as light a feather to eat. Chill evaporated milk for 2 hours, then whip until thick. Dissolve jelly crystals in 125 ml (4 fl oz) of boiling water, then drizzle into whipped milk. Beat to incorporate. Spoon into serving bowl(s) and allow to set. This is traditionally made with lemon-flavoured jelly, but any jelly is okay. MC

Coffee and cardamom mousse

We are keen on blending the flavours of coffee and cardamom, so you'll find it in lots of our dessert recipes, including here, in this mousse.

10 g gelatine* sheets
125 ml (4 fl oz) hot strong black coffee
3 medium eggs, separated

90 g (3 oz) caster sugar
¼ tsp ground cardamom
250 g (8 oz) mascarpone

Dissolve gelatine in hot coffee, stir well and strain. Set aside until cool and just beginning to set, about 10–15 minutes.

Beat egg yolks, sugar and cardamom until white and creamy. Add mascarpone and the cooled coffee/gelatine. Mix well. Beat egg whites until stiff peaks form. Stir 1 tablespoon of egg white into coffee mixture, then fold rest through gently.

Spoon into serving bowl(s) and allow to set. Serve with orange and walnut florentines, page 316. Serves 4–6

Chocolate meringue and coffee mousse stack
Make 3 discs of chocolate meringue, page 278. When meringue is cool, layer with coffee mousse (before fully set). Top with grated chocolate and chill until mousse sets.

Chocolate soufflé

We expect that the name chocolate soufflé will get your attention, then you'll put it into the too-hard basket and move on to the next page ... Well, don't!

This way of making a soufflé is how I was taught at catering college and if seventeen-year-old apprentices can make it, so can you. Go on, give it a go, just this once ... and you might not want to stop. AC

2 medium eggs, separated
60 g (2 oz) caster sugar
2 tbsp plain flour
500 ml (1 pt) milk

125 g (4 oz) dark chocolate, chopped
2 egg whites, additional
6 × 175 ml (6 fl oz) soufflé dishes, buttered and sprinkled with caster sugar

In a bowl, beat egg yolks and sugar until pale, stir in flour until smooth. Heat milk and chocolate in a saucepan until chocolate melts. Whisk milk on to egg yolk mixture and return to a clean saucepan over low heat. Stir constantly as custard comes to the boil and thickens. Remove from heat.

Preheat oven to 200°C (390°F).

Whip egg whites until stiff, then carefully fold them into warm chocolate mix.

Place buttered soufflé dishes on a flat ovenproof tray. Divide soufflé mixture between dishes, allowing room for rising. Cook in preheated oven until the soufflés are well risen and firm to the touch, about 12–15 minutes. Remove carefully from the oven and serve immediately. Serves 6.

Coffee soufflé
Omit chocolate. Instead add 2–3 tbsp strong black coffee to the milk as it comes to the boil.

Raspberry soufflé
Omit chocolate. Purée 60 g (2 oz) raspberries and strain to remove the seeds. Stir purée into cooked custard. Scatter a few extra raspberries onto the top of each soufflé as they go into the oven.

Vanilla panna cotta

This is a simple yet stylish dessert. You can add just about any flavouring to the base mix, such as citrus zest, spices or flavour extracts, to get other tastes. Panna cotta is delicious served with fresh berries, figs or roasted stone fruit.

375 ml (⅔ pt) milk
375 ml (⅔ pt) cream
75 g (2⅔ oz) caster sugar

1 tsp vanilla extract
15 g gelatine* sheets
Fruit to serve

Bring milk, cream, sugar and vanilla to the boil. Remove from heat. Add gelatine and stir until dissolved. Strain liquid, then pour into 6 × 125 ml (4 fl oz) moulds. Refrigerate overnight.

To serve use a small spatula or knife to work the pudding away from the edges, then stand mould in boiling water for 4–5 seconds. Place a plate on top of each mould, then turn over carefully so the plate is on the bottom. Shake to dislodge the pudding. Remove the mould and serve with fruit of your choice. Serves 6.

Rosewater panna cotta
Add 2 tbsp rosewater to strained liquid.

Liquorice panna cotta
Add 1–2 tsp liquorice extract to strained liquid.

Cardamom panna cotta
Crush 2 cardamom pods and add to milk/cream and heat. Add 2 tbsp orange blossom water to strained liquid. Serve with 500 g (1 lb) raspberries tossed with 2 tbsp orange blossom water.

Lime panna cotta
Add the chopped zest of 2 limes to the milk/cream, then bring to the boil.

Coffee panna cotta
Substitute 125 ml (4 fl oz) of milk for strong black coffee. Add 2 crushed cardamom pods to milk/cream mixture for additional pleasures.

Jelly-topped panna cotta
Heat 125 ml fruit juice, such as raspberry, add 1 gelatine sheet and dissolve. Divide between 7 × 125 ml (4 fl oz) moulds and set. Pour cool panna cotta onto firm jelly and refrigerate until set.

Caroline's (vodka and blood orange) jelly

Caroline is a new friend. As we're all ex-chefs we've had many food discussions, mostly centred around dessert, and jelly kept popping up in conversation. It became a bit of an in joke and I promised her a jelly recipe with her name, so here it is. MC

250 ml (8 fl oz) blood orange juice
125 g (4 oz) caster sugar
400 ml (13 fl oz) water
60 ml (2 fl oz) vodka, optional
20 g gelatine* sheets

4 tangelos
3 pink grapefruits
4 blood oranges
60 ml (2 fl oz) Cointreau
2 tbsp lemon juice

Place juice, sugar, water and vodka (if using) in a saucepan and bring to the boil. Remove from heat. Add gelatine and stir until dissolved. Strain and pour into 6 × 125 ml (4 fl oz) moulds. Refrigerate until set, 3–4 hours or overnight.

Use a sharp knife to remove the skins and pith of the citrus fruits. Remove the segments from the membranes so that each segment is free from any pith or seeds. Combine all fruits in a bowl with Cointreau and lemon juice and set aside to marinate for up to 4 hours.

To serve, stand moulds in boiling water for a few seconds. Place serving plate on top of each mould and shake to unmould jelly. Warm citrus salad by heating gently in a pan until steaming, or microwave on medium heat for 2–3 minutes. Serve jellies with fruit segments. Serves 6.

Steamed lemon pudding

A good steamed pudding is one of the most popular of desserts. Despite the few ingredients and the easy cooking method, a huge variety of different puddings can be made by swapping the lemon with other flavours.

125 g (4 oz) soft butter
125 g (4 oz) caster sugar
2 medium eggs

200 g (7 oz) self-raising flour
Chopped zest and juice of 2 lemons

Cream butter and sugar until light and fluffy. Add eggs one by one, allowing each to be incorporated before adding the next. Stir in flour, then stir in lemon zest and juice.

Butter a 1-litre (1⅔ pt) pudding bowl and spoon in the pudding mixture. Cover with buttered greaseproof paper and foil. Tie down tightly with string under the rim of the pudding bowl or, easier still, use a large elastic band.

Place pudding bowl into a large pot and pour in enough water to come three-quarters of the way up the bowl. Bring water to the boil; reduce to a simmer, place the lid on the saucepan and cook for 1½ hours. Check the water level from time to time and add more if needed.

Remove pudding bowl from the water and allow to stand for 10 minutes. Remove the foil and greaseproof paper. Run a small spatula around the edge of the pudding and unmould onto a platter. Serve with thin custard. Serves 4–6.

Steamed orange pudding
Substitute orange, tangelo or blood orange zest and juice for lemon.

Steamed chocolate pudding
Replace 60 g (2 oz) of the flour with cocoa. Sift the two together. Omit lemon zest and juice. Add 90 g (3 oz) small chocolate chips as an optional extra.

Steamed jam or marmalade pudding
Spoon 100 g (3½ oz) of your favourite jam or marmalade into bottom of bowl, then spoon pudding mix over the top. Omit lemon juice and zest and add ½ tsp vanilla extract.

Steamed ginger pudding
Add 2 tsp ground ginger to the pudding mix and omit lemon juice and zest. Stir in 60 g (2 oz) chopped glace ginger.

Steamed treacle or maple syrup pudding
Spoon 100 g (3½ oz) golden syrup or maple syrup into bottom of bowl, then spoon pudding mix over the top. Omit lemon juice and zest and add ½ tsp vanilla extract.

Steamed rhubarb pudding
Chop 1 bunch rhubarb into 1 cm (⅓ in) pieces. Toss with 2 tbsp raw sugar, ½ tsp nutmeg and ½ tsp cinnamon. Omit lemon juice and zest and stir in rhubarb, sugar and spices instead.

Sticky date pudding

175 g (6 oz) pitted dates, chopped
1 tsp bicarbonate of soda
250 ml (8 fl oz) boiling water
60 g (2 oz) butter
150 g (5 oz) soft brown sugar
2 medium eggs

175 g (6 oz) self-raising flour
150 g (5 oz) soft brown sugar, additional
250 ml (8 fl oz) cream
½ tsp vanilla extract
1 tbsp butter

Preheat oven to 180°C (350°F).

Mix dates and bicarb in a bowl. Pour boiling water over and leave to stand.

Cream butter and sugar until pale and thick. Add eggs, one by one, incorporating each before adding next. Fold in flour until well mixed, then fold through date mixture. Spoon into a greased and lined 20 cm (8 in) springform cake tin. Bake for 35–40 minutes, or until a skewer comes out clean when tested.

To make toffee sauce place additional brown sugar, cream, vanilla and butter in a saucepan and cook over a medium heat, stirring often until sauce comes to boil.

Cut cake into wedges to serve and pour hot toffee sauce over. Serves 6.

Chocolate self-saucing pudding

This is an incredibly popular style of dessert – partly because it is so easy and partly because of the apparently magical way the sauce starts on the top of the pudding and ends up on the bottom.

60 g (2 oz) melted butter
125 ml (4 fl oz) milk
75 g (2⅔ oz) caster sugar
1 medium egg
150 g (5 oz) self-raising flour
20 g (⅔ oz) cocoa

20 g (⅔ oz) cocoa, additional
100 g (3½ oz) caster sugar, additional
250 ml (8 fl oz) boiling water
1 litre (1⅔ pt) ovenproof dish, buttered and sprinkled with caster sugar

Preheat oven to 180°C (350°F).

Whisk melted butter, milk, sugar and egg together lightly. Sift flour and cocoa together, then whisk in to the milk. Pour this into an ovenproof dish.

Place additional cocoa and sugar together into a bowl, whisk in boiling water until smooth, then pour this over the chocolate pudding.

Place in preheated oven and cook for 30–40 minutes, or until skewer comes out clean when tested. Serves 4.

Chocolate and peppermint pudding
Add 1 tsp peppermint essence with melted butter.

Chocolate and walnut pudding
Add 60 g (2 oz) chopped walnuts with flour and cocoa.

Butterscotch pecan self-saucing pudding

This combination of flavours is decadent to the extreme.

60 g (2 oz) brown sugar
180 g (6 oz) self-raising flour
125 ml (4 fl oz) milk
1 medium egg
80 g (2¾ oz) melted butter
2 tbsp golden syrup
75 g (2⅔ oz) pecan nuts, chopped

90 g (3 oz) brown sugar, additional
15 g (½ oz) cornflour
300 ml (10 fl oz) boiling water
2 tbsp golden syrup, additional
1 litre (1⅔ pt) ovenproof dish, buttered and sprinkled with caster sugar
Cream to serve

Preheat oven to 180°C (350°F).

Stir brown sugar and flour together. Whisk together milk, egg, melted butter and golden syrup until smooth, then pour onto flour mixture. Add nuts and mix together until smooth. Spoon into greased pudding bowl.

Mix additional brown sugar and cornflour together and sprinkle over pudding mix. Pour boiling water onto additional golden syrup and pour over pudding. Place in preheated oven and cook for 45 minutes, or until skewer comes out clean when tested. Serve with cream. Serves 4–6.

Lemon delicious pudding

Few people can resist lemon delicious pudding. Its light-as-a-feather crust floats over a decadently tangy lemon sauce. It's the type of pudding that is perfectly at home as a weeknight family dessert and at a weekend dinner party. We often make it with other citrus fruits such as limes, oranges or tangelos.

75 g (2⅔ oz) soft butter
Grated zest of 2 lemons
330 g (11½ oz) caster sugar
3 medium eggs, separated
125 ml (4 fl oz) lemon juice

250 ml (8 fl oz) milk
100 g (3½ oz) self-raising flour
1 litre (1⅔ pt) ovenproof dish, buttered and sprinkled with caster sugar

Preheat oven to 180C (350F).

Cream butter with zest and sugar. Add egg yolks and mix well. Add lemon juice, milk and flour, mix to incorporate. Beat egg whites until stiff and fold through the batter.

Spoon mixture into the pudding bowl. Place bowl in a deep baking dish and pour hot water into the dish until it comes halfway up the bowl

Cook in preheated oven for 45 minutes, or until golden-brown and puffed. Serves 4–6.

Christmas pudding

This is the pudding recipe we have been making for years and no doubt will continue to make for years to come, as Christmas just wouldn't be the same without it. It uses stout to give it a delicious richness, which is the giveaway that it originated in Ireland, from where my family and I emigrated in 1973. This mix makes three large puddings – one for the day itself, one as a gift and one to put away for mid-year Christmas. AC

175 g (6 oz) self-raising flour
½ tsp ground nutmeg
1 tsp ground cinnamon
1 tsp mixed spice
225 g (7½ oz) fresh breadcrumbs
500 g (1 lb) brown sugar
450 g (15 oz) currants
225 g (7½ oz) raisins
225 g (7½ oz) sultanas
50 g (1¾ oz) slivered almonds

100 g (3½ oz) mixed peel or candied orange peel
Zest of 1 orange
Zest of 1 lemon
225 g (7½ oz) margarine
3 medium eggs
65 ml (2⅓ fl oz) brandy
275 ml (9 fl oz) Guinness
3 × 1 litre (1⅔ pt) pudding bowls, buttered

Sift together flour and spices. Stir in breadcrumbs, brown sugar, currants, raisins, sultanas, mixed peel, almonds and citrus zest. Melt margarine and mix with eggs, brandy, stout and margarine. Stir wet mix into dry mix, combining both fully. It may look quite runny at this stage but will thicken in the refrigerator. Cover mixture and refrigerate overnight.

Divide pudding mixture between three bowls. Cover with buttered greaseproof paper and foil. Tie down tightly with string under the rim of each pudding bowl or, easier still, use a large elastic band.

Place each pudding bowl into a large pot. Pour in enough water to come three-quarters of the way up the bowl. Bring to the boil, reduce to a simmer, cover and cook for 4 hours.

Check water level from time to time and add more if needed. Test the puddings with a skewer as you would a cake, to make sure they are cooked. Either serve while still hot or wrap carefully and store in a cool dark place for up to 6 months. Each pudding serves 10.

Australian Christmas pudding
This is the variation we developed as we grew to love great Australian ingredients – including glace ginger; dark rum from Queensland; and wattle seed, a wonderful native bush food. It is quite different to the original, but delicious also. Add to the pudding mix 1 tsp ground ginger, ¾ tsp ground wattle seed, 175 g (6 oz) chopped glace ginger in place of mixed peel and 150 g (5 oz) macadamias in place of almonds. Swap Australian dark rum for brandy and South Australian stout for Guinness.

Bread and butter pudding

Bread and butter pudding is best made with day-old bread to absorb the egg mixture better. A simple dish that any member of the family could make.

10 slices white bread, crusts removed
Butter as required
30 g (1 oz) sultanas
3 medium eggs
60 g (2 oz) caster sugar
500 ml (1 pt) milk
1 tsp vanilla extract

Preheat oven to 180°C (350°F).

Lightly butter each slice of bread, then cut each into quarters to form triangles. Butter a pie dish and lay the bread triangles into it so that they overlap each other. Scatter the sultanas over the top. Beat eggs, sugar, milk and vanilla extract together in a bowl. Pour egg mixture over the bread slices. Allow to stand for 10–15 minutes, then push bread down to soak up egg mixture, adding the remaining egg mix if there is any.

Bake in preheated oven for 45 minutes. When ready, the pudding will be puffed and golden. Serves 4.

Bread and jam pudding
Spread strawberry or raspberry jam onto the buttered bread triangles.

Pain au chocolat pudding
Substitute 2–3 pains au chocolat (chocolate-filled 'croissants') for bread and butter.

Panettone pudding
Substitute 10 thin slices of panettone for bread and butter.

Rice pudding

This is the easiest rice pudding recipe we know. Anyone of virtually any level of kitchen skills could make it. We often add a dollop of raspberry jam to serve.

1 litre (1⅔ pt) milk
100 g (3½ oz) caster sugar
1 tsp vanilla extract
100 g (3½ oz) short grain rice

Place milk, sugar, vanilla and rice in a large heavy-based saucepan.

Bring to the boil, reduce to a very low heat and cook for 20 minutes, stirring often. When rice is tender remove from heat, cover and allow to rest for 15 minutes before serving. This will allow time for any remaining liquid to be absorbed.

Spoon warm rice into serving bowls. Serves 4.

Middle-Eastern rice pudding
Prepare pudding as directed, then add 60 g (2 oz) toasted pine nuts and 60 g (2 oz) currants. Drizzle with pomegranate syrup to serve.

Baked rice pudding
Make the rice pudding as described. After 20 minutes of simmering, stir in 100 ml (3½ fl oz) cream. Pour into a buttered baking dish (an attractive one that can be served at the table), sprinkle with 100 g (3½ oz) brown sugar and bake in preheated oven 180°C (350°F) for 20 minutes, or until top is caramelised. Allow to cool for 5 minutes before serving. Delicious with quinces.

Adult's rice pudding
Soak 100 g (3½ oz) sultanas in 125ml (4 fl oz) liqueur muscat or tokay as the rice is simmering, then add it to the pudding.

Chocolate rice pudding
Add 60 g (2 oz) of chopped dark chocolate to the pudding once cooked. Stir until melted.

Sticky black rice pudding
Substitute short grain rice for 200g (7½ oz) black glutinous rice, swap milk for water and caster sugar for palm sugar. Cook for 1–1½ hours over a low heat until rice is tender. Serve with coconut milk and fresh lime wedges.

Sago plum pudding

Sago is hardly the most popular of desserts, being commonly described as fish eggs but it can be a great textural and taste sensation. We like it.

1 litre (1⅔ pt) milk
125 g (4 oz) caster sugar
½ tsp vanilla extract

70 g (2⅔ oz) sago
4 plums, pitted and quartered

Bring milk, sugar and vanilla to the boil in a heavy-based saucepan. Sprinkle in sago, stirring all the time. Reduce to a simmer and cook for 25–30 minutes, stirring occasionally until seeds are tender.
    Divide between bowls. And serve with plums on top. Serves 4.

Banana sago pudding with butterscotch sauce
Serve with butterscotch sauce, page 261, and sliced bananas in place of plums.

Thin custard

Nothing compares to a really good pot of custard, especially when served with a steamed pudding or over fruit crumble, stewed fruit or baked apples. Be warned, though: there is an art to making good custard, and it's one that develops with plenty of practice. Classically known as crème Anglaise.

5 egg yolks
125 g (4 oz) caster sugar

500 ml (1 pt) milk
½ tsp vanilla extract

In a bowl beat egg yolks and sugar until pale and thick. Place milk and vanilla into a saucepan and bring to simmering point. Whisk hot milk into egg yolk mixture, then pour it into a clean saucepan.

Place custard over a medium–low heat and stir constantly with a wooden spoon in a figure of eight to prevent the custard catching on the bottom of the saucepan. As it approaches (but isn't allowed to reach) the boil, the mixture will begin to thicken. Remove immediately from the heat and strain into a cold bowl. This will slow the cooking and remove any eggy bits from the custard. Serves 6–8.

Muscat custard
Add 60 ml (2 fl oz) of liqueur muscat or tokay to the custard just before serving.

Banana custard
Slice 2–3 bananas; divide between bowls and pour custard over the top.

Brandy custard
Add 60 ml (2 fl oz) of brandy to the custard just before serving.

Thick custard

This is for those who like their custard thick and gluggy. It's also the custard that is used in other desserts and tarts. Often called pastry cream (crème patisserie).

2 egg yolks
60 g (2 oz) caster sugar
1 tbsp plain flour

500 ml (1 pt) milk
½ tsp vanilla extract

In a bowl, beat egg yolks and sugar until pale, then stir in flour until smooth. Place milk and vanilla into a saucepan and bring to a simmering point. Whisk milk into egg yolk mixture and return to a clean saucepan over low heat. Stir constantly as custard comes to the boil and thickens. Remove from the heat.

This can be made in advance and reheated gently over low heat when needed. Cover with cling film if not using immediately to stop a skin forming. Serves 6–8.

Crème caramel

Crème caramel is a light, refreshing dessert. Do you need more temptation? No? Good, then make it tonight.

90 g (3 oz) caster sugar
60 ml (2 fl oz) water
600 ml (19 fl oz) milk
½ tsp vanilla extract

Zest of 1 orange
3 medium eggs
3 egg yolks
60 g (2 oz) caster sugar, additional

Place sugar and water in a saucepan. Cook, stirring over a low heat until sugar dissolves. Raise heat and boil liquid. Stop stirring once liquid is clear; otherwise mixture will caramelise. Cook for 12–15 minutes, or until liquid begins to colour; the desired colour is a lovely mix of gold and caramel, not dark brown. If needed, carefully swirl the saucepan to mix the caramel. Allow to cool for 1 minute, then pour the caramel into 6 × 175 ml (6 fl oz) individual ovenproof moulds. Tilt and turn the dish so that the caramel covers the base and goes up the sides a little.

Preheat the oven to 160°C (320°F).

Warm milk, vanilla and orange zest in a saucepan over a medium heat. Remove just as it comes to the boil and infuse for 10 minutes. Beat eggs, egg yolks and additional sugar together until pale and thick. Whisk warm milk into egg mixture. Strain the mixture, then pour it in on top of the caramel.

Place dish into a deep baking tray. Pour hot water around to come halfway up the sides. Cook in preheated oven for 35–45 minutes. Custard should be firm to touch, with a slight wobble when ready. Refrigerate overnight.

To serve run a knife around the edge of the custard, then place a plate upside-down over the top of the dish and quickly turn over. Serves 6.

Baked passionfruit custard

We have several passionfruit vines in our garden and as a result we make more than our fair share of passionfruit desserts. These custards are delicious with a fruit sorbet, or with tuile biscuits, page 317.

6 medium eggs
125 g (4 oz) mascarpone
250 ml (8 fl oz) passionfruit pulp, from about 12–15 passionfruit

200 g (7 oz) caster sugar
Grated zest of 2 lemons
80 ml (2¾ fl oz) lemon juice

Beat together eggs, mascarpone, sugar, passionfruit, and lemon zest and juice. Allow to stand for 30 minutes, then strain to remove passionfruit seeds. Pour strained filling into 6 × 125 ml (4 fl oz) dariole moulds. Pour mixture into 6 × 125 ml (4 fl oz) ramekin dishes and place them in a deep baking tray. Pour hot water around dishes to come halfway up the sides. Cover with foil and cook in a preheated oven for 45 minutes, or until custard is just set.

Remove from the water immediately and refrigerate. These are best left overnight to set fully. To serve run a knife around the edge of each custard, then quickly tip custard onto serving plate. Add poached fruit if preferred. Serves 6.

Zabaglione

Zabaglione is a rich marsala-flavoured Italian dessert. It's usually made, poured into tall glasses and served while still warm. It can also be chilled and used in many other ways. It is a particularly impressive and decadent dish to offer friends.

6 egg yolks
110 g (3¾ oz) caster sugar
60 ml (2 fl oz) marsala

Place egg yolks, sugar and marsala in a large stainless-steel bowl and whisk lightly. Sit bowl over a pot of simmering water and whisk mixture continually until it thickens and doubles in bulk, about 5 minutes.

Pour zabaglione into tall glasses and serve immediately. Serves 4.

Zabaglione mousse
Remove from heat and continue to whisk until zabaglione cools. Whisk in 200 g (7 oz) mascarpone and spoon into glasses to set.

Zabaglione ice-cream
Stir zabaglione into homemade vanilla ice-cream, page 279.

Tiramisu

No book about contemporary Australian cooking would be complete without a recipe for tiramisu. This creamy, chocolate- and coffee-flavoured Italian trifle is always popular when it is served, and there is virtually no cooking involved, other than making the coffee essence.

6 medium eggs, separated
3 tbsp caster sugar
500 g (1 lb) mascarpone
3 tbsp sweet Marsala

24 Italian sponge finger biscuits
125 ml (4 fl oz) strong black coffee
Cocoa powder, or grated chocolate

Beat egg yolks with sugar until pale and creamy. Gently whisk in mascarpone and marsala. Whip egg whites until stiff, then fold them into the mascarpone mix.

Lay half the sponge fingers in the bottom a serving dish and drizzle with half of the coffee. Pour half of the mascarpone mix over. Top with remaining biscuits, drizzle with remaining coffee. Top with remaining mascarpone mix. Refrigerate for 3–4 hours to allow the flavours to develop fully. Sift cocoa, or grate chocolate, over the top just before serving. Serves 4–6.

Pavlova

The pavlova is a marvellous version of meringue, almost always topped with cream, then finished with berries and passionfruit. There's no real secret to making one; if you can whip egg whites you can whip up a pavlova. It's traditionally served at barbecues all through summer, so who are we to break a great custom?

6 egg whites
440 g (15 oz) caster sugar
1 tsp vanilla extract
1 tbsp cornflour

1½ tsp white vinegar
250 ml (8 fl oz) whipping cream
Pulp from 6 passionfruit
200 g (7 oz) raspberries

Preheat oven to 180°C (390°F).
    Beat egg whites until stiff peaks form. Add sugar, one third at a time, allowing each third to be well incorporated so that you well end up with a thick glossy meringue. Fold through vanilla, cornflour and vinegar.
    Either spoon into a greased and lined 23 cm (9 in) springform cake tin or spread in a high circle on a sheet of baking paper on a tray. Place in oven, lower temperature to 120°C (245°F) and bake for 45 minutes. Turn the oven off, leaving the pavlova to cool inside the oven overnight preferably.
    Place cool pavlova on a serving platter and cover with whipped cream. Scoop passionfruit pulp on top and scatter raspberries over. Serves 8–10.

Baby pavs
Spoon pavlova mix into 12 individual rounds and bake for 30 minutes. Allow to cool in oven. Serve one per guest.

Meringues

A delicate white meringue is one of the wonders of baking. How is it that two basic ingredients, namely egg whites and sugar, can be transformed into such a delicious food by mere beating and cooking? The technique becomes irrelevant with the first mouthful of these crispy delights with their marshmallow centres.

6 egg whites
300 g (10 oz) caster sugar

Preheat oven to 160°C (320°F).
    Beat egg whites until stiff. Add the caster sugar a third at a time and continue beating until the meringue is glossy and firm. Spoon large dollops of meringue onto lined baking trays (you should get around 20 meringues). Bake in preheated oven for 30 minutes. Turn oven off, and leave to cool for 30 minutes more. Enjoy them as they are! Makes about 20.

With chocolate sauce
Place one meringue on each plate. Add a dollop of whipped cream and another meringue. Pour over hot chocolate sauce, page 278, and serve.

With berries
Layer meringues with whipped cream and berries.

Chocolate meringue
Sprinkle 40 g (1⅓ oz) of cocoa over meringue mixture, then add 1 tsp vinegar and fold in carefully, before baking.

Chocolate meringue discs
Make meringue as described. Line 3 flat trays with paper and divide meringue between them. Smooth into large circles, about 20 cm (8 in). They don't have to be perfect. Cook for 1 hour and leave in oven overnight. Use these 3 circles to make meringue mousse stacks, below.

Chocolate mousse and meringue stack
Make chocolate meringues as described. Top each meringue with coffee mousse, page 265, before it sets and layer meringues on top of each other. Refrigerate for 2–3 hours until mousse sets before serving.

Chocolate sauce

Sometimes I make this sauce with Mars Bars (instead of dark chocolate), which adds that little something extra. Just use same weight of Mars Bars as chocolate (approximately 1⅓ bar) MC

90 g (3 oz) dark chocolate, chopped
1 tbsp butter

2 tbsp brandy
90 ml (3 fl oz) cream

Place all ingredients into a bowl. Set bowl over a pot of simmering water and cook for 5–6 minutes. Stir often until everything has melted together smoothly. Serve while hot or warm.

Pancakes

Pancakes are easily made. Besides, they can also be adapted for the individual tastes of each family member. Perhaps adults will prefer lemon and a sprinkle of sugar while younger members will prefer a little jam in theirs. Then everyone can be happy.

1 medium egg
250 ml (8 fl oz) milk
Pinch of salt

150 g (5 oz) plain flour
30 g (1 oz) melted butter

Place eggs, milk and salt into a bowl and whisk lightly. Whisk in flour a little at a time until the pancake batter has the consistency of thin custard. Allow to rest for 30 minutes. Strain the batter if there are any lumps.

    Heat a heavy-based pan over a medium heat. When hot brush the base of the pan with melted butter, then pour in just enough batter to coat the bottom of the pan thinly. Allow to cook until golden, then turn pancake over and cook the other side. Place the pancake onto a plate and repeat the process until all pancakes are ready.

    Serve pancakes warm with the filling or topping of choice. Serves 4.

Berry pancakes
Top pancakes with fresh berries (or stewed apricots or sliced banana) and roll up. Place filled pancakes in a buttered ovenproof dish and cook in preheated oven 180°C (350°F) for 10 minutes. Serve with cream or ice-cream.

Custard pancakes
Make thick custard, page 274, and allow to cool. Top the pancakes with some of the custard and add a few berries or slices of peach, then roll up. Place filled pancakes in a buttered ovenproof dish and cook in preheated oven 180°C (350°F) for 10 minutes. Serve with a sprinkle of icing sugar.

Cheese blintzes
Mix together 250 g (8 oz) ricotta, 150 g (5 oz) cream cheese, 1 medium egg, zest and juice of 1 lemon, ½ tsp vanilla extract and enough caster sugar to sweeten to your liking. Spoon 1–2 tbsp ricotta mix onto pancakes, roll up and place them in a buttered oven proof dish and cook in a preheated oven 180°C (350°F) for 10 minutes. Warm 250 g (8 oz) blueberries in a saucepan with 2 tbsp caster sugar, lemon juice and a little water, and serve on top of the blintzes with sour cream.

Vanilla ice-cream

This recipe, which has a high proportion of cream, enabled us to get by for years without an ice-cream machine. The cream is folded through at the last minute before the mix goes into the freezer. You just have to give it a stir each hour until it freezes – roughly 4–5 times.

4 medium eggs
125 g (4 oz) caster sugar

2 tsp vanilla extract
500 ml (1 pt) whipping cream

Beat eggs, caster sugar and vanilla until thick and doubled in size, about 5 minutes. Whip cream until it forms stiff peaks. Fold whipped cream gently into egg mixture.

If you have an ice-cream machine, churn ice-cream according to machine's instructions; if not, pour the mixture into a bowl. Place in freezer. Remove after one hour and stir well to break up ice particles. Return to the freezer and repeat every hour for 4–5 hours or until just about frozen. On the last stir transfer ice-cream into a sealable container.

Allow to set in the freezer for at least 24 hours before serving. Serves 8–10.

Christmas cake ice-cream
Add ¼ tsp ground cinnamon, ¼ tsp ground nutmeg and 3 tbsp brandy to the mixture with eggs and sugar. Follow the basic recipe. When the ice-cream is almost frozen, stir in 100 g (3½ oz) mixed fruit, 50 g (1⅔ oz) roasted almonds and 50 g (1⅔ oz) candied cherries.

Chocolate ice-cream
Add 250 g (8 oz) melted dark chocolate to the mix just before adding the whipped cream. You can also add 100 g (3½ oz) chocolate chunks.

Hazelnut ice-cream
Add 200 g (7 oz) roasted hazelnuts and 60 g (2 oz) ground roasted hazelnuts to the mix just before adding the whipped cream.

Coffee semifreddo

Delicious with butterscotch sauce over the top and a brownie on the side.

6 egg yolks
125 g (4 oz) caster sugar
150 ml (5 fl oz) strong black coffee

2 tbsp alcohol, such as Tia Maria
350 ml (12 fl oz) cream

Beat egg yolks with sugar until pale and thick. Add coffee and alcohol and beat to incorporate. Whip cream to soft peaks. Fold through egg mixture until incorporated. Spoon into either a sealable plastic container or a lined loaf tin 23.5 × 13.5 × 7 cm (9 × 5 × 2½ in).

Freeze overnight. To serve, allow to stand at room temperature for 10 minutes. If set in a loaf tin, turn out and cut slices, or scoop using an ice-cream scoop. Serves 8–10.

Lemon and lime semifreddo
Substitute 150 ml (5 fl oz) lemon and lime juice for coffee and alcohol and add chopped zest of 3 lemons.

Passionfruit semifreddo
Substitute 150 ml (5 fl oz) passionfruit pulp for coffee and omit alcohol.

Frozen nougat

Melbourne chef Arnie Sleeman created this method for what he calls frozen nougat. We've persuaded him to allow us to use it here. His recipe uses glucose, which means the ice-cream never really freezes, so in many ways it's more like a semifreddo than an ice-cream. It doesn't require an ice-cream machine and can have virtually any flavour added. How good is that?

100 g (3½ oz) honey
65 g (2 oz) glucose* (available from chemist shops)
8 egg whites

4 egg yolks
125 g (4 oz) caster sugar
330 ml (11 fl oz) cream
165 g (5½ oz) flavouring of your choice

Place honey and glucose in a saucepan, cook over a medium heat until it boils, remove and allow to cool slightly.

Beat egg whites until soft peaks appear, then slowly pour honey mixture onto whites and continue beating until incorporated.

In a separate bowl beat egg yolks and sugar until white and silky in appearance. Whip cream until soft peaks form.

Gently whip a large spoonful of beaten egg white and whipped cream into egg yolks. When this is fully incorporated gently fold in remaining egg white and cream. Fold in flavouring of your choice.

Place the mixture in a freezer-proof bowl, cover with foil and freeze overnight. Serves 8–10.

Liquorice frozen nougat
Use 165 g (5½ oz) liquorice, melt with honey and glucose, it will take an extra 2–3 minutes to melt.

Chocolate and chestnut frozen nougat
Add 90 g (3 oz) melted chocolate and 90 g (3 oz) peeled chestnuts (or hazelnuts).

Frozen nougat ice-cream cake
Because of the no-churn policy this can be poured into a 22 cm (8½ in) springform cake tin and frozen. Perfect for birthday parties. Add strawberry sauce, page 263 or 165 g (5½ oz) of melted chocolate.

Raspberry and Campari sorbet

This is where an ice-cream machine becomes indispensable. If you don't have one you can still give it a go, best within 2 days of making it.

200 g (7 oz) caster sugar
375 ml (12 fl oz) water
300 g (10 oz) raspberries

30 ml (1 fl oz) lemon juice
2 tbsp Campari
Additional Campari for serving

Prepare syrup by placing sugar and water in a saucepan. Stir over a medium heat until sugar dissolves. Allow to cool for 5 minutes.

Place berries, lemon juice and cooled syrup in a food processor and whiz until smooth. Strain liquid to remove the raspberry seeds. Add Campari to the strained liquid.

Pour into ice-cream machine and churn according to the manufacturer's instructions. Alternatively pour the liquid into a shallow freezer-proof tray and freeze for 1 hour. Remove tray and stir the sorbet well. Freeze for 1 hour more and repeat the stirring. Pour into a freezer-proof bowl, cover and freeze overnight. Place sorbet in refrigerator for 10 minutes before serving.

Serve scoops of sorbet with additional Campari drizzled over. Serves 6–8.

Praline

Use praline to garnish desserts such as panna cotta or pavlova, or fold through mousse and ice-cream. Almost any nut can be swapped for the almonds.

80 g (2¾ oz) caster sugar
2 tbsp water
80 g (2¾ oz) blanched almonds, toasted

Place sugar and water in a small saucepan, heat gently to dissolve sugar, then bring to the boil. Swirl the liquid over the heat (do not stir) to prevent sugar crystals forming, and cook to a light brown colour. Remove from heat and stir in toasted almonds. Pour onto a lightly oiled baking tray and leave until set hard. When completely cold, remove from tray and chop into bite-size pieces.

Lemon tea cake
Almond cake
Orange and yoghurt syrup cake
Lemon sour cream cake
Green cake
Coconut cake
Gingerbread cake
One-pot chocolate cake
Chocolate fudge cake
Rich chocolate and almond cake
Choc chip pound cake
Boil-and-bake fruit cake
Banana and walnut cake
Apple, fig and pecan cake
Carrot cake
Pumpkin cake
Orange and almond cake
Date and coconut loaf
Pecan coffee cake
Plum cake
Moist berry pudding cake
Rich apple and walnut cake
Chocolate and hazelnut panforte
Spiced Italian fruit cake
Icings and ganache
Linzertorte made easy
No-cook orange cheesecake
My kind of cheesecake
Cherry cheesecake
Scones
Strawberry shortcakes
Basic muffins
Carrot and nut muffins
Chocolate cheesecake muffins
Peanut butter muffins
Banana muffins
Morning glory muffins
Coffee and walnut muffins
'Doughnut' muffins
Flourless chocolate muffins
Spicy cheddar muffins
Polenta herb muffins

Cakes and muffins

SIMPLE AND DECADENT CAKES, CHEESECAKES AND ENDLESS MUFFINS

There's a domestic goddess (or god) waiting to escape from all of us — one who loves to whip up a batch of muffins or make a decadent apple cake on a Sunday morning.

The truth is, most people find an excuse not to do these things. If it were not so, they would find out just how pleasurable cakes and muffins can be — in the making as well as, obviously, in the eating. One of life's simple pleasures is to make a cake, then have to fight with the children for the right to lick the bowl and spoon!

I tend to make only simple cakes; anything that requires more than two bowls gets put into the too-hard basket, which is the real reason I like muffins.

Anything more complicated and it's over to Allan, who has far more patience. MC

THINGS YOU NEED TO KNOW ABOUT CAKES AND MUFFINS

- Always line tins with baking paper to make sure cakes come out easily and to keep washing up to a minimum. The easiest way to line a round cake tin is to tear a square piece of paper big enough to sit the tin on without much excess. Fold in half, then half again (sideways), then half again diagonally to end with a wedge-shaped piece of paper. Using scissors mark a curve using the cake tin as a gauge, then cut. Unfold and it should fit perfectly.
- Grease tins with the fat you are cooking with. This means butter with most cakes, oil when used, and so on. Grease tin, line with paper, then grease again.
- Basic cake tins to have:
  - 20 cm (8 in)
  - 22 cm (8½ in)
  - 23 cm (9 in)
  - A loaf tin, about 23.5 × 13.5 × 7 cm (9 × 5 × 2½ in)
  - Muffin tins, either 2 × 6 large or 3 × 6 small
  - And a cooling rack.
- It's much easier to make a cake with soft butter than with hard. Zap hard butter in the microwave for 20 seconds, or grate to soften it quickly. We usually use unsalted butter for baking.
- Vanilla extract has a far superior flavour to vanilla essence. Yep, it's more expensive too, but you only have to use half as much.
- When a recipe calls for chocolate, use cooking *couverture*; and the better the quality, the better your cakes. Dark *couverture* is best, and buttons (or chips) melt more easily.
- Use Dutch cocoa for better flavour; again the better the quality, the better the cake.
- For preference use espresso coffee where coffee is called for, using extra coffee grounds for a stronger brew. A stovetop espresso machine makes great cooking coffee. Otherwise the simplest thing to do is to dissolve 1–2 tsp of instant coffee in the required amount of boiling water.
- All eggs are medium (59 g), unless otherwise stated.
- To test whether a cake is ready, insert a skewer or cake tester into the centre of the cake. The skewer should come out free of cake mix or crumbs. If it doesn't, cook for a further 5 minutes, then try again.
- When the cake is cooked, place on a cooling rack and allow to stand for 10–15 minutes before removing the cake tin.
- Needless to say, a mixer will make light work of any beating, whisking or blending to be done.
- A simple way to jazz up a cake is to dust it with icing sugar or cocoa.

Lemon tea cake

Also known as Madeira cake, this is one of our favourite types of cake: quiet and unassuming, but somehow extremely more-ish. If you can leave it alone for a few days, it gets better with age.

220 g (7⅔ oz) soft butter
180 g (6 oz) caster sugar, plus additional for sprinkling
Grated zest of 2 lemons, chopped
3 medium eggs
200 g (7 oz) self-raising flour
90 g (3 oz) plain flour
3 tbsp lemon juice

Preheat oven to 170°C (340°F).
    Cream butter and sugar until light and fluffy. Add lemon zest. Add eggs one at a time, allowing each to be incorporated before adding the next. Stir in flour and lemon juice and keep stirring until incorporated.
    Spoon into a greased and lined loaf tin 23.5 × 13.5 × 7 cm (9 × 5 × 2½ in), sprinkle with additional caster sugar and bake for 1 hour. Test the cake by inserting a skewer; if it comes out clean the cake is ready. If it doesn't, cook for a further 5 minutes and test again. Allow to cool in tin before removing. Serves 6–8.

Lemon and poppyseed tea cake
Add 1 tbsp of poppyseeds to flour.

Cinnamon and lemon tea cake
Add 1 tsp ground cinnamon to flour.

Orange tea cake
Substitute orange zest and juice for lemon.

Lime and poppyseed tea cake
Substitute orange zest and juice for lemon.
Add 1 tbsp poppyseeds.

Almond cake

This almond cake is perfect for afternoon tea, it's so beautifully moist and rich.

125 g (4 oz) soft butter
220 g (7⅔ oz) caster sugar
2 medium eggs
125 g (4 oz) ground almonds
225 g (7¾ oz) self-raising flour
250 g (8 oz) natural yoghurt
A few drops of almond essence
Icing sugar for dusting

Preheat oven to 180°C (350°F).
    Cream butter and sugar until light and fluffy. Add eggs one by one, fully incorporating each one before adding the next. Fold in almonds and flour, yoghurt and almond essence. Spoon into a greased and lined 22 cm (8½ in) springform cake tin and bake in preheated oven.
    Test the cake after 35 minutes by inserting a skewer. If it comes out clean the cake is ready; if it doesn't, cook for a further 5 minutes and test again. When cool, dust cake with icing sugar and serve. Serves 6–8.

Orange and yoghurt syrup cake

This style of cake is always wonderfully moist because you pour flavoured syrup over it not long after it comes from the oven.

125 g (4 oz) soft butter
220 g (7½ oz) caster sugar
3 medium eggs, separated
Zest of 2 oranges
60 ml (2 fl oz) orange juice
250 g (8 oz) natural yoghurt

300 g (10½ oz) self-raising flour
Grated zest of 2 oranges
100 ml (3½ fl oz) orange juice
2 tbsp lemon juice
90 g (3 oz) caster sugar

Preheat oven to 180°C (350°F).

Cream butter and sugar until light and fluffy. Add egg yolks along with the zest. Add orange juice and yoghurt. Mix briefly, then add flour and beat until smooth. Beat egg whites until stiff, then fold through cake mix. Spoon into a greased and lined 22 cm (8½ in) springform cake tin and bake in preheated oven for 40 minutes. Test the cake by inserting a skewer. If it comes out clean the cake is ready; if it doesn't, cook for a further 5 minutes and test again.

Prepare syrup by placing zest and juice in a small saucepan with sugar. Stir to dissolve, then bring to the boil. Allow to simmer for 2–3 minutes. Pour warm syrup topping over cake and allow to cool. Serves 6–8.

Orange poppyseed cake
Add 150 g (5 oz) poppyseeds. Forget the syrup topping.

Lemon sour cream cake

This has a great gutsy lemon flavour and stays moist because of the sour cream in it.

125 g (4 oz) soft butter
200 g (7 oz) caster sugar
Zest of 1 lemon
3 medium eggs
2 tbsp lemon juice

150 g (5 oz) plain flour
60 g (2 oz) self-raising flour
100 g (3½ oz) sour cream
Icing sugar for dusting

Preheat oven to 180°C (350°F).

Cream butter and sugar until light and fluffy. Add lemon zest, then add eggs one by one, fully incorporating each one before adding the next. Stir through lemon juice. Sift flours together and fold in carefully, alternating with sour cream. Spoon into a greased and lined 20 cm (8 in) springform cake tin.

Bake for 40 minutes. Test the cake by inserting a skewer. If it comes out clean the cake is ready; if it doesn't, cook for a further 5 minutes and test again.

Allow to cool for 15 minutes, then remove from tin. Dust with icing sugar to serve. Serves 6–8.

Green cake

Don't be put off by the name; this is a great tasting cake with a hint of almond flavour. My mum made this cake for my brother and me for every birthday we had as children, and it always came with chocolate icing. Even now, I find it irresistible. Our children, though, want to change it to a blue, or even a red, cake; but for me it was always, and will always be, green cake. MC

200 g (7oz) soft butter
250 g (8 oz) caster sugar
3 medium eggs

225 g (7½ oz) self-raising flour
1½ tsp almond essence
1 tsp green food colouring

Preheat oven to 180°C (350°F).

Cream butter and sugar until light and fluffy. Add eggs one by one, fully incorporating each one before adding the next. Add flour with almond essence and colouring. Beat until smooth.

Spoon into a greased and lined 23 cm (9 in) springform cake tin and bake in preheated oven for 40 minutes. Test the cake by inserting a skewer. If it comes out clean the cake is ready; if it doesn't, cook for a further 5 minutes and test again.

Allow to cool for 15 minutes, then remove from tin. When cool, top with chocolate icing, page 299. Serves 6–8.

Coconut cake

This is a beautiful cake with a dense texture that can easily be sliced and passed around. Try it as your next birthday cake.

270 ml (8⅔ fl oz) coconut milk
100 g (3½ oz) desiccated coconut
200 g (7 oz) soft butter

300 g (10½ oz) caster sugar
4 medium eggs
250 g (8 oz) self-raising flour

Preheat oven to 180°C (350°F).

Place coconut milk and coconut in a small saucepan over a medium heat. Allow to simmer for 2–3 minutes, then allow to cool.

Cream butter and sugar until light and fluffy. Add eggs one by one, fully incorporating each one before adding the next. Alternatively fold in sifted flour and coconut mixture until well combined. Spoon mixture into greased and lined 22 cm (8½ in) springform cake tin. Bake in preheated oven for 40 minutes.

Test the cake by inserting a skewer. If it comes out clean the cake is ready; if it doesn't, cook for a further 5 minutes and test again. Allow to cool, dust with icing sugar and serve. Serves 6–8.

Gingerbread cake

This cake comes from the oven smelling sweetly of ginger, mixed spice, treacle and golden syrup. Tempting, eh?

100 g (3½ oz) soft butter
100 g (3½ oz) treacle
100 g (3½ oz) brown sugar
100 g (3½ oz) golden syrup
300 g (10½ oz) self-raising flour

3 tsp ground ginger
1 tsp mixed spiced
2 medium eggs
125 ml (4 fl oz) milk

Preheat oven to 170C°C (340°F).

Melt butter, treacle, sugar and golden syrup together in a saucepan. Allow to cool. Sift flour with spices and fold into the butter and sugar mixture. Add eggs and milk and combine well. Spoon into a greased and lined loaf tin 23.5 × 13.5 × 7 cm (9 × 5 × 2½ in) and bake in preheated oven for 30 minutes.

Test the cake by inserting a skewer. If it comes out clean the cake is ready; if not, cook for a further 5 minutes and test again. Allow to cool before slicing. Serves 6–8.

One-pot chocolate cake

Aha, the best, simplest chocolate cake in the whole world. No need for a mixer, or anything difficult, just a pot and a wooden spoon. This cake is ideal for adults because we love the rich chocolate and coffee, but it's also a great cake for a children's party because it's so dense. And it's perfect all round because it gets better with age. The longer in advance you make it, the moister and deeper the flavours become.

250 g (8 oz) soft butter
150 g (5 oz) dark chocolate, chopped
300 g (10½ oz) caster sugar
250 ml (8 fl oz) strong coffee

150 g (5 oz) plain flour
100 g (3½ oz) self-raising flour
50 g (1¾ oz) cocoa
2 medium eggs

Preheat oven to 180°C (350°F).

Place butter, chocolate, sugar and coffee into a large saucepan. Cook over a medium heat until everything melts, stir occasionally. Remove from the heat and allow to cool slightly. Sift flours and cocoa together and add to cool chocolate mixture along with eggs and beat well until everything combines. Spoon into a greased and lined 22 cm (8½ in) springform cake tin.

Bake for 45 minutes. Test the cake by inserting a skewer. If it comes out clean the cake is ready; if it doesn't, cook for a further 5 minutes and test again. Serves 6–8.

Moist chocolate squares
Bake mixture in a greased and lined lamington tin, top with ganache, page 299.

Chocolate fudge cake

Similar to the one-pot chocolate cake, but just a tad more sophisticated and fudgy.

250 g (8 oz) soft butter, diced
150 g (5 oz) dark chocolate, chopped
250 g (8 oz) caster sugar
250 ml (8 fl oz) strong coffee
150 g (5 oz) self-raising flour

50 g (1¾ oz) cocoa
2 medium eggs
100 g (3½ oz) ground almonds
Ganache, page 299, or extra cocoa powder, for topping

Preheat oven to 180°C (350°F).

Place butter, chocolate, sugar and coffee in a large saucepan. Cook over a medium heat, stirring occasionally, until everything melts. Remove from the heat and allow to cool slightly. Sift flour and cocoa together and add to cooled chocolate mixture, along with eggs and ground almonds. Beat well until all ingredients are combined. Spoon into a greased and lined 22 cm (8½ in) springform cake tin. Bake for 45 minutes.

Test the cake by inserting a skewer. If it comes out clean the cake is ready; if it doesn't, cook for a further 5 minutes and test again. Top with ganache or dust with cocoa powder. Serves 6–8.

Rich chocolate and almond cake

Our variation on this classic Elizabeth David cake, which we find every bit as good as everyone says it is.

250 g (8 oz) dark chocolate, chopped
1 tbsp brandy
130 g (4⅓ oz) ground almonds
250 g (8 oz) soft butter

220 g (7⅔ oz) caster sugar
6 medium eggs, separated
2 tbsp caster sugar, additional
Ganache, page 299, for topping

Preheat oven to 180°C (350°F).

Melt chocolate gently, then mix in brandy and ground almonds. Cream the butter and sugar until light and fluffy. Add egg yolks, then beat to incorporate. Add chocolate and almond mixture, stir lightly to blend. Beat egg whites with additional caster sugar until they form stiff peaks. Add 1 tablespoon of egg whites to chocolate mixture and stir in well. Gently fold through remaining egg white.

Spoon into a greased and lined 23 cm (9 in) springform tin and bake in preheated oven for 50 minutes.

Test with a skewer. If it comes out clean, the cake is ready; if it doesn't, cook cake for a further 5 minutes before trying again. Allow cake to cool in tin for 15 minutes before removing on to a cooling rack.

When cool, cover with ganache. Serves 6–8.

Rich chocolate and hazelnut cake
Replace the ground almonds with roasted ground hazelnuts.

Choc chip pound cake

This is afternoon tea fare at its best – a simple plain cake studded with chocolate chips.

200 g (7oz) soft butter
200 g (7 oz) soft cream cheese
330 g (11½ oz) caster sugar
3 medium eggs

Grated zest of 1 lemon
3 tbsp sour cream, or natural yoghurt
350 g (12⅓ oz) self-raising flour
250 g (8 oz) small chocolate chips

Preheat oven to 180°C (350°F).

Cream together butter, cream cheese and sugar until white. Add eggs, one by one, until incorporated. Add lemon zest and sour cream and mix well. Finally add flour, then stir through chocolate chips. Spoon into a greased and lined 22 cm (8½ in) springform cake tin. Bake in preheated oven for 40 minutes. Check the cake with a skewer. If it comes out clean the cake is cooked; if it doesn't, cook for a further 5–10 minutes and try again. Serves 6–8.

Blueberry pound cake
Substitute blueberries for chocolate chips.

Mascarpone and raspberry pound cake
Substitute mascarpone for cream cheese and fresh raspberries for chocolate chips.

Boil-and-bake fruit cake

This is easy to make and great for bringing away on a weekend camping trip or just for having on hand in the cupboard.

150 g (5 oz) butter
300 g (10½ oz) sultanas
300 g (10½ oz) currants
180 g (6 oz) demerara sugar
1 tsp ground allspice
1 tsp ground cinnamon

1 tsp ground ginger
1 tsp bicarbonate of soda
250 ml (8 fl oz) water
2 medium eggs, beaten
150 g (5 oz) plain flour
150 g (5 oz) self-raising flour

Preheat oven to 180°C (350°F).
   Combine butter, sultanas, currants, sugar, spices, soda and water in a saucepan. Cook over a medium heat until mixture comes to the boil, stirring often. Remove from heat and allow to cool.
   Add eggs and beat well. Sift flours together, add to the mixture and beat well. Spoon into a greased and lined 22 cm (8½ in) springform tin and bake for 1 hour. Check the cake with a skewer. If it comes out clean the cake is cooked; if it doesn't, cook for a further 5–10 minutes and try again. Serves 8–10.

Apple fruit cake
Swap half of the dried fruit for grated fresh apple.

Fig or date fruit cake
Replace half of the currants with figs or dates.

Banana and walnut cake

At last, something to do with the bananas lurking at the bottom of the fruit bowl. The riper the bananas and the blacker the skins, the better this cake will be.

125 g (4 oz) soft butter
220 g (7⅔ oz) caster sugar
2 medium eggs
225 g (7⅔ oz) self-raising flour

1 tsp vanilla extract
2 ripe bananas, mashed
90 g (3 oz) walnuts, chopped, optional

Preheat oven to 180°C (350°F).
   Cream butter and sugar until light and fluffy. Add eggs, one by one, incorporating well after each addition. Stir through flour, vanilla, mashed banana and walnuts.
   Spoon into a greased and lined log tin 23.5 × 13.5 × 7 cm (9¼ × 5¼ × 2¾ in) and bake in preheated oven for 20–25 minutes. Check the cake with a skewer. If it comes out clean the cake is cooked; if not, cook for a further 5–10 minutes and try again. Serves 6–8.

Apple, fig and pecan cake

This is a rich, moist cake that will keep well for several days.

Zest of 1 orange
125 ml (4 fl oz) orange juice
150 g (5 oz) raw sugar
150 g (5 oz) honey
100 g (3½ oz) dried figs, chopped
60 g (2 oz) raisins
1 apple, grated
150 g (5 oz) plain flour

150 g (5 oz) self-raising flour
1 tsp baking powder
½ tsp ground cinnamon
1 tsp mixed spice
2 medium eggs, lightly beaten
60 ml (2 fl oz) vegetable oil
90 g (3 oz) pecan nuts, roughly chopped
Cream cheese frosting, page 299

Preheat oven to 180°C (350°F).

Combine orange zest, juice, sugar, honey, figs and raisins in a saucepan. Bring to the boil over a medium heat, then remove and allow to cool. Add the grated apple. Sift flours, baking powder and spice together and add to mixture. Add eggs, oil and pecans and mix well until combined.

Spoon into a greased and lined 22 cm (8½ in) spring form tin. Bake for 45 minutes. Check the cake with a skewer. If it comes out clean the cake is cooked; if it doesn't, cook for a further 5–10 minutes and try again. Allow to cool in tin for 15 minutes, then remove and cool on a cooling rack.

Top with cream cheese frosting. Serves 6–8.

Carrot cake

When we first heard about carrot cakes in the 1980s, we were very sceptical of the whole idea. This delicious cake goes to prove just how wrong we were.

300 g (10½ oz) self-raising flour
1 tsp cinnamon
1 tsp mixed spice
4 medium eggs
350 g (12 oz) caster sugar
1 tsp vanilla extract
300 ml (10 fl oz) olive or vegetable oil

Pinch of salt
60 g (2 oz) hazelnuts
60 g (2 oz) walnut pieces
150 g (5 oz) sultanas
3 large grated carrots
Lemon cream cheese frosting, page 299

Preheat oven to 180°C (350°F).

Sift flour, cinnamon and mixed spice together into a large bowl. Add eggs, sugar, vanilla, oil and a pinch of salt. Mix lightly, then incorporate hazelnuts, walnuts, sultanas and grated carrots.

Pour into a greased and lined 23 cm (9 in) greased cake tin. Bake in preheated oven for 1 hour. Check the cake with a skewer. If it comes out clean, the cake is cooked; if it doesn't, cook for a further 5–10 minutes and try again. Allow to cool in tin for 15 minutes, then remove and cool on cooling rack.

Top with lemon cream cheese frosting. Serves 8–10.

Pumpkin cake

Pumpkin is a particularly sweet vegetable and it produces a cake that has a lovely crust on the outside and is moist on the inside.

100 g (3½ oz) sultanas
250 ml (8 fl oz) hot tea
225 g (7¾ oz) soft butter
220 g (7⅔ oz) caster sugar
3 medium eggs
375 g (13 oz) self-raising flour

500 g (1 lb) pumpkin, steamed or boiled and puréed
1 tsp mixed spice
Icing sugar for dusting or cream cheese frosting, page 299

Preheat oven to 180°C (350°F).

Soak sultanas in hot tea for 15 minutes, drain well and discard tea. Set sultanas aside. Cream butter and sugar until light and fluffy. Add eggs one by one, beating well after each addition. Add flour and pumpkin purée, beat well. Stir in sultanas and mixed spice. Pour into a greased and lined 22 cm (8½ in) springform cake tin and bake in preheated oven for 50–60 minutes.

Check the cake with a skewer. If it comes out clean the cake is ready; if it doesn't, cook for a further five minutes and try again.

To serve, dust with icing sugar or cream cheese frosting. Serves 6–8.

Orange and almond cake

This is great for dessert served with mixed berries or even just cream.

2 oranges
5 medium eggs
220 g (7⅔ oz) caster sugar

250 g (8 oz) ground almonds
1 tsp baking powder

Place oranges in a small saucepan, cover with water and bring to the boil. Reduce heat to a simmer and cook for 30–40 minutes, or until fruit is soft. Allow to cool. Remove all pips. Purée oranges in a food processor until smooth.

Preheat oven to 180°C (350°F).

Beat eggs and sugar until pale and doubled in bulk, about 5 minutes. Mix almonds and baking powder together. Add orange purée and almond mixture to the beaten eggs and beat to incorporate completely. Pour mixture into a greased and lined 22 cm (8½ in) springform cake tin. Bake in preheated oven until light brown and firm in the centre, about 1 hour. Allow to cool. Dust with icing sugar to serve. Serves 6–8.

Tangelo and almond cake
For a twist on this classic, replace oranges with tangelos when in season.

Date and coconut loaf

This very healthy looking, and tasting, cake will keep for up to a week in an airtight container.

175 g (6 oz) dates, chopped
125 ml (4 fl oz) boiling water
125 g (4 oz) soft butter
100 g (3½ oz) caster sugar

1 medium egg
100 g (3½ oz) self-raising flour
60 g (2 oz) desiccated coconut

Preheat oven to 180°C (350°F).
    Soak chopped dates in boiling water until well softened and water has been absorbed. Cream butter and sugar until light and fluffy. Beat in egg.
    Add flour and beat until smooth. Add dates and coconut and stir well until combined.
    Spoon into a greased and lined loaf tin 23.5 × 13.5 × 7 cm (9 × 5 × 2½ in) and bake in preheated oven for 40 minutes. Test by inserting a skewer. If it comes out clean, it's ready; if it doesn't, cook for a further 5 minutes and try again. Serves 6–8.

Pecan coffee cake

This is a very simple tea cake, or should that be a coffee cake?

150 g (5 oz) soft butter
90 g (3 oz) caster sugar
2 medium eggs
150 g (5 oz) self-raising flour

1 tsp baking powder
3 tbsp strong coffee
90 g (3 oz) chopped pecans
Pecan halves and coffee icing, page 299

Preheat oven to 180°C (350°F).
    Cream butter and sugar until light and fluffy. Add eggs, one by one, incorporating well after each addition. Sift together flour and baking powder. Add flour and coffee and mix until well combined. Fold through chopped nuts.
    Spoon into a greased and lined 20 cm (8 in) springform cake tin and bake in preheated oven for 30–35 minutes. Check the cake with a skewer. If it comes out clean the cake is cooked; if it doesn't, cook for a further 5 minutes and try again.
    Allow to cool, then top with coffee icing and pecan halves. Serves 6–8.

Steamed marmalade pudding (recipe page 268)

Lemon tea cake (recipe page 285)

My kind of cheesecake (recipe page 300)

Plum cake

Every summer we have oodles of plums from a tree in our garden, and this cake is just one of our favourite things to do with them.

200 g (7 oz) soft butter
165 g (6 oz) caster sugar
4 medium eggs
1 tsp vanilla extract
125 g (4 oz) plain flour

100 g (3½ oz) self-raising flour
Pinch of salt
12 blood plums
Icing sugar for dusting

Preheat oven to 180°C (350°F).

Cream butter and sugar until light and fluffy. Add eggs, one at time, allowing each one to be incorporated well. Add vanilla, sifted flours and salt together and stir in well.

Spoon into a greased and lined 23 cm (9 in) springform cake tin. Cut fruit in half, remove stones and arrange on top of cake mixture. Bake in preheated oven for 30–35 minutes. Check that cake is cooked by inserting skewer. If it comes out clean, the cake is cooked; if it doesn't, cook for a further 5 minutes and try again. Allow to cool, dust with icing sugar to serve. Serves 6–8.

Moist berry pudding cake

A rich, moist full-flavoured cake, great for any time of day.

125 g (4 oz) plain flour
1 tsp baking powder
Pinch of salt
60 g (2 oz) caster sugar
60 g (2 oz) soft butter, finely diced
1 medium egg

3 tbsp milk
250–350 g (8–12 oz) berries
60 g (2 oz) raw sugar
½ tsp ground cinnamon
2 tbsp melted butter
Icing sugar for dusting

Preheat oven to 180°C (350°F).

Sift flour, baking powder, salt and sugar together into a large bowl. Add butter and rub together until mixture develops a rough breadcrumb texture. In a separate bowl beat egg and milk together, add to flour mix and stir until a smooth dough forms. Spoon into a greased and lined 20 cm (8 in) springform cake tin. Scatter the berries on top.

Mix together raw sugar, cinnamon and melted butter. Drizzle over top of cake. Bake cake in preheated oven for 30–35 minutes. Check that cake is cooked by inserting a skewer. If it comes out clean, the cake is cooked; if it doesn't, cook for a further 5 minutes and try again. Allow to cool, dust with icing sugar to serve. Serves 6–8.

Rich apple and walnut cake

This cake has a top layer of buttery apple slices and lots of crunchy walnuts inside.

1 kg (2 lb) apples
60 g (2 oz) butter
100 ml (3½ fl oz) sweet wine
150 g (5 oz) soft butter
150 g (5 oz) caster sugar, additional
3 medium eggs
½ tsp vanilla extract
300 g (10½ oz) self-raising flour
250 ml (8 fl oz) cream
150 g (5 fl oz) walnuts, roughly chopped
1 tbsp raw sugar

Preheat oven to 180°C (350°F).

Peel and core the apples, then cut into wedges. Heat a heavy-based saucepan over medium heat, melt butter and add apple slices. Stir apple slices for 5–6 minutes. Do not allow to brown. Add wine and cook until liquid has evaporated. Set aside to cool.

Cream additional butter and sugar until light and fluffy. Begin adding eggs one by one, fully incorporating each before adding the next. Add vanilla and flour and mix until smooth. Stir through cream, walnuts and ⅓ of the cooked apples.

Spoon into a greased and lined 23 cm (9 in) springform cake tin. Top cake with the remaining apple slices. Sprinkle with raw sugar. Bake for 45 minutes in preheated oven. Check that cake is cooked by inserting skewer. If it comes out clean, the cake is cooked; if it doesn't, cook for a further 5 minutes and try again. Best served warm with pure cream. Serves 6–8.

Chocolate and hazelnut panforte

This is our own version of panforte, a firm toffee-like cake of Italian origin. Use new season's hazelnuts and the best chocolate you can afford. You must line the cake tin with greaseproof paper for this recipe.

150 g (5 oz) dark chocolate, chopped
150 g (5 oz) caster sugar
350 g (12 fl oz) honey
500 g (1 lb) hazelnuts, skins removed
200 g (7 oz) citron*, diced
50 g (1¾ oz) plain flour
50 g (1¾ oz) Dutch cocoa
2 tsp ground cinnamon
1 tsp ground nutmeg
¼ tsp ground black pepper
¼ tsp ground cloves
¼ tsp mixed spice

Preheat oven to 150°C (300°F). Prepare a 23 cm (9 in) springform cake tin by lining base and sides with greaseproof paper. Lightly grease with hazelnut or olive oil.

Place chocolate, sugar and honey in a large saucepan and dissolve over low heat, stirring regularly.

Place hazelnuts and citron in a large bowl. Sift flour, cocoa and spices, add to nut mix and combine well. Pour hot chocolate mixture over dry ingredients and stir together quickly. Press firmly into prepared tin. Bake in preheated oven for 60 minutes.

During cooking the mixture will start to bubble at the edges of the tin. When bubbles have almost reached the middle, the cake is ready. Remove and, if necessary, smooth top using a butter knife. Cool for 15 minutes, then remove from tin. Allow to cool completely before cutting.

To serve, cut into quarters then into thin slices with a sharp knife and serve with coffee.

Panforte can be wrapped in silicon paper and stored in a cool dark place for up to 6 months. Serves 18–20.

Spiced Italian fruit cake

This is a glorious blending of candied fruits, chocolate, a multitude of spices and the heady aroma of Marsala. Resistance is useless.

When the cake mix is in the tin you can add additional sliced glace fruit in a decorative pattern on top if you wish.

125 g (4 oz) sultanas
80 ml (2¾ fl oz) Marsala
250 g (8 oz) blanched almonds, chopped
90 g (3 oz) pine nuts
250 g (8 oz) candied fruit, such as orange, apricots, figs, pears or lemon, chopped
125 g (4 oz) dark chocolate, chopped
125 g (4 oz) caster sugar
125 g (4 oz) plain flour

1 tsp ground cinnamon
¼ tsp ground cloves
½ tsp nutmeg
½ tsp ground cardamom
½ tsp baking powder
2 tbsp honey
60 g (2 oz) butter
3 medium eggs

Soak sultanas in Marsala for at least 1 hour, but ideally overnight. Cooking the sultanas in the Marsala for 1–2 minutes in the microwave will hurry the soaking along.

Preheat oven to 180°C (350°F).

Mix sultanas with nuts, candied fruit and chocolate. Add sugar and mix together. Sift flour with spices and baking powder. Mix through nut mixture. Melt honey and butter together. Beat eggs until light and fluffy and doubled in size. Add warm butter and honey mixture to eggs and fold through fruit/nut mixture until well combined.

Spoon into a greased and lined 22 cm (8½ in) springform cake tin. Bake in preheated oven for 45–50 minutes, or until a skewer comes out clean. Serves 8–10.

ICINGS AND GANACHE

Basic icing
This basic icing is what you'll need for everyday cakes.

1½ tbsp water
30 g (1 oz) melted butter

150 g (5 oz) sifted icing sugar

Mix water and butter together. Add to icing sugar bit by bit until you reach the desired consistency.

Lemon icing
Substitute lemon juice for water and add the finely chopped zest of 1 lemon.

Chocolate icing
Substitute cocoa powder for 30 g (1 oz) of the icing sugar.

Orange icing
Substitute orange juice for water and add the finely chopped zest of 1 orange.

Passionfruit icing
Strain 2 passionfruit and add same amount of juice as water.

Coffee icing
Substitute strong coffee for water.

Chocolate ganache
This is the shiny icing used on European cakes. Be sure to place your cake on a cooling rack over a plate before pouring the warm ganache over.

90 ml (3 fl oz) cream

125 g (4 oz) dark chocolate, chopped

Warm the cream to just below boiling, then remove from heat. Add chocolate and whisk to incorporate. Pour over cake, taking care to cover sides as well as top.

White chocolate ganache
Substitute white chocolate for dark.

Cream cheese frosting
This is the classic icing for carrot cake, but we love its fresh, creamy flavour and use it on lots of other cakes too.

200 g (7 oz) soft cream cheese
100 g (3½ oz) caster sugar

2 tbsp lemon juice

Place all ingredients in food processor and blend until smooth.

Linzertorte made easy

Here we replace the traditional Linzertorte pastry lattice top with flaked almonds. But if you have one of the lattice gadgets, feel free to reserve a small amount of the dough to form the lattice strips and lay them across the top.

175 g (6 oz) plain flour
75 g (2⅔ oz) ground hazelnuts
60 g (2 oz) icing sugar
Zest of 1 lemon
1 tsp ground cinnamon

100 g (3½ oz) soft butter, diced
2 egg yolks
350 g (12⅓ oz) plum jam
1 tbsp lemon juice
60 g (2 oz) flaked almonds

Preheat oven to 180°C (350°F).

Combine flour, hazelnuts, icing sugar, lemon zest and cinnamon in a large bowl. Rub in butter until mixture develops a breadcrumb texture. Add egg yolks and form mixture into a smooth dough. Press dough into a greased and lined 22 cm (8½ in) springform cake tin, pushing some of the dough up the sides to form an edge, like a tart.

Mix plum jam and lemon juice together and spoon onto dough, taking care not to let it go over the edge. Sprinkle flaked almonds on top and bake in preheated oven for 30–40 minutes, or until filling is beginning to set.

Allow the torte to cool completely before cutting and serving. Serves 6–8.

No-cook orange cheesecake

The simplest cheesecake of all, and very nice it is too.

150 g (5 oz) digestive biscuits
60 g (2 oz) melted butter
500 g (1 lb) soft cream cheese
150 g (5 oz) caster sugar

150 ml (5 fl oz) orange juice
10 g gelatine* sheets
100 ml (3½ fl oz) cream
Zest of 2 oranges

Place biscuits in a food processor and whiz to form small crumbs, add melted butter and process briefly. Press biscuit mix into the bottom of 20 cm (8 in) springform cake tin. Place in the refrigerator to set, for at least 20 minutes.

Beat cream cheese with sugar until well softened and creamy. Place orange juice in a saucepan and bring to the boil, add gelatine sheets and stir until dissolved. Add cream, orange zest and gelatine mixture to cream cheese and stir until well combined. Pour on top of biscuit base and chill until set. Serves 6–8.

Lemon cheesecake
Substitute lemon for orange, reduce juice to 90 ml (3 fl oz).

Chocolate cheesecake
Omit gelatine, zest and juice. Add 150 g (5 oz) melted chocolate and 125 ml (4 oz) sour cream to beaten cream cheese.

My kind of cheesecake

This cheesecake is made in the traditional way but is cooked in a deep baking tray surrounded by hot water. This gentle cooking means the cheesecake cooks slowly. The result is our kind of cheese cake: one with an extraordinarily soft, silky texture. MC

150 g (5 oz) digestive biscuits
60 g (2 oz) melted butter
500 g (1 lb) cream cheese
125 g (4 oz) caster sugar
Zest of 2 lemons

2 medium eggs
3 egg yolks
150 ml (5 fl oz) cream
100 ml (3½ oz) lemon juice

Place biscuits in a food processor and whiz to form small crumbs, add melted butter and process briefly. Press biscuits into the bottom of 22 cm (8½ in) springform cake tin. Place in the refrigerator to set, for at least 20 minutes.

Preheat oven to 170°C (340°F).

Beat cream cheese until smooth, add sugar and lemon zest, then whisk in eggs and yolks one at a time. Stir in cream and lemon juice. Take the cake tin and wrap the outside base with foil, using two pieces to cover the base. This prevents water seeping into the cake during cooking.

Place the cake tin in a deep baking tray. Pour in cheesecake filling over biscuit base. Pour boiling water into the baking dish to come halfway up the cake tin. Place carefully in the oven. Cook for 1 hour, or until the cake is just set, still with some hint of wobble. Allow to cool on a cooling rack before refrigerating, preferably overnight. Serves 6–8.

Passionfruit cheesecake
Substitute strained passionfruit pulp for lemon juice and serve chilled cake with additional pulp on top.

Baked orange cheesecake
Substitute orange juice and zest for lemon juice and zest.

Cherry cheesecake

This cheesecake has a similar texture to My kind of cheesecake as it is also cooked in a deep baking tray surrounded by hot water. The cherry topping makes it even more enjoyable.

150 g (5 oz) digestive biscuits
60 g (2 oz) melted butter
200 g (7 oz) soft cream cheese
125 g (4 oz) caster sugar
Zest of 1 lemon
2 medium eggs
150 g (5 oz) curd cheese or ricotta

200 g (7 oz) cottage cheese
500 g (1 lb) pitted cherries, halved
90 ml (3 fl oz) water
2 tbsp caster sugar
1 tbsp arrowroot
1 tbsp cold water, additional

Place biscuits in a food processor and whiz to form small crumbs, add melted butter and process briefly. Press biscuits into the bottom of 22 cm (8½ in) springform cake tin. Place in the refrigerator to set, for at least 20 minutes.

Beat cream cheese, sugar and lemon zest until smooth. Add eggs one at a time, beating after each addition. Fold through curd and cottage cheese.

Take the cake tin and wrap the outside base with foil, using two pieces to cover the base. This prevents water seeping into the cake during cooking.

Place the cake tin in a deep baking tray. Pour in cheesecake filling over biscuit base. Pour boiling water into the baking dish to come halfway up the cake tin. Place carefully in the oven. Cook for 1 hour, or until the cake is just set, with some hint of wobble still. Allow to cool on a cooling rack before refrigerating, preferably overnight.

Place water and sugar in a saucepan and bring to the boil. Add cherries. Dissolve arrowroot in cold water and add to cherry mixture, stir until thick. Pour cherry mixture over cold cheesecake and return to the refrigerator for about 30 minutes, or until set. Serves 6–8.

Raspberry cheesecake
Substitute cherries for raspberries.

Scones

Many people claim that they, and only they, know how to make the perfect scone. Try the recipe below and you'll realise that now you have that knack too!

300 g (10½ oz) self-raising flour
Pinch of salt
2 tsp caster sugar
125 ml (4 fl oz) cream
125 ml (4 fl oz) milk

Additional cream
Jam
Whipped cream

Preheat oven to 200°C (390°F).

Sift together flour, salt and sugar into a bowl. Mix cream and milk together, then stir the wet mix onto the dry mix. Stir gently until the mixture is just combined. Tip mixture onto a lightly floured bench top.

Pat scone dough out with lightly floured hands until it is 2 cm thick. Cut out scones with a 5½ cm (2 in) cutter. Mix together leftover bits and roll and cut them out also.

Place scones on a lined baking tray touching together, brush tops with additional cream. Cook in preheated oven for 12–15 minutes.

Remove tray and cover scones with a clean tea towel until cool. Split scones and spread with jam and whipped cream. Makes 10–12.

Cinnamon scones
Sift 1 tsp of cinnamon with the flour.

Date scones
Add 6–8 finely chopped dates to the scone dough.

Strawberry shortcakes

These shortcakes make a great Sunday afternoon tea treat.

325 g (12 oz) plain flour
Pinch of salt
1 tbsp baking powder
60 g (2 oz) caster sugar
125 g (4 oz) soft butter, chopped
1 medium egg, beaten

125 ml (4 fl oz) cream
2 tbsp caster sugar, additional
1 egg white, lightly beaten
300 g (10 oz) strawberries, sliced
250 ml (8 fl oz) whipped cream

Preheat oven to 220°C (425°F).

Sift flour, salt and baking powder into a bowl. Add sugar and butter and rub in to produce a fine breadcrumb texture. Whisk egg into cream and pour into flour mixture, bit by bit, stirring it with a fork until mixture holds together.

Turn dough out onto a lightly floured surface and roll to a thickness of 2 cm (1 in). Cut out circles using a 6 cm (2½ in) cutter. Continue re-rolling dough and cutting out circles – you should get 8 in total.

Place shortcakes on a greased baking tray, brush with egg white and sprinkle with remaining caster sugar. Bake for 10–15 minutes, until golden brown. Split while still warm and fill with sliced strawberries and whipped cream and serve immediately. Makes 8.

Basic muffins

This is our everyday muffin mixture that's exceptionally easy to make. You can vary it in many ways by adding berries, chocolate chips or anything else that takes your fancy.

150 g (5 oz) self-raising flour
Pinch of salt
100 g (3½ oz) caster sugar
1 tsp vanilla extract

125 ml (4 fl oz) milk
3 tbsp melted butter
1 egg

Preheat oven to 180°C (350°F).

Mix flour, salt and sugar together. Add vanilla, milk, butter and egg and beat until smooth. Spoon into greased muffin trays and bake in preheated oven for 15–20 minutes, or until risen and golden brown. Makes 6 large or 12 small muffins.

Chocolate muffins
Substitute cocoa for 30 g (1 oz) of the flour.

Blueberry muffins
Add 125 g (4 oz) of blueberries to the mix.

Carrot and nut muffins

These muffins are a delish combination of sweet, grated carrot, currants and crunchy walnuts. You're bound to love them as much as we do.

100 g (3½ oz) caster sugar
90 ml (3 fl oz) vegetable oil
1 medium egg
1 tsp vanilla extract

100 g (3½ oz) self-raising flour
1 carrot, grated
50 g (1¾ oz) walnuts, chopped
50 g (1¾ oz) currants

Preheat oven to 180°C (350°F).

Place sugar, oil, egg and vanilla in a large bowl and beat until smooth. Add flour, carrot, nuts and currants and stir well until combined. Spoon into greased muffin trays and bake in preheated oven for 15–20 minutes, or until golden brown and risen. Makes 6 large or 12 small muffins.

Apple and hazelnut muffins
Replace carrot with apple and walnuts with hazelnuts.

Chocolate cheesecake muffins

These are a bit tricker to make than some of our other muffin recipes, but they well worth the extra hassle.

90 g (3 oz) cream cheese
30 g (1 oz) caster sugar
150 g (5 oz) self-raising flour
30 g (1 oz) cocoa
Pinch of salt

100 g (3½ oz) caster sugar, additional
1 medium egg, beaten
175 ml (6 fl oz) milk
80 ml (2¾ fl oz) vegetable oil

Preheat oven to 180°C (350°F).

Beat cream cheese and sugar until soft and smooth. Set aside.

Sift flour, cocoa and salt together into a large bowl. Add additional sugar and mix together. Beat egg, milk and oil together, then add to the flour mix and beat until well combined.

Half-fill greased muffin tins with chocolate batter. Add about 1 tsp of cream cheese mix, then cover with remaining chocolate batter. Bake in preheated oven for 15–20 minutes, or until risen and golden brown. Makes 8 large or 16 small muffins.

Peanut butter muffins

These are incredibly easy to make and will appeal to peanut butter lovers everywhere.

125 g (4 oz) soft crunchy peanut butter
75 g (2⅔ oz) soft butter
100 g (3½ oz) caster sugar

2 medium eggs
250 ml (8 fl oz) milk
225 g (7½ oz) self-raising flour

Preheat oven to 180°C (350°F).

Cream butters, sugar and eggs together until smooth. Add milk, mix well, then add flour and stir to combine. Spoon into greased muffin tins. Bake in preheated oven for 15–20 minutes until risen and golden brown. Makes 12 large muffins.

Banana muffins

The banana in these muffins gives them a great fruity flavour and texture.

3 ripe bananas, mashed
180 g (6 oz) caster sugar
1 medium egg

75 g (2⅔ oz) melted butter
225 g (7½ oz) self-raising flour

Preheat oven to 180°C (350°F).

Mix mashed bananas and sugar together well. Beat egg in, add melted butter, stir to combine, then add flour, stirring well until combined.

Spoon into greased muffin tins and bake in preheated oven for 20 minutes, or until risen and golden brown. Makes 6 large or 12 small muffins.

Banana and walnut muffins
Add 60 g (2 oz) chopped walnuts.

Banana, pecan and maple syrup muffins
Substitute 2 tbsp maple syrup for 30 g (1 oz) of the sugar. Add 60 g (2 oz) chopped pecans.

Morning glory muffins

Apparently these are the ultimate morning muffin, but we never seem to get around to making them until at least lunchtime.

150 g (5 oz) self-raising flour
1 tsp ground cinnamon
Pinch of salt
125 g (4 oz) caster sugar
1 carrot, grated
60 g (2 oz) raisins

60 g (2 oz) chopped nuts
60 g (2 oz) desiccated coconut
1 apple, grated
2 medium eggs
60 ml (2 fl oz) vegetable oil
1 tsp vanilla extract

Preheat oven to 180°C (350°F).

Sift flour, cinnamon and salt into a large bowl. Add sugar, carrot, raisins, nuts, coconut and apple and mix until combined. Add eggs, oil and vanilla and mix until combined.

Spoon into greased muffin tins and bake in preheated oven for 20 minutes, or until risen and golden brown. Makes 12 large muffins.

Coffee and walnut muffins

These muffins are great as they are, but if you want to jazz them up even further you can spoon a little coffee icing on top and add a walnut half.

125 ml (4 fl oz) strong coffee
125 ml (4 fl oz) cream
1 medium egg, lightly beaten
125 ml (4 fl oz) vegetable oil

225 g (7½ oz) self-raising flour
Pinch of salt
80 g (2¾ oz) caster sugar
100 g (3½ oz) chopped walnuts

Preheat oven to 180°C (350°F).

Whisk coffee, cream, egg and oil together. Sift flour and salt together into a separate bowl. Add sugar and nuts and stir through. Pour coffee mixture onto flour mixture and whisk until well combined. Spoon into greased muffin tins and bake in preheated oven for 20 minutes, or until risen and golden brown. Makes 8 large or 16 small muffins.

'Doughnut' muffins

No tricky names here, just muffins that taste like a doughnut, with only a fraction of the work.

250 g (8 oz) self-raising flour
Pinch of salt
1 tsp ground cinnamon
80 ml (2¾ fl oz) vegetable oil
150 g (5 oz) caster sugar

1 medium egg
175 ml (6 fl oz) milk
75 g (2⅔ oz) melted butter
150 g (5 oz) caster sugar, additional
1 tsp ground cinnamon, additional

Preheat oven to 180°C (350°F).

Sift flour, salt and cinnamon into a large bowl. In a separate bowl mix oil, sugar, egg and milk together. Add to flour and stir well until combined. Spoon into greased muffin tins and bake in preheated oven for 20 minutes, or until risen and golden brown. While cooking mix melted butter, additional sugar and cinnamon together.

When muffins are cooked, remove from tins and dip tops into cinnamon/sugar mixture, then place on a cooling rack to cool. Makes 10–12 large muffins.

Jam doughnut muffins
Half-fill muffin tins, then add ½ tsp strawberry jam to each muffin. Cover with more batter and cook in the same way.

Flourless chocolate muffins

As with all flourless cakes, these muffins use ground almonds to keep them moist.

150 g (5oz) dark chocolate, chopped
125 g (4 oz) soft butter
3 medium eggs, separated

90 g (3 oz) caster sugar
90 g (3 oz) ground almonds
2 tbsp caster sugar, additional

Preheat oven to 170°C (340°F).

Place chocolate and butter in a bowl over a pot of simmering water to melt. Remove from heat and add egg yolks, sugar and ground almonds. Whisk egg whites until stiff peaks form, then fold in additional sugar. Fold egg mixture into chocolate mixture. Spoon into greased muffin trays and bake in preheated oven for 30–35 minutes, or until a skewer comes out clean when tested. Makes 20 small or 10 large muffins.

Spicy cheddar muffins

It's worth searching out the best farmhouse cheddar you can for these muffins as they are well worth any extra expense. The recipe was supplied by food writer and friend Siu Ling Hui.

250 ml (8 fl oz) milk
2 tbsp melted butter
1 medium egg, lightly beaten
Generous pinch of cayenne pepper
200 g (7 oz) plain flour
1 tbsp baking powder

1 tbsp caster sugar
A pinch of salt
150 g (5 oz) grated farmhouse cheddar
100 g (3½ oz) walnuts, lightly roasted and chopped; or 1 grated apple

Preheat oven to 180°C (350°F).

Combine milk, butter, egg and cayenne pepper in a large bowl. Sift together the flour, baking powder, sugar and salt. Toss grated cheddar with flour to mix well. Add the cheese and flour mixture to the wet mixture and stir well. Add the walnuts or grated apple.

Spoon into greased muffin trays, cook in preheated oven for 15–20 minutes, or until risen and golden brown. Makes 6 large or 12 small muffins.

Polenta herb muffins

These are a great savoury option for when you want to give the sweet things a miss.

90 g (3 oz) polenta
150 g (5 oz) self-raising flour
1 tsp baking powder
60 g (2 oz) soft butter, diced

2 medium eggs
100 ml (3½ fl oz) milk
2 tbsp chopped fresh herbs

Preheat oven to 180°C (350°F).

Stir polenta, flour and baking powder together. Add butter and rub in until mixture resembles fine breadcrumbs. Add eggs, milk and herbs, then mix well. Spoon into greased muffin tins and bake in preheated oven for 20 minutes, or until muffins are risen and golden brown in colour. Makes 6 large muffins or 12 small ones

Macadamia Anzacs
Biscotti
Raspberry jam drops
Almond macaroons
Viennese biscuits
Shortbread
Snickerdoodles
Coconut wafers
Passionfruit yoyo biscuits
Hazelnut and vanilla creams
Gingerbread hearts
Orange and walnut florentines
Cardamom spiced wafers
Mini rum and raisin garibaldi
Oatcakes
Goat's cheese biscuits
Cheese bickies
Almond bread
Brandy snaps
Chocolate chip cookies
Peanut cookies
Chocolate brownies
Raspberry coconut slice
Millionaire's shortbread (caramel slice)
Hedgehog
Toffee almond squares
Munchie muesli slice
Raspberry, vanilla and almond slice
Mars Bar slice
Honey joys
Caramel popcorn

Biscuits and slices

JAM DROPS TO BROWNIES AND CHILDREN'S STUFF TOO

In this chapter you'll find many of our (and probably some of your) favourite sweet things. Some are old fashioned, others relatively modern. Some of them, we enjoyed as children ourselves – like shortbread, yoyos, raspberry coconut slice and honey joys. While others are recipes we've collected as adults and enjoy today – such as hazelnut and vanilla creams, oatcakes and goat's cheese biscuits.

Biscuits are a great thing to bake because a batch seems to go quite a long way – unlike a cake, which seems to disappear almost as soon as it's made. It is also possible to make a simple biscuits (like macaroons, for instance) and jazz them up no end by sandwiching two together with chocolate ganache.

The simplest type of slice takes only a few minutes to stir together and requires nothing more than to be poured into a baking tin and popped into the oven, and there is very little chance that it will fail.

So essentially there's a recipe here for every occasion, from afternoon tea right through to children's birthday parties. Or just when it's a rainy Saturday afternoon and you're in need of a little something sweet.

THINGS YOU NEED TO KNOW ABOUT BISCUITS AND SLICES

- To make biscuits and slices you will need 1 lamington tin, 20 x 30 cm (8 x 12 in), 2–3 flat baking trays and a cooling rack.
- Greasing trays with butter and lining with greaseproof paper will give you a better chance of removing slices in one piece, and will keeps washing up to a minimum.
- It's difficult to say how many people each recipe will feed, because it depends how much you can eat. On average, each slice recipe can be cut into 12 large slices.
- We often cut into smallish squares 3 cm (1 in) and offer a selection.
- Test to see whether a slice is cooked in the same way as for cakes: insert a skewer or cake tester into the centre of the slice. The skewer should come out free of mix or crumbs. If it doesn't, cook for a further 5 minutes, then try again.
- It's much easier to make a slice or biscuits with soft butter than with hard. Zap hard butter in the microwave for 20 seconds, or grate to soften it quickly. We usually use unsalted butter for baking.
- Vanilla extract has a far superior flavour to vanilla essence. Yep, it's more expensive too, but you only have to use half as much.
- When a recipe calls for chocolate, use cooking *couverture*; and the better the quality, the better your cakes. Dark *couverture* is best, and buttons (or chips) melt more easily.
- Use Dutch cocoa for better flavour; again the better the quality, the better the cake.
- For preference use espresso coffee where coffee is called for, using extra coffee grounds for a stronger brew. A stovetop espresso machine makes great cooking coffee. Otherwise the simplest thing to do is to dissolve 1–2 tsp of instant coffee in the required amount of boiling water.
- All eggs are medium (59 g), unless otherwise stated.
- Needless to say, a mixing machine will make light work of any beating, whisking or blending to be done.

Chocolate fudge cake (recipe page 289)

Chocolate brownies (recipe page 321)

Selection of biscuits including Passionfruit yoyo biscuits and Hazelnut and vanilla creams (recipes page 315), Peanut cookies (recipe page 321) and Raspberry jam drops (recipe page 312)

Macadamia Anzacs

Every Australian knows that Anzac biscuits were sent to our forces in World War I. Not every Australian knows that they taste even better with macadamias in them, rather than coconut.

100 g (3½ oz) rolled oats
70 g (2½ oz) macadamia nuts, chopped
180 g (6 oz) plain flour
125 g (4 oz) brown sugar

125 g (4 oz) butter
3 tbsp water
2 tbsp golden syrup
1 tsp bicarbonate of soda

Preheat oven to 180°C (350°F).

Line 2 baking trays with baking paper. Mix together oats, macadamias, flour and sugar in a large bowl. Place butter, water and golden syrup in a small saucepan. Bring to the boil, remove from heat, add bicarb and stir until mixture become frothy.

Pour mixture onto dry ingredients and mix quickly. Roll into small balls and place on trays, allowing some room for spreading, and press down gently.

Bake in preheated oven for 15–20 minutes or until golden brown but still slightly soft. Allow to cool for 5 minutes. Remove from trays and leave to cool on a cooling rack, then store in an airtight container. Makes 20–24.

Traditional Anzacs
Substitute dessicated coconut for macadamias.

Biscotti

Biscotti are an Italian-style dry biscuit, usually served after a meal with coffee and grappa. We prefer them at 11 a.m. with a cup of tea.

250 g (8 oz) plain flour
1 tsp baking powder
250 g (8 oz) caster sugar
1 tsp vanilla extract

2 medium eggs
1 egg yolk
100 g (3½ oz) blanched toasted almonds

Preheat oven to 180°C (350°F).

Sift flour, baking powder and sugar into a large bowl. Add vanilla, eggs and egg yolk to the mixture and mix until ingredients form a ball. Add almonds and knead until they are combined.

Divide dough into two and form into two log-shaped pieces, about 25 cm (10 in) in length. Place both pieces on a lined baking tray, allowing room for spreading. Bake in preheated oven for 30 minutes, or until firm to touch and golden brown. Remove and allow to cool.

Reduce oven temperature to 140°C (275°F). Slice logs on the diagonal, 1 cm (½ in) thickness. Place slices on lined baking trays and return to the oven for 20 minutes, or until quite dry. Makes 24–30.

Pistachio biscotti
Substitute pistachios for almonds.

Chocolate and hazelnut biscotti
Substitute hazelnuts for almonds and cocoa for 30 g (1 oz) of the flour.

Raspberry jam drops

These have become a real favourite at our place in recent years – no doubt due to the two mini food lovers named Mia and Luke. The quality of the jam you use will make a big difference, and you can use other than raspberry jam if preferred.

125 g (4 oz) soft butter
75 g (2⅔ oz) caster sugar
1 tsp vanilla extract
175 g (6 oz) plain flour

1 tsp baking powder
2 tbsp milk
150 g (5 oz) raspberry jam

Preheat oven to 180°C (350°F).
Cream butter, sugar and vanilla until light and fluffy. Sift flour and baking powder together. Add flour and milk to mixture, then stir to combine.
Roll into small balls and place on a greased baking tray. Flatten each biscuit slightly, then use a teaspoon to make an indent in the middle. Spoon jam into indent. Bake in preheated oven for 10–15 minutes until cooked but not coloured. Allow to cool completely. Makes 30.

Lemon gems
Substitute lemon curd for jam.

Chocolate drops
Replace jam with one large chocolate chip on each biscuit (or use Smarties if the biscuits are for a child's party).

Almond macaroons

The variations on these biscuits are enormous and are limited only by the different types of nuts available.

3 eggs whites
300 g (10½ oz) caster sugar
300 g (10½ oz) ground almonds

2 tbsp plain flour
Additional plain flour as required

Preheat oven to 180°C (350°F).

Beat egg whites to stiff peaks. Slowly beat in sugar until thick and glossy. Mix together almonds and flour. Fold dry mix into beaten egg whites.

Dust hands with a little flour and roll heaped teaspoonfuls of the biscuit mixture into balls. Place biscuits on a lined baking tray. Bake in preheated oven for 10–15 minutes, or until golden brown and firm to touch. Makes 48.

Cinnamon almond macaroons
Add 1½ tsp ground cinnamon to the almond/flour mix.

Coconut macaroons
Substitute desiccated coconut for ground almonds.

Chocolate macaroons
Substitute cocoa powder for 30 g (1 oz) of the ground almonds. Be really decadent and sandwich cooked macaroons with chocolate ganache, page 299.

Viennese biscuits

This is a classic biscuit mixture that has its origins in Austria. It is perfect when you want to make a biscuit mixture that can be used in a piping bag. You can pipe rounds or fingers as you need. They can then be sandwiched together with butter icing or dipped into melted chocolate.

250 g (8 oz) soft butter
125 g (4 oz) icing sugar

2 medium eggs
250 g (8 oz) plain flour

Preheat oven to 200°C (390°F).

Cream butter and sugar until white and fluffy. Add eggs, beat well, then beat in flour. Place mixture into a piping bag and pipe onto buttered baking trays or trays lined with baking paper.

Bake in preheated oven for 8–10 minutes, or until beginning to brown at the edges. Makes 40.

Shortbread

There's something essentially wholesome about shortbread; it's always so crisp and satisfying. It can also be adapted to produce new versions such as orange, chocolate or spice

260 g (8½ oz) plain flour
115 g (3½ oz) rice flour
250 g (8 oz) soft butter, diced

125 g (4 oz) caster sugar
Pinch of salt
Water, if required

Preheat oven to 170°C (340°F).

Rub together flours, butter, sugar and salt. Knead well until combined. Add a little water if it is very dry. Roll to ½ cm (¼ in) thickness and cut into large fingers or 5 cm (2 in) circles. Bake in preheated oven until crisp, about 10–12 minutes. Makes 30.

Orange shortbread
Add the zest of 2 oranges to the basic mixture.

Spiced shortbread
Add 1 tsp mixed spice to the basic mixture.

Chocolate shortbread
Substitute cocoa for 30 g (1 oz) of the plain flour.

Snickerdoodles

Love the name, but we have no idea what it means. Which is pretty irrelevant when they taste so good.

125 g (4 oz) soft butter
165 g (5¾ oz) caster sugar
1 medium egg
1 egg yolk
225 g (7⅔ oz) self-raising flour

½ tsp nutmeg
165 g (5¾ oz) walnuts, chopped
65 g (2⅓ oz) currants
2 tsp caster sugar, additional
2 tsp ground nutmeg, additional

Preheat oven to 180°C (350°F).

Cream together butter and sugar until light and fluffy. Beat in egg and egg yolk. Add flour, nutmeg, walnuts and currants and mix until smooth. Drop teaspoonfuls onto a greased baking tray. Mix together additional sugar and nutmeg and sprinkle onto biscuits. Bake in preheated oven for 10–15 minutes. Makes 20–24.

Coconut wafers

Coconut wafers are excellent to serve with desserts such as mousses, chilled puddings and panna cotta.

100 g (3½ oz) soft butter
100 ml (3½ fl oz) coconut cream
110 g (3¾ oz) caster sugar

75 g (2⅔ oz) self-raising flour
25 g (¾ oz) flaked coconut

Preheat oven to 180°C (350°F).

Cream butter, coconut cream and sugar together until smooth. Stir in flour and flaked coconut. Gently shape heaped teaspoonfuls of the mixture into rounds, place on a floured baking tray and flatten slightly. Cook in preheated oven for 10–12 minutes, or until golden brown. Makes 12–15.

Passionfruit yoyo biscuits

Yoyo biscuits are a classic combination where two simple biscuits are joined with a vanilla filling. We like to think we have improved on this classic by using a passionfruit filling – we'll leave it to you decide whether we have or not.

300 g (10½ oz) plain flour
300 g (10½ oz) soft butter
100 g (3½ oz) icing sugar
100 g (3½ oz) custard powder
Pinch of salt

½ tsp vanilla extract
2 passionfruit
60 g (2 oz) melted butter
250 g (8 oz) icing sugar

Preheat oven to 180°C (350°F).

Beat together flour, butter, icing sugar, custard powder, salt and vanilla. Roll into small balls and place on a greased baking tray. Press down with the prongs of a fork to form a round biscuit. Bake in preheated oven for 10–15 minutes, until cooked but not coloured. Allow to cool completely.

Strain the pulp from passionfruit to remove seeds. Mix with butter and icing sugar until smooth. Spoon a small amount of passionfruit butter onto one biscuit half and top with another biscuit. Continue until all biscuits are ready. Makes 18.

Hazelnut and vanilla creams

These are quite rich, full-flavoured biscuits that are great with a strong, long black coffee.

125 g (4 oz) soft butter
150 g (5 oz) brown sugar
1 medium egg
½ tsp ground nutmeg
300 g (10½ oz) self-raising flour

75 g (2⅔ oz) roasted hazelnuts, skins removed
125 g (4 oz) soft butter, additional
250 g (8 oz) icing sugar
½ tsp vanilla extract

Preheat oven to 180°C (350°F).

Cream butter and sugar until light and fluffy. Beat in egg until well combined, then stir in nutmeg and flour. Roughly chop hazelnuts and add to mixture.

Roll teaspoonfuls of the biscuit mixture into balls and place on a lined baking tray. Press down with the prongs of a fork to form a round biscuit. Bake in preheated oven for 10–15 minutes, or until golden brown. Remove and allow to cool.

Make vanilla cream by beating additional butter with until light and fluffy. Add icing sugar and vanilla and beat until smooth.

Match up same-size biscuits in pairs. Spoon a small amount of vanilla cream on to one biscuit and top with its match. Continue until all biscuits are ready. Makes 18.

Gingerbread hearts

The flavour of ginger is one that people either love or can't stand at all; this one is for all the ginger lovers we know.

125 g (4 oz) soft butter
70 g (2½ oz) brown sugar
Zest of 1 orange, finely chopped
1 medium egg
125 ml (4 fl oz) warm honey
450 g (15 oz) self-raising flour

4 tsp ground ginger
½ tsp ground cinnamon
30 blanched almonds
1 medium egg, lightly beaten
Raw sugar

Preheat oven to 170°C (340°F).

Cream butter and sugar until light and fluffy. Add zest and egg and beat until smooth. Stir in honey. Sift together flour, ginger and cinnamon and stir into wet mixture. Wrap biscuit mixture in cling film and chill for 30 minutes.

Roll biscuit mixture out onto a floured surface and cut out heart shapes. Lay biscuits on a lined baking tray. Push an almond into the centre of each. Brush each biscuit with beaten egg and sprinkle raw sugar over. Bake in preheated oven for 8–10 minutes.

Allow biscuits to cool. Makes 30 biscuits.

Orange and walnut florentines

This twist on the classic florentine recipe brings a great orange taste to the existing toffee and chocolate flavours.

45 g (1½ oz) butter
125 ml (4 fl oz) pure cream
125 g (4 oz) caster sugar
100 g (3½ oz) walnuts, roughly chopped

Zest of 1 orange, finely chopped
50 g (1⅔ oz) plain flour
100 g (3½ oz) dark chocolate, chopped

Preheat oven to 160°C (320°F).

Place butter, cream and sugar in a small saucepan and bring to the boil over a medium heat, then remove immediately. Stir in the nuts, orange zest and flour. Leave to cool for 5 minutes.

Drop heaped teaspoons of the mix onto lined baking trays, leaving 4 cm (1½ in) between each one.

Bake in preheated oven for 15–20 minutes. Biscuits should be golden at the edges and firm to the touch. Allow to cool on the trays.

Melt chocolate and spread onto the back of each biscuit. Allow chocolate to set completely before storing. Makes 24 biscuits.

Cardamom spiced wafers

This recipe is based on tuile biscuits, which made obligatory appearances on all restaurant dessert menus in the 1980s.

60 g (2 oz) soft butter
60 g (2 oz) caster sugar
2 egg whites

60 g (2 oz) plain flour
¼ tsp ground cardamom

Preheat oven to 180°C (350°F).

Beat butter and sugar until pale and light. Lightly whisk in egg whites. Sift together the flour and ground cardamom, then fold into the mixture.

Drop teaspoons of the mix onto lined baking trays. Use a spatula to spread it paper thin into 10 cm (4 in) long wafers. Bake in preheated oven for 5 minutes. They should be just golden at the edges and pale in the centre. Allow to cool, then transfer to an airtight container. Makes 18–20 biscuits.

Tuiles
Omit the ground cardamom to make plain tuiles. These biscuits can be made in any shape but traditionally they are shaped into 10 cm (4 in) circles; baked; and draped over moulds, or rolled around rolling pins, while still warm to make basket shapes.

Mini rum and raisin garibaldi

These are a decadent sandwich-style biscuit, with crisp pastry circles enveloping a rich, moist, rum-flavoured fruit filling. They deserve to be eaten regularly.

60 g (2 oz) raw sugar
75 ml (2½ fl oz) water
30 ml (1 fl oz) muscat
20 ml (⅔ fl oz) dark rum
Pinch of mixed spice

Pinch of cinnamon
320 g (11 oz) sultanas
1 quantity sweetcrust pastry, page 241
Egg wash*
Caster sugar

Preheat oven to 180°C (350°F).

Place sugar, water, muscat, rum and spices in a saucepan. Heat to simmering and stir until sugar dissolves. Add the sultanas and simmer for 10 minutes, stirring regularly. If most of the liquid has not been absorbed into the fruit, continue cooking for a few minutes more. Allow mix to cool but do not refrigerate.

Roll pastry to 3mm (½ in) thickness. Cut out 7.5 cm (3 in) circles. Lay half of the pastry circles onto lined baking trays.

Brush edges of pastry circles with egg wash. Spoon a tablespoon of sultanas onto each pastry circle, then press another pastry circle on top. Press down gently. Brush pastry tops with egg wash and sprinkle with a little sugar.

Bake in preheated oven for 10–12 minutes, or until golden brown. Makes 15 biscuits.

Oatcakes

These are wonderful with cheese – cheddar in particular – and make a change from packets of water crackers, which are pretty unexciting.

110 g (3¾ oz) wholemeal flour
75 g (2⅔ oz) plain flour
110 g (3¾ oz) oatmeal

110 g (3¾ oz) soft butter, diced
3 tbsp brown sugar
1 medium egg

Preheat oven to 190°C (375°F).

Mix flours and oatmeal together and rub in butter to produce a breadcrumb texture. Add sugar and egg and mix together until a smooth dough forms. Roll out with a rolling pin until 3 mm thick and cut into 5 cm (2 in) circles. Place circles on a tray lined with baking paper and cook for 20–25 minutes, or until biscuits are crisp. Store in an airtight container. Makes 20.

Goat's cheese biscuits

These biscuits are great spread with a little tapenade, or topped with fresh goat's curd and a slice of roasted tomato. A formal thank you to Grace.

350 g (12⅓ oz) soft butter
250 g (8 oz) fresh goat's cheese
60 g (2 oz) parmigiano, grated

Pinch of salt
½ tsp cayenne
425 g (15 oz) plain flour

Preheat oven to 160°C (320°F).

Beat butter, goat's cheese, parmigiano, salt and cayenne to a smooth paste in a food processor. Place in a bowl and mix in flour. Roll into 5 cm (2 in) logs and wrap in cling film. Freeze for 30 minutes to allow easy slicing. Slice logs into discs 1 cm (½ in) thick. Place on a tray lined with baking paper and bake in preheated oven for 20–25 minutes, until pale gold in colour. Allow to cool, then store in an airtight container. Makes 40.

Cheese bickies

Easy to make, easy to cook and easy to eat. What more could you want in life?

150 g (5 oz) soft butter
225 g (7½ oz) plain flour
125 g (4 oz) grated cheddar

Pinch of salt
½ tsp cayenne pepper

Place all ingredients in mixing bowl. Beat until mixture forms a ball. Roll into 2 long sausage shapes, about 3 cm (1 in) thick. Wrap in cling film and refrigerate for 30 minutes.
   Preheat oven to 180°C (350°F).
   Slice logs into discs 1 cm (½ in) thick. Place on a tray lined with baking paper and bake in preheated oven for 10–12 minutes or until slightly browned. Makes 25–30.

Almond bread

A perfectly crisp slice of almond bread is a beautiful thing, particularly when served alongside a dessert or simply piled in multiples on a plate for afternoon tea.

6 egg whites
180 g (6 oz) caster sugar

180 g (6 oz) plain flour
180 g (6 oz) blanched almonds

Preheat oven to 180°C (350°F).
   Beat egg whites to stiff peaks. Slowly beat in sugar until mixture is thick and glossy. Fold through flour and almonds. Spoon into a greased log tin 23.5 × 13.5 × 7 cm (9¼ × 5¼ × 2¾ in) and bake in preheated oven for 45 minutes. Allow to cool, then slice very thinly.
   Lower oven temperature to 140°C (280°F). Place slices on baking tray and dry in preheated oven until crisp, about 10 minutes.

Pistachio bread
Substitute pistachios (or any other nut that takes your fancy) for almonds.

Brandy snaps

Brandy snaps are considered the epitome of dinner party chic by many. We don't hold them quite that high, but they are a traditional biscuit, often filled with brandy cream and berries, that are well worth knowing how to make.

90 g (3 oz) butter
90 g (3 oz) golden syrup
200 g (7 oz) icing sugar

90 g (3 oz) plain flour
Pinch of salt
1 tsp ground ginger

Place butter, golden syrup and icing sugar in a saucepan over a medium heat. Stir until melted, then remove from heat. Sift flour, salt and ginger together and add to melted mixture. Beat until well combined.

Drop teaspoons of the mix onto lined baking trays. Use a spatula to spread the mixture into 8 cm (3 in) circles. Bake in preheated oven for 5 minutes. They should be just golden at the edges and pale in the centre. Allow to cool then transfer to an airtight container. Makes 20–24.

Brandy snap baskets
Brandy snaps, while still warm, can be draped over moulds to form basket shapes or rolled around the handle of a large wooden spoon to form tubes.

Chocolate chip cookies

These cookies are very difficult to say 'no' to, as they are rich, decadent, chewy and studded with chocolate chips.

150 g (5 oz) melted butter
150 g (5 oz) caster sugar
125 g (4 oz) demerara sugar
1 medium egg

300 g (10½ oz) self-raising flour
1 tsp vanilla extract
150 g (5 oz) small chocolate chips

Preheat oven to 180°C (350°F).

Cream butter and sugars until light and fluffy. Add egg, then beat well until combined. Add flour and vanilla, beat until combined. Fold through the chocolate chips.

Drop teaspoons of the mix onto lined baking trays. Use a spatula to spread the mixture into 3 cm (1 in) circles. Bake in preheated oven for 10–15 minutes. They should be just golden at the edges and pale in the centre. Makes 36.

Chocolate and hazelnut cookies
Add 90 g (3 oz) of hazelnuts with chocolate chips.

White chocolate and walnut cookies
Add 90 g (3 oz) of walnuts and substitute white chocolate chips.

Double chocolate chip cookies
Substitute cocoa for 30 g (1 oz) of the flour.

Peanut cookies

If you like peanut butter it's pretty much guaranteed you're going to enjoy these biscuits too.

100 g (3½ oz) soft butter
100 g (3½ oz) crunchy peanut butter
90 g (3 oz) caster sugar
90 g (3 oz) demerara sugar

2 medium eggs
225 g (7½ oz) self-raising flour
¼ tsp vanilla extract
250 g (8 oz) roasted peanuts

Preheat oven to 180°C (350°F).

Cream butters and sugars until light and fluffy. Add eggs, one at a time, beating well until combined. Add flour and vanilla, beat until combined. Fold through peanuts.

Drop teaspoonfuls of the mix onto lined baking trays. Use a spatula to spread the mixture into 3 cm (1 in) circles. Bake in preheated oven for 10–15 minutes. The cookies should be just golden at the edges and pale in the centre. Makes 36.

Chocolate brownies

A good chocolate brownie is a wondrous thing, and that's exactly what you'll get with this recipe.

180 g (6 oz) butter
180 g (6 oz) dark chocolate, chopped
3 medium eggs
1 tsp vanilla extract

250 g (8 oz) caster sugar
110 g (3½ oz) plain flour
½ tsp salt
150 g (5 oz) chopped walnuts

Preheat oven to 180°C (350°F).

Melt butter and chocolate together. Beat eggs, vanilla and sugar until light and doubled in bulk. Sift flour and salt together. Add flour, melted chocolate and nuts to beaten eggs and mix to combine.

Pour into lined lamington tin and bake in preheated oven for 25 minutes. Take care not to overcook brownies or they will lose their delicious richness and gooey texture. Makes 12.

Raspberry coconut slice

This slice, with its raspberry jam base and coconut topping, appeals to children and adults alike.

90 g (3 oz) soft butter
90 g (3 oz) caster sugar
1 medium egg
60 g (2 oz) self-raising flour
90 g (3 oz) plain flour

2 medium eggs, lightly beaten, additional
75 g (2⅔ oz) caster sugar
180 g (6 oz) desiccated coconut
125 ml (4 fl oz) raspberry jam

Preheat oven to 180°C (350°F).

Cream butter and sugar until light and fluffy. Add egg, beating well. Sift flours together and add to mix, stir to combine. Spread mixture in lined lamington tin. Bake in preheated oven for 15–20 minutes, or until cooked and golden brown.

Meanwhile beat additional eggs, sugar and coconut together. Remove baked slice from oven. Spread with raspberry jam, then spread with coconut topping. Return to the oven for a further 20 minutes. Cool in pan before slicing. Makes 12.

Millionaire's shortbread (caramel slice)

We always knew this recipe as caramel slice, but have recently found out that it's also called Millionaire's shortbread – a much more fitting name.

90 g (3 oz) soft butter
90 g (3 oz) raw sugar
1 medium egg
60 g (2 oz) self-raising flour
60 g (2 oz) desiccated coconut

400 ml (13 fl oz) condensed milk
125 g (4 oz) butter, additional
125 g (4 oz) caster sugar, additional
150 g (5 oz) dark chocolate, chopped

Preheat oven to 180°C (350°F).

Cream butter and sugar until light and fluffy. Add egg, beat well. Add flour and coconut and stir to combine. Spread mixture in lined lamington tin. Bake in preheated oven for 15–20 minutes, or until just cooked. (It's going to go back into the oven for another 15 minutes, so it doesn't have to be brown.)

Place condensed milk, butter and additional sugar in a small saucepan. Place over a medium heat and bring to the boil, stirring often to prevent condensed milk catching and burning. When sugar is dissolved and mixture has just started to boil, pour it over the cooked pastry base. Return to oven and cook for a further 10–15 minutes, or until caramel has turned golden brown. Set aside to cool.

When caramel is set, melt chocolate and coat caramel. Top evenly, leave to set, then cut into squares. Makes 12.

Hedgehog

This is one of those 'stir together and pour into a tin' recipes that is incredibly quick and easy to make. Hedgehog is best kept chilled as it softens at room temperature.

250 g (8 oz) Marie biscuits
75 g (2½ oz) walnuts, chopped
250 g (8 oz) butter
150 g (5 oz) caster sugar

50 g (1¾ oz) cocoa
2 medium eggs
100 g (3½ oz) dark chocolate, chopped

Preheat oven to 180°C (350°F).

Break biscuits into approximately 1 cm (⅓ in) pieces. Mix with walnuts and set aside. Melt butter over a medium heat. Add sugar and cocoa to the saucepan; return to the heat and stir until sugar dissolves. Remove from heat and allow to cool.

Beat in eggs, then add broken biscuits and nuts. Spoon into a lined lamington tin, press down well until biscuits are covered with chocolate mix and refrigerate until set. Melt chocolate and coat top evenly. Allow to set, then cut into small squares. Makes 24.

Toffee almond squares

These squares are delicious and quite rich, certainly decadent enough to stand up to a strong espresso after dinner.

60 g (2 oz) soft butter
125 g (4 oz) ground almonds
100 g (3½ oz) caster sugar
2 medium eggs

2 tbsp plain flour
90 g (3 oz) butter, additional
125 g (4 oz) caster sugar, additional
60 g (2 oz) flaked almonds

Preheat oven to 180°C (350°F).

Cream butter, almonds and sugar until light and fluffy. Add eggs and flour and beat well to combine. Spoon into greased and lined lamington tin. Bake in preheated oven for 15–20 minutes, or until set and golden brown.

Place additional butter and sugar in a small saucepan. Bring to the boil over a medium–high heat and cook for 5–10 minutes, or until sugar starts to caramelise, stirring often. Remove from heat, add flaked almonds and pour and spread evenly over baked base. Set aside to cool before slicing into squares. Makes 12.

Munchie muesli slice

This is packed with good things, including dried fruit, rolled oats, sunflower seeds and honey. We've been making it for years and it never fails to satisfy.

100 g (3½ oz) caster sugar
150 g (5 oz) self-raising flour
90 g (3 oz) shredded coconut
90 g (3 oz) rolled oats
75 g (2½ oz) sultanas
75 g (2½ oz) raisins

75 g (2½ oz) chopped dates
60 g (2 oz) sunflower seeds, optional
125 g (4 oz) butter
2 tbsp water
60 g (2 oz) honey
1 medium egg

Preheat oven to 180°C (350°F).

Mix together sugar, flour, coconut, oats, dried fruit and seeds. Melt butter, water and honey together and pour over combined ingredients while still hot. Stir well until mixture comes together, then stir in the egg. Spoon mixture into a lined lamington tin and bake in preheated oven for 40 minutes, or until set and golden brown. Allow to cool before cutting into slices. Makes 12.

Raspberry, vanilla and almond slice

This is a simple slice to make. All you have to do is make a simple base and place half of it in a tin and bake it. The remaining mixture is combined with berries and almonds to create the topping.

350 g (12⅓ oz) caster sugar
300 g (10 oz) self-raising flour
125 g (4 oz) soft butter
250 ml (8 fl oz) milk

1 tsp vanilla extract
1 medium egg
250 g (8 oz) raspberries
60 g (2 oz) flaked almonds

Preheat oven to 180°C (350°F).

Rub together sugar, flour and butter. Divide mixture in half. Press half into lined 23 cm (9 in) cake tin and press down firmly. Bake in preheated oven for 20 minutes.

Add milk, vanilla and egg to remaining mix. Scatter baked half with raspberries and pour remaining mixture over. Sprinkle almonds on top.

Return to the oven and cook for a further 30 minutes, or until risen and firm to touch. Slice into wedges to serve. Serves 8.

Mars Bar slice

I'd like to claim that I only make this for kids' parties, but then I would be a liar. MC

180 g (6 oz) Mars Bars® (3 bars)
90 g (3 oz) butter

90 g (3 oz) Rice Bubbles®

Chop Mars Bars roughly and place in a small saucepan with butter. Cook over a medium heat until Mars Bars and butter have melted. Whisk together well to combine the two.

Place Rice Bubbles in good-sized bowl and pour hot melted ingredients over. Stir well to combine the two together. Pour mixture into a lamington tin and refrigerate until set. Or spoon into 24 patty pans for individual cakes. Makes 12 large.

Honey joys

It wouldn't be a proper party without honey joys.

100 g (3½ oz) butter
100 g (3½ oz) honey

125 g (4 oz) Corn Flakes®
24 paper patty pans

Preheat oven to 180°C (350°F).

Place butter and honey in a small saucepan and cook over a low heat, stirring until sugar has dissolved. Then bring to the boil and remove from heat.

Place Corn Flakes in a bowl and stir in hot butter mixture. Divide mixture between patty pans. Bake for 10 minutes. Makes 24.

Caramel popcorn

2–3 tbsp olive oil
90 g (3 oz) popping corn
150 g (5 oz) butter

200 g (7 oz) Jersey caramels
30 paper patty pans

Heat a saucepan over a medium heat. Add oil, heat, then add popping corn. Cover and allow to cook until all the corn is popped. Shake the saucepan regularly to encourage this. Tip the popcorn into a bowl.

Place butter and Jersey caramels in a small saucepan and cook over a low heat. Stir until melted, then pour over the popcorn. Stir until popcorn is completely coated with the caramel, then spoon into patty pans. Makes 30.

Guide to ingredients

acidulated water   Water that has had lemon juice added to prevent ingredients such as artichokes and quinces discolouring during preparation. 1 litre (1⅔ pt) of water requires 60 ml (2 fl oz) lemon juice.

arborio rice   A short-grain rice from northern Italy used for making risotto.

barbecue pork   This roast meat, also known as Char siew, is a boneless piece of pork marinated in soy sauce, hoisin, salt, sugar and colouring, then roasted in a traditional Chinese manner while hanging in a special oval-shaped oven.

black beans   Fermented salted black beans that require soaking for at least 10 minutes before being rinsed, drained and chopped. Available at Asian grocers.

black pepper   All pepper in these recipes is freshly ground black pepper, unless otherwise stated.

blanch   Briefly cook ingredients in boiling water.

bok choy   Small green bundles of leafy cabbages.

bouquet garni   A bundle of fresh herbs that includes bay leaves, thyme, parsley and celery leaves, tied with string or wrapped in muslin. It is added to stocks and soups for flavour and removed during straining.

chickpea flour   Flour made from chickpeas; also known as besan flour.

chilli paste   A fiery chilli mixture also called sambal oelek. Available widely. Adjust amounts to suit your taste.

Chinese rice wine   Chinese rice wine, also known as shao hsing rice wine, has a delicate amber colour and fragrance. Dry sherry can be substituted at a pinch.

chocolate   When we cook with chocolate we usually use *couverture*. This chocolate, specially made for cooking, has a high fat content and less sugar than other chocolate. Dark chocolate is a pretty good substitute if you can't get *couverture*.

citron   Candied citrus fruit. Available from Italian delicatessens.

clarified butter   A butter that has been melted and from which milk solids have been removed. It has very good keeping qualities and will not burn during cooking. Also known as ghee.

coconut milk and cream   Made from grated coconut soaked in hot water. Coconut milk is lighter and thinner than coconut cream and usually purchased in tins.

cornichons   Baby pickled cucumbers.

couscous   This staple of North African cooking comes in different grades. 'Instant' couscous just requires soaking in boiling water to be ready.

couverture	see chocolate.
crispy shallots	Crispy shallots are deep-fried shallots. These can be made at home by deep-frying sliced shallots until golden-brown. A much better idea is to buy them in plastic containers from Asian grocery shops.
dashi	A Japanese ingredient made from bonito (fish) used as a base flavouring for soups.
dukkah	Egyptian mixture consisting of roasted and crushed spices, nuts and sesame seeds.
egg wash	Lightly beaten egg yolk with a splash of milk, usually brushed onto raw pastry and bread dough to add a shiny finish when cooked.
fish sauce	A tangy thin sauce made from salted fish and essential in many Asian cuisines. Wonderful for adding a salty flavour burst to food.
galangal	Thick rhizome, not dissimilar to ginger. Very tough and fibrous.
gelatine	Substance used to set desserts and puddings. Sheet gelatine is considerably better than powdered; note that this comes in various sheet sizes.
ghee	See clarified butter.
glucose	Dense sugar syrup. Can be easily bought at chemist shops.
goat's curd	Soft fresh cheese made from goat's milk.
grated ginger	Approx. 5 cm (2 in) of fresh root ginger will produce 1 tsp of grated ginger. Ginger graters (small white textured ceramic 'plates') are available from Asian grocers.
harissa	Tunisian chilli paste with a smoky flavour.
herbs	All herbs in these recipes are fresh unless otherwise stated.
hot bean paste	Mixture of chillies and soy beans. Available from Asian grocers.
kaffir lime leaves	Search out fresh leaves from Asian grocers. Each leaf consists of two oval sections with a pungent citrus flavour. Mostly used whole in broths for flavour, or shredded finely for salads and marinades.
kecap manis	Thick, sweet Indonesian soy sauce. You can substitute a combination of soy sauce and sugar, but this sauce in now widely available at all Asian grocery stores and larger supermarkets.
Lebanese cucumber	Short thin cucumbers.
mascarpone	Fresh Italian cheese with a rich sour cream flavour.
mesquite wood chips	Wood chips that impart a smoky flavour to barbecued food. Available from barbecue retailers.
mirin	Sweetened Japanese sake used for cooking.
miso paste	Miso is a Japanese paste made from soy beans. You can purchase different colours, though usually red or brown are used to form the base of soups and entrées.

moscato — Italian sweet sparkling wine. You will find it at good bottle shops.

nori sheets — Sheets of dried seaweed that is essential in Japanese cooking, particularly in making California rolls.

olive oil — Extra virgin olive oil has a finer flavour than olive oil, but use one that suits your tastes and budget.

palm sugar — Sugar made from the sap of palm trees and set into thick dense cakes. Best shaved with a sharp knife when needed, or it can be grated. Usually dissolved in an acidic liquid such as lemon juice or fish sauce. Can be substituted with raw or brown sugar.

pancetta — An Italian ham shaped like a fat sausage.

pandan leaves — A fresh green leaf from the pandanus tree that is often wrapped around food before grilling. The leaves impart a delicate perfume to the food.

parmigiano reggiano — True parmigiano comes only from Italy. Be sure you are buying parmigiano (or grana padano), rather than imitation parmesan.

polenta — Ground cornmeal much used in Italy to produce either a soft mixture to accompany stews or firm blocks to be grilled or pan-fried.

pomegranate syrup — Thick bittersweet fruit syrup available from Middle-Eastern grocery stores.

prosciutto — Also known as Parma ham, this salted air-dried ham adds a salty bacon flavour to dishes.

red chilli — Small red chillies (not bird's eye) are used unless otherwise stated. Take care removing seeds and membrane as these contain the capsaicin (the source of the heat).

rice flour — Finely ground rice used to make shortbread and other biscuits.

rice vinegar — A Japanese vinegar. Make sure you purchase pure rice vinegar, not flavoured 'sushi vinegar'.

rosewater — Rose-scented liquid from the Middle East. Available at good delicatessens and Middle-Eastern grocery stores.

saffron — Saffron is one of the world's most expensive spices, with each thread coming from the centre of the crocus flower. Luckily, only a few threads are needed to enjoy saffron's aroma and flavour.

salt — Use sea salt for preference, as it has a finer mineral flavour than common table salt. Some recipes call for sea salt flakes.

seasoned flour — Flour with the addition of salt and pepper. Usually used to coat meat or fish before frying.

sesame oil — A rich aromatic oil made from roasted sesame seeds. Only a small amount is needed to add flavour to dishes.

shallots — Small brown or red onion-shaped vegetables. The red onions are used extensively in Asian cuisines, and have a flavour between garlic and onion.

shoyu	Japanese soy sauce.
Sichuan pepper	Also called as 'Szechwan' pepper. These small red berries, not actually a member of the pepper family, have a peppery taste. Best toasted before use.
sumac	Ground red berries with a sweet flavour. Available from Middle-Eastern grocery stores.
tahini	Paste made from sesame seeds. Look in Middle-Eastern grocery stores or the health food section of the supermarket.
tamari	Japanese wheat-free soy sauce.
tamarind	A pulp of the tamarind fruit, sold in clear plastic packets. Soak 60 g (2 oz) of the sour tamarind pulp in 250 ml (8 fl oz) of boiling water. Strain, cool then use remaining water.
tofu	Soy milk set into firm blocks, also called bean curd.
tom yum	A Thai paste usually used to make spicy soup and broths.
tomato sugo	Tomato sugo is simply a ready-to-use Italian tomato sauce. The best tasting sugos come from Italy and are an essential cupboard item in our kitchen. We use them in pasta sauces and in casseroles.
vanilla extract	As the name suggests, this is a pure extract from crushed vanilla pods producing a thick, aromatic liquid. Use it wherever vanilla is called for. Vanilla essence is a poor substitute.
verjuice	Unfermented grape juice, can use dry white wine instead.
wasabi	Fiery lime-green paste extracted from the wasabi root, used extensively in Japanese cuisine.

References and inspirations

We are inspired by the many books below, as well as countless meals in restaurants and at the dining tables of home cooks who have welcomed us. Our sincere thanks to all.

Alexander, Stephanie. *The Cook's Companion.* Viking 1996

Beck, Simone, Bertholle, Louisette & Child, Julia. *Mastering the Art of French Cooking.* Penguin Books, Vols 1 & 2, 1983

Brissenden, Rosemary. *South-East Asian Food.* Penguin Books Australia 1996

Ceserani and Kinton. *Practical Cookery.* The Chaucer Press 1983

David, Elizabeth. *French Provincial Cookery.* Penguin 1970

Dupliex, Jill. *Old Food.* Allen & Unwin 1998

Freeman, Meera. *Vietnamese Cookbook.* Viking 1995

Hazan, Marcella. *Marcella's Kitchen.* Macmillan 1988

Kikkoman. *What's Cooking in Japan.* Kikkoman Corporation 1993

Lawson, Nigella. *How to Be a Domestic Goddess.* Chatto & Windus 2000

Luard, Elisabeth. *European Peasant Cookery.* Corgi 1988

Manfield, Christine. *Spice.* Viking 1999

Passmore Jackie. *Encyclopaedia of Asian Food & Cooking.* Doubleday Books 1991

Perry, Neil. *Simply Asian.* Viking 2000

Reader's Digest Services. *The Kitchen Handbook.* 1982

Roden, Claudia. *A New Book of Middle-Eastern Food.* Penguin Books, 1985

Solomon, Charmaine. *Charmaine Solomon's Encyclopaedia of Asian Food.* William Heineman Australia 1996

Solomon, Charmaine. *Thai Cookbook.* Viking 1989

Thompson, David. *Classic Thai Cuisine.* Simon & Schuster 1993

Some of the recipes in this book have appeared in our other books, too:

The Seasonal Produce Diary. Allan Campion & Michele Curtis. 1995–2000

Tucker for Tots. Allan Campion & Michele Curtis. Lothian, 1996

Chilli Jam – Choosing and Using Asian Ingredients. Allan Campion & Michele Curtis. Allen & Unwin 1997

Sizzle! Modern Barbecue Food. Allan Campion & Michele Curtis. Purple Egg, 2000

Fresh. The Seasonal Produce Cookbook. Allan Campion & Michele Curtis. Purple Egg, 2001

Index

A
A great crusty loaf 226
Adult's rice pudding 273
Allan's gravy 148
almonds
   almond bread 319
   almond cake 285
   almond macaroons 312
   almond pear tart 246
   almond sweetcrust pastry 241
   apricot and frangipane tart 243
   asparagus, almond and feta salad 212
   green bean, almond and feta salad 212
   orange and almond cake 293
   pear frangipane tart 243
   poached pear and almond pudding 260
   raspberry, vanilla and almond slice 324
   rich chocolate and almond cake 289
   tangelo and almond cake 294
anchovies
   anchovy dressing 218
   pissaladière 231
   tomato and anchovy tart 240
apples
   apple and hazelnut muesli 11
   apple and hazelnut muffins 303
   apple and raspberry pie 247
   apple and rhubarb crumble tart 247
   apple and rhubarb pie 247
   apple fruit cake 291
   apple porridge 13
   apple tart 245
   apple, fig and pecan cake 292
   tarte tatin 251
apricot
   apricot and almond muesli 11
   apricot and frangipane tart 243
Aromatic vegetable tagine 205
Artichoke, prosciutto and buffalo mozzarella parcels 48
Asian chicken stock 21
Asian coleslaw 212
Asian greens
   barbecue pork and bok choy stir-fry 99
   chicken and bok choy stir-fry 95
   ginger-steamed choy sum 104
   simple bok choy salad 213
   Thai red beef and bok choy curry 164
   wok-fried Asian greens 103
Asian noodle salad 212
Asian-inspired pumpkin soup 25
asparagus
   asparagus and prawn risotto 130
   asparagus omelette 5
   asparagus quiche 239
   asparagus soup 24
   asparagus, almond and feta salad 212
   chicken and asparagus risotto 129
   smoked trout and asparagus cream sauce 85
Australian Christmas pudding 271
avocado
   smoked trout and avocado toasts 60
   guacamole 43

B
Baba ghanoush 41
Baby burgers 116
Baby pavs 277
bacon
   bacon and eggs 2
   broad bean and bacon pasta sauce 84
   egg and bacon pie 250
   grilled tomatoes with basil butter and bacon 10
Baked eggs with spinach and cheddar 5
Baked fish parcels with coconut milk and kaffir lime 61
Baked orange cheesecake 300
Baked passionfruit custard 275
Baked rice pudding 273
bananas
   banana and walnut cake 291
   banana and walnut muffins 304
   banana custard 274
   banana muffins 304
   banana pikelets 8
   banana sago pudding with butterscotch sauce 273
   banana, pecan and maple syrup muffins 304
barbecue 108-123
   beef fillet with chilli and garlic marinade 115
   chermoula prawns 121
   duck and hokkien noodles 100
   onion rings 122
   oysters 64
   pork and bok choy stir-fry 99
   pork and noodle stir-fry 99
   pork and sweet chilli noodles 100
   pork ribs 119
   pork sausage with spiced lentils 140
   sauce 123
   vegetable salad 213
   whole fish 120
Basic beef stew 196
Basic beef stew with dumplings 196
Basic beef stew with mushrooms 196
Basic muffins 302
Basic pasta 77
Basic wine marinade 109
basil
   basil and pine nut stuffed lamb 155
   basil tzatziki 41
   grilled tomatoes with basil butter and bacon 10
   spiced beef balls in basil leaves 117
beans, dried
   beef, black bean and cashew nut stir-fry 96
   chicken and black bean stir-fry 95
   Indian-spiced beans 138
   kidney bean and vegetable chilli 139
   spicy pipis with black bean and ginger 72
   stir-fried crabs with black beans and ginger 71
   white bean dip 44
   see also: chickpeas; lentils
beans, fresh
   broad bean and bacon pasta sauce 84
   broad bean soup 26
   green bean, almond and feta salad 212
beef
   baby burgers 116
   barbecue beef fillet with chilli and garlic marinade 115
   basic beef stew 196
   basic beef stew with dumplings 196
   basic beef stew with mushrooms 196
   beef and Guinness pie 197
   beef and mushroom bolognaise 89
   beef and prune tagine 198
   beef burgers with red wine and onion gravy 178
   beef burgers with roasted vegetables 116
   beef lasagna 90
   beef pot-roast 154
   beef rendang 165
   beef satay kebabs 114
   beef stock 21
   beef stroganoff 184
   beef, black bean and cashew nut stir-fry 96
   braised steak and onions 195
   chilli beef stir-fry 97
   chilli con carne 179
   corned beef (silverside) 198
   cottage pie 179
   hot and sour beef curry 166
   Indian beef curry 168
   Indian beef, spinach and potato curry 169
   Mexican mince 179
   mustard roast beef 153
   pan-fried steak with mushroom sauce 183
   quick-and-easy bolognaise 89
   roast beef with Yorkshire puddings 153

roast rib of beef   153
savoury mince   179
sour and spicy beef braise   199
sour beef with lemongrass   97
spiced beef balls in basil leaves   117
spicy bolognaise sauce   89
steak with oven chips   184
tacos   179
Thai red beef and bok choy curry   164
the perfect steak   114
Vietnamese beef noodle salad   219
beetroot
  dips   42
  salads   215, 216
  beetroot soup   33
berries
  berry jam   15
  berry pancakes   279
  cherry berry pudding   263
  meringues with berries   278
  moist berry pudding cake   295
  summer berry pikelets   8
  summer pudding   263
  see also: blueberries; raspberries; strawberries
Bircher muesli   12
Birgit's easy mousse   265
Birgit's frikadella   180
biscuits   309-325
  almond bread   319
  biscotti   311, 312
  brandy snap baskets   320
  brandy snaps   319
  cardamom spiced wafers   317
  cheese bickies   319
  chocolate and hazelnut cookies   320
  chocolate chip cookies   320
  chocolate drops   312
  coconut wafers   314
  double chocolate chip cookies   320
  gingerbread hearts   316
  goat's cheese biscuits   318
  hazelnut and vanilla creams   315
  honey joys   325
  lemon gems   312
  macadamia Anzacs   311
  mini rum and raisin garibaldi   317
  oatcakes   318
  orange and walnut Florentines   316
  passionfruit yoyo biscuits   315
  peanut cookies   321
  pistachio bread   319
  raspberry jam drops   312
  snickerdoodles   314
  traditional Anzacs   311
  tuiles   317
  Viennese biscuits   313
  white chocolate and walnut cookies   320
  see also macaroons; shortbread; slices
Bitter chocolate tarts   246
Blinis   45
Blood orange and fennel salad   216
blueberry
  blueberry muffins   302
  blueberry pikelets   7
  blueberry pound cake   290
Boil-and-bake fruit cake   291
Boreks   52
Braised red cabbage   157

Braised steak and onions   195
Brandy custard   274
Brandy snap baskets   320
Brandy snaps   319
bread   223-235
  a great crusty loaf   226
  bread and butter pudding   272
  bread and jam pudding   272
  bread rolls   226
  cheese and sesame seed pita crisps   45
  crisp breads   45
  crostini   45
  duck and pine mushroom bread soup   31
  foccacia   228
  French toast   9
  fruit bread   227
  fruity soda bread   225
  garlic foccacia   229
  garlic naan   229
  knot rolls   226
  lemon pepper pita crisps   45
  mushrooms on toast   11
  naan bread   229
  olive foccacia   229
  orange brioche   233
  pita crisps   44
  polenta bread   228
  poppyseed rolls   226
  rhubarb and ricotta toast   14
  rosemary foccacia   229
  rosemary polenta bread   228
  sesame seed rolls   226
  simple brioche   232
  smoked trout and avocado toasts   60
  soda bread   225
  spice naan   229
  see also buns; pizza
broccoli
  broccoli frittata   6
  chicken and broccoli stir-fry   95
buns
  cheat's hot cross buns   234
  Chelsea buns   234
  jam swirls   234
  sticky cinnamon buns   234
  sticky currant buns   233
  Swiss buns   234
burgers
  baby burgers   116
  beef burgers with red wine and onion gravy   178
  beef burgers with roasted vegetables   116
  Birgit's frikadella   180
  burgers with the lot   116
  caramelised onion and chickpea burgers   141
  ginger-chicken burgers with satay sauce   178
  lentil and ricotta burgers   141
Butterscotch pecan self-saucing pudding   270
Butterscotch sauce   261

C
cabbage
  braised red cabbage   157
Caesar salad   217
cakes   283-307

almond cake   285
apple fruit cake   291
apple, fig and pecan cake   292
banana and walnut cake   291
blueberry pound cake   290
boil-and-bake fruit cake   291
carrot cake   292
choc chip pound cake   290
chocolate and hazelnut panforte   296
chocolate brownies   321
chocolate fudge cake   289
cinnamon and lemon tea cake   285
coconut cake   287
date and coconut loaf   294
fig or date fruit cake   291
frozen nougat ice-cream cake   281
gingerbread cake   288
green cake   287
lemon and poppyseed cake   285
lemon sour cream cake   286
lemon tea cake   285
lime and poppyseed tea cake   285
Linzertorte made easy   299
mascarpone and raspberry pound cake   290
moist berry pudding cake   295
moist chocolate squares   289
one-pot chocolate cake   288
orange and almond cake   293
orange poppyseed cake   286
orange tea cake   285
oranges and yoghurt syrup cake   286
pecan coffee cake   294
plum cake   295
pumpkin cake   293
rich apple and walnut cake   296
rich chocolate and almond cake   289
rich chocolate and hazelnut cake   290
spiced Italian fruit cake   297
strawberry shortcakes   302
tangelo and almond cake   294
see also cheesecakes; muffins; scones
calamari
  calamari with soy and chilli glaze   98
  deep-fried Thai calamari   73
  pan-fried calamari   72
  seared calamari with chilli and balsamic dressing   73
California rolls   53
Caponata   176
capsicum
  caponata   176
  chicken casserole with red capsicum   191
  roasted tomato and red capsicum sauce   81
  tomato and roast capsicum salad   214
caramel
  caramel oranges   261
  caramel popcorn   325
  caramel sauce   261
Caramelised onion and chickpea burgers   141
Caramelised onion quiche   239
Caramelised onions, feta and rocket combo   82
cardamom
  coffee and cardamom mousse   265

cardamom panna cotta 267
cardamom spiced wafers 317
Caribbean fish marinade 110
Caroline's (vodka and blood orange)
  jelly 267
carrots
  carrot and coriander soup 24
  carrot and nut muffins 303
  carrot cake 292
  Middle-Eastern carrot salad 211
casseroles and stews
  basic beef stew 196
  basic beef stew with dumplings 196
  basic beef stew with mushrooms 196
  braised steak and onions 195
  chicken casserole with mushrooms 191
  chicken casserole with red
    capsicum 191
  chicken casserole with wine 191
  corned beef (silverside) 198
  Hungarian chicken casserole 192
  lamb hot pot 201
  Mediterranean chicken casserole 192
  Moroccan chicken with tomatoes
    and olives 193
  Moroccan chickpea and pumpkin
    stew 138
  osso buco 203
  pot-roasted veal shanks 204
  rabbit casserole 204
  simple chicken casserole 191
  sour and spicy beef braise 199
  soy-braised chicken 193
  Spanish lamb stew 200
  The pork dish 202
  Tunisian lamb shanks 202
  see also tagines
Cheat's hot cross buns 234
cheese
  artichoke, prosciutto and buffalo
    mozzarella parcels 48
  baked eggs with spinach and
    cheddar 5
  beetroot salad with tomato and
    mozzarella 215
  boreks 52
  cheese and potato pies 240
  cheese and sesame seed pita crisps
    45
  cheese bickies 319
  cheese blintzes 279
  cheesy choux puffs 252
  cheesy schnitzel 175
  cherry tomato and parmigiano frittata
    6
  Greek cheese pastries or spanakopita
    254
  macaroni cheese 87
  parmigiano crumbed veal cutlets
    with caponata 176
  pecorino and pancetta vine leaf
    parcels 47
  spicy cheddar muffins 307
  see also goat's cheese; feta; ricotta
cheesecake
  baked orange cheesecake 300
  cherry cheesecake 300
  chocolate cheesecake 299
  lemon cheesecake 299
  my kind of cheesecake 300
  no-cook orange cheesecake 299

passionfruit cheesecake 300
passionfruit cheesecake 300
raspberry cheesecake 301
Chelsea buns 234
cherries
  cherry berry pudding 263
  cherry cheesecake 300
  cherry clafouti 262
Cherry tomato and parmigiano frittata 6
chestnut
  chocolate and chestnut frozen
    nougat 281
  chestnut stuffing 149
chicken
  Asian chicken stock 21
  cheesy schnitzel 175
  chicken and asparagus risotto 129
  chicken and corn soup 28
  chicken and mushroom pie 195
  chicken and mushroom risotto 129
  chicken and pea risotto 129
  chicken and roasted sweet potato
    risotto 129
  chicken and roasted sweet potato
    risotto 129
  chicken and spinach risotto 129
  chicken and veal polpettini 180
  chicken casserole with mushrooms 191
  chicken casserole with red capsicum 191
  chicken casserole with wine 191
  chicken laksa 31
  chicken liver pâté 46
  chicken noodle soup 28
  chicken nuggets 175
  chicken risotto 129
  chicken saltimbocca 186
  chicken saltimbocca skewers 112
  chicken satay kebabs 113
  chicken schnitzel 175
  chicken stock 21
  chicken tandoori in naan bread 113
  chicken, sultana and sweet spice
    pilaf 128
  Chinese crispy-skin chicken 151
  coconut chicken and noodle salad 218
  coconut chicken curry 169
  ginger-chicken burgers with satay
    sauce 178
  Hungarian chicken casserole 192
  Indian chicken curry 167
  Indian chicken, potato and spinach
    curry 168
  Indian spiced schnitzel 175
  lemon and herb schnitzel 175
  lime and chilli chicken wings 112
  linguini with smoked chicken and
    peas 84
  Mediterranean chicken casserole 192
  Moroccan chicken pie 194
  Moroccan chicken salad 220
  Moroccan chicken with tomatoes
    and olives 193
  Oriental roast chicken 150
  pandan chicken parcels 48
  pan-fried chicken with mushroom
    sauce 185
  pan-fried herb chicken fillets 185
  pot-roasted chicken with 40 cloves
    of garlic 151
  rich chicken stock 21
  roast chicken (and variations) 148

sesame schnitzel 175
simple chicken casserole 191
soy-braised chicken 193
spicy chicken fillets with coriander
  couscous 135
steamed ginger chicken 104
stir-fries 95-96
Thai chicken balls 179
Thai chicken salad 218
Thai green chicken and spinach
  curry 164
Thai green chicken curry 163
Thai red chicken curry 164
chickpeas
  caramelised onion and chickpea
    burgers 141
  hummus 42
  Indian chickpea and spinach
    curry 168
  lamb, chickpea and saffron pilaf 128
  Moroccan chickpea and pumpkin
    stew 138
  nine-spiced roasted vegetables with
    chickpeas 158
  pumpkin, chickpea and saffron
    pilaf 128
chilli
  barbecued pork and sweet chilli
    noodles 100
  calamari with soy and chilli
    glaze 98
  chicken and sweet chilli noodles 96
  chilli and garlic marinade 115
  chilli beef stir-fry 97
  chilli con carne 179
  chilli stir-fried vegetables with
    noodles 103
  kidney bean and vegetable chilli 139
  lime and chilli chicken wings 112
  lime and chilli lamb cutlets 112
  lime and chilli mayonnaise 67
  seared calamari with chilli and
    balsamic dressing 73
  sweet chilli and mirin steamed
    tofu 105
Chinese crispy-skin chicken 151
Chinese noodle soup 28
Chinese roast duck 157
Chinese stir-fried vegetables with
  noodles 102
chocolate
  bitter chocolate tarts 246
  choc chip pound cake 290
  chocolate and chestnut frozen
    nougat 281
  chocolate and hazelnut biscotti 312
  chocolate and hazelnut cookies 320
  chocolate and hazelnut panforte 296
  chocolate and peppermint pudding 269
  chocolate and walnut pudding 269
  chocolate brandy mousse 264
  chocolate brownies 321
  chocolate cheesecake 299
  chocolate cheesecake muffins 303
  chocolate chip cookies 320
  chocolate coffee mousse 264
  chocolate drops 312
  chocolate fudge cake 289
  chocolate ice-cream 279
  chocolate macaroons 313
  chocolate meringue and coffee

mousse stack 265
chocolate meringue discs 278
chocolate meringues 278
chocolate mousse 264
chocolate mousse and meringue stack 278
chocolate muffins 302
chocolate rice pudding 273
chocolate sauce 278
chocolate self-saucing pudding 269
chocolate shortbread 314
chocolate soufflé 266
double chocolate chip cookies 320
flourless chocolate muffins 306
frozen chocolate mousse 264
jaffa mousse 264
meringues with chocolate sauce 278
moist chocolate squares 289
one-pot chocolate cake 288
rich chocolate and almond cake 289
rich chocolate and hazelnut cake 290
steamed chocolate pudding 268
white chocolate and walnut cookies 320
Choux pastry 251
Christmas cake ice-cream 279
Christmas pudding 271
cinnamon
  cinnamon almond macaroons 313
  cinnamon and lemon tea cake 285
  cinnamon rhubarb crumble 262
  cinnamon scones 301
  sticky cinnamon buns 234
Classic beef and mushroom kebabs 115
coconut
  baked fish parcels with coconut milk and kaffir lime 61
  coconut cake 287
  coconut chicken and noodle salad 218
  coconut chicken curry 169
  coconut macaroons 313
  coconut rice 127
  coconut wafers 314
  date and coconut loaf 294
  pan-fried fish with coconut curry sauce 59
  prawn and coconut tom yum 31
  raspberry coconut slice 322
coffee
  chocolate coffee mousse 264
  coffee and cardamom mousse 265
  coffee and walnut muffins 305
  coffee panna cotta 267
  coffee semifreddo 280
  coffee soufflé 266
  pecan coffee cake 294
cookies see biscuits
coriander
  carrot and coriander soup 24
  chicken and coriander noodles 96
  coriander pesto 89
  pumpkin and coriander soup 24
  spicy chicken fillets with coriander couscous 135
corn
  chicken and corn soup 28
  corn chowder 35
  corn fritters 8
  sweet paprika corn cobs 122

Corned beef (silverside) 198
Cottage pie 179
couscous 134-136
  herb couscous 134
  Moroccan couscous salad 214
  Moroccan spiced breakfast couscous 12
  quick couscous 134
  saffron couscous 134
  seven-spice lamb fillets with onion couscous 136
  spicy chicken fillets with coriander couscous 135
  traditional couscous 135
Crab cakes with Thai cucumber salad 70
Creamy onion soup 32
Creamy tomato sauce 80
Crème caramel 274
Creole fish fillets 59
Creole spice blend 111
Crisp breads 45
Crispy polenta wedges 143
Crispy skin fish with spring onions 61
Croque monsieur 10
Crostini 45
Crumbed lamb chops 175
crumbles
  cinnamon rhubarb crumble 262
  nutty rhubarb crumble 262
  rhubarb crumble 262
  rhubarb oat crumble 262
cucumber
  crab cakes with Thai cucumber salad 70
  Thai cucumber salad 71
curries 162-171
  beef rendang 165
  coconut chicken curry 169
  fragrant vegetable curry 170
  hot and sour beef curry 166
  Indian beef curry 168
  Indian beef, spinach and potato curry 169
  Indian chicken curry 167
  Indian chicken, potato and spinach curry 168
  Indian chickpea and spinach curry 168
  Indian lamb, spinach and potato curry 169
  Indian vegetable curry 168
  Indian-spiced beans 138
  Kashmiri lamb 170
  Malaysian curry prawns 66
  Malaysian fish curry 167
  pan-fried fish with coconut curry sauce 59
  red curry of duck 165
  red curry of quail 165
  sweet potato and cashew nut curry 171
  Thai green chicken and spinach curry 164
  Thai green chicken curry 163
  Thai red beef and bok choy curry 164
  Thai red chicken curry 164
  Thai red fish curry 164
curry pastes
  Rendang curry paste 163
  Thai green curry paste 163
  Thai red curry paste 162

custard
  baked passionfruit custard 275
  banana custard 274
  brandy custard 274
  crème caramel 274
  custard pancakes 279
  Muscat custard 274
  thick custard 274
  thin custard 273
  zabaglione 276

D

dates
  date and coconut loaf 294
  date and orange ricotta tart 243
  date and walnut muesli 11
  date scones 301
  fig or date fruit cake 291
  sticky date pudding 269
Deep-fried fish fillets in beer batter 60
Deep-fried Thai calamari 73
Dessert wine poached fruit 259
dips
  baba ghanoush 41
  beetroot dip 42
  creamy beetroot dip 42
  dukkah 44
  guacamole 43
  hummus 42
  tapenade 43
  tzatziki 41
  white bean dip 44
Double chocolate chip cookies 320
Doughnut' muffins 306
Doughnuts 235
dressings
  anchovy dressing 218
  mirin dressing 213
  red wine dressing 53
  spice-crusted quail salad with pomegranate dressing 219
  yoghurt dressing 214
duck
  barbecue duck and hokkien noodles 100
  Chinese roast duck 157
  duck and macadamia wonton soup 29
  duck and pine mushroom bread soup 31
  duck stock 21
  pomegranate and sumac glazed duck 114
  red curry of duck 165
  roast duck 157
  roast duck rice paper rolls 50
  roast duck, chilli and coriander rolls 49
  sumac and pomegranate roast duck 157
  udon soup with shiitake and roast duck 30
Duck liver pâté 47
Dukkah 44
Dumplings 196

E

Eclairs 252
eggplant
  Baba ghanoush 41
  caponata 176

moussaka 182
roasted eggplant risotto cakes 133
eggs
  bacon and eggs 2
  baked eggs with spinach and cheddar 5
  Caesar salad 217
  egg and bacon pie 250
  eggs Benedict 3
  eggs Florentine 4
  French toast 9
  fresh tuna Nicoise 218
  herbed scrambled eggs 4
  poached eggs 3
  saffron scrambled eggs 4
  salmon Nicoise 218
  stir-fried vegetables and egg with noodles 103
  tuna Nicoise a la our house 217
  zabaglione 276
  zabaglione ice-cream 276
  zabaglione mousse 276
  see also custards; frittatas; meringues; omelettes; soufflés
Egyptian bread and butter pudding 254

F
fennel
  fish and fennel chowder 36
  blood orange and fennel salad 216
  Moroccan mussel and fennel salad 221
feta cheese
  asparagus, almond and feta salad 212
  caramelised onions, feta and rocket combo 82
  green bean, almond and feta salad 212
  roast pumpkin, feta and pine nut risotto 131
  roasted pumpkin and feta frittata 6
figs
  apple, fig and pecan cake 292
  fig or date fruit cake 291
fish 57-73
  baked fish parcels with coconut milk and kaffir lime 61
  barbecued whole fish 120
  Creole fish fillets 49
  crispy skin fish with spring onions 61
  deep-fried fish fillets in beer batter 60
  fish and fennel chowder 36
  fish fingers 175
  fish stock 22
  Malaysian fish curry 167
  pan-fried fish fillets 58
  pan-fried fish with coconut curry sauce 59
  pan-fried swordfish with olive ratatouille 62
  seven-spice fish fillets 59
  seven-spice with whole fish 120
  steamed ginger fish 105
  Thai fish balls 51
  Thai red fish curry 164
  see also: smoked fish; specific fish
Flourless chocolate muffins 306
Foccacia 228
Fragrant vegetable curry 170

Free-form fruit pie 247
French onion soup 32
French toast 9
Fresh tuna Nicoise 218
frittata
  broccoli frittata 6
  cherry tomato and parmigiano frittata 6
  cherry tomato and parmigiano frittata 6
  prosciutto and olive frittata 6
  roast vegetable frittata 6
  roasted pumpkin and feta frittata 6
Frozen chocolate mousse 264
Frozen nougat 280
Frozen nougat ice-cream cake 281
fruit
  apple fruit cake 291
  boil-and-bake fruit cake 291
  dessert wine poached fruit 259
  free-form fruit pie 247
  fruit bread 227
  fruit mince pies 248
  fruity soda bread 225
  grilled peaches with goat's curd and honey 13
  Middle-Eastern fruit and nut stuffing 150
  seasonal winter fruit compote 17
  spiced Italian fruit cake 297
  spiced poached fruit 259
  spiced roasted stone fruit 261
  stewed fruit porridge 13
  sugar-grilled stone fruit 261
  sugar-roasted stone fruit with fresh cheese and honey 260
  summer fruit compote 13
  vanilla poached fruit 258
  winter fruit compote 17
  see also: specific fruit

G
Game stock 22
garlic
  chilli and garlic marinade 115
  garlic foccacia 229
  garlic mushrooms 122
  garlic naan 229
  grilled polenta with garlic vegetables 143
  herb and garlic roast lamb 154
  pot-roasted chicken with 40 cloves of garlic 151
  rosemary and garlic potatoes 159
  sizzlin' garlic prawns 67
  soy and garlic marinade 110
  steamed mussels with garlic 68
ginger
  chicken and ginger noodles 96
  gingerbread cake 288
  gingerbread hearts 316
  ginger-chicken burgers with satay sauce 178
  ginger-steamed choy sum 104
  parsnip, ginger and lemon soup 27
  soy and ginger salmon kebabs 120
  spicy pipis with black bean and ginger 72
  steamed ginger chicken 104
  steamed ginger fish 105
  steamed ginger pudding 268
  stir-fried crabs with black beans and

  ginger 71
  sweet potato and ginger soup 24
  tofu and ginger noodles 96
  tofu and ginger stir-fry 103
goat's cheese
  goat's cheese biscuits 318
  goat's cheese soufflé 54
  grilled peaches with goat's curd and honey 13
  leek and goat's cheese quiche 239
  roast vegetable and goat's cheese lasagna 90
  sugar-roasted stone fruit with fresh cheese and honey 260
Greek cheese pastries or spanakopita 254
Greek leg of lamb 118
Greek salad 209
Green bean, almond and feta salad 212
Green cake 287
Green olive salsa 143
Green pea soup 26
Green salad 209
Grilled peaches with goat's curd and honey 13
Grilled polenta with garlic vegetables 143
Grilled tomatoes with basil butter and bacon 10
Guacamole 43

H
ham, pancetta and prosciutto
  artichoke, prosciutto and buffalo mozzarella parcels 48
  ham omelette 5
  pecorino and pancetta vine leaf parcels 47
  penne with prosciutto, peas and mint 84
  pot-roasted veal with pancetta and mushrooms 158
  prosciutto and olive frittata 6
  roast tomato, pancetta and sweet onions with gnocchi 82
hazelnut
  apple and hazelnut muesli 11
  apple and hazelnut muffins 303
  chocolate and hazelnut panforte 296
  hazelnut and vanilla creams 315
  hazelnut ice-cream 279
  rich chocolate and hazelnut cake 290
Hedgehog 323
herbs
  herb and garlic roast lamb 154
  herb couscous 134
  herb polenta 143
  herbed scrambled eggs 4
  lemon and herb schnitzel 175
  mushrooms with fresh herbs 123
  pan-fried herb chicken fillets 185
  polenta herb muffins 307
  roast chicken with herbs 148
  tomato and fresh herb salsa 46
  see also specific herbs
Hollondaise sauce 4
honey
  grilled peaches with goat's curd and honey 13
  honey joys 325
  roast chicken with honey 148

Sichuan pepper and honey pork
    fillet 119
sugar-roasted stone fruit with fresh
    cheese and honey 260
Horseradish dumplings 197
Horseradish Yorkshire pudding 153
Hot and sour beef curry 166
Hot water pastry 253
Hummus 42
Hungarian chicken casserole 192

I

ice-creams and sorbets
    chocolate ice-cream 279
    Christmas cake ice-cream 279
    coffee semifreddo 280
    frozen chocolate mousse 264
    frozen nougat 280
    frozen nougat ice-cream cake 281
    hazelnut ice-cream 279
    lemon and lime semifreddo 280
    liquorice frozen nougat 281
    passionfruit semifreddo 280
    raspberry and Campari sorbet 281
    vanilla ice-cream 279
    zabaglione ice-cream 276
icings
    basic icing (and variations) 298
    chocolate ganache 298
    cream cheese frosting 298
    white chocolate ganache 298
Indian beef curry 168
Indian beef, spinach and potato
    curry 169
Indian chicken curry 167
Indian chicken, potato and spinach
    curry 168
Indian chickpea and spinach curry 168
Indian lamb, spinach and potato
    curry 169
Indian spiced schnitzel 175
Indian tikka lamb kebabs 118
Indian vegetable curry 168
Indian-spiced beans 138

J

Jaffa mousse 264
jam
    berry jam 15
    bread and jam pudding 272
    jam doughnut muffins 306
    jam swirls 234
    orange marmalade 15
    plum jam 14
    raspberry jam drops 312
    steamed jam or marmalade pudding 268
Jelly-topped panna cotta 267

K

Kashmiri lamb 170
Kashmiri marinade 109
Katsudon (Japanese crumbed pork) 177
kebabs
    barbecued chermoula prawns 121
    beef satay kebabs 114
    chicken saltimbocca skewers 112
    chicken satay kebabs 113
    chicken tandoori in naan bread 113
    classic beef and mushroom
        kebabs 115
    Indian tikka lamb kebabs 118

lamb kofta skewers 182
rosemary lamb kebabs 117
seven-spice salmon kebabs 120
soy and ginger salmon kebabs 120
spiced beef balls in basil leaves 117
tuna teriyaki skewers 121
Kidney bean and vegetable chilli 139
Knot rolls 226

L

Laksa 31
lamb
    basil and pine nut stuffed lamb 155
    Greek leg of lamb 118
    herb and garlic roast lamb 154
    Indian tikka lamb kebabs 118
    Kashmiri lamb 170
    lamb cutlets with red wine
        onions 186
    lamb hot pot 201
    lamb kofta skewers 182
    lamb steaks with oregano and spiced
        onions 187
    lamb tagine 200
    lamb topsides with ratatouille 156
    lamb, chickpea and saffron pilaf 128
    lime and chilli lamb cutlets 112
    Moroccan lamb cutlets 118
    moussaka 182
    rosemary lamb kebabs 117
    seven-spice lamb fillets with onion
        couscous 136
    Spanish lamb stew 200
leeks
    leek and goat's cheese quiche 239
    potato and leek soup 23
lemons
    and herb schnitzel 175
    and lime semifreddo 280
    and poppyseed cake 285
    Birgit's easy mousse 265
    butter sauce 63
    cinnamon and lemon tea cake 285
    curd (butter) 16
    delicious pudding 270
    gems 312
    lemon cheesecake 299
    mayonnaise 66
    meringue pie 245
    microwave lemon curd 16
    mousse 264
    parsnip, ginger and lemon soup 27
    pepper pita crisps 45
    roast chicken with lemon 148
    sour cream cake 286
    spaghetti with breadcrumbs, tuna,
        parsley and lemon 86
    steamed lemon pudding 268
    tart 244
    tea cake 285
lentils
    barbecued pork sausage with spiced
        lentils 140
    lentil and ricotta burgers 141
    lentil dhal 139
    Moroccan lentil broth 34
    spiced pumpkin and lentil soup 24
limes
    lemon and lime semifreddo 280
    lime and chilli chicken wings 112
    lime and chilli lamb cutlets 112

lime and chilli mayonnaise 67
lime and poppyseed tea cake 285
lime panna cotta 267
Linguini with smoked chicken and
    peas 84
Linzertorte made easy 299
Lion's-head meatballs 181
Liquorice frozen nougat 281
Liquorice panna cotta 267

M

Macadamia Anzacs 311
Macaroni cheese 87
Macaroni cheese with corn 87
Macaroni cheese with ham 87
macaroons
    almond macaroons 312
    chocolate macaroons 313
    cinnamon almond macaroons 313
    coconut macaroons 313
Malaysian curry prawns 66
Malaysian fish curry 167
marinades 109-112
    basic wine marinade 109
    Caribbean fish marinade 110
    chilli and garlic marinade 115
    Creole spice blend 111
    Kashmiri marinade 109
    Oriental marinade 110
    salt and pepper spice 112
    simple Moroccan blend 111
    soy and garlic marinade 110
    spicy barbecue marinade 109
    spicy Mexican marinade 110
    sweet sticky marinade 111
Mars Bar slice 325
Mashed potato 197
mayonnaise
    lemon mayonnaise 66
    lime and chilli mayonnaise 67
    mayonnaise 210
meatballs
    chicken and veal polpettini 180
    lion's-head meatballs 181
    spaghetti and meatballs 88
Mediterranean chicken casserole 192
meringues
    baby pavs 277
    chocolate meringue and coffee
        mousse stack 265
    chocolate meringue discs 278
    chocolate meringues 278
    chocolate mousse and meringue
        stack 278
    lemon meringue pie 245
    meringues 277
    meringues with berries 278
    meringues with chocolate sauce 278
    pavlova 277
Mexican mince 179
Microwave lemon curd 16
Middle-Eastern carrot salad 211
Middle-Eastern fruit and nut stuffing 150
Middle-Eastern rice pudding 273
Millionaire's shortbread (caramel
    slice) 322
Minestrone 36
Mini rum and raisin garibaldi 317
mint
    chocolate and peppermint pudding 269

mint sauce 155
penne with prosciutto, peas and mint 84
Mirin dressing 213
Moist berry pudding cake 295
Moist chocolate squares 289
Morning glory muffins 305
Moroccan chicken pie 194
Moroccan chicken salad 220
Moroccan chicken with tomatoes and olives 193
Moroccan chickpea and pumpkin stew 138
Moroccan couscous salad 214
Moroccan lamb cutlets 118
Moroccan lentil broth 34
Moroccan mussel and fennel salad 221
Moroccan roast turkey 152
Moroccan spiced breakfast couscous 12
Moussaka 182
mousses
  Birgit's easy mousse 265
  chocolate brandy mousse 264
  chocolate coffee mousse 264
  chocolate mousse 264
  chocolate mousse and meringue stack 278
  coffee and cardamom mousse 265
  jaffa mousse 264
  lemon mousse 264
  passionfruit mousse 265
  zabaglione mousse 276
muesli
  apple and hazelnut muesli 11
  apricot and almond muesli 11
  Bircher muesli 12
  date and walnut muesli 11
  munchie muesli slice 324
muffins
  apple and hazelnut muffins 303
  banana and walnut muffins 304
  banana muffins 304
  banana, pecan and maple syrup muffins 304
  basic muffins 302
  blueberry muffins 302
  carrot and nut muffins 303
  chocolate cheesecake muffins 303
  chocolate muffins 302
  coffee and walnut muffins 305
  'doughnut' muffins 306
  flourless chocolate muffins 306
  jam doughnut muffins 306
  morning glory muffins 305
  peanut butter muffins 304
  polenta herb muffins 307
  spicy cheddar muffins 307
Muscat custard 274
mushrooms
  basic beef stew with mushrooms 196
  beef and mushroom bolognaise 89
  chicken and mushroom pie 195
  chicken and mushroom risotto 129
  chicken casserole with mushrooms 191
  classic beef and mushroom kebabs 115
  duck and pine mushroom bread soup 31
  garlic mushrooms 122
  mushroom omelette 5
mushroom quiche 239
mushroom risotto cakes 132
mushroom risotto with truffle oil 132
mushroom soup 24
mushrooms on toast 11
mushrooms with fresh herbs 123
pan-fried chicken with mushroom sauce 185
pan-fried steak with mushroom sauce 183
pot-roasted veal with pancetta and mushrooms 158
udon soup with shiitake and roast duck 30
mussels
  Moroccan mussel and fennel salad 221
  mussels with Thai chilli broth 69
  steamed mussels with garlic 68
Mustard roast beef 153
My kind of cheesecake 300

N

Naan bread 229
Nasi Goreng (stir-fried rice) 100
Nine-spiced roasted vegetables with chickpeas 158
No-cook orange cheesecake 299
noodles
  Asian noodle salad 212
  barbecue duck and hokkien noodles 100
  barbecue pork and noodle stir-fry 99
  barbecued pork and sweet chilli noodles 100
  chicken and coriander noodles 96
  chicken and ginger noodles 96
  chicken and sweet chilli noodles 96
  chicken noodle soup 28
  chilli stir-fried vegetables with noodles 103
  Chinese noodle soup 28
  Chinese stir-fried vegetables with noodles 102
  coconut chicken and noodle salad 218
  Pad Thai (Thai rice noodles) 100
  Singapore noodles 101
  spicy Sichuan noodles 102
  stir-fried vegetables and egg with noodles 103
  tofu and ginger noodles 96
  udon soup with shiitake and roast duck 30
  Vietnamese beef noodle salad 219
nuts
  beef, black bean and cashew nut stir-fry 96
  carrot and nut muffins 303
  chicken and cashew nut stir-fry 95
  duck and macadamia wonton soup 29
  macadamia Anzacs 311
  Middle-Eastern fruit and nut stuffing 150
  nutty rhubarb crumble 262
  peanut cookies 321
  spiced nut rice 127
sweet potato and cashew nut curry 171
see also specific nuts

O

Oatcakes 318
Olive and spinach quiche 239
Olive foccacia 229
olives
  green olive salsa 143
  Moroccan chicken with tomatoes and olives 193
  olive and spinach quiche 239
  pan-fried swordfish with olive ratatouille 62
  pissaladière 231
  prosciutto and olive frittata 6
  tapenade 43
omelettes
  asparagus omelette 5
  ham omelette 5
  mushroom omelette 5
  omelettes 5
  Spanish potato omelette 6
  tomato omelette 5
  truffle omelette 5
One-pot chocolate cake 288
onions
  barbecue onion rings 122
  braised steak and onions 195
  caramelised onion and chickpea burgers 141
  caramelised onion quiche 239
  creamy onion soup 32
  crispy skin fish with spring onions 61
  French onion soup 32
  lamb steaks with oregano and spiced onions 187
  onion bahjis 51
  onion pilaf 127
  pissaladière 231
  roast tomato, pancetta and sweet onions with gnocchi 82
  sage and onion stuffing 149
  sausages with onion gravy 178
  seven-spice lamb fillets with onion couscous 136
  veal, sage and onion meatloaf 183
oranges
  baked orange cheesecake 300
  blood orange and fennel salad 216
  caramel oranges 261
  Caroline's (vodka and blood orange) jelly 267
  date and orange ricotta tart 243
  jaffa mousse 264
  no-cook orange cheesecake 299
  orange and almond cake 293
  orange and walnut florentines 316
  orange and yoghurt syrup cake 286
  orange brioche 233
  orange marmalade 15
  orange poppyseed cake 286
  orange shortbread 314
  orange tea cake 285
  steamed orange pudding 268
oregano
  lamb steaks with oregano and spiced onions 187
Oriental marinade 110
Oriental roast chicken 150

Osso buco 203
Other pâté flavours 47
Oxtail soup 37
oysters
  barbecued oysters 64
  steamed oysters with Asian flavours 65

P
Pad Thai (Thai rice noodles) 100
Paella 133
Pain au chocolat pudding 272
pancakes
  banana pikelets 8
  berry pancakes 279
  blinis 45
  blueberry pikelets 7
  cheese blintzes 279
  corn fritters 8
  custard pancakes 279
  pancakes 278
  ricotta hotcakes with banana and maple syrup 8
  smoked salmon with polenta pancakes 9
  smoked salmon with polenta pancakes 9
  summer berry pikelets 8
Pandan chicken parcels 48
Panettone pudding 272
pan-fried
  calamari 72
  chicken with mushroom sauce 185
  fish fillets 58
  fish with coconut curry sauce 59
  herb chicken fillets 185
  steak with mushroom sauce 183
  swordfish with olive ratatouille 62
panna cotta
  cardamom panna cotta 267
  coffee panna cotta 267
  jelly-topped panna cotta 267
  lime panna cotta 267
  liquorice panna cotta 267
  rosewater panna cotta 267
  vanilla panna cotta 266
Parmigiano crumbed veal cutlets with caponata 176
Parsley sauce 199
Parsnip, ginger and lemon soup 27
passionfruit
  baked passionfruit custard 275
  passionfruit cheesecake 300
  passionfruit mousse 265
  passionfruit profiteroles 252
  passionfruit semifreddo 280
  passionfruit tart 244
  passionfruit yoyo biscuits 315
pasta 75-91
  basic pasta 77
  beef lasagna 90
  linguini with smoked chicken and peas 84
  macaroni cheese 87
  macaroni cheese with corn 87
  macaroni cheese with ham 87
  pasta with tuna and artichokes 83
  penne with prosciutto, peas and mint 84
  potato gnocchi 78
  roast pumpkin, pancetta and sweet onions with gnocchi 83
  roast tomato, pancetta and sweet onions with gnocchi 82
  roast vegetable and goat's cheese lasagna 90
  semolina gnocchi 79
  spaghetti and meatballs 88
  spaghetti with breadcrumbs, tuna, parsley and lemon 86
  spaghetti with pesto 88
  spaghetti with seafood and tomato sauce 86
  spaghettini carbonara 85
  traditional lasagna 90
pasta sauces 75-91
  beef and mushroom bolognaise 89
  broad bean and bacon pasta sauce 84
  caramelised onions, feta and rocket combo 82
  coriander pesto 89
  creamy tomato sauce 80
  linguini with smoked chicken and peas 84
  pesto 89
  quick-and-easy bolognaise 89
  roasted tomato and red capsicum sauce 81
  smoked trout and asparagus cream sauce 85
  spaghetti with seafood and tomato sauce 86
  spaghettini carbonara 85
  spicy bolognaise sauce 89
  tomato sauce (and variations) 79, 80, 81
  veal ragu 90
pastries
  boreks 52
  cheesy choux puffs 252
  éclairs 252
  Egyptian bread and butter pudding 254
  Greek cheese pastries or spanakopita 254
  passionfruit profiteroles 252
  pistachio, almond and orange-blossom baklava 255
  profiteroles 252
  sausage rolls 250
  vegetable pasties 253
  see also pies; quiches; tarts
pastry
  almond sweetcrust pastry 241
  choux pastry 251
  hot water pastry 253
  puff pastry 248
  rich sweetcrust pastry 242
  rough puff pastry 249
  shortcrust pastry 238
  sweetcrust pastry 241
Pavlova 277
Peanut butter muffins 304
Peanut cookies 321
Pear frangipane tart 243
pâtés
  chicken liver pâté 46
  duck liver pâté 47
  other pâté flavours 47
  smoked trout pâté 47
pears
  pear frangipane tart 243
  poached pear and almond pudding 260
  spiced poached pears 260
peas
  chicken and pea risotto 129
  linguini with smoked chicken and peas 84
  penne with prosciutto, peas and mint 84
pecans
  apple, fig and pecan cake 292
  banana, pecan and maple syrup muffins 304
  butterscotch pecan self-saucing pudding 270
  pecan coffee cake 294
Pecorino and pancetta vine leaf parcels 47
Penne with prosciutto, peas and mint 84
peppers, *see* capsicum and chilli
Pesto 89
pies, sweet
  apple and raspberry pie 247
  apple and rhubarb pie 247
  free-form fruit pie 247
  fruit mince pies 248
pies, savoury
  beef and Guinness pie 197
  cheese and potato pies 240
  chicken and mushroom pie 195
  egg and bacon pie 250
  Moroccan chicken pie 194
pine nuts
  basil and pine nut stuffed lamb 155
  pine nut and saffron pilaf 128
  roast pumpkin, feta and pine nut risotto 131
Pissaladière 231
pistachios
  pistachio biscotti 312
  pistachio bread 319
  pistachio, almond and orange blossom baklava 255
Pita crisps 44
pizza
  pissaladière 231
  pizza dough 230
  roasted vegetable calzone 232
  thin and crispy pizza 230
  toppings 231
Plum cake 295
Plum jam 14
Poached eggs 3
Poached pear and almond pudding 260
Poached quinces 259
Poached salmon 62
polenta 142-143
  crispy polenta wedges 143
  grilled polenta with garlic vegetables 143
  herb polenta 143
  polenta bread 228
  polenta herb muffins 307
  rosemary polenta bread 228
  smoked salmon with polenta pancakes 9
  the best soft polenta 142
pomegranate
  pomegranate and sumac glazed duck 114
  pomegranate and sumac glazed quail 114

sumac and pomegranate roast duck 157
Poppyseed rolls 226
pork
   barbecue pork and bok choy stir-fry 99
   barbecue pork and noodle stir-fry 99
   barbecue pork ribs 119
   barbecued pork and sweet chilli noodles 100
   barbecued pork sausage with spiced lentils 140
   Birgit's frikadella 180
   katsudon (Japanese crumbed pork) 177
   roast rack of pork 156
   Sichuan pepper and honey pork fillet 119
   the pork dish 202
porridge
   apple porridge 13
   porridge 12
   stewed fruit porridge 13
   sultana porridge 13
potato
   cheese and potato pies 240
   cottage pie 179
   Indian beef, spinach and potato curry 169
   Indian chicken, potato and spinach curry 168
   mashed potato 197
   potato and leek soup 23
   potato and watercress soup 24
   potato gnocchi 78
   potato salad 210
   rosemary and garlic potatoes 159
   salmon and potato cakes 177
   Spanish potato omelette 6
   steak with oven chips 184
pot-roasts
   beef pot-roast 154
   pot-roasted chicken with 40 cloves of garlic 151
   pot-roasted veal shanks 204
   pot-roasted veal with pancetta and mushrooms 158
Praline 281
prawns
   asparagus and prawn risotto 130
   barbecued chermoula prawns 121
   Malaysian curry prawns 66
   prawn and coconut tom yum 31
   prawn cocktail 67
   prawn rice paper rolls 50
   sizzlin' garlic prawns 67
   smoked salmon and prawn kedgeree 7
   Thai prawn salad 218
Profiteroles 252
puddings
   banana sago pudding with butterscotch sauce 273
   bread and butter pudding 272
   bread and jam pudding 272
   Egyptian bread and butter pudding 254
   lemon delicious pudding 270
   pain au chocolat pudding 272
   panettone pudding 272
   poached pear and almond pudding 260

sago plum pudding 273
tiramisu 276
Puff pastry 248
pumpkin
   Asian-inspired pumpkin soup 25
   Moroccan chickpea and pumpkin stew 138
   pumpkin and coriander soup 24
   pumpkin cake 293
   pumpkin, chickpea and saffron pilaf 128
   roast pumpkin, feta and pine nut risotto 131
   roasted pumpkin and feta frittata 6
   spiced pumpkin and lentil soup 24

Q
quail
   pomegranate and sumac glazed quail 114
   red curry of quail 165
   spice-crusted quail salad with pomegranate dressing 219
Quiche (and variations) 239
Quick couscous 134
Quick-and-easy bolognaise 89
quinces
   poached quinces 259

R
Rabbit casserole 204
raspberry
   apple and raspberry pie 247
   mascarpone and raspberry pound cake 290
   raspberry and Campari sorbet 281
   raspberry and mascarpone tart 243
   raspberry cheesecake 301
   raspberry coconut slice 322
   raspberry jam drops 312
   raspberry sauce 263
   raspberry soufflé 266
   raspberry, vanilla and almond slice 324
Red curry of duck 165
Red curry of quail 165
Red wine dressing 53
Rendang curry paste 163
rhubarb
   apple and rhubarb crumble tart 247
   apple and rhubarb pie 247
   rhubarb and ricotta toast 14
   rhubarb crumble (and variations) 262
   steamed rhubarb pudding 268
rice 125-133
   California rolls 53
   chicken, sultana and sweet spice pilaf 128
   coconut rice 127
   lamb, chickpea and saffron pilaf 128
   Nasi Goreng (stir-fried rice) 100
   onion pilaf 127
   paella 133
   pine nut and saffron pilaf 128
   pumpkin, chickpea and saffron pilaf 128
   roasted eggplant risotto cakes 133
   saffron rice 127
   smoked salmon and prawn kedgeree 7
   spiced nut rice 127

spiced pipis with risoni 70
steamed rice 127
sushi rice 52
see also risoni
Rice pudding (and variations) 272, 273
Rich apple and walnut cake 296
Rich chicken stock 21
Rich chocolate and almond cake 289
Rich chocolate and hazelnut cake 290
Rich sweetcrust pastry 242
ricotta
   date and orange ricotta tart 243
   lentil and ricotta burgers 141
   rhubarb and ricotta toast 14
   ricotta hotcakes with banana and maple syrup 8
   ricotta tart 242
risotto
   asparagus and prawn risotto 130
   chicken and asparagus risotto 129
   chicken and mushroom risotto 129
   chicken and pea risotto 129
   chicken and roasted sweet potato risotto 129
   chicken and spinach risotto 129
   chicken risotto 129
   mushroom risotto cakes 132
   mushroom risotto with truffle oil 132
   risotto with porcini mushrooms 132
   roast pumpkin, feta and pine nut risotto 131
   roasted eggplant risotto cakes 133
   Spring risotto 130
roast
   beef with Yorkshire puddings 153
   chicken (and variations) 148
   duck 157
   duck rice paper rolls 50
   duck, chilli and coriander rolls 49
   eggplant risotto cakes 133
   pumpkin and feta frittata 6
   pumpkin, pancetta and sweet onions with gnocchi 83
   rack of pork 156
   rib of beef 153
   root vegetable chips 159
   tomato and red capsicum sauce 81
   tomato soup 25
   tomato, pancetta and sweet onions with gnocchi 82
   vegetable and goat's cheese lasagna 90
   vegetable calzone 232
   vegetable frittata 6
   vegetable gazpacho 33
   vegetable stock 23
   see also pot-roasts
Rocket tabbouleh 211
rosemary
   rosemary and garlic potatoes 159
   rosemary foccacia 229
   rosemary lamb kebabs 117
   rosemary polenta bread 228
   rosemary polenta bread 228
Rosewater panna cotta 267
Roast pumpkin, feta and pine nut risotto 131
Rough puff pastry 249

S

saffron
  lamb, chickpea and saffron pilaf 128
  pine nut and saffron pilaf 128
  pumpkin, chickpea and saffron pilaf 128
  saffron couscous 134
  saffron rice 127
  saffron scrambled eggs 4
sage
  sage and onion stuffing 149
  veal, sage and onion meatloaf 183
sago
  banana sago pudding with butterscotch sauce 273
  sago plum pudding 273
salads 207-221
  Asian coleslaw 212
  Asian noodles salad
  asparagus, almond and feta salad 212
  barbecued vegetable salad 213
  beetroot fattouche 216
  beetroot salad 215
  beetroot salad with tomato and mozzarella 215
  blood orange and fennel salad 216
  Caesar salad 217
  coconut chicken and noodle salad 218
  fresh tuna Niçoise 218
  Greek salad 209
  green bean, almond and feta salad 212
  green salad 209
  Middle-Eastern carrot salad 211
  Moroccan chicken salad 220
  Moroccan couscous salad 214
  Moroccan mussel and fennel salad 221
  potato salad 210
  rocket tabouleh 211
  salad of fennel, walnuts and parmigiano 215
  salmon Niçoise 218
  simple bok choy salad 213
  spice-crusted quail salad with pomegranate dressing 219
  spinach salad 213
  Thai chicken salad 218
  Thai cucumber salad 71
  Thai prawn salad 218
  tomato and roast capsicum salad 214
  tomato and white bean salad 210
  tuna Niçoise a la our house 217
  Vietnamese beef noodle salad 219
  watercress tabbouleh 211
salmon
  poached salmon 62
  salmon and potato cakes 177
  salmon Niçoise 218
  seven-spice salmon kebabs 120
  smoked salmon with polenta pancakes 9
  soy and ginger salmon kebabs 120
  whole smoky salmon 63
  see also smoked fish
Salt and pepper spice 112
San choy bau 98
sauces, savoury
  Allan's gravy 148
  barbecue sauce 123
  coconut curry sauce 59
  green olive salsa 143
  hollandaise sauce 4
  lemon butter sauce 63
  mint sauce 155
  mushroom sauce 183, 185
  onion gravy 178
  parsley sauce 199
  red wine and onion gravy 178, 186
  tartare sauce 66
  tomato and fresh herb salsa 46
  Vietnamese dipping sauce 50
sauces, sweet
  butterscotch sauce 261
  caramel sauce 261
  chocolate sauce 278
  lemon butter sauce 63
  raspberry sauce 263
  strawberry sauce 263
sausages
  barbecued pork sausage with spiced lentils 140
  sausage rolls 250
  sausages with onion gravy 178
Savoury mince 179
schnitzel
  cheesy schnitzel 175
  chicken schnitzel 175
  Indian spiced schnitzel 175
  lemon and herb schnitzel 175
  sesame schnitzel 175
  veal schnitzel 175
scones
  cinnamon scones 301
  date scones 301
  scones 301
Seared calamari with chilli and balsamic dressing 73
Seasonal winter fruit compote 17
Semolina gnocchi 79
sesame
  cheese and sesame seed pita crisps 45
  sesame schnitzel 175
  sesame seed rolls 226
  sesame sweet potato wedges 123
Seven-spice fish fillets 59
Seven-spice lamb fillets with onion couscous 136
Seven-spice salmon kebabs 120
Seven-spice with whole fish 120
shellfish 57-73
  crab cakes with Thai cucumber salad 70
  shellfish chowder 36
  shellfish stock 22
  spaghetti with seafood and tomato sauce 86
  spiced pipis with risoni 70
  spicy pipis with black bean and ginger 72
  stir-fried crabs with black beans and ginger 71
  see also mussels; oysters; prawns
shortbread 313
  chocolate shortbread 314
  millionaire's shortbread (caramel slice) 322
  orange shortbread 314
  spice shortbread 314
Shortcrust pastry 238
Sichuan pepper and honey pork fillet 119
Simple bok choy salad 213
Simple brioche 232
Simple chicken casserole 191
Simple Moroccan blend 111
Singapore noodles 101
Sizzlin' garlic prawns 67
slices
  chocolate brownies 321
  hedgehog 323
  Mars Bar slice 325
  millionaire's shortbread (caramel slice) 322
  munchie muesli slice 324
  raspberry coconut slice 322
  raspberry, vanilla and almond slice 324
  toffee almond squares 323
smoked fish
  smoked salmon and prawn kedgeree 7
  smoked salmon with polenta pancakes 9
  smoked trout and asparagus cream sauce 85
  smoked trout and avocado toasts 60
  smoked trout pâté 47
Snickerdoodles 314
Soda bread 225
soufflés
  chocolate soufflé 266
  coffee soufflé 266
  goat's cheese soufflé 54
  raspberry soufflé 266
soups 19-37
  Asian-inspired pumpkin soup 25
  asparagus soup 24
  beetroot soup 33
  broad bean soup 26
  carrot and coriander soup 24
  chicken and corn soup 28
  chicken laksa 31
  chicken noodle soup 28
  Chinese noodle soup 28
  corn chowder 35
  creamy onion soup 32
  duck and macadamia wonton soup 29
  duck and pine mushroom bread soup 31
  fish and fennel chowder 36
  French onion soup 32
  green pea soup 26
  laksa 31
  minestrone 36
  Moroccan lentil broth 34
  mushroom soup 24
  oxtail soup 37
  parsnip, ginger and lemon soup 27
  potato and leek soup 23
  potato and watercress soup 24
  prawn and coconut tom yum 31
  pumpkin and coriander soup 24
  roast tomato soup 25
  roasted vegetable gazpacho 33
  shellfish chowder 36
  spiced pumpkin and lentil soup 24
  sweet potato and ginger soup 24
  tom yum 30
  udon soup with shiitake and roast duck 30

udon soup with tofu 30
vegetable and barley broth 35
Vietnamese noodle soup 28
wonton soup 29
Sour and spicy beef braise 199
Sour beef with lemongrass 97
sour cream
   beef stroganoff 184
   lemon sour cream cake 286
   smoked salmon with sour cream and horseradish 46
   smoked salmon, sour cream, freshly ground black pepper and dill 46
Soy and garlic marinade 110
Soy and ginger salmon kebabs 120
Soy-braised chicken 193
Spanish lamb stew 200
Spanish potato omelette 6
spatchcocking 108
   spice-crusted quail salad with pomegranate dressing 219
   pomegranate and sumac glazed quail 114
spiced
   beef balls in basil leaves 117
   Italian fruit cake 297
   nut rice 127
   pipis with risoni 70
   poached fruit 259
   pears 260
   pumpkin and lentil soup 24
   roasted stone fruit 261
spicy
   barbecue marinade 109
   bolognaise sauce 89
   cheddar muffins 307
   chicken fillets with coriander couscous 135
   Mexican marinade 110
   pipis with black bean and ginger 72
   Sichuan noodles 102
Spice naan 229
Spice shortbread 314
Spice-crusted quail salad with pomegranate dressing 219
spinach
   baked eggs with spinach and cheddar 5
   chicken and spinach risotto 129
   Indian beef, spinach and potato curry 169
   Indian chicken, potato and spinach curry 168
   Indian chickpea and spinach curry 168
   olive and spinach quiche 239
   spinach salad 213
   Thai green chicken and spinach curry 164
Spring risotto 130
Spring rolls 49
Steak with oven chips 184
steamed
   ginger chicken 104
   ginger fish 105
   ginger-steamed choy sum 104
   mussels with garlic 68
   oysters with Asian flavours 65
   steamed rice 127
   sweet chilli and mirin steamed tofu 105
steamed puddings

Australian Christmas pudding 271
butterscotch pecan self-saucing pudding 270
chocolate and peppermint pudding 269
chocolate and walnut pudding 269
chocolate pudding 268
chocolate self-saucing pudding 269
Christmas pudding 271
ginger pudding 268
jam or marmalade pudding 268
lemon pudding 268
orange pudding 268
rhubarb pudding 268
sticky date pudding 269
treacle or maple syrup pudding 268
Stewed fruit porridge 13
stews see casseroles
Sticky black rice pudding 273
Sticky cinnamon buns 234
Sticky currant buns 233
sticky date pudding 269
stir-fries 93-105
   barbecue pork and bok choy 99
   barbecue pork and noodle 99
   beef, black bean and cashew nut 96
   calamari with soy and chilli glaze 98
   chicken and black bean 95
   chicken and bok choy 95
   chicken and broccoli 95
   chicken and cashew nut 95
   chicken and oyster sauce 95
   chilli beef 97
   chilli stir-fried vegetables with noodles 103
   Chinese stir-fried vegetables with noodles 102
   sour beef with lemongrass 97
   crabs with black beans and ginger 71
   vegetables and egg with noodles 103
   vegetables with tofu with noodles 103
   tofu and ginger 103
   wok-fried Asian greens 103
   see also noodles; rice
stocks 19-37
   Asian chicken stock 21
   beef stock 21
   chicken stock 21
   duck stock 21
   fish stock 22
   game stock 22
   rich chicken stock 21
   roasted vegetable stock 23
   shellfish stock 22
   turkey stock 21
   veal stock 22
   vegetable stock 23
strawberries
   strawberry sauce 263
   strawberry shortcakes 302
Stuffed turkey breast 152
stuffings
   basil and pine nut stuffed lamb 155
   chestnut stuffing 149
   sage and onion stuffing 149
   Middle-Eastern fruit and nut stuffing 150
Sugar syrup 233
Sugar-grilled stone fruit 261
Sugar-roasted stone fruit with fresh

cheese and honey 260
Sultana porridge 13
Sumac and pomegranate roast duck 157
Summer berry pikelets 8
Summer fruit compote 13
Summer pudding 263
Summer vegetable terrine 53
Sushi rice 52
Sweet chilli and mirin steamed tofu 105
Sweet paprika corn cobs 122
sweet potatoes
   chicken and roasted sweet potato risotto 129
   sesame sweet potato wedges 123
   sweet potato and cashew nut curry 171
   sweet potato and ginger soup 24
Sweet sticky marinade 111
sweetcorn, see corn
Sweetcrust pastry 241
Swiss buns 234

T
Tacos 179
tagines
   aromatic vegetable tagine 205
   beef and prune tagine 198
   lamb tagine 200
   Tunisian lamb shanks 202
Tangelo and almond cake 294
Tapenade 43
Tartare sauce 66
Tarte tatin 251
tarts, savoury
   tomato and anchovy tart 240
tarts, sweet
   almond pear tart 246
   apple and rhubarb crumble tart 247
   apple tart 245
   apricot and frangipane tart 243
   bitter chocolate tarts 246
   date and orange ricotta tart 243
   lemon meringue pie 245
   lemon tart 244
   passionfruit tart 244
   pear frangipane tart 243
   port-soaked prune and ricotta tart 242
   quince and ricotta tart 242
   raspberry and mascarpone tart 243
   ricotta tart 242
   tarte tatin 251
Thai chicken salad 218
Thai cucumber salad 71
Thai fish balls 51
Thai green chicken and spinach curry 164
Thai green chicken curry 163
Thai green curry paste 163
Thai prawn salad 218
Thai red beef and bok choy curry 164
Thai red chicken curry 164
Thai red curry paste 162
Thai red fish curry 164
The best soft polenta 142
The perfect steak 114
The pork dish 202
Thick custard 274
Thin and crispy pizza 230

Thin custard 273
Tiramisu 276
Toffee almond squares 323
tofu
   stir-fried vegetables with tofu with noodles 103
   sweet chilli and mirin steamed tofu 105
   tofu and ginger noodles 96
   tofu and ginger stir-fry 103
Tom yum 30
tomatoes
   beetroot salad with tomato and mozzarella 215
   cherry tomato and parmigiano frittata 6
   creamy tomato sauce 80
   grilled tomatoes with basil butter and bacon 10
   Moroccan chicken with tomatoes and olives 193
   roast tomato soup 25
   roast tomato, pancetta and sweet onions with gnocchi 82
   roasted tomato and red capsicum sauce 81
   spaghetti with seafood and tomato sauce 86
   tomato and anchovy tart 240
   tomato and fresh herb salsa 46
   tomato and roast capsicum salad 214
   tomato and white bean salad 210
   tomato omelette 5
   tomato sauce #1 79
   tomato sauce #2 80
   tomato sauce with bacon 81
   tomato sauce with basil 80
   tomato sauce with capers 80
   tomato sauce with chilli 80
   tomato sauce with mushroom 81
   tomato sauce with olives 80
   tomato sauce with pesto 81
   tomato sauce with roasted capsicum 80
   tomato sauce with roasted eggplant 80
   tomato sauce with spinach 81
   tomato sauce with tuna 80
   tomato, olive and anchovy pasta sauce 81
Toppings for crostini and blini 46
Traditional Anzacs 311
Traditional couscous 135
Traditional lasagna 90
truffles
   truffle omelette 5
   mushroom risotto with truffle oil 132
Tuiles 317
tuna
   fresh tuna Nicoise 218
   pasta with tuna and artichokes 83
   spaghetti with breadcrumbs, tuna, parsley and lemon 86
   tuna Nicoise a la our house 217
   tuna teriyaki skewers 121
Tunisian lamb shanks 202
turkey
   Moroccan roast turkey 152
   stuffed turkey breast 152
   turkey stock 21
Tzatziki 41

U
Udon soup with shiitake and roast duck 30

V
vanilla
   hazelnut and vanilla creams 315
   raspberry, vanilla and almond slice 324
   vanilla ice-cream 279
   vanilla panna cotta 266
   vanilla poached fruit 258
veal
   Birgit's frikadella 180
   chicken and veal polpettini 180
   osso buco 203
   parmigiano crumbed veal cutlets with caponata 176
   pot-roasted veal shanks 204
   pot-roasted veal with pancetta and mushrooms 158
   veal ragu 90
   veal schnitzel 175
   veal stock 22
   veal, sage and onion meatloaf 183
vegetables
   aromatic vegetable tagine 205
   barbecued vegetable salad 213
   beef burgers with roasted vegetables 116
   chilli stir-fried vegetables with noodles 103
   Chinese stir-fried vegetables with noodles 102
   fragrant vegetable curry 170
   grilled polenta with garlic vegetables 143
   Indian vegetable curry 168
   kidney bean and vegetable chilli 139
   lamb topsides with ratatouille 156
   nine-spiced roasted vegetables with chickpeas 158
   pan-fried swordfish with olive ratatouille 62
   roast chicken and vegetables 148
   roast vegetable and goat's cheese lasagna 90
   roast vegetable frittata 6
   roasted root vegetable chips 159
   roasted vegetable calzone 232
   roasted vegetable gazpacho 33
   roasted vegetable stock 23
   stir-fried vegetables and egg with noodles 103
   stir-fried vegetables with tofu with noodles 103
   summer vegetable terrine 53
   vegetable and barley broth 25
   vegetable pasties 253
   vegetable stock 23
Viennese biscuits 313
Vietnamese beef noodle salad 219
Vietnamese dipping sauce 50
Vietnamese noodle soup 28
vine leaves
   pecorino and pancetta vine leaf parcels 47

W
walnuts
   banana and walnut cake 291
   banana and walnut muffins 304
   chocolate and walnut pudding 269
   coffee and walnut muffins 305
   date and walnut muesli 11
   orange and walnut florentines 316
   rich apple and walnut cake 296
   white chocolate and walnut cookies 320
Watercress tabouleh 211
White bean dip 44
White chocolate and walnut cookies 320
Whole smoky salmon 63
Winter fruit compote 17
Wok-fried Asian greens 103
Wonton soup 29

Y
yoghurt
   basil tzatziki 41
   orange and yoghurt syrup cake 286
   tzatziki 41
   yoghurt dressing 214

Z
Zabaglione 276
Zabaglione ice-cream 276
Zabaglione mousse 276